Black Olympian Medalists

Black Olympian Medalists

JAMES A. PAGE

Introduction by
Reynold S. O'Neal

1991
LIBRARIES UNLIMITED, INC.
Englewood, Colorado

LIBRARIES UNLIMITED, INC.
P.O. Box 3988
Englewood, CO 80155-3988

Library of Congress Cataloging-in-Publication Data

Page, James A. (James Allen), 1918-
    Black olympian medalists / James A. Page ; introduction by Reynold
S. O'Neal, track and field statistician (consultant).
    xxiii, 190 p. 22x28 cm.
    Includes bibliographical references and index.
    ISBN 0-87287-618-7
    1. Athletes, Black--Biography--Dictionaries. 2. Afro-American
athletes--Biography--Dictionaries. 3. Olympics. I. Title.
GV697.A1P284   1990
796'.092'2--dc20
    [B]   90-46660
                                                 CIP

Dedicated to my wife, Ethel Stene (Ross) Page.

Table of Contents

Preface

The 24th Olympiad at Seoul, Korea, in the summer of 1988 produced an astounding number of Black or African-descended male medal winners. An impressive number were in track and field. The following events were all-Black sweeps: 100 meters, 200 meters, 400 meters (all U.S.), 800 meters, 110-meter hurdles, and 400-meter hurdles.

In addition, there were Black winners in the 1,500 meters, 3,000-meter steeplechase, 5,000 meters, 10,000 meters, marathon, 4 x 100-meter relay, and 4 x 400-meter relay. Finally, there were Kenyan long distance gold medal sweeps in the 800 meters, 1,500 meters, 3,000-meter steeplechase, and 5,000 meters. If one adds the 10,000 meters (won by a Moroccan) to these other distance races, it becomes an African sweep.

In the women's events there were also outstanding stars. There was the "electrifying FloJo" (Florence Griffith-Joyner) in the sprints; there was the dedicated "World's Greatest Woman Athlete," Jackie Joyner-Kersee; and there were other proven medalists, such as Evelyn Ashford and Kim Gallagher, who performed brilliantly.

In swimming and diving, Anthony Nesty of Surinam won a gold medal in the 100-meter butterfly, to become the first medal winner from his country (as well as the second Black ever) to win a medal in swimming.

Women's basketball proved to be a crowning achievement, with the gold going to the talented women of the United States.

Black fighters held their own, winning four gold, two silver, and two bronze medals in boxing.

Women's tennis contributed Zina Garrison, gold and bronze winner, who became the first Black medalist ever in tennis.

But African-descended athletes have been garnering Olympic honors since 1904 in an ever-expanding triumph of dedication, skill, and prominence. The 1988 Olympics were simply the most recent and most dramatic flowering of that process.

The idea for this biographical dictionary of Black Olympic medalists, first occurred to me when I became enthralled by the twenty-third Olympiad, which I attended in Los Angeles in the summer of 1984. My interest was enhanced by the fact that the newly established California Afro-American Museum used "The Black Olympians" as its initial exhibit. I later obtained photographs from that museum.

My subsequent research followed the usual method of drawing up and sending out questionnaires, inquiring from knowledgeable persons, and burying myself in the subject. Thus, I attempted to ascertain who these 472 Black Olympian medalists were, beginning with the first medalists in 1904. I researched in the First Interstate Bank Athletic Foundation Sports Museum and Library (as it was then designated) and talked to, as well as interviewed, persons who were or had been involved one way or another with the athletes or the Olympic Games. I also sought information from the Los Angeles Public Library, Los Angeles County Public Library, University of Southern California, University of California at Los Angeles, Beverly Hills Public Library, California State University at Los Angeles, Pasadena Public Library, Southwest Community College Library, and El Camino College Library.

In addition, I contacted the United States Olympic Committee in Colorado Springs, Colorado; The International Olympic Committee in Lausanne, Switzerland; and the Los Angeles Olympic Committee. I was referred to the Olympians individually and to various Olympic committees throughout the world.

Four persons who were extremely helpful were Bruce McIntosh, Braven "Bud" Dyer, Wayne Wilson, and Shirley Ito of the newly designated Amateur Athletic Foundation Library (where the great bulk of my information and many photographs were found). Former Olympians I interviewed were Barbara Ferrell, John Carlos, Wyomia Tyus, Ulis Williams, John Rambo, and Anita DeFrantz (current president of the Amateur Athletic Foundation). I also interviewed Olympic coach Leon Coleman; Don Sanders, brother of deceased boxer "Ed" Sanders; and sports columnist Jesse Robinson, who has covered Olympic Games since 1960. In a panel discussion at the California Afro-American Museum, I heard "Mack" Robinson, Audrey Patterson, and Tommie Smith speak on the topic, "After the Olympics." Questionnaires were returned by many of the Olympians.

I have been fortunate in having Reynaldo Brown, Olympic high jumper, and his wife, Carol, assist me. Nathaniel Davis, author/librarian, has been very efficient and dedicated in helping me complete the manuscript. Raymond Roney, Director, Instructional Services, El Camino College, has been one of the most important advisors on this project. Finally, the most important ongoing relationship with a person removed from the scene has been with Reynold O'Neal, president of the British Virgin Islands Olympic Committee, who has been tremendously supportive. He has been a valuable consultant and collaborator and wrote the introduction.

Of course many reference books and other materials have been consulted. Some of the more notable are *Who's Who in Track and Field, The Complete Book of the Olympic Games, The Black Olympians, An Approved History of the Olympic Games, Guinness Book of Olympic Records, Encyclopaedia of Track and Field Athletics, The 1984 Olympics Handbook, The History of the Olympics, United States Track and Field Olympians, The Negro in Sports, Negro Firsts in Sports, Quest for Gold, Track and Field News, New York Times,* and *Los Angeles Times.* (The bibliography contains the entire list.)

Some entries included in this reference work lack as much detail or depth as others. This is especially true in the case of the Cubans. The United States has had very poor relations with Cuba during Fidel Castro's regime. As a result, information from there is all but non-existent. The same is true to a great extent also for African and some other Third World countries. In addition, information is practically unavailable on many of the less prominent athletes of the past.

Black Olympian Medalists was written to answer the many questions that sports enthusiasts, sports teams, and athletic programs and departments have. If it has helped to overcome the gray areas in these events, it will have served its purpose. We shall appreciate any errors or omissions called to our attention.

This work has been in progress for a long time. As time has passed, some of the family and career information for living individuals will inevitably have changed.

James A. Page
Los Angeles, California

James Page researching *Black Olympian Medalists* in the library of the Amateur Athletic Foundation, Los Angeles California. (Photo courtesy of Los Angeles Daily News.)

Acknowledgments

I wish to thank Anita DeFrantz, President of the Amateur Athletic Foundation of Los Angeles and to acknowledge the Foundation's special consideration in the development of this project.

Introduction

By Reynold S. O'Neal

Chronicling the performances of Black athletes in the Olympic Games demanded extensive research, checking, and double-checking of material and, to some extent, delving into the sociological factors that made athletics the vehicle for several of the early champions to gain recognition in societies that otherwise denied them most opportunities for self-expression.

My interest in the subject of Black Olympians, and especially Black medalists in track and field athletics, was "ignited" by a fellow student at Interamerican University in Puerto Rico, a hurdler from Guyana named Winston Jerrick. He made past Olympic heroes like Harrison "Bones" Dillard, Eddie Tolan, and Herb McKenley more than names in a record book to me. Through him, I became aware of the fact that several of the Olympic medals won by European countries were the fruits of the efforts of competitors of African or Afro-Caribbean origin.

For several years I had been engaged in the compilation of all-time lists of Black performers in various track and field disciplines, but it was not until I was contacted by Jim Page of Los Angeles through the British Virgin Islands Olympic Committee that I became interested in his project as a separate work. While I had a pretty good idea of who most of the Black Olympic medalists were, it was through his research that I became aware that Black athletes had won Olympic medals for Great Britain as early as 1920.

Since the introduction of the modern Olympics in 1896, Black competitors have won medals in 13 Olympic sports—basketball, boxing, cycling, fencing, figure skating, judo, rowing, swimming, tennis, track and field athletics, volleyball, weightlifting, and wrestling. The first Black Olympic medalist was American 400-meter hurdler George Poage, who won a bronze medal in the 1904 Games in St. Louis, Missouri.

By far the lion's share of Olympic medals won by Black competitors have been awarded to athletes from the United States.

However, countries not particularly well known for their success in international sports have also produced Olympic medalists. Included among them are Haiti, whose Silvio Cator won a silver medal in the long jump in 1928; the Cameroons, for whom boxer Joseph Bessala won a silver medal in 1968; and Bermuda, whose Clarence Hill won a bronze medal as a heavyweight boxer in 1976.

The earliest Black Olympic medalists were all competitors in track and field. After George Poage, other Black athletes to win Olympic medals were: Joseph Stadler, who won first a silver medal for the standing high jump and then a bronze for the standing long jump in 1904 (both discontinued), and John B. Taylor, Jr., who won a gold medal for the 4 x 400-meter relay in 1908. Then there was sprinter Harry Edward of Great Britain, who won medals in both the 100 and 200 meters at the 1920 Games. Like fellow sprinter Jack London, who was to win a silver medal in the 100-meter sprint 8 years later, Edward had migrated to England from Guyana, then the South American colony of British Guiana. They were the forerunners of a large-scale exodus from the British Caribbean, and the emigrants from the region and their descendants later entered the Olympic record books as representatives of Great Britain, Canada, the United States, Cuba, Panama, and Venezuela.

Black Americans began to make their mark in the 1924 Games when DeHart Hubbard and Edward Gourdin occupied the first two places in the long jump. There were no successes in 1928, but in 1932 Eddie Tolan won both the 100 and 200 meters, with Ralph Metcalfe placing second in the 100 and third in the longer dash. Oddly, neither was selected to run the 400-meter relay. In the long jump, which would become the event that would produce more Black gold medalists than any other, Edward Gordon emerged victorious.

The Berlin Olympics of 1936 provided Black athletes the opportunity to disprove Adolf Hitler's theory of a master race. Jesse Owens won four gold medals and the other Black males on the U.S. squad added nine more medals in track and field. The total might have been higher had the American relay teams not excluded Mack Robinson (silver medalist in the 200) from the 400-meter event, and Archie Williams and James LuValle (first and third in the open 400), as well as 800-meter winner John Woodruff from the four-lapper. Canada's Phil Edwards, a medical student from British Guiana, added an 800-meter bronze to similar medals won four years earlier in both the 800- and 1,500-meter events.

The first post-war Olympics in 1948 was notable for the emergence of Black female competitors of the highest international class. Alice Coachman of the United States won the high jump, and her teammate Audrey Patterson placed third in the 200 meters. Jamaican women also performed creditably, although their real impact was to come much later. For the first time, Black athletes won medals in sports other than athletics. Don Barksdale and Jackie Robinson both won gold medals as members of the U.S. basketball team, while in weightlifting big American John Davis won the heavyweight division and Trinidad's Rodney Wilkes earned a silver medal in the featherweight class.

On the track, Black athletes gained more medals than ever before. The athletes of the Caribbean made their first major impact, with Jamaica's Arthur Wint and Herb McKenley scoring a historic 1-2 in the 400 meters. Also making a great impression were Americans Mal Whitfield, who won his first of two Olympic golds in the 800 meters, another gold in the longer relay, and a bronze in the individual 400 meters. Harrison "Bones" Dillard, not selected in his specialty, the 110-meter hurdles, scored an upset win in the 100-meter over teammate Barney Ewell and the "Panama Express," Lloyd LaBeach.

The 1952 Olympics in Helsinki revealed the awesome potential of the Black American boxers. Led by middleweight Floyd Patterson and heavyweight Ed Sanders, they made a mark that was to be emphasized 8 years later in Rome. Hitherto most of the more capable Black fighters had turned to the professional ranks without being exposed to international competition as amateurs. Black weightlifters had their most successful Games. Heavyweight John Davis defended his title with teammate James Bradford second. Trinidadians Rodney Wilkes in the featherweight class and Lennox Kilgour in the middle heavyweight division presented the Caribbean country with bronze medals.

In track and field, the Black sprinters from the United States and the Caribbean once again sparkled, although the title of "World's Fastest Human" as the winner of the 100 meters went to Italian-American Lindy Rimigino. The 1952 Games saw the arrival of Adhemar Ferreira da Silva, the first of a triumvirate of great Black Brazilian triple jumpers. His gold medal at Helsinki was followed by another at Melbourne 4 years later. His countryman, José Telles da Conceição, better known as a sprinter and hurdler, took third in the high jump. Another South American, Arnoldo Devonish of Venezuela, placed third in the triple jump at the age of 19. It was the most successful Olympic competition to date in the field events for Black men, with Americans Jerome Biffle and Meredith Gourdine heading the long jump, American schoolboy Milt Campbell finishing second in the decathlon, and Bill Miller of the United States winning the silver medal in the javelin throw.

In 1956 Black women began to play a more important role on the American track and field teams. An all-Black team finished third in the 400-meter relay. At Helsinki three Black runners had played a part in an American victory in the event. Making her Olympic debut on the 1956 squad was young Wilma Rudolph, destined for greatness at home. American Mildred McDaniel won the high jump and broke the Olympic record. Sixteen-year-old Willye White placed second in the long jump in her Olympic debut. She would go on to compete in the next four Games and would add another silver medal in the 400-meter relay in 1964.

Among the men, sprint medals were harder to come by, although Charlie Jenkins took gold in the 400 meters and Lee Calhoun the first of two such medals in the high hurdles. Milt Campbell went one place better than he did at Helsinki and teammate Rafer Johnson took the silver medal. Another Black winner was high jumper Charles Dumas, a teenager destined to be the first to clear 7 feet.

Basketball players Bill Russell and K. C. Jones, teammates at the University of San Francisco, led the United States team to victory. Puerto Rico-born José "Chegui" Torres, a member of the American team, was the only Black medalist in the sport, winning a silver medal in the light middleweight class in boxing.

The stars of the 1960 Rome Olympics were three personable Black Americans—Cassius Clay, Rafer Johnson, and Wilma Rudolph—and a barefoot Ethiopian by the name of Abebe Bikila.

Clay, later Muhammad Ali, prefaced a distinguished professional career with a stirring gold medal victory in the light heavyweight division. The articulate junior middleweight Wilbert "Skeeter" McClure, who also won a gold medal, helped to restore his reputation, which had been tarnished by a poor showing at Melbourne.

On what was arguably the strongest amateur basketball squad ever, the three Black members, Oscar Robertson, Walt Bellamy, and Bob Boozer, all played key roles. All went on to professional stardom as did their teammates Jerry West, Jerry Lucas, Adrian Smith, and Terry Dischinger.

In weightlifting, Louis Martin, a Jamaican competing for Great Britain, won a bronze medal as a middle heavyweight. He improved to a silver in 1964 in winning what was to be the last major honor to date for a lifter with origins in the English-speaking Caribbean.

Black Africa won its first two Olympic medals at the 1960 Rome Games. Light welterweight boxer Clement Quartey of Ghana won a silver medal, but the story that made the headlines was the unexpected victory in the marathon by a barefoot member of the Ethiopian Emperor Haile Selassie's palace guard, Abebe Bikila, who, by winning in an Olympic record time, made Ethiopian runners who followed him a powerful force in world athletics.

In women's track and field, Wilma Rudolph of Tennessee State University confirmed her promise of 4 years earlier by winning both the 100 and 200 meters and anchoring an all-Black U.S. quartet to victory in the 400-meter relay. Massive Earlene Brown of the United States became the first Black woman to win an Olympic medal in a throwing event when she finished third in the shot put.

Among the men, two other standouts were Rafer Johnson and Ralph Boston, both of the United States. Johnson had placed second to Milton Campbell in the decathlon at Melbourne. At Rome, his epic struggle with UCLA teammate C. K. Yang of Taiwan was one of the most gripping in Olympic history. Boston, who won the long jump at Rome, was a superb all-round athlete who went on to take the silver medal at Tokyo and, 8 years after his first victory, he managed a bronze medal in the same event at Mexico City.

Tokyo in 1964 saw the return to prominence of the Black sprinter when Bob Hayes and Henry Carr of the United States led Black medal sweeps in both the 100 and 200 meters. Wilson Kiprugut of Kenya won a bronze medal in the 800 to become the first Black African to win an Olympic award on the track. Bikila, wearing shoes on this occasion, repeated his Rome marathon triumph. Although they won no medals in Tokyo, Kenya's Kip Keino and Mamo Wolde of Ethiopia served notice that they would become forces to be reckoned with in the middle distances.

Among the women, the Americans found worthy successors to Wilma Rudolph in the persons of Wyomia Tyus and Edith McGuire, both students at Tennessee State University. Tyus won the 100 with McGuire second. McGuire added to the 200-meter title and teamed with Tyus, Willye White, and Marilyn White to win the 400-meter relay.

The American basketball squad continued their nation's unbeaten string in Olympic competition. Among the stars were Black collegians Walt Hazzard, Luke Jackson, Joe Caldwell, and Jim "Bad News" Barnes.

In boxing, the only gold medal won by a Black fighter went to the stocky heavyweight Joe Frazier of Philadelphia. Bronze medals went to fighters from Ghana and the United States, but it was not a very successful tournament for Black pugilists.

In 1968 the Mexico City Games were the Games of the Black Africans. No doubt the effects of high altitude played a part in their success, but subsequent performances by athletes from East Africa tend to indicate that talent was just as important a factor.

Aided no doubt by the thin air of Mexico City, Black Americans achieved fantastic results in the sprints and long jump. Two of the performances, Lee Evans's time of 43.86 seconds in the 400 meters and Bob Beamon's 29-foot 2½-inch long jump still stand—the oldest individual records in the sport. Brazilian triple jumper Nelson Prudencio also became a brief holder of the world record but had to settle for a silver medal behind the Soviet jumper Viktor Saneyev.

In the sprints, American and Caribbean sprinters occupied the places of honor, except for an upset in the 200 where Australian Peter Norman snatched the silver medal from the highly fancied John Carlos. For the first time ever, all-Black squads placed first and second in both men's relays and the women's 400-meter relay. In both sprint relays the American quartets were followed home by the Cubans, while in the 1,600-meter event the Kenyans took the silver medals.

From 800 meters up, the promise showed by the East Africans in Tokyo turned into a frightening reality. Not totally unexpected, especially in light of the altitude, were the victories of Kip Keino in the 1,500 meters and Naftali Temu in the 10,000. But few would have anticipated a marathon win by an Ethiopian other than Abebe Bikila (Mamo Wolde), and not even Kenyan Amos Biwott himself could have forecast his win in the 3,000-meter steeplechase.

In the women's track events, Wyomia Tyus became the first sprinter, male or female, to successfully defend an Olympic title in the 100-meter dash. In winning the 800-meter event, Madeline Manning, also of Tennessee State, became the first Black woman to win an Olympic final at a distance beyond 200 meters.

Three Black basketball stars—Charlie Scott, Jo Jo White, and Spencer Haywood—propelled an otherwise ordinary U.S. squad to victory in the Olympic tournament while maintaining their unbeaten record.

Boxer George Foreman, later to become a professional champion, won the heavyweight title in devastating fashion. Another Black champion was the unorthodox Ronald Harris. East Africans began to make an impact in the ring and the Cuban boxing machine had started to stir.

The Mexico Games were fraught with controversy, as would be all those to follow. The first issue, the expulsion of South Africa from the Olympic movement, was resolved despite the opposition of Avery Brundage, president of the International Olympic Committee. More ominous was the threat of a boycott by leading Black American athletes. In the event, few standouts stayed away, with the notable exception of basketball's star, Lew Alcindor.

The Mexico City Games themselves were the scene of a major incident when sprinters Tommie Smith and John Carlos, on the victory stand following their being awarded their medals for placing first and third respectively in the 200-meter dash, raised their fists in a Black Power salute. In short order they were expelled from the Olympic Village (which, as it turned out, they had already left), as Brundage decreed that the Olympics could not be used for "political" purposes.

Munich will be remembered as much for the Israeli massacre in the Olympic Village as for the 1972 Games themselves. And, once more, two Black athletes, American 400-meter runners Vince Matthews and Wayne Collett, were banished from further competition for a political statement on the victory stand.

The Munich Games saw Cuba emerge as, temporarily at least, a dominant power in world boxing. Their effort was spearheaded by the powerful heavyweight Teófilo Stevenson, who would go on to win two further Olympic titles. Also outstanding was light welterweight Ray Seales, an American from the island of St. Croix.

The American basketball team tasted defeat for the first time in Olympic competition in a bitter loss to the Soviets. Among the leading lights of the American team were guard Thomas Henderson and front-line players Dwight Jones, Mike Bantom, and Jim Brewer. A very physical Cuban team, starring burly center Pedro Chappe, forward Ruperto Herrera, and playmaker Tomas Herrera, won the bronze medals.

On the track, the 1972 Olympics were not extremely successful for Black athletes. In the women's events, the only competitor to win a medal in an individual event was Cuban teenager Silvia Chivas, third in the 100. The Cuban women finished third in the 400-meter relay and three Black Americans—Mable Fergerson, Cheryl Toussaint, and Madeline (Manny) Jackson—joined Kathy Hammond to take the U.S. squad to a second place finish in the first Olympic women's 1,600-meter relay.

The most outstanding male performance on the track probably came from the colorful Ugandan 400-meter hurdler John Akii-Bua. Although he was forced to run in the tight inside lane, he easily broke the world record in romping to victory. The African presence was also evident in the middle distances. Kip Keino had been upset in defense of his 1,500-meter title, but succeeded in overcoming his inexperience in the 3,000-meter steeplechase to seize the gold medal from teammate Ben Jipcho.

Black American athletes who gained individual honors included Rod Milburn, the nonpareil 110-meter hurdler who broke the world record; Vince Matthews in the 400, and teenaged long jumper Randy Williams. Both men's relays were won by Black teams, the U.S. taking the 400-meter event with a world record performance and Kenya running to victory in the 1,600-meter relay in the absence of the Americans.

The 1976 Olympics saw the first of three successive Games that would be plagued by boycotts. Piqued by the decision of New Zealand to allow South African rugby players to tour their country, the Organization of African Unity called for its member nations to boycott the Montreal Games if New Zealand participated. Except for the Ivory Coast and Senegal, every country answered the OAU's call, and they were joined by Guyana. The absence of the Africans deprived spectators of several epic contests in the middle and long distance track events, as well as the 400-meter hurdles in which Edwin Moses would have faced Munich champion John Akii-Bua.

The boxing ring provided some of the most interesting competition of the 1976 Games. A powerful American team, headed by Ray Leonard, Howard Davis, and the Spinks brothers, Leon and Michael, defeated the Cubans in several finals. For the Cubans, Teófilo Stevenson won again and Angel Herrera gained his first Olympic title.

Women's basketball was introduced in 1976, and an American team led by the talented Luisa Harris, placed second to the much taller Soviet squad. In the men's competition, the Americans survived a scare from a Puerto Rican team, some of whom like Butch Lee, Hector Blondet, Raymond Dalmau, and Ruben Rodriguez, had made their mark on New York City playgrounds. The U.S. team faced Yugoslavia, rather than the Soviet Union, in the final, and Phil Ford, Scott

May, Walter Davis, and Adrian Dantley ensured that there would be no repeat of 1972.

In rowing, Anita DeFrantz of the United States became the first Black athlete, male or female, to win a medal in that sport with a bronze in the eights. Other firsts were scored by the all-Black Cuban male volleyball players who finished third and Dutch freestyle swimmer, Enith Brigitha, who won two bronze medals.

In track and field athletics, the male athletes of the Central American and Caribbean area had their most impressive showing yet, winning all track events under 1,500 meters, as well as the 20-kilometer walk. The undoubted star was Alberto Juantorena of Cuba, who succeeded where such luminaries as Jamaica's Arthur Wint and American Mal Whitfield, had failed in winning both the 400- and 800-meter events. Jamaica's Don Quarrie won the gold and silver medals of a set that would be completed 4 years later with a 200-meter bronze medal. A new face on the scene, Edwin Moses of the United States, broke Akii-Bua's world record in route to becoming the best-ever practitioner of the 400-meter hurdles event.

There were no successes for Black females in individual track events and, in fact, the U.S. quartet of Pam Jiles, Debra Sapenter, Sheila Ingram, and Rosalyn Bryant, second in the 1,600-meter relay, joined DeFrantz and teenaged American long jumper Kathy McMillan, who also finished second, as the only Black females to win medals at Montreal.

The 1980 Moscow Games were beset by another boycott. This time the Americans and most of their allies, especially in the Third World, stayed away in protest of the Soviet presence in Afghanistan. For some of the better African athletes, notably Kenyan world-raters like Mike Boit and Henry Rono, it would represent 8 years in the wilderness.

In the absence of the Americans, the Cubans dominated the boxing competition, winning six gold medals and two silvers. Surprisingly, only one African made an impression, the Ugandan middleweight John Mugabi.

Cuba's Daniel Nuñez became the first from his country to win a medal in weightlifting, setting a new Olympic record in the bantamweight class. Cubans were also among the medals in judo, although there were to be no golds.

On the track, the absence of many of the Western athletes was felt in most events. The leading Black performers were British decathlete Daley Thompson, whose win at Moscow would be followed by victories in the First World Championships and the 1984 Olympics, and the ageless Ethiopian runner Miruts Yifter. Yifter had been one of the world's leading distance runners since

1971, but because of the African boycott he had been denied the opportunity of gaining Olympic glory in 1976. He made no mistake in Moscow, winning both the 5,000 and 10,000 meters as Finn Lasse Viren had done in the two previous Games. Ethiopians and Tanzanians figured prominently in the three longest track races. In the sprints, favored Cubans Silvio Leonard (100 and 200) and 110-meter hurdler Alejandro Casañas flattered to deceive, though each managed to take home a silver medal. More disappointed than disappointing was the Brazilian triple jump world holder, Joao Carlos de Oliveira, who was apparently the victim of some unusual officiating, which would leave him with his second Olympic bronze medal in the last major meet of his ill-starred career.

The Moscow Games were the first in which more than one Black athlete won a medal in the throws. Unlike her favored compatriot, discus thrower Luis Delis, who was relegated to third place in the manner of Oliveira, javelin thrower María Caridad Colón upset the pundits in winning with a new games record. The West Indians on the British women's relay teams contributed four of the eight bronze medals.

As might have been expected, most Eastern Bloc countries chose not to attend the 1984 Games in Los Angeles. Also absent were their ideological supporters Cuba and Ethiopia. The United States captured the lion's share of the gold medals, but the lesser honors were fairly well distributed.

The U.S. boxers dominated the tournament even more comprehensively than had the Cubans 4 years earlier. Seven of the eight gold medals won by Americans went to Black fighters, the most outstanding of whom were featherweight Meldrick Taylor, lightweight Pernell Whitaker, and welterweight Mark Breland. Once again the Africans were less than impressive with only one silver medal and three bronzes going to the continent.

Both American basketball teams won as they pleased, the gold for the women being their first such medals. The women's team was headed by charismatic Cheryl Miller and included such other collegiate stars as Lynette Woodard and Janice Lawrence. The men's quintet, like their female counterparts, encountered no real roadblocks on their road to victory. Frontliners Wayman Tisdale and Patrick Ewing, along with guards Michael Jordan and Alvin Robertson, made this team one of the strongest ever to play in amateur competition.

Blacks struck new ground in winning medals in cycling (Nelson Vails taking second in the individual sprint) and fencing, where Peter Westbrook captured a bronze medal in sabre competition. In women's volleyball the American women lost to China in the final but boasted the world's best amateur in statuesque spiker Flo Hyman. Another major contributor to the U.S. effort was Rita Crockett.

On the track the star of the Games was American Carl Lewis, who equaled Jesse Owens's 1936 feat in winning gold medals in the 100, 200, long jump, and 400-meter relay. In the latter event, the American quartet set a new world record, while Lewis added a new Olympic mark in the 200 meters. As dominant as Lewis was among the men, so too was Valerie Brisco-Hooks in the women's events. The American took the 200 and 400 and ran on the victorious 1,600-meter relay team.

Repeat wins came from the British decathlete Daley Thompson and 400-meter hurdler Edwin Moses of the United States. Actually, Moses's initial win had come 8 years earlier, but he had been deprived of the opportunity in 1980 by the U.S. boycott.

Impressive wins came from Joaquim Cruz of Brazil in the 800, Morocco's Said Aouita in the 5,000, Roger Kingdom of the United States in the 100-meter hurdles, and Evelyn Ashford, another American, in the 100 meters. All set new Olympic records.

West African athletes, surprisingly, won their first Olympic medals on the track, as Gabriel Tiacoh of the Ivory Coast followed American Alonzo Babers home in the 400 and the Nigerian quartet won bronze medals in the 1,600-meter relay. Sprinters of Caribbean origin from Canada and the United Kingdom, and those representing Jamaica, also showed well in the relay races.

Of 52 athletic medals won by the United States, 43 went to Black competitors, the highest percentage ever. Among the medals were a gold for triple jumper Al Joyner and a silver for his sister, Jackie Joyner, in the heptathlon, a first-time occurrence for siblings in Olympic track and field.

As a whole, then, African-descended athletes from 1904 through 1988, have labored mightily to achieve a great measure of dedication, skill, and prominence and have proved to the world that they have indeed earned the many honors they have won.

We hope that this overview of Black participation in the Olympic Games will help the reader to better appreciate and interpret the thumbnail sketches and brief profiles that follow.

Modern Olympic Games

I	1896	Athens		XIII**	1944	London
II	1900	Paris		XIV	1948	London
III	1904	St. Louis		XV	1952	Helsinki
*	1906	Athens		XVI	1956	Melbourne
IV	1908	London		XVII	1960	Rome
V	1912	Stockholm		XVIII	1964	Tokyo
VI**	1916	Berlin		XIX	1968	Mexico City
VII	1920	Antwerp		XX	1972	Munich
VIII	1924	Paris		XXI	1976	Montreal
IX	1928	Amsterdam		XXII	1980	Moscow
X	1932	Los Angeles		XXIII	1984	Los Angeles
XI	1936	Berlin		XXIV	1988	Seoul
XII**	1940	Tokyo, then Helsinki				

*Held to mark 10th anniversary of Games; not numbered
**Canceled

Abbreviations

Athletic Groups, Terms, and Expressions

AAA	Amateur Athletic Association
AAC	Amateur Athletic Club
AAU	Amateur Athletic Union
ABA	American Basketball Association
ABF	American Boxing Federation
AFL	American Football League
AR	American record
AIAW	Association for Intercollegiate Athletics for Women
ATFS	Association of Track and Field Statisticians
CIF	California Interscholastic Federation
ESPN	Eastern Sports Network
FIBA	International Amateur Basketball Federation
ft.	feet
hrs.	hours
IAAF	International Amateur Athletic Federation
IC4A	Intercollegiate Association of Amateur Athletes of America
in.	inches
IOC	International Olympic Committee
ITA	International Track Association
JUCO	junior college
kg	kilograms
km	kilometers
lbs.	pounds
m	meters
MVP	most valuable player
NAIA	National Association of Intercollegiate Athletics
NBA	National Basketball Association
NCAA	National Collegiate Athletic Association
NFL	National Football League
NSF	National Sports Festival
OR	Olympic record
PAC	Pacific Athletic Conference
PAC-10	Pacific 10
PCAA	Pacific Coast Athletic Association
Pan Am	Pan American
PR	Personal record

pts.	points
SEC	Southeastern Conference
TAC	The Athletic Congress
USBWA	United States Basketball Writers Association
USOC	United States Olympic Committee
WAAA	Women's Amateur Athletic Association
WR	world record

General Terms

AP	Associated Press
B.A.	Bachelor of Arts
B.S.	Bachelor of Science
d.n.a.	data not available
ESPN	Entertainment and Sports Programming Network
Jr.	Junior
M.A.	Master of Arts
M.D.	Medical Doctor
M.S.	Master of Science
Ph.D.	Doctor of Philosophy
UCLA	University of California, Los Angeles
UPI	United Press International
USA/ABF	United States of America/Amateur Boxing Federation
USC	University of Southern California

Nations

Bah	Bahamas
Ber	Bermuda
Bra	Brazil
BWI	British West Indies (Jamaica and Trinidad)
Cam	Cameroon
Can	Canada
Cub	Cuba
Dji	Djibouti
Eth	Ethiopia
Fra	France
Gbr	Great Britain
Gha	Ghana
Guy	Guyana
Hai	Haiti
Hol	Netherlands
Ivc	Ivory Coast
Jam	Jamaica
Ken	Kenya
Mex	Mexico
Mor	Morocco
Ngr	Nigeria
Nig	Niger
Pan	Panama
Pur	Puerto Rico
Sen	Senegal
Tan	Tanzania
Tog	Togo
Tri	Trinidad and Tobago

Tun	Tunisia	Ven	Venezuela
Uga	Uganda	Zam	Zambia
USA	United States of America	Zim	Zimbabwe
USSR	Union of Soviet Socialist Republics		

The Athletes

ADKINS, CHARLES (USA). Born April 27, 1932.

1952 Gold Medal: Light Welterweight Boxing

Charles Adkins won the national AAU lightweight title in 1949. He won a boxing scholarship to San Jose State in California, where he was coached by DeWitt Portel. Adkins beat out Joe Reynolds in the Olympic trials and won the gold medal rather easily in Helsinki. Adkins turned professional and fought as a lightweight for 5 years during which he had a record of 16 wins and 5 losses. Adkins returned to college in the 1970s and graduated from Ohio State University.

Sources: *Approved History of Olympic Games; Black Olympians; XVth Olympiad, Helsinki, 1952; Guinness Book of Olympic Records; Helsingin Olympiakisat, 1952; Tales of Gold.*

AGUILAR, JOSÉ (Cuba). Born in Cuba.

1980 Bronze Medal: Light Welterweight Boxing

At the 1980 Olympic Games in Moscow in the preliminary rounds, José Aguilar, 140 pounds, won in a decision over Bun Hwa Rye of North Korea. In the semifinals, Serik Konakbaev, 140 pounds, of the USSR, decisioned Aguilar.

Sources: *Approved History of Olympic Games;* British Virgin Islands, Olympic Committee; *Guinness Book of Olympic Records;* "Today's Olympic Results," *Los Angeles Times* (July 27, 1980); "Track and Field, Boxing," *Los Angeles Times* (August 1, 1980).

AKABUSI, KRISS (Great Britain). Born November 28, 1958, of Nigerian parentage.

1984 Silver Medal: 4 x 400-Meter Relay (2:59.13)

Kriss Akabusi's personal best in the 400 meters is 45.37 seconds (1984). Before the 1984 Olympics he won a bronze medal in the 4 x 400-meter relay in the 1983 World Championships and a gold medal in the 4 x 400 in the European Championships. Akabusi is a member of Britain's Royal Air Force.

Sources: British Virgin Islands, Olympic Committee; *1984 Olympic Games; Sarajevo/Los Angeles;* "The Games," *Olympian* (October/November 1984).

AKII-BUA, JOHN (Uganda). Born December 3, 1950, in Uganda.

1972 Gold Medal: 400-Meter Hurdles (47.82, Olympic record)

The only Ugandan ever to win an Olympic gold medal, John Akii-Bua set the world 400-meter hurdles record in 1972 in Munich. He came into promise in 1971 at the Pan African-U.S. meet with a time of 49.0 seconds, defeating both Americans and Kenyans. That same year he was champion in the U.S.-USSR World All-Star meet with the world's second fastest time of 50.1 seconds. Akii-Bua began as a high hurdler but turned to the intermediates for the 1970 Commonwealth Games, where he placed fourth with 51.1 seconds. He qualified for both events, but didn't make the 110-meter finals. In the Munich Olympic Games in 1972, Akii-Bua set the world record with a time of 47.82, becoming Uganda's first track medalist. His hopes for the 1976 Games were dashed by the African boycott, and his world record and Olympic title fell in Montreal when Edwin Moses ran a time of 47.64 seconds. Akii-Bua was one of 43 children whose father had 8 wives. A police officer by vocation, he was forced to escape his country with his family because of political conflicts there, a move facilitated by his connections with a major manufacturer of athletic shoes in West Germany. He was later invited back to Uganda where he returned to his old job of colonel in the police force and where he became an Olympic coach. In 1972 he was the winner of the Citizens Savings (Helms) World Trophy Award in Africa.

Sources: *Approved History of Olympic Games;* British Virgin Islands, Olympic Committee; *Complete Book of the Olympics; Die Spiele, Official Report of XXth Olympiad; Guinness Book of Olympic Records;* "Akii-Bua Wins a Bigger Race—for His Life," *Los Angeles Times* (August 2, 1984); Uganda Olympic Committee; *Who's Who in Track and Field.*

ALBRITTON, DAVID DONALD (USA). Born April 13, 1913, in Danville, Alabama.

1936 Silver Medal: High Jump (6 ft. 6¾ in./2m)

David Albritton graduated from East Technical High School in Cleveland, Ohio, and Ohio State University. In high school he was Cleveland All-City in football and basketball. He was twice Golden Gloves champion, three times Ohio State boxing champion, and held the world, national, and collegiate record in the running high jump. He was named outstanding high jumper of the first half of the century by the Western Intercollegiate Athletic Association and the National AAU. He was selected 13 times All-American, and was an All-Collegiate high jumper. Albritton, at the 1936 Olympic trials, cleared 6 feet, 9¾ inches to become the first Black athlete to hold a world high jump record. In 1939 Dave Albritton made a 6-foot 9¼-inch leap—a world record. In the *World Encyclopedia of Sports*, the record was described this way: "Beaten by Cornelius Johnson in the Berlin Games (1936), David Albritton made a sensation there by using a technique resembling the California Roll." His career extended from 1936 through 1951. Albritton is a member of the Hall of Fame, Ohio Track Coaches, Ohio State University, and Helms Athletic Foundation Track and Field and National Track and Field. He was a member of the 13 All-Star U.S. Track Teams touring Europe, the Far East, and Central and South America. He has been a member of the President's Council on Physical Fitness and Sports, a member of the Ohio Criminal Justice Commission, and president and organizer of Ohio Olympians. For 14 years he was a member of the Ohio General Assembly. He married Margaret A. Holliday and has a son, David D. II.

Sources: Albritton, David D. Questionnaire, 1984; *Black Olympians; International Athletics Annual; XIth Olympic Games, Berlin, 1936; Guinness Book of Olympic Records; Quest for Gold; Who's Who in Track and Field* "The High Jump," *World Encyclopedia of Sports*.

ALDAMA, ANDRÉS (Cuba). Born in Cuba.

1976 Silver Medal: Light Welterweight Boxing
1980 Gold Medal: Welterweight Boxing

At the Moscow Games Andrés Aldama defeated John Mugabi of Uganda in the 1980 welterweight boxing division. He had won the light welterweight boxing silver medal in 1976 at Montreal, where Ray Leonard won the gold.

Sources: *Approved History of Olympic Games*; British Virgin Islands, Olympic Committee; *Complete Book of the Olympics; Games of the XXIInd Olympiad; Guinness Book of Olympic Records*; "Summer Games, Boxing," *New York Times* (August 3, 1980); "Olympic Winners," *New York Times* (August 4, 1980).

ALI, MUHAMMAD (Cassius Marcellus Clay) (USA). Born January 17, 1942, in Louisville, Kentucky.

1960 Gold Medal: Light Heavyweight Boxing

Muhammad Ali won the 1959 Golden Gloves Championship. He repeated the victory in 1960 and added to it the

AAU title and Olympic light heavyweight crown (thus becoming "The Greatest"). He won the world heavyweight title in 1964. Ali turned professional after the Rome Olympics in 1960 and worked his way up to the heavyweight ranks. As fast as he was, he wasn't given much of a chance of beating Sonny Liston. But Ali beat him by a technical knockout in the seventh round on February 25, 1964. Ali joined the Black Muslims and changed his name. He later refused to fight in the Vietnamese War on religious grounds. He was charged with draft evasion and banned from boxing for 3 years. The Supreme Court finally ruled in his favor, and his license was restored in 1970. The Muhammad Ali of the late 1960s was an awesome fighting machine. He possessed great speed, deceptive power, and an unequaled ability to take a punch. He was never beaten or seriously challenged. He defended his heavyweight championship nine times before being stripped of his titles and banned from boxing. Ali won back his heavyweight title in 1974 by defeating George Foreman (after losing to Joe Frazier in a 15-round decision). He lost the title again, this time to Leon Spinks, in 1978, but regained it from Spinks later that same year. In the late 1970s, Ali attempted to regain the title but he was not the same man. He lost to Larry Holmes in 1980. Muhammad Ali was a flamboyant personality and a man of strong convictions; he once threw his Olympic medal in the Ohio River at Louisville when he was refused service in a restaurant.

Sources: *Black Olympians; Guinness Book of Olympic Records; Quest for Gold*.

AMARTEY, PRINCE (Ghana). Born in Ghana.

1972 Bronze Medal: Middleweight Boxing

During the 1972 Olympic Games at Munich, Prince Amartey defeated José Luis Espinosa of Mexico on points, 5-0. He defeated Poul Knudsen of Denmark, 3-2, but lost to Reima W. Virtanen of Finland, 3-2.

Sources: *Approved History of Olympic Games; Complete Book of the Olympics; Die Spiele, Official Report of the Games of the XXth Olympiad; Guinness Book of Olympic Records; Munich, 1972; Results of the Games of the XXth Olympiad*.

ANDERSON, WILLIE (USA). Born January 8, 1967.

1988 Olympic Bronze Medal: Basketball

Willie Anderson graduated in 1988 from the University of Georgia where he majored in education. Anderson was an All-Southeastern Conference selection, both in 1987 and 1988. He ranked among SEC leaders in 1988 in: scoring, field goal percentage, free throw percentage, assists, blocked shots, and steals. As a senior he led Georgia in scoring, assists, and blocks. Willie Anderson was SEC Player of the Week for performances against Florida and

Alabama when he scored 53 points and had 10 rebounds, 6 assists, 7 steals, and 5 blocks. He went over the 20-point mark 11 times as a senior. Anderson was a member of the U.S. team at the Pan Am Games in 1987.

Sources: "Black American Medal Winners," *Ebony* (December 1988); "The Seoul Games/Medal Winners," *Los Angeles Times* (October 3, 1988); *1988 United States Olympic Team, Media Guide; Seoul '88*; "Olympics Record," *USA Today* (October 3, 1988).

ANTHONY, MICHAEL (Guyana). Born in Guyana.

1980 Bronze Medal: Bantamweight Boxing

At the 1980 Games in Moscow, Michael Anthony defeated Nuremi Ghabamosi of Nigeria and Fayez Zaghloul of Syria. He went on in the quarterfinal to defeat Daniel Zaragoza of Mexico when the referee stopped the match in the second round.

Sources: *Approved History of Olympic Games*; British Virgin Islands, Olympic Committee; *Complete Book of the Olympics; Games of the XXIInd Olympiad, Moscow, 1980; Guinness Book of Olympic Records.*

AOUITA, SAÏD (Morocco). Born November 2, 1960, in Kenitra, Morocco (of Berber parentage).

1984 Gold Medal: 5,000-Meter Run (13:05.59, Olympic record)
1988 Bronze Medal: 800-Meter Run (1:44.06)

At the International Amateur Federation Mobil Grand Prix meet at Crystal Palace in London, Saïd Aouita won the 1,500 in 3:36.50. At another international meet, he won the 1,000 meters in 2:15.16, the fastest time in the world (1988). By so doing he maintained his unbeaten seasonal record after 17 races at a variety of distances. Aouita is world record holder at 1,500 and 5,000 meters as well as the Olympic 5,000-meter champion. Saïd Aouita is the oldest of seven children; his father was a factory foreman in Morocco, and his younger brother, Khalid, is an excellent junior runner. Aouita has trained both in France and in Italy. He ran an amazing 3:32.54 in Florence in 1983. On the same track a year later, he ran the 5,000 meters in 13:04.78, the second fastest ever at the time. He took the lead at 1,000 meters in the 1,500 World Championships in Helsinki, but couldn't hold off Steve Oram and Steve Scott. Aouita's gold medal-winning score in Los Angeles set a new Olympic record. The manner of his victory was quite impressive. He passed Canario of Portugal and strode away very comfortably with a 55-second last lap to win. He set world records in 1985 at 1,500 and 5,000 meters— 3:29.45 for 1,500 and 13:00.40 for 5,000. Aouita is a very versatile runner with bests of 46.9 for 400 meters, 1:44.38 for 800, 3:46.92 for the mile, 8:40.2 for the 3,000-meter

steeplechase, and 7:32.94 for 3,000 meters. He was the world's number 1 athlete in 1985, when he was chosen Athlete of the Year. He also received the *Track & Field News* Athlete of the Year Award. In 1985 Aouita became the eighth 5,000/10,000 doubler. At the Golden Gala Meet in Rome he broke the race open at 3,000 meters and carried on to a stunning 12:58.39. He thus became the first runner to cover the 12½ laps under 13:00. This was the second global mark for him in 6 days. He had set a 2,000 meter record of 4:50.81 in Paris. (He had won a World Championships bronze medal in the 1983 1,500 meters.) Aouita won the men's 2-mile in 8:13.09 at Casablanca, Morocco, in the spring of 1988, breaking his own record of 8:13.45 set the previous year. He won only one medal in Seoul, the 800 bronze, although he had predicted victories also in the 1,500 and the 5,000. He withdrew from the 1,500 semifinal with a pulled hamstring.

Sources: British Virgin Islands, Olympic Committee; *International Athletics Annual*; "World Records Are Broken," *Los Angeles Times* (June 12, 1988); "Aouita Stretches Win Streak," *Los Angeles Times* (August 29, 1988); *1984 Olympic Games; Sarajevo/Los Angeles*; "The Games," *Olympian* (October/November 1984); "Aouita through the Eyes of Others," *Track & Field News* (January/February 1986); "Something Old ... Something New," *Track & Field News* (January 1987); "Historic WR for Aouita," *Track & Field News* (September 1987); "Glory and Disappointment," *USA Today* (October 3, 1988).

ARMSTEAD, RAY (USA). Born May 27, 1960, in Kirksville, Missouri.

1984 Gold Medal: 4 x 400-Meter Relay (2:57.91)

Ray Armstead attended Northeast Missouri University. His best time in the 400 meters of 44.83 seconds was recorded in 1984 in Los Angeles. He also ran on the victorious U.S. 4 x 400-meter relay team at the 1985 World Cup in Canberra, Australia.

Sources: "The 1984 Olympics," *Ebony* (October 1984); *Games of the XXIIIrd Olympiad, Los Angeles; International Athletics Annual*; "The Champions," *Los Angeles Times* (August 14, 1984); *1984 Olympic Games; Sarajevo/Los Angeles*; "The Games," *Olympian* (October/November 1984); *Research Information, Games of the XXIIIrd Olympiad*; "Olympic Medal Results," *Sporting News* (August 20, 1984).

ASATI, CHARLES (Kenya). Born in 1945 in Kisii, Kenya.

1968 Silver Medal: 4 x 400-Meter Relay (2:59.64)
1972 Gold Medal: 4 x 400-Meter Relay (2:59.83)

Charles Asati was inspired by the performances of his fellow countryman Kipchoge Keino in the metric mile. He is probably Kenya's best-ever all-around sprinter with personal bests of 10.2 for the 100 meters, 20.66 for the 200, and 46.01 for the 400. He was Commonwealth 400-meter champion in 1970. Asati was leadoff man in 1972. In 1968 he was 30 yards behind the first-place winner, Lee Evans.

Sources: *Approved History of Olympic Games*; British Virgin Islands, Olympic Committee; *Complete Book of the Olympics*; *Die Spiele, Official Report of the XXth Olympiad*; *The Games, Organizing Committee, XIXth Olympiad*; *Guinness Book of Olympic Records*.

ASHFORD, EVELYN (USA). Born April 15, 1957, in Shreveport, Louisiana.

1984 Gold Medal: Women's 100-Meter Run (10.97, Olympic record)
1984 Gold Medal: Women's 4 x 100-Meter Relay (41.65)
1988 Gold Medal: Women's 4 x 100-Meter Relay (41.98)
1988 Silver Medal: Women's 100-Meter Run (10.83)

Evelyn Ashford grew up in Roseville, California. She attended UCLA where she received one of the school's first athletic scholarships to women. She is married to Ray Washington, a former assistant junior college basketball coach (San Jacinto College) who became her coach. The couple have a daughter, Raina, born after the 1984 Olympics. During her career Evelyn Ashford accomplished dual goals: a world record and an Olympic gold medal. (Wilma Rudolph had been her role model). She defeated Marlies Gohr at the World Class Invitational (Gohr ranked number 1 in the world five times). Ashford was virtually unchallenged as fastest woman in the West (before the Seoul Games). Evelyn Ashford was chosen for the 1976 Olympic Team in the 100 meters and came in fifth at Montreal. She left UCLA to concentrate on achieving world-class level. Her coach, Pat Connolly, also left UCLA and trained Ashford on a volunteer basis. Ashford was TAC champion in the 100 and 200 (1983). Her other TAC titles in 1977, 1979, and 1981 set her personal record of 51.57 in the 400 (1979). In 1979 she set the American 200-meter record (21.83). Her affiliation was with the Puma and Energizer Track Clubs. She was a member of a national 4 x 100-meter relay team that set an American record of 41.61, also at the National Sports Festival in 1983. She wound up with world rankings of third in the 100 and fifth in the 200 (1983), but in 1979 and 1981 she was top-ranked in the 100 and in 1981 had the number 1 rating in the 200. She was fifth in the 100 at the 1976 Olympics and at the World Cup in 1977, and fourth in the 200. Evelyn Ashford was the best sprinter in the world in 1979, winning the 100 and 200 in the World Cup at Montreal. She beat East Germans Marlies Gohr and Marita Koch in the World Class Invitational. She dropped out of the 200 at the U.S. Olympic trials because of a pulled hamstring muscle. She was primed to meet the East Germans again

EVELYN ASHFORD (Above photo courtesy of Rich Clarkson, Denver, Colorado. Top photo courtesy of Amateur Athletic Foundation, Los Angeles, California, and Michael Yada AAF/LPI 1984.)

and claim a gold medal at the World Championships at Helsinki, Finland. However, she strained a muscle before the competition. Ashford stated in the *Los Angeles Times*: "I wanted to win the Olympic Games and prove that I was the World's fastest woman. For people to discover me after that would be soon enough." She set the world record of 10.79 at the National Sports Festival in Colorado Springs in 1983. She set the world record at a Zurich meet (in which the Eastern bloc countries were represented) after the 1984

Olympics; there she beat her own world record of 10.79 (with 10.76). Evelyn Ashford was chosen Athlete of the Year in 1984. No woman Olympic winner had ever run faster than her 10.97 dash. In February 1986 Ashford won the 55-meter dash in 6.6 seconds at the Vitalis Olympic Invitational. Ashford finished second behind Florence Griffith-Joyner in the 100 meters at the 1988 Olympic trials (10.8). ("FloJo" had shattered Ashford's world record at Indianapolis with a 10.49). This second-place finish was repeated at Seoul when she was outclassed by Griffith-Joyner's spectacular sprinting. Ashford made a kind of comeback in the 400-meter relay when she took a rather weak passoff from Griffith-Joyner to anchor the team to a 41.98 silver win. Evelyn Ashford has been a reporter for "World Class Woman," a cable television program on female athletics. She signed a 4-year contract with Mazda to be a runner and spokesperson for their track club.

Sources: "The 1984 Olympics," *Ebony* (October 1984); "World's Fastest Mom," *Ebony* (June 1986); *For the Record*; "U.S. Coach is Playing Wait-and-See on Finalists," *Los Angeles Times* (July 30, 1984); "Olympic Games," *Los Angeles Times* (August 6, 1984); "Ashford Runs World Record 10.76," *Los Angeles Times* (August 23, 1984); "Seoul Games/Medal Winners," *Los Angeles Times* (October 3, 1988); "Olympic Medal Results" *Sporting News* (August 13, 1984); "Ashford Gets Gold and More," *Track & Field News* (December 1984); *United States Olympic Team, Media Guide* (1984, 1988); "Olympics Record," *USA Today* (October 3, 1988); "Evelyn Ashford," *Women's Sports* (August 1984).

AUGMON, STACEY (USA). Born August 1, 1968, in Pasadena, California.

1988 Bronze Medal: Basketball

Stacey Augmon attended John Muir High School, Pasadena, and the University of Nevada, majoring in social work. Augmon was PCAA Freshman of the Year and a member of PCAA's All-Freshman team. He established a University of Nevada (Las Vegas) first by recording a triple-double against Providence: 21 points, 10 rebounds, and 10 assists. He set a career high of 14 rebounds against Pacific. Augmon was a member of the U.S. Jr. World Championship team in 1987.

Sources: "Black American Medal Winners," *Ebony* (December 1988); "The Seoul Games/Medal Winners," *Los Angeles Times* (October 3, 1988); *1988 United States Olympic Team, Media Guide; Seoul '88;* "Olympics Record," *USA Today* (October 3, 1988).

BA, ELHADJDIA (Senegal). Born August 22, 1958, in Dakar, Senegal.

1988 Silver Medal: 400-Meter Hurdles (47.23)

In Seoul Edwin Moses finished third behind the surprising Elhadjdia Ba of Senegal. Ba ran 47.23 to Moses' 47.56. Ba's 400-meter hurdles record speaks for itself: Olympic Games, 1984-5th, 1988-2nd; World Championships, 1983-7th, 1987-5th; World Student Games, 1983-2nd; African Games, 1987-1st; African Championships, 1982-1st (1st at 400 meters), 1984-1st; World Cup, 1985-4th. His high jump record is: African Games, 1978-3rd; World Cup, 1981-7th. Elhadjdia Ba is a member of the Racing Club de France.

Sources: British Virgin Islands, Olympic Committee; *International Amateur Athletic Federation;* "Phillips Upset Moses," *Los Angeles Times* (September 25, 1988); "Seoul Games/Medal Winners," *Los Angeles Times* (October 3, 1988); *Seoul '88;* "Olympics Record," *USA Today* (October 3, 1988).

BABERS, ALONZO (USA). Born October 31, 1961, in Montgomery, Alabama.

1984 Gold Medal: 400-Meter Run (44.27)
1984 Gold Medal: 4 x 400-Meter Relay (2:57.91)

Alonzo Babers grew up in Kaiserlauten, West Germany, where his father was a career air force officer. He attended Air Force Base High School, Kaiserlauten, and graduated from the U.S. Air Force Academy in 1983. He was affiliated with Bud Light Track America. Babers became the fifth fastest man ever in the 400 meter event with a time of 44.27, although he didn't emerge as a world class quartermiler until 1983. In the athlete's first season of international experience he ranked seventh in the world, placing fourth in the NCAA and fifth at TAC; that same year he achieved a personal record of 45.07 at Zurich (where he beat Bert Cameron in Cameron's only loss of 1983). Babers ran a leg of the U.S. 4 x 400-meter relay at Helsinki and won a gold medal at the Pan Am Games (where he led off the relay team with 45.21). He earned gold medals as a member of the winning 4 x 400 teams at the World University Games and at the Pan Am Games. Babers is a second lieutenant in the U.S. Air Force and a jet pilot. He has flown a variety of aircraft, including the T-38 jet, the F-15 fighter plane, and the huge C-141 transport.

Sources: "The 1984 Olympics," *Ebony* (October 1984); "After Others Did the Talking," *Los Angeles Times* (August 9, 1984); "Babers Close to Fastest Ever," *Track & Field News* (September 1984); "Commission Decommissions

Babers," *Track & Field News* (June 1985); "Babers Has No Fear of Flying," *Track & Field News* (June 1987); *United States Olympic Guide*.

BAILES, MARGARET JOHNSON (USA). Born January 23, 1951, in The Bronx, New York.

1968 Gold Medal: 4 x 100-Meter Relay (42.88, Olympic record, world record)

Margaret Bailes graduated from Winston Church High School in Portland, Oregon, in 1969. She was a member of the Oregon Track Club. Bailes placed first at the AAU in the 100 and 200 meters in 1968 and first in the first and second 200 meters in the Olympic trials. She competed in the 1968 Olympics while still attending high school, finishing fifth in the 100 meters and seventh in the 200 meters. That year she won the AAU national title in the 100 meters.

Sources: *Approved History of Olympic Games; Black Olympians; Guinness Book of Olympic Records; United States Olympic Team, Games of the XIXth Olympiad; United States Track and Field Olympians*.

BAILEY, ANGELA (Canada). Born February 28, 1962, in Coventry, England, of Jamaican parentage.

1984 Silver Medal: 4 x 400-Meter Relay (42.77)

Angela Bailey was a finalist in the 100 and 200 meters at the 1983 World Championships and in the 100 at the 1984 Olympics. She had bests of 11.17 (100 meters), 22.64 (200), and 51.96 (400). Bailey won the silver in 1978 at the Commonwealth Games when she was only 16. Her coach was John Mumford at the University of Ontario. She attended UCLA.

Sources: *British Virgin Islands, Olympic Committee; Canadian Olympic Association; 1984 Olympic Games; Sarajevo/Los Angeles; Who's Who in 1984 Olympics*.

BAILEY, EMMANUEL MCDONALD (Great Britain). Born December 8, 1920, in Williamsville, Trinidad.

1952 Bronze Medal: 100-Meter Run (10.83)

Champion sprinter E. McDonald Bailey was encouraged by his father, an outstanding cricketer. He was junior champion at Queen's Royal College where he finished his education. Bailey ranked first in Britain for the 100 yards in 9.5 seconds and first in the 220 yards with 21.3. This was all in 1949. One of his best performances was the 100 meters at Antwerp in 1947 (10.3). He also ran 100 meters in 10.4 in the grass at Glasgow—considered by some to be the world's fastest; 200 meters in 21.2 at Prague in 1947;

and 220 yards in 21.2 in British Guiana in 1944. Bailey was top-ranked in the world at 200 meters in 1951. He held the record for the greatest number of American Amateur Athletic titles, with 14 victories, excluding relays, between 1946 and 1953. E. McDonald Bailey joined the Royal Air Force in 1945. He later lived in Port-of-Spain, Trinidad.

Sources: *Approved History of Olympic Games*; British Virgin Islands, Olympic Committee; *Encyclopaedia of Track and Field Athletics; Guinness Book of Olympic Records; Official Report of the XVth Olympiad; World's All-Sports Who's Who for 1950*.

BALDWIN, JOHN (USA). Born August 26, 1949, in Detroit, Michigan.

1968 Bronze Medal: Light Middleweight Boxing

John Baldwin won the Michigan AAU Championships in 1966 and 1968 and was runner-up in the National AAU in 1968. He lost a close decision to Rolando Garbey of Cuba at the Olympics in Mexico City. Baldwin began fighting as a professional in 1970 and ran up a good record. Through 1976, in 32 fights as a middleweight, he lost only twice, both times to "Marvelous" Marvin Hagler, the future middleweight champion.

Sources: *Black Olympians*; British Virgin Islands, Olympic Committee; *Games of the XIXth Olympiad; Guinness Book of Olympic Records; Quest for Gold*.

BAMBUCK, ROGER (France). Born November 29, 1945, in Guadeloupe.

1968 Bronze Medal: 4 x 100-Meter Relay (38.43)

Roger Bambuck was European champion at 200 meters in 1966. He finished 15th in both sprints at the Mexico City Olympics. He had personal bests of 10.11 (100 meters) and 20.47 (200). He established a world record in the 100 with 10.0 on June 20, 1968. Bambuck is currently a physician in France. He is married to two-time French Olympian Ghislaine Barney of Martinique.

Sources: British Virgin Islands, Olympic Committee; *Complete Book of the Olympics; Encyclopaedia of Track and Field Athletics; Guinness Book of Olympic Records*.

BANTOM, MICHAEL ALLEN (USA). Born December 3, 1951, in Philadelphia, Pennsylvania.

1972 Silver Medal: Basketball

Michael Bantom started his basketball career at St. Joseph's University in Philadelphia. After participating in the 1972 Olympics, he was drafted in the first round by the Phoenix Suns; he was the eighth pick overall in that year's NBA draft. He made the NBA All-Rookie team that same year (1973) and averaged 10.1 points per game. Bantom has been a member of the Indiana Pacers since 1977.

Sources: *Black Olympians; Die Spiele, Official Report of XXth Olympiad; Guinness Book of Olympic Records; Quest for Gold.*

BAPTISTE, KIRK (USA). Born June 20, 1963, in Beaumont, Texas.

1984 Silver Medal: 200-Meter Run (19.96)

At Madison High School in Houston, Kirk Baptiste ran the 200 and 400 meters and ranked fifth among American high schoolers in the 440 yards in 1980. He attended the University of Houston where he majored in hotel and restaurant management. Baptiste decided to forgo his final year of intercollegiate eligibility in 1986 and to compete instead for the Athletics West Track Club. The apex of Kirk Baptiste's record was his performance at the Los Angeles Olympics where he ran the 200 in 19.96, the sixth fastest time ever to win the silver medal. His teammate Carl Lewis won the gold. Baptiste ranked second in the world in the 200 in 1984 and first in 1985, despite losing the IAAF Grand Prix Final to Calvin Smith and suffering the ignominy of a disqualification after a fairly comfortable win in the World Cup 200. He had, however, won both the NCAA and TAC half-lap titles. In the 100 meters, Baptiste, whose personal best is 10.11, has been much less consistent, although he did win the TAC Championship in 1985 and was third at the 1985 World Cup. In the 100 he was ranked number 3 in the world in 1984 and fourth in 1985 by *Track & Field News*. Baptiste's personal record in the 400, achieved in 1986, is 45.95. Baptiste has also proven himself an outstanding runner in the sprint relay. Together with Harvey Glance, Calvin Smith, and Dwayne Evans, he ran an outstanding time of 38.10 to win the event at the 1985 World Cup in Canberra, Australia. Kirk Baptiste has twice defeated Carl Lewis, once in 1985 when he beat him in a post-Olympic 300-meter race in London with a world best 31.70.

Sources: British Virgin Islands, Olympic Committee; "The 1984 Olympics," *Ebony* (October 1984); "The Champions," *Los Angeles Times* (August 14, 1984); "The Games," *Olympian* (October/November 1984); *Research Information, Games of the XXIIIrd Olympiad*; "Olympic Medal Results," *Sporting News* (August 20, 1984); "Baptiste Is Taking Giant Steps," *Track & Field News* (August 1985).

BARKSDALE, DONALD ARGEE (USA). Born March 31, 1923, in Berkeley, California.

1948 Gold Medal: Basketball

Donald Barksdale attended UCLA and starred for the UCLA Bruins in 1942-43 and 1946-47. He won the 1944 AAU

triple jump championship. He was also an outstanding UCLA track star. Barksdale was the first Black to play on the U.S. Olympic basketball team. At that time Blacks were not allowed on the professional teams. He played 4 years of AAU ball with the Oakland Bittners before the ban on Blacks in the NBA was lifted. He averaged 12.6 and 13.8 points per game as top player in the days of much lower scores. In the NBA Barksdale played 2 years with the original Baltimore Bullets and 2 years with the Boston Celtics. He was a member of the All-Time Pacific Coast Conference team. He was selected to the NBA All-Star Game in 1953, the first Black to participate. Don Barksdale majored in business administration at UCLA and minored in art. His business interests over the years have included real estate, radio, and nightclubs. He is now president of Save High School Sports in the San Francisco Bay Area, and hopes to go statewide with the project.

Sources: *Black Olympians; Great Black Athletes; Guinness Book of Olympic Records; Quest for Gold; Tales of Gold; United States Olympic Team, Games of XIVth Olympiad.*

BARNES, JIM (USA). Born August 13, 1941, in Tuckerton, Arkansas.

1964 Gold Medal: Basketball

Jim Barnes attended Texas Western (now University of Texas at El Paso). Following his participation in the Olympics he played professionally with the New York Knicks and the Baltimore Bullets. "Bad News" Barnes played mostly center at Texas Western and also played center for the 1964 Olympic team, alternating with Mel Counts in that position. As first-round choice of the New York Knicks in 1964, he played well for 2 years, averaging in the double figures. In 1966 Barnes, a forward in the NBA, was traded to the Baltimore Bullets (now the Washington Bullets). He finished up his career as a journeyman with four more teams before his 1971 retirement.

Sources: *Black Olympians; Great Black Athletes; Guinness Book of Olympic Records; Quest for Gold.*

BAUTISTA, DANIEL (Mexico). Born August 4, 1952, in Mexico.

1976 Gold Medal: 20-Kilometer Walk (1 hr. 24:40.6, Olympic record)

Daniel Bautista became Mexico's first-ever Olympics athletic champion when he won the 20-kilometer walk in Montreal. His time in the 1976 Olympics was the fastest yet recorded in a major championship race. Earlier in the 1976 season, he had set an unofficial world's best for the event on the road with a time of 1 hour, 23 minutes, 39 seconds. In the Olympic race, Bautista broke away from East Germany's Hans-Georg Reismann and Peter Frankel, at 18 kilometers to win by over half a minute. By winning the Lugano Cup Finals of 1977 and 1979, Bautista continued to dominate the 20-kilometer walk. In 1979 he won in the phenomenal time of 1h.20:49.0. He was disqualified at the 1980 Olympics and soon retired. His 1h.20:6.8 on the track and 15,121 meters (9 miles, 697 yards) in the hour were other world bests. Bautista's best 50-kilometer time was 3hs.51:14.0. Daniel Bautista had been top-ranked in the 20-kilometer walk for 6 years, from 1974 to 1979, and in his final competitive season (1980), he ranked second. Bautista attended the 1984 Olympics as an assistant walking coach.

Sources: *Approved History of Olympic Games*; British Virgin Islands, Olympic Committee; *Encyclopaedia of Track and Field Athletics*; *Guinness Book of Olympic Records*; *Montreal 1976, Games of the XXIst Olympiad*.

BAYI, FILBERT (Tanzania). Born June 23, 1953 in Karatu, Tanzania.

1980 Silver Medal: 3,000-Meter Steeplechase (8:12.5, personal record)

Born a Mbulu near Mt. Kilimanjaro, Filbert Bayi grew up on a maize and bean farm, which provided nearly the totality of his diet. This diet perhaps accounts for his delicate build: as a 6-foot 1-inch Olympian he weighed 130 pounds. The most intense gold-medal struggle at Lenin Stadium in Moscow took place on the last lap of the 3,000-meter steeplechase. "For Bayi, the race meant the culmination of a career sidetracked by the black African boycott of 1976 and by frequent bouts with malaria" (*New York Times*). In 1973 Bayi set a Commonwealth record of 3:34.0. He accomplished his second world record in 1975, when he covered a mile in 3:51.0 in Jamaica—with quarter-mile timings of 56.9, 59.7, and 55.7 seconds. Bayi had produced the most uncompromising run ever seen in a major international 1,500-meter championship when he led from gun to tape at the 1974 Commonwealth Games for a world record of 3:32.2. He won the African 1,500-meter title in 1973 in 3:37.2, well ahead of Kenya's Kip Keino, and was again African champion in 1977. Filbert Bayi struck superb form in the Moscow Olympics as a steeplechaser. He passed 1,000-meters in 2:36.8 and finished second to Bronislaw Malinowski of Poland in 8:12.5. His best marks include 1:45.3 for 800-meters, 7:39.3 for 3,000 and 13:18.2 for 5,000. Bayi, an air force mechanic, became Tanzania's first Olympic medalist.

Sources: *Approved History of Olympic Games*; "Bayi Looms as Best of African Imports," *Black Sports* (August 1975); British Virgin Islands, Olympic Committee; *Complete Book of the Olympics*; *Encyclopaedia of Track and Field Athletics*; *Games of XXIInd Olympiad*; *Guinness Book of Olympic Records*; "Malinowski Defeats Bayi in Steeplechase," *New York Times* (August 1, 1980).

ROBERT BEAMON (Photo courtesy of U.S. Olympic Committee, Colorado Springs, Colorado.)

BEAMON, ROBERT (USA). Born August 29, 1946, in Jamaica, New York.

1968 Gold Medal: Long Jump (29 ft. 2½ in./8.90 m, Olympic record/world record)

Robert Beamon's long jump of 29 feet, 2½ inches was the shortest field event competition in history. (Experts forecast that the record could survive for 50 years). This long jump stunned the world. Beamon's record is untouched and regarded as the greatest achievement in some 3,000 years of track. Bob Beamon set a national high school triple jump record in 1965 and in 1967 won the AAU long jump. He won both the AAU and NCAA indoor long jump—all in 1968. Beamon long-jumped 25 feet, 2½ inches in 1965 and set a national high school record of 50 feet, 3¾ inches in the triple jump. The next year, at 19, he improved to

25 feet, 8 inches and placed fourth and ninth in the AAU. In 1967, he won the outdoor long jump at 26 feet, 11½ inches. Outdoors he was third in the AAU and second in the Pan Am Games, with 26 feet, 5¾ inches. He jumped 26 feet, 8 inches with wind assistance. Indoors, in 1968, Beamon became the longest jumper in history. He won the NAIA Championships with a world indoor record of 27 feet, 1 inch. He won in the AAU at 26 feet, 11½ inches again (plus 52 feet, 7 inches for third in the triple jump). He won both events in the NCAA at 52 feet, 3 inches in the triple jump and a world record of 27 feet, 2¾ inches in the long jump. Outdoors Bob jumped 27 feet, 4 inches with wind, won in the AAU at 27 feet, 4 inches, and leaped 27 feet, 6½ inches, with a 7.1 mile per hour wind, in the final trials. Beamon moved from being a ghetto lad who had been in trouble, to winning an Olympic gold medal, to earning a degree in sociology and physical education from the University of Texas at El Paso, to completing a master's in psychology and counseling at San Diego State University, to becoming a track coach at two universities. He has spent most of his career in social work.

Sources: *Black Olympians; Guinness Book of Olympic Records; Hard Road to Glory; 1980 Olympic Handbook; Quest for Gold; Spirit Team Profiles, Los Angeles Olympic Organizing Committee; Who's Who in the Olympic Games.*

BELL, GREGORY C. (USA). Born July 11, 1930, in Terre Haute, Indiana.

1956 Gold Medal: Long Jump (25 ft. 8¼ in./7.83 m)

Greg Bell broad jumped 25 feet, 8¼ inches to beat by half a foot his teammate John Bennett, the Marquette alumnus. Except for the two Americans, the broad jumping was definitely inferior, presumably because of the wind. In addition to being a gold medal-winning long jumper, Greg Bell is a successful dentist. He is also a poet, sculptor, and an accomplished motivational speaker. Bell, who uses his own life as an example of someone who rose above the circumstances of a humble birth, speaks candidly on controversial issues.

Sources: *Approved History of Olympic Games; Black Olympians; British Virgin Islands, Olympic Committee; Complete Book of the Olympics; Encyclopaedia of Track and Field Athletics; Guinness Book of Olympic Records; Story of the Olympic Games; Tales of Gold; United States 1956 Olympic Book.*

BELLAMY, WALTER (USA). Born July 24, 1939, in New Bern, North Carolina.

1960 Gold Medal: Basketball

As a student at Indiana University Walter Bellamy made most All-American teams in 1960 and 1961. Bellamy was starting center at the 1960 Olympics and was one of the top centers during his 14-year professional career, which saw him play for five teams. He ended up with career averages of over 20 points and 14 rebounds per game. When he joined the New Orleans Jazz, he was entering his 14th year as a professional. He became the last of the 1960 Olympians to still be playing professional basketball. Walt Bellamy was drafted by the Chicago Packers in 1961. An NBA team star, he was Rookie of the Year in 1962, leading the league in field goals percentages (with a new record of .519) and averaging 31.6 points and 19 rebounds per game. He played just one game with the New Orleans Jazz. Bellamy invested wisely in real estate while still playing professional basketball; he is now managing his investments and doing public relations for several southern firms. He was a Georgia delegate to the 1984 Democratic National Convention.

Sources: *Black Olympians;* British Virgin Islands, Olympic Committee; *Guinness Book of Olympic Records; Quest for Gold.*

BERNARD, KENT BEDE (Trinidad). Born May 27, 1942, in Port-of-Spain, Trinidad.

1964 Bronze Medal: 4 x 400-Meter Relay (3:01.7)

Kent Bernard was a member of the quartet that set a world record in the 1-mile relay in Jamaica in 1966 at the Commonwealth Games. Somewhat injury-prone, the University of Michigan graduate had a personal best of 45.7 in the 400 meters. He was an outstanding indoor runner. Bernard was the winner of five Big Ten Championships: 400 meters (outdoors) and 600 yards (indoors). He has been a member of the Baltimore Olympic Club, Ann Arbor Track Club, and Caribbean Connection Track Club. Bernard still shares the 440 record (46.0) at Michigan. Bernard earned, in addition to his Olympic bronze, silver medals in the 1966 and 1970 British Commonwealth Games and a bronze in the Pan Am Games of 1971. He is a member of the Trinidad Hall of Fame. Bernard attended Belmont Boys Catholic High School in Trinidad, and received a B.S. and a masters of social work from the University of Michigan. He has worked as a market researcher in New York City and as a counselor at the W.J. Maxey Boys' Training School. He is currently assistant track coach at the University of Michigan and enjoys international politics as a hobby. He and his wife, Carol Moe, have a son, Kolin.

Sources: *Approved History of Olympic Games;* Bernard, Kent. Questionnaire. 1984; British Virgin Islands, Olympic Committee; *Complete Book of the Olympics; Encyclopaedia of Track and Field Athletics; Games of the XVIIIth Olympiad; Guinness Book of Olympic Records.*

BESSALA, JEAN JOSEPH (Cameroon). Born in 1941 in Obala, Cameroon.

1968 Silver Medal: Welterweight Boxing

In welterweight boxing at the Mexico City Games in 1968, Joseph Bessala followed gold winner Manfred Wolke of East Germany. Vladimir Musalinov of the USSR won the bronze.

Sources: *Approved History of Olympic Games*; British Virgin Islands, Olympic Committee; *Complete Book of the Olympics*; *Guinness Book of Olympic Records*; *Olympic Games: The Record*.

BIFFLE, JEROME COUSINS (USA). Born March 20, 1928, in Denver, Colorado.

1952 Gold Medal: Long Jump (24 ft. 10 in./7.57 m)

Jerome Biffle won the 1950 NCAA long jump title. In 1952 he placed third in the AAU and finished second to Meredith Gourdine at the final Olympic trials. In Helsinki Biffle was lying second to Gourdine after two rounds but moved into the lead with his third jump. Even though his final three jumps were fouls, that third round effort of 24 feet, 10 inches brought him the gold medal. An alumnus of the University of Denver, Jerome Biffle has worked in the Denver school system for many years. He is now a counselor at a Denver high school.

Sources: *Black Olympians*; *Guinness Book of Olympic Records*; *Official Report of XVth Olympiad*; *Quest for Gold*.

BIGGS, TYRELL (USA). Born December 22, 1960 in Philadelphia, Pennsylvania.

1984 Gold Medal: Super Heavyweight Boxing

Tyrell Biggs attended West Philadelphia High School and Hampton Institute, Virginia, where he excelled on the basketball court. He won the 1984 Olympic trials and the 1983 U.S. Amateur and Pan Am trials and finished third at the Pan Am Games. Biggs was world amateur champion; he won his first global title in 1982 and was three-time U.S. champion. Biggs had 6 losses in 109 fights, with 40 or 45 knockouts.

Sources: "The 1984 Olympics," *Ebony* (October 1984); *Guinness Book of Olympic Records*; "The Champions," *Los Angeles Times* (August 14, 1984); *United States Olympic Team, Media Guide*.

ABEBE BIKILA (Photo courtesy of U.S. Olympic Committee, Colorado Springs, Colorado.)

BIKILA, ABEBE (Ethiopia). Born August 7, 1932, in Mont, Ethiopia.

1960 Gold Medal: Marathon (2 hrs.15:16.2, Olympic record/world best)
1964 Gold Medal: Marathon (2 hrs.12:11.2, Olympic record/world best)

Abebe Bikila, the son of a shepherd, was the first person to win the Olympic marathon twice and the first gold medal winner in track and field from Black Africa. He beat the

Olympic record of Czechoslovakian Emil Zatopek by almost 8 minutes in 1960. Bikila's appendix was removed a month before the 1964 race, but he beat the silver medal winner by 4 minutes. Bikila won his first gold medal for the marathon running barefoot through the streets of Rome in world-best time, and the second wearing shoes in Tokyo. But his attempt for the third gold medal in 1968 (Mexico City) failed as he dropped out of the race after 10 miles because of a broken fibia. Sports writer Jesse Robinson who had attended the Olympic Games for the past 24 years, said: "One of my greatest athletes was Abebe Bikila. As a matter of fact in 1972, I made a trip into Africa [Ethiopia] on my way to the Olympic Games in Munich, just to visit him. I had seen him running…. I was so tremendously impressed with his winning, and winning barefooted!… I went, in 1964, to Tokyo. When he ran in Tokyo, he won…. I decided to pay due respect to him." Abebe Bikila became one of Emperor Haile Selassie's imperial bodyguards, and was later elevated to captain in the palace guard. Brave and fatalistic, Bikila believed that successful people met with tragedy, and that it was God's will that he should become famous and be paralyzed in an accident. He was also patriotic and idealistic. An automobile injury rendered him a paraplegic and he died October 25, 1973.

Sources: *All That Glitters Is Not Gold; Complete Book of the Olympics; Guinness Book of Olympic Records; Lincoln Library of Sports Champions;* "A. Bikila (Ethiopia) Wins Marathon," *New York Times* (September 11, 1960); *1980 Olympic Handbook; Who's Who in Track and Field.*

BILALI, IRAHIM (Kenya). Born in Kenya.

1984 Bronze Medal: Flyweight Boxing

At the 1984 Olympics Irahim Bilali defeated Patrick Mwamba of Zambia, Alvaro Mercado of Colombia, and Laureano Ramírez of the Dominican Republic. Bilali lost to Radzep Redzepavski of Yugoslavia, points 5-0.

Sources: "The Champions," *Los Angeles Times* (August 14, 1984); *Official Report of the Games of the XXIIIrd Olympiad;* "The Games," *Olympian* (October/November 1984).

BIWOTT, AMOS (Kenya). Born September 8, 1947, in Uasin Gishee, Kenya.

1968 Gold Medal: 3,000-Meter Steeplechase (8:51.02)

Amos Biwott was inspired by his fellow countryman Kipchoge Keino's performances in the metric mile. In winning, Biwott won Kenya's second gold medal, 8 seconds faster than any one had run the steeplechase at an altitude that high. Biwott "displayed [the] most extraordinary, crowd-pleasing, and exciting style taking the water jump ever witnessed anywhere in this event" (*United States Olympic Book*). He would jump onto the hedge and hop, triple-jump style, over

the water. Then he would land on dry ground with the same foot.

Sources: *Guinness Book of Olympic Records; Complete Book of the Olympics; 1968 United States Olympic Book; Track & Field News* (October/November 1968).

BLACK, LARRY (USA). Born July 20, 1951, in Miami, Florida.

1972 Gold Medal; 4 x 100-Meter Relay (38.19, Olympic record/world record)
1972 Silver Medal: 200-Meter Run (20.19)

Larry Black had a fine collegiate season in 1971 at North Carolina Central University. He won the NCAA, NAIA, and NCAA (College Division) all in the same year. He also ran a 440-yard relay leg in 43.8 seconds at the 1972 Penn Relays. Black led off the Olympic 4 x 100-meter relay team that gained the world record. He twice ran 20.0 before the Munich Games, but lost the Olympic title to Valery Borzov of the USSR by 2 meters. Larry Black later became director of Miami's Parks and Recreation Department.

Sources: *Black Olympians; Guinness Book of Olympic Records; Quest for Gold; United States Olympic Team, Games of the XXth Olympiad.*

BLAY, EDDIE (Ghana). Born in Ghana.

1964 Bronze Medal: Light Welterweight Boxing

At the 1964 Tokyo Games, Eddie Blay defeated Preben R. S. Rasmussen of Denmark on points and knocked out Nol Touch of Cambodia in the second round. Blay was defeated on points by Joao da Silva of Brazil.

Sources: *Approved History of Olympic Games; Complete Book of the Olympics; Games of the XVIIIth Olympiad; Guinness Book of Olympic Records.*

BOIT, MICHAEL (Kenya). Born January 6, 1949, in Nandi, Kenya.

1972 Bronze Medal: 800-Meter Run (1:46.01)

Michael Boit graduated from the University of Eastern New Mexico with an excellent competitive record. He was Commonwealth champion at 800 meters in 1978 and won the 1,500 with 3:39.9 at the African Games in 1979. His bests include 1:43.57 for 800 meters, 3:33.67 for 1,500, 3:49.45 for 1 mile, and 7:45.61 for 3,000 meters. Additional records include: Commonwealth Games, 800 silver (1974) and 1,500 bronze (1982); World Cup, 800 silver (1979); African Games 800 (1:43.57) (1976) and 800 (1:43.45) (1981). Boit, along with another Kenyan, Robert Ouko, took an early lead in the 800 meters at

Munich, but they soon faded as Arzhanov and Worttle passed them. Boit, who retired in 1985, was still one of the world's best middle distance runners 13 years after 1972. Although he lost two opportunities for further Olympic honors in 1976 and 1980, because of boycotts, he still represented his country in the first World Athletics Championships in 1983, reaching the finals in the 1,500 meters.

Sources: *Approved History of Olympic Games*; British Virgin Islands, Olympic Committee; *Complete Book of the Olympics*; *Encyclopaedia of Track and Field Athletics*; *Guinness Book of Olympic Records*; *United States Olympic Team, Games of the XXth Olympiad*; *Who's Who in the 1984 Olympics*.

BOLDEN, JEANETTE (USA). Born January 26, 1960, in Los Angeles, California.

1984 Gold Medal: 4 x 100-Meter Relay (41.65)

Jeanette Bolden had a 6.54 world record tie at the *L.A. Times* meet and was twice a member of NCAA Championships at UCLA. She fashioned her second-fastest time ever (6.57 seconds) in defeating Marlies Gohr and Alice Brown, two of the best starters in the world. She set a personal record in her first meet in Europe (11.09 in Zurich). Bolden set the world indoor record at 60 yards in 1982 (6.60) and equaled it in 1986 (6.54). Bolden has a total of five indoor American records and seven indoor personal records at various distances. She made the 1980 U.S. Olympic team as an alternate 4 x 100-meter relay runner. In 1981 she ran second in the 100 meters at the U.S. Nationals with a 11.27. The same year she also won second place in the World Cup 4 x 100 relay with 42.82. In the 1984 Olympic trials she finished third in the 100 with 11.24. Over the years Jeanette Bolden has overcome many obstacles to achieve her goals. For example, she was born with club feet and severe asthma. She went on to graduate from Centennial High School in Compton, California, in 1978, and from UCLA in 1983. She competes for the World Class Athletic Club and is coached by Bob Kersee.

Sources: British Virgin Islands, Olympic Committee; "The 1984 Olympics," *Ebony* (October 1984); "The Champions," *Los Angeles Times* (August 14, 1984); "The Games," *Olympian* (October/November 1984); *Research Information, Games of the XXIIIrd Olympiad*; "Bolden Finally Sees the Light," *Track & Field News* (April 1986); "Jeanette Bolden," *Women's Sports* (October 1984).

BON, NAFTALI (Kenya). Born October 9, 1945, in Kapsabet, Kenya.

1968 Silver Medal: 4 x 400-Meter Relay (2:59.64)

Naftali Bon's role was primarily that of an 800-meter runner in international competition, even though he won an Olympic medal as an anchor man in the Mexico City Games. He

had personal bests of 46.22 seconds for the 400 meters and 1:46.5 for the 800.

Sources: *Approved History of Olympic Games*; British Virgin Islands, Olympic Committee; *Complete Book of the Olympics*; *Games of the XIXth Olympic Organizing Committee*; *Guinness Book of Olympic Records*; *Mexico City 1968, Participants in the XIXth Olympiad*.

BOOZER, ROBERT (USA). Born April 26, 1937, in Omaha, Nebraska.

1960 Gold Medal: Basketball

Robert Boozer graduated in 1959 from Kansas State University, where he was an All-American forward. Boozer had a dream of playing in the Olympics. Although he was drafted by Cincinnati in 1959, he had them wait a year while he played AAU basketball with the Peoria Cats. He won a gold medal with them. Boozer turned professional with the Cincinnati Royals and later played with the Milwaukee Bucks, helping them win the championship in 1971. Although he played with Cincinnati for only 4 years, he had an 11-year NBA career during which he averaged 15 points per game. Boozer went on to work for a regional phone company in the northwest and served as sportscaster for local basketball games. He owns several radio stations in partnership with baseball great Bob Gibson.

Sources: *Approved History of Olympic Games*; *Black Olympians*; *Games of the XVIIth Olympiad*; *Guinness Book of Olympic Records*; *Quest for Gold*.

BOSTON, RALPH HAROLD (USA). Born May 9, 1939, in Laurel, Mississippi.

1960 Gold Medal: Long Jump (26 ft. 7¾ in./8.12 m, Olympic record)
1964 Silver Medal: Long Jump (26 ft. 4¼ in./8.03 m)
1968 Bronze Medal: Long Jump (26 ft. 9¼ in./8.16 m)

Ralph Boston attended Tennessee A&I University. He was the 1960 NCAA titlist and held the American collegiate record with 27 feet, 1½ inches in 1961. He was undefeated in the high hurdles in 1961. Boston took the gold medal in 1960 with the unbelievable leap of 26 feet, 7¾ inches. (Later he would pass the 27-foot barrier.) He toppled Jesse Owens's famous long jump mark of 26 feet, 5½ inches, which had stood for 24 years. Ralph Boston won the 1961 through 1966 AAU Outdoor Championships and the indoor AAU in 1961 and 1965. He placed fourth in the Pan Am Games high jump, and headed U.S. lists in the triple jump. Boston first set the long jump record at Walnut, California, August 8, 1960—leaping 26 feet, 11¼ inches. He next moved up to 27 feet, ½ inch at Modesto, California, on May 27, 1961. He defeated rival Ter-Ovanesyan and advanced the record to 27½ feet in Moscow in July 1961.

Ter-Ovanesyan took the record back with 27 feet, 3¼ inches in 1962. On July 15, 1964, Boston tied the mark in Jamaica. At the 1964 L.A. Olympic trials on August 12, he regained sole possession of the record with a 27-foot 4¼-inch jump. In Modesto on May 29, 1965, he made his last record jump of 27 feet, 5 inches. Boston was superseded by Bob Beamon in 1968 with a 29-foot 2½-inch long jump that stunned the world (and gained Bob Beamon a gold medal). Ralph Boston was top long jumper of the 1960s and was once rated premier long jumper of all time. But he was also talented in other events. In the 1961 Conference Meet, he won the javelin at 185 feet and vaulted 15 feet. Ralph Boston became a biochemist and administrator at Tennessee A&I and also a television track commentator.

Sources: *Approved History of Olympic Games; Black Olympians; Complete Book of the Olympics; Encyclopaedia of Track and Field Athletics; Guinness Book of Olympic Records; Quest for Gold;* "Then There Were Three," *Time* (March 29, 1968); *Track and Field: The Great Ones; Who's Who in Track and Field.*

BOSWELL, CATHY (USA). Born November 10, 1962, in Joliet, Illinois.

1984 Gold Medal: Basketball

Cathy Boswell graduated from Illinois State University, Normal, in 1983. As a forward she set six career records and was the first woman to ever have a jersey retired at her school. Boswell was a standout for 4 years. She scored 2,005 points and 1,060 rebounds. She was selected three times to the Kodak All-Region team and was twice Wade Trophy finalist. She was named to the 1983 J.C. Penney All-American Five. She was second only in scoring to the great NBA and Illinois State athlete Doug Collins and was an alternate to the 1983 Pan Am Games team. Boswell has competed on the following teams: 1983 World University team; 1982 USA Select team; 1981 USA Dial Jr. Women's team; and 1980 Jones Cup team. She also played in the 1979 and 1981 National Festival. Boswell established 6 school records in her 4 years and ended her career as the all-time leading scorer in Lady Redbird Basketball with 2,005 points. Her sophomore year at Illinois State was her best, when she hit an 18-point scoring average. Her other records include: most points scored (649), most field goals scored (274), most field goals attempted (537), highest field goal percentage (.599), most free throws scored (101), most free throws attempted (119), and highest free throws percentage (.848). She is the all-time women's scoring leader at Illinois State University in Normal. Boswell's father, Hank, said, "Cathy twice was one of 30 players nominated for the Wade Trophy. That's one of her proudest possessions.... She also won the Willye White Award as the top female high school athlete in Illinois in 1979" (*Herald News*, Joliet).

Sources: Boswell, Cathy. Questionnaire. 1984; "The 1984 Olympics," *Ebony* (October 1984); "Parents Consider Olympian..." *Herald News*, Joliet, Illinois (July 28, 1984); "The Champions," *Los Angeles Times* (August 14, 1984); "Basketball," *Olympian* (October/November 1984); *United States Olympic Team, Media Guide*.

BOUTAIB, MOULAY BRAHIM (Morocco). Born August 15, 1967, in Morocco.

1988 Gold Medal: 10,000-Meter Run (27:21.46, new Olympic record)

Brahim Boutaib stole the Moroccan limelight from Aouita in 1988 in Seoul by overpowering him in the 10,000 meters. Kenyan Kipkemboi Kimeli finished third, and Salvatore Antibo of Italy, second. Boutaib won in the fourth fastest time ever, 27:21.46. Boutaib's personal bests are 3,000, 7:43.22 (1988) and 5,000, 13:18.68 (1988).

Sources: British Virgin Islands, Olympic Committee; *International Amateur Athletic Federation*; "Seoul Games/Medal Winners," *Los Angeles Times* (October 3, 1988); *Seoul '88;* "Olympics Record," *USA Today* (October 3, 1988).

BOWE, RIDDICK (USA). Born August 10, 1967, in Brooklyn, New York.

1988 Silver Medal: Super Heavyweight Boxing

Riddick Bowe beat first-round winner Robert Salters twice at the U.S. Olympic box-offs to seal a spot on the U.S. Olympic boxing team. He won despite his having had surgery on his right hand in late April 1988. At the 1988 U.S. Amateur Championships, he was beaten by Salters in the semifinal round. Bowe took the bronze medal at the 1987 Pan Am Games. He was the super heavyweight gold medalist at the 1987 U.S. Olympic Festival. He lost to Nurmagomed Shanavazov of the USSR at the 1985 World Cup. Bowe beat Peter Hart of Hungary, thus winning the Jr. World Championships in 1985. Bowe studied business administration and drama at Kingsborough Community College in Brooklyn.

Sources: "Black American Medal Winners," *Ebony* (December 1988); "The Seoul Games/Medal Winners," *Los Angeles Times* (October 3, 1988); *1988 United States Olympic Team, Media Guide; Seoul '88;* "Olympics Record," *USA Today* (October 3, 1988).

BOYD, JAMES FELTON (USA). Born November 30, 1930, in Rocky Mount, North Carolina.

1956 Gold Medal: Light Heavyweight Boxing

James Boyd, All-American and All-Service champion in both 1955 and 1956, had no difficulty winning the gold medal at Melbourne. He turned professional in 1959 after serving in the army.

Sources: *Approved History of Olympic Games; Black Olympians; Guinness Book of Olympic Records; Quest for Gold.*

BRADFORD, JAMES EDWARD (USA). Born November 1, 1928, in Washington, D.C.

1952 Silver Medal: Heavyweight Weightlifting (964½ lbs./ 437.5 kg)
1960 Silver Medal: Heavyweight Weightlifting (1,129¾ lbs./512.5 kg)

James Bradford won the AAU heavyweight title in both 1960 and 1961. He had won the AAU Jr. Championship in 1950. Bradford lost out to John Davis at the 1952 Olympics and 1952 World Championships. He was second to Norb Schemansky at the 1954 World Championships, and Paul Anderson defeated him in 1955. The great Russian lifter Yuri Vlasov defeated Bradford in the 1959 World Championships and in the 1960 Olympics. Even though he got off to a good start, "Bradford had the misfortune to be lifting against some of the greatest weightlifters in history" (*Quest for Gold*).

Sources: *Black Olympians; Guinness Book of Olympic Records; Quest for Gold; United States Olympic Team, Games of the XVth Olympiad.*

BRELAND, MARK (USA). Born May 11, 1963, in Brooklyn, New York.

1984 Gold Medal: Welterweight Boxing

Mark Breland graduated from Brooklyn's Eastern District High School in 1981. He was three-time World champion in 1982, 1983, and 1984. He was two-time U.S. Amateur champion (1982-83) and was named Boxer of the Year in 1982 and 1983 (USA/ABF). He was selected outstanding boxer at the 1982 World Championships. Breland is believed to have the best record in the history of the sport. According to Colonel Don Hull, president of International Amateur Boxing Federation, "Sugar Ray Robinson, Laszlo Papp, Floyd Patterson, Cassius Clay ... none of those people had a record like that as amateurs" (*United States Olympic Team, Media Guide*). Breland's trainer, Emanuel Steward, believes that Mark is the most talented boxer he has ever worked with. For many years his coach was George Washington, an old sparring partner of Joe Louis. Breland began by winning a New York Golden Gloves Championship and has since won five of them. Said Rolly Schwartz of the U.S. Amateur Boxing Federation, "He's got one of the greatest straight rights in the history of Amateur Boxing, and I include Stevenson.... When Breland gets you with that right, the lights go out" (*U.S. Olympic Team, Media*

Guide). After winning 18 professional fights, Mark Breland lost his World Boxing Association welterweight crown to Marlon Starling in an 11th-round knockout on August 22, 1987. Meanwhile, he had become a popular figure as a model and film actor as well as a boxer.

Sources: "The 1984 Olympics," *Ebony* (October 1984); "104 and 1," *Los Angeles Times* (July 1984); "Breland and Whitaker Turn Pro. in November," *Los Angeles Times* (September 11, 1984); "Starling Takes Breland's Crown," *Los Angeles Times* (August 23, 1987); "Breland Has to Face Test Under Fire," *Los Angeles Times* (April 16, 1988); "Olympic Medal Results," *Sporting News* (August 27, 1984); *United States Olympic Team, Media Guide.*

BREWER, JAMES TURNER (USA). Born December 3, 1951, in Maywood, Illinois.

1972 Silver Medal: Basketball

James Brewer attended Proviso East High School in Maywood, where he was an All-State player. In college basketball at the University of Minnesota (where he held a Williams Scholarship) he was a power forward under coach Bill Musselman. He made several All-American teams and graduated in 1973. Jim Brewer was named to the NBA All-Defensive second team twice. He was part of the Big Ten Tour of Australia in 1971. In 1971-72, he scored 9.8 points and in 1970-71, 16.6. In 1971-72 he was MVP for Minnesota and in 1972 Big Ten Conference MVP. He averaged seven blocked shots a game in 1971-72. As a professional Brewer was a second-round draft selection for the Cleveland Cavaliers and played for 6 years.

Sources: *Black Olympians; Guinness Book of Olympic Records; Lexicon der 12000 Olympianiken; 1972 United States Olympic Book; United States Olympic Teams, Games of the XXIInd Olympiad.*

BRIGITHA, ENITH SALLE (Netherlands). Born April 15, 1955, in the Netherlands.

1976 Bronze Medal: Women's 100-Meter Freestyle Swimming (56.65)
1976 Bronze Medal: Women's 200-Meter Freestyle Swimming (2:01.40)

Enith Brigitha set records in the heats of both the women's 100-m freestyle swimming and the women's 200-meter freestyle swimming. Her Olympic statistics were: semi-finals, 100-meter freestyle, 57.08; finals, 100-meter freestyle, 56.65; heats, 200-meter freestyle, 2:01.54 (Olympic record); finals, 200-meter freestyle, 2:01.40.

Sources: *Approved History of Olympic Games; British Virgin Islands, Olympic Committee; Guinness Book of Olympic Records; Lexicon der 14000 Olympianiken (Who's Who at the Olympics); Montreal 1976, Games of the XXIst Olympiad.*

VALERIE BRISCO-HOOKS (Photo courtesy of the Amateur Athletic Foundation, Los Angeles, California, and Robert Long AAF/LPI 1984.)

BRISCO-HOOKS, VALERIE (USA). Born July 6, 1960, in Greenwood, Mississippi.

1984 Gold Medal: 200-Meter Run (21.81/Olympic record)
1984 Gold Medal: 400-Meter Run (48.83/Olympic record)
1984 Gold Medal: 4 x 400-Meter Relay (3:18.29/Olympic record)
1988 Silver Medal: 4 x 400-Meter Relay (3:15.51)

Valerie Brisco-Hooks attended Locke High School in Los Angeles where she was a short sprinter. She also attended California State, Northridge, where she was AIAW champion and AAU runner-up in the 200 meters (1979). She clocked a best of 23.16 and earned a number 10 world ranking. She ran the 400 in 52.08 (1979) and set an American record of 49.83 in the TAC Championships. In winning the 400 meters in 48.83 in 1984, Brisco-Hooks not only lowered the American record but broke the Olympic record of 48.88 set by East German Marita Koch in 1980. Brisco-Hooks

became the fourth fastest performer of all time in the event and the first Olympian ever to win at both 200 and 400 meters. She set Olympic records in both events: 21.81 and 48.83. Her 400 time put her fourth on the All-Time World Performers list, her 200 placed her third, and by being on the winning relay team, which also set an American record (3:19.29), she became the first U.S. woman track and field athlete to win three gold medals since Wilma Rudolph in 1960. (Her Locke High School coach had given her Rudolph's biography to read when she was 15.) Brisco-Hooks began as a 200-meter specialist who moved up to 400. She was out of competition in 1980 and 1982, but after her son was born in 1982, she seemed to be stronger than ever. She trained most of 1982 with coach Bob Kersee and lost 40 pounds in the process. Brisco-Hooks characterizes the 400 as a "frightening event," but decided to try it to enhance her chances. "My goal this year mainly was to run 400m" (*Track & Field News*). But 49.83? She couldn't possibly expect to become the first American woman under 50 seconds. She didn't realize she was going that fast. She doesn't like to think of herself as one of the all-time greats. "I just think I'm a good runner," she said. "I don't want to take it [celebrity] to heart. You could get a big head" (*Los Angeles Times*). This three-time medalist went on to race in Europe after the 1984 Olympics. Her former husband, Alvin Hooks (wide receiver for the Philadelphia Eagles), served as his wife's manager. Brisco-Hooks ranked second in the 200 and third in the 400 in the world in 1985. She finished third in the 200 and 400 and fifth in the 100 in the world in 1986. She won the U.S. Olympic Festival in 1987 but finished fourth at TAC. She ran the third leg in the 1,600 to win the silver in 1988 (3:15.51).

Sources: *American Athletics Annual*; "The 1984 Olympics," *Ebony* (October 1984); *For the Record*; "Brisco-Hooks: Good As Gold," *Los Angeles Times* (August 14, 1984); "Gold Medalist Urges Kids...," *Los Angeles Times* (October 10, 1984); "Seoul Games/Medal Winners," *Los Angeles Times* (October 3, 1988); *1988 United States Olympic Team, Media Guide*; "Motherhood a Boon to Brisco-Hooks," *Track & Field News* (July 18, 1984).

BROOKS, NATHAN EUGENE (USA). Born August 4, 1933, in Cleveland, Ohio.

1952 Gold Medal: Flyweight Boxing

During his career as a professional after his Olympic triumph, Nate Brooks chalked up seven victories and one defeat. On February 8, 1954, he won the North American Bantamweight Championship by knocking out Billy Peacock in the eighth round. He retired soon thereafter.

Sources: *Approved History of Olympic Games*; *Black Olympians*; *Guinness Book of Olympic Records*; *Helsingin Olympiakisat, 1952*; *Quest for Gold*; *United States Team, Games of the XVth Olympiad*.

BROWN, ALICE REGINA (USA). Born September 20, 1960, in Jackson, Mississippi.

1984 Gold Medal: 4 x 100-Meter Relay (41.65)
1984 Silver Medal: 100-Meter Run (11.13)
1988 Gold Medal: 4 x 100-Meter Relay (41.98)

Alice Brown graduated from Muir High School in Pasadena, California in 1978 and attended California State, Northridge. She was a member of World Class Athletic Club and was coached by Bob Kersee. Brown competed at Cal State in 1979 and 1980. In 1980 she finished second in the AIAW 200. She came in third at TAC in 1981 and fifth in 1982 (both in the 100). In the 100 her personal record in 1983 was 11.08; that year she was fourth at TAC and competed at the World Championships. Her personal record in the 200 was 22.41 in 1983. Brown won the TAC and AIAW titles in 1980 and wound up in eighth place in the world. One year she had a very good indoor season—five times she ran 6.65 or better, culminating with her 6.56 at TAC. Brown finished fifth at the Olympic trials with 11.04 in the 100m and ranked third in the 100 and eighth in the 200 in the U.S. (1987). She tied for sixth on the All-Time U.S. list in the 100, with a best time of 11.01. She competed at the World Championships in 1987 and ran the first leg in the women's 400-meter relay at Seoul. Bob Kersee believes that Alice Brown is America's most durable sprinter: "For years coaches have been telling me, 'Alice doesn't have talent.' And I tell them, 'Alice is always there.' "

Sources: "The 1984 Olympics," *Ebony* (October 1984); "Ashford Adds Golden Anchor," *Los Angeles Times* (August 12, 1984); "The Champions," *Los Angeles Times* (August 14, 1984); *1984 Olympic Games; 1988 United States Olympic Team, Media Guide;* "The Games," *Olympian* (October/November 1984); "Brown Is Relieving the Tension," *Track & Field News* (April 1985); "Olympics Record," *USA Today* (October 3, 1988); "Alice Brown," *Women's Sports* (October 1984).

BROWN, BENJAMIN GENE (USA). Born September 27, 1953, in San Francisco, California.

1976 Gold Medal: 4 x 400-Meter Relay (2:58.65)

Benjamin Brown finished in fourth place at the 1976 final Olympic trials. This placed him on the 1600-meter relay team at Montreal where he ran the third leg in 44.6. He had won the NCAA championship earlier. Benny Brown attended UCLA and was a member of the Maccabi Track Club.

Sources: *Black Olympians; Guinness Book of Olympic Records;* "Olympic Summaries," *New York Times* (August 1, 1976); "Olympic Summaries," *New York Times* (August 2, 1976); *Quest for Gold; United States Olympic Team, Games of the XXIst Olympiad.*

BROWN, CHARLES (USA). Born February 28, 1939, in Cincinnati, Ohio.

1964 Bronze Medal: Featherweight Boxing (tied)

Charles Brown had a fine year in 1964. He won the AAU title and final Olympic trials before moving on to Tokyo. In the Olympics he won three decisions before losing a 4-1 decision to the Filipino Anthony Villanueva in the semi-finals.

Sources: *Black Olympians; Guinness Book of Olympic Records; Quest for Gold; United States Team, Games of the XVIIIth Olympiad.*

BROWN, CINDY (USA). Born March 16, 1965.

1988 Gold Medal: Basketball

Cindy Brown graduated in 1987 from Long Beach State, California, with a degree in criminal justice. After a brilliant career at Long Beach State, she played basketball in Ancona, Italy, for a year. She was selected to the 1987 Pan Am Games team but was unable to participate. She was a 1987 Kodak All-America pick while leading Long Beach to the Final Four. As a senior Cindy Brown averaged 27.8 points and 9.9 rebounds while shooting 57.9 percent from the field. In a single game against San Jose State her senior year, she scored an NCAA record 60 points. In her collegiate career Brown scored 2,696 points and grabbed 1,184 rebounds. Her international experience was playing on the gold medal-winning U.S. teams at the 1986 FIBA World Championships and Goodwill Games. She earned a silver medal for the U.S. during the 1985 World University Games.

Sources: "Black American Medal Winners," *Ebony* (December 1988); "The Seoul Games/Medal Winners," *Los Angeles Times* (October 3, 1988); *1988 United States Olympic Team, Media Guide; Seoul '88;* "Olympics Record," *USA Today* (October 3, 1988).

BROWN, EARLENE DENNIS (USA). Born July 11, 1935, in Latero, Texas.

1960 Bronze Medal: Shot Put (53 ft. 10½ in./16.42 m)

Earlene Brown held the outdoor record in the shot put and the discus throw. She was eight times AAU National champion in shot put and won seven titles in a row, from 1956 through 1961. On July 16, 1960, Earlene Brown threw the discus 176 feet, 10 inches in Abilene, Texas. On September 21, 1960, she put the shot 54 feet, 9 inches at Helsinki. She took first place in the 1958 U.S./USSR duel meet in Moscow, with a put of 54 feet, 3 inches. She placed second in the discus with a throw of 161 feet, 1½ inches. Brown was Pan Am shot and discus champion in 1959. In Melbourne in 1956, she was fourth in the discus with a toss of 168 feet,

5½ inches and sixth in the shot with a put of 49 feet, 7½ inches (both new U.S. records). Earlene Brown, housewife, mother, and beautician, as well as athlete, made the 1956, 1960, and 1964 Olympic teams. Jesse Robinson, sports writer who attended the Olympic Games for 24 years, stated: "My great woman athlete ... is Miss Earlene Brown.... She became, I would say, one of the three great women athletes in the U.S. in track and field. I'm sure Wilma Rudolph is up there as number one. And Tyus has to be up there *with* number one.... No one has been as strong and dominant as Earlene Brown over the series of Olympic Games" (interview with author). After amateur sports Brown became a superstar in the Roller Derby. She died in 1983.

Sources: *Black Olympians; Compton's Gift to Olympic Games; Guinness Book of Olympic Records; 100 Greatest Women in Sports; Quest for Gold;* Robinson, Jesse. Personal interview. 1984; *Who's Who in Track and Field.*

BROWN, JUDI (USA). Born July 14, 1961, in East Lansing, Michigan.

1984 Silver Medal: 400-Meter Hurdles (55.20, American record)

Judi Brown attended high school in Milwaukee, Wisconsin. In 1983 she graduated from Michigan State University with a degree in speech and audiology. Brown was coached by former Polish Olympic gold medalist Ella Krzesinska (1960 long jump winner). Brown states that Krzesinska's effect on her career is immeasurable and that she never would have gotten to where she is now without her. Judi Brown finished second in the 1984 U.S. Nationals 400-meter intermediate hurdles with 54.99 seconds (American record). She finished first in the U.S. Olympic trials 400-meter intermediate hurdles with 54.93 (American record)—and broke her own record. In 1984 Brown was top American long hurdler and first to break 55 flat. She had relinquished her American record to Latanya Sheffield early in 1985. But in Brussels, in August, she got back a share, equaling Sheffield's 54.66 set in May. She was 10th on the all-time world list in 1985.

Sources: British Virgin Islands, Olympic Committee; "The 1984 Olympics," *Ebony* (October 1984); "The Games," *Olympian* (October/November 1984); *Research Information, Games of the XXIIIrd Olympiad;* "Brown-King Equals 400H AR," *Track & Field News* (October 1985); "Bridges to the Future," *Track & Field News* (October 1985).

BROWN, PHILIP (Great Britain). Born January 6, 1962, in Birmingham, England.

1984 Silver Medal: 4 x 400-Meter Relay (2:59.13)

Philip Brown's father is Jamaican and his mother is Trinidadian. He started running in elementary school. At 18 he just missed making the 1980 British Olympic team. He later ran for the Birchfield Harriers, the oldest club in Britain. A former 200-meter specialist, Brown's personal best in the 400 meters is 45.26 seconds. He is an outstanding relay runner who anchored British 4 x 400 quartets to second and third place finishes at the Los Angeles Olympics and Helsinki World Championships, respectively. Most impressive was his tremendous finish in the 4 x 400 relay, in which he nearly overtook European champion Hartnut Weber of West Germany.

Sources: British Virgin Islands, Olympic Committee; *1984 Olympic Games; Sarajevo/Los Angeles; Research Information, Games of the XXIIIrd Olympiad.*

BROWN, RON (USA). Born March 31, 1961, in Los Angeles, California.

1984 Gold Medal: 4 x 100-Meter Relay (37.83 Olympic record/world record)

A burly sprinter and football player, Ron Brown turned down a lucrative contract offer from the Cleveland Browns in 1983 in order to retain his amateur status for an Olympic bid the following year. After a collegiate track career at Arizona State University, marked more by potential than performance, Brown hit pay dirt in 1983 with a victory in the 100 meters over the world's best sprinter, Carl Lewis. Lewis later exacted his revenge, several times, but Brown's clocking of 10.06 seconds at the Welt Klasse meet in Zurich moved him high on the list of contenders for Olympic honors. In 1984 Brown, then running for the Stars and Stripes Track Club, created a stir by defeating Lewis three times in events over 60 meters indoors. Outdoors he continued to run well and finished third in the 100 at the U.S. trials. At the Olympics in Los Angeles he experienced mixed fortune. He barely qualified for the final of the 100, finishing fourth in his semifinal in a photo finish. In the final he again finished fourth, apparently slightly injured. Brown's moment of glory was to come later in the 4 x 100-meter relay. Running the second leg for the powerful American quartet (consisting of Calvin Smith, Carl Lewis, and Sam Graddy), Brown stormed down the backstretch to give Smith a comfortable lead, which Lewis converted into a new World and Olympic record of 37.83 seconds. Brown, whose 200-meter best of 20.74 seconds was achieved in 1982, turned to professional football shortly after the Olympics, signing as a wide receiver with the Rams in his hometown, Los Angeles. Ron Brown retired from football after four seasons with the Rams to resume a career in track and field.

Sources: British Virgin Islands, Olympic Committee; "The 1984 Olympics," *Ebony* (October 1984); "The Champions," *Los Angeles Times* (August 14, 1984); "Rams' Ron Brown Retires from Football," *Los Angeles Times* (April 20, 1988); "The Games," *Olympian* (October/November 1984); *Research Information, Games of the XXIIIrd Olympiad;* "Olympic Medal Results," *Sporting News* (August 13, 1984); *United States Olympic Team, Media Guide.*

BRYANT, ROSALYN (USA). Born January 7, 1956, in Chicago, Illinois.

1976 Silver Medal: 4 x 400-Meter Relay (3:22.81)

Rosalyn Bryant attended Von Steuben High School in Chicago and graduated from California State University, Los Angeles, in 1977. Bryant finished second in the 1976 AAU 100 meters, setting an American record. She was first both in the 1976 AIAW 100 and the 200. She had been first in the AAU 100 and second in the 200. In the 1975 indoor AAU 220 yards she finished first. She was affiliated with the L.A. Mercurettes and with the UCLA Ali Track Club. In the 1976 Olympic trials, Bryant ran third in the 400. Rosalyn Bryant returned to competition in 1986 as a 400-meter hurdler after being out of competition for several years.

Sources: *Black Olympians*; British Virgin Islands, Olympic Committee; *United States Olympic Team, Games of the XXIst Olympiad*; *United States Track and Field Olympians*.

BUCKNER, WILLIAM QUINN (USA). Born August 20, 1954, in Phoenix, Illinois.

1976 Gold Medal: Basketball

William Buckner had a tough decision to make. He was a star at Indiana University on both the football and basketball teams and, had he wanted to, probably could have played defensive back in the NFL. He chose professional basketball, playing first with the Milwaukee Bucks and later with the Boston Celtics. He was known primarily as a defensive specialist. In 1976 Buckner was a member of both an NCAA and an Olympic Championship team—a rare achievement. His later membership on a professional championship team (The NBA All-Defensive team) made him the first ever to gain that triple honor.

Sources: *Black Olympians*; *Guinness Book of Olympic Records*; *Quest for Gold*; *United States Olympic Team, Games of the XXIst Olympiad*.

BULLETT, VICKY (USA). Born October 4, 1967.

1988 Gold Medal: Basketball

During her junior year at the University of Maryland, Bullett finished sixth in the ACC in points per game average (18.2), third in rebounding (95), third in field goal percentage (60.1), fifth in blocked shots (1.3), and seventh in steals (2.2). Bullett was a first team all-ACC selection after receiving second team honors as a sophomore. She scored a season-high 33 points in the NCAA tournament against Ohio State, and led Maryland to the final eight before being eliminated by Auburn. Bullett is 10th on the all-time Maryland scoring list (1,242 points) and fifth on the rebounding list (681). Vicky Bullett majored in early childhood education at the university.

Sources: "Black American Medal Winners," *Ebony* (December 1988); "Seoul Games/Medal Winners," *Los Angeles Times* (October 3, 1988); *1988 United States Olympic Team, Media Guide; Seoul '88*; "Olympic Record," *USA Today* (October 3, 1988).

BUTTS, JAMES A. (USA). Born May 9, 1950, in Los Angeles, California.

1976 Silver Medal: Triple Jump (56 ft. 4½ in./17.18 m)

James Butts graduated from UCLA in 1974. A member of the Tobias Striders, he won the NCAA triple jump in 1972 and the AAU title in 1978. When Butts placed second at the Montreal Games he became the first U.S. athlete to win an Olympic triple jump since 1928, when Levi Casey won the event. He narrowly missed making the Olympic team in both 1972 and 1980. Butts placed third in the 1979 Pan Am Games in which Brazilian Joao Carlos de Oliveira broke the world record in the triple jump.

Sources: *Black Olympians*; *Guinness Book of Olympic Records*; "Results of Olympic Games at Montreal," *New York Times* (July 31, 1976); *Quest for Gold*; *United States Olympic Team, Games of the XXIst Olympiad*.

CAIN, CARL CECIL (USA). Born August 2, 1934, in Freeport, Illinois.

1956 Gold Medal: Basketball

Carl Cain graduated from the University of Iowa in 1956 where he was the star of Iowa's basketball team when they twice won the Big Ten Championship and went to the finals of the NCAA Tournament. Cain never played professional basketball. He later became a bookkeeper.

Sources: *Black Olympians*; *Guinness Book of Olympic Records*; *Quest for Gold*; *United States Olympic Team, Games of the XVIth Olympiad*.

CALDERÓN-GÓMEZ, MIGUEL (Cuba). Born October 30, 1950, in Havana, Cuba.

1972 Bronze Medal: Basketball

Miguel Calderón-Gómez's team's scores during the Munich 1972 Games were: (preliminaries) match #2, Cuba-Egypt, 105-64; match #13, Cuba-Spain, 74-53; match #24, U.S.-Cuba, 67-48; match #29, Czechoslovakia-Cuba, 65-77; match #34, Australia-Cuba, 70-84; match #44, Japan-Cuba, 63-108; match #56, Cuba-Brazil, 64-63; (semifinals) match #62, USSR-Cuba, 67-61; (finals) match #68, Cuba-Italy, 66-65. The Cuban team consisted of Calderón-Gómez, Rafael Canizares, Pedro Chappé, Ruperto Herrera, Tomás Herrera, Juan Ortega, Conrado

Pérez, Franklin Standard, Alejandro Urgelles, and Oscar Varona. Calderón-Gómez, a guard, is now head coach of Cuba's junior team.

Sources: *Approved History of Olympic Games*; British Virgin Islands, Olympic Committee; *Die Spiele, Official Report for the Games of the XXth Olympiad; Guinness Book of Olympic Records; Munchen, 1972, Results of the Games of the XXth Olympiad; Official Report of the Olympic Games, 1972; Sportsworld*.

CALDWELL, JOE LOUIS (USA). Born November 1, 1941, in Texas City, Texas.

1964 Gold Medal: Basketball

Jumping Joe Caldwell, "the human pogo stick," attended Arizona State University in the early 1960s. He moved from there to play for 11 years in the NBA and the ABA, always as a top performer. Although short for a forward, he played the position well. In 1970 Caldwell switched leagues, going from Atlanta of the NBA to the Carolina Cougars of the ABA.

Sources: *Black Olympians; Guinness Book of Olympic Records; Quest for Gold; United States Olympic Team, Games of the XVIIIth Olympiad*.

CALHOUN, LEE QUENCY (USA). Born February 23, 1933, in Laurel, Mississippi.

1956 Gold Medal: 110-Meter Hurdles (13.70, Olympic record)
1960 Gold Medal: 110-Meter Hurdles (13.98)

Lee Calhoun, a graduate of North Carolina Central State College, was the first athlete to win the 110-Meter hurdles event twice. He equaled the world record of 13.2 seconds in 1960. Calhoun won the AAU indoor and outdoor, the NAIA, and the NCAA in 1956. He then successively defended all four titles in 1957. He won the third AAU Outdoor Championship in 1959 and also the Pan Am Games title. Calhoun was technically one of the most accomplished high hurdlers of all time. He was helped by his predecessor Harrison Dillard. His best marks in other events were 9.7 seconds for the 100-yard hurdles, 22.9 for the 220-yard hurdles (turn), and 1.90 meters in the high jump. He was suspended for the 1958 season when his amateur status was questioned as a result of his receiving gifts after being married on television. He later returned to prominence. Subsequently, Lee Calhoun coached at Grambling College and became head track coach at Yale. Since 1980 he has been coaching at Western Illinois University in Macomb. He was also assistant coach at the 1971 and 1979 Pan Am Games and at the Montreal Games in 1976.

Sources: "More about Winning," *American Visions*, Volume 3, 1988; *Approved History of Olympic Games; Black Olympians; Guinness Book of Olympic Records; Quest for Gold; Tales of Gold; Track and Field: The Great Ones; United States Track and Field Olympians; Who's Who in the Olympic Games*.

CAMERON, BERT (Jamaica). Born November 16, 1959, in Spanish Town, Jamaica.

1988 Silver Medal: 4 x 400-Meter Relay (3:00.30)

Bert Cameron is a graduate of University of Texas, El Paso, and a member of the Converse Track Club. At 400 meters in the 4 x 400-meter relay, Cameron placed sixth in Seoul in 1988, second in the 1987 Pan Am Games, first in the 1983 World Championships, first in the 1982 Commonwealth Games, first in the 1982 Central America and Caribbean Games, third in the 1981 World Cup (three relays), and first in the 1980 NCAA Championships. Cameron's personal bests are 20.74 seconds at 200 meters (1983) and 1 minute, 49.57 seconds at 800 meters (1982).

Sources: British Virgin Islands, Olympic Committee; *International Amateur Athletic Federation*; "Seoul Games/Medal Winners," *Los Angeles Times* (October 3, 1988); *Seoul '88*; "Olympics Record" *USA Today* (October 3, 1988).

CAMPBELL, MILTON GRAY (USA). Born December 9, 1934, in Plainfield, New Jersey.

1952 Silver Medal: Decathlon (6,975 pts.)
1956 Gold Medal: Decathlon (7,937, Olympic record)

Milton Campbell graduated from Indiana University in 1957. In 1953 he won the AAU decathlon, and in 1955 he finished first in both the AAU and NCAA high hurdles. While at Indiana University, where he won letters in both football and track, he set a world record of 13.4 seconds for the 120-yard hurdles. Campbell was one of the first great Black decathletes and the first Black to win the Olympic decathlon. He had won the silver medal in 1952 at age 18. His 1956 decathlon scores, totaling 7,708 points, were: 100-meter run, 10.8 seconds; 400-meter run, 48.8 seconds; long jump, 7.33 meters; 110-meter hurdles, 14.0 seconds; high jump, 1.89 meters; pole vault, 3.40 meters; shot put, 14.76 meters; javelin, 57.08 meters; discus, 48.5 meters; 1,500-meter run, 4:50.6. Milton Campbell more recently has worked with underprivileged youth in New Jersey and is a well-known lecturer.

Sources: *Approved History of Olympic Games; Black Olympians*; British Virgin Islands, Olympic Committee; *Guinness Book of Olympic Records; Quest for Gold; United States Olympic Team, Games of the XVth Olympiad*.

CAMPBELL, TONIE (USA). Born June 14, 1960, in Los Angeles, California.

1988 Bronze Medal: 110-Meter Hurdles (13.38)

Tonie Campbell finished second after Roger Kingdom with a time of 13.25 seconds at the 1988 Olympic trials. He won the 60-meter hurdles at the 1987 World Indoor Championships. In 1987 he ranked second in the U.S. in the 110-meters. He has run with Greg Foster and Renaldo Nehemiah, although in their shadows. Campbell won the TAC meet in 1984 and the World Cup Championship in 1985. Campbell attended USC and was a member of the Bee-Fit Track Club.

Sources: "Black American Medal Winners," *Ebony* (December 1988); "Seoul Games/Medal Winners," *Los Angeles Times* (October 3, 1988); *1988 United States Olympic Team, Media Guide*; "Tonie Campbell," *Track & Field News* (June 1987); "Olympic Record," *USA Today* (October 3, 1988).

CANIZARES POEY, RAFAEL (Cuba). Born March 4, 1950, in Alacs Mtnzs, Cuba.

1972 Bronze Medal: Basketball

For a summary of Rafael Canizares's team's record at the 1972 Munich Games, see Calderón-Gómez.

Sources: *Approved History of Olympic Games*; British Virgin Islands, Olympic Committee; *Die Spiele, Official Report of the Games of the XXth Olympiad*; *Guinness Book of Olympic Records*; *Munchen, 1972, Results of the Games of the XXth Olympiad*.

CARILLO, GILBERTO (Cuba). Born in Cuba.

1972 Silver Medal: Light Heavyweight Boxing

The Cubans made headlines in boxing at the 1972 Olympic Games, improving from their Mexico City successes. They led the world in Munich, winning three golds, a silver, and a bronze. Gilberto Carillo defeated Ernesto Sanchez of Venezuela, with a knockout in the first round (time: 2 minutes, 24 seconds). Carillo defeated Harald Skog of Norway in the first round, when the referee stopped the contest (time: 2 minutes, 41 seconds).

Sources: *Approved History of Olympic Games*; British Virgin Islands, Olympic Committee; *Complete Book of the Olympics*; *Die Spiele, Official Report for the Games of the XXth Olympiad*; *Guinness Book of Olympic Records*; *Munchen, 1972, Results of the Games of the XXth Olympiad*.

JOHN CARLOS (John Carlos [right] and Tommie Smith give Black Power salute at 1968 Olympics. Photo courtesy of U.S. Olympic Committee, Colorado Springs, Colorado.)

CARLOS, JOHN WESLEY (USA). Born June 5, 1945 in New York City.

1968 Bronze Medal: 200-Meter Run (20.10)

John Carlos attended San Jose State College in San Jose, California. He won the AAU and NCAA 200-meter run and equaled the world record for the indoor 60 and the outdoor 100. Carlos's finest performance was 19.7 seconds for the 200 meters at the 1968 final trials. (Because he was wearing illegal brush spikes, this time, which was three-tenths of a second inside the world record, was never ratified.) John Carlos and Tommie Smith made a political impact at the 1968 Olympics in Mexico City. When they were on the victory stand they refused to acknowledge the American flag and the "Star Spangled Banner." Head lowered, each raised a black-gloved fist. This protest against the treatment of Blacks in the United States resulted in the expulsion of both athletes from the Olympic Village. The culmination of a decade of protest of Blacks' civil rights in the United States, the movement was led by Harry Edwards, academic and former athlete. Carlos was probably the best sprinter in the world in both 1969 and 1970 but, with future Olympic involvement closed to him, he participated in the professional International Track Association from 1973 to 1975. Carlos was also for a short time a professional football player. In a revealing interview with the author, John Carlos expressed himself as follows: "[Peter] Uberroth is a very strong individual, and a very meek [humane] individual. He lets Blacks play very many major roles. He didn't *have* to let a Black light the Olympic torch. He didn't *have* to honor Jesse Owens' granddaughter. He didn't *have* to go behind the scenes to have Jim Thorpe's medals restored... [or] have Wilma Rudolph come in and run public service announcements.... Mack (Robinson) has had the opportunity of giving speeches to many business people, to many of the schools. He had the opportunity to run the torch, and he's been very public." Carlos went on to say: "I used to coordinate young kids.... I was community coordinator working with the community to meet challenges. I went from there to liaison between the community and the L.A. Olympic Organizing Committee.... The kids were very enthused about what was happening. The committee would take 100,000 kids to the Olympics through the school system" (interview with author, 1984).

Sources: *Approved History of Olympic Games; Black Olympians;* Carlos, John W. Interview. 1984; *Guinness Book of Olympic Records; Quest for Gold; Spirit Team Profiles, Los Angeles Olympic Organizing Committee; United States Olympic Team, Games of the XIXth Olympiad.*

CARNEY, LESTER (USA). Born March 21, 1934, in Bellaire, Ohio.

1960 Silver Medal: 200-Meter Run (20.69)

Lester Carney attended Ohio University and was affiliated with Akron Track Club. Although better known as a football player at Ohio University, he was a match for all but the very best of his contemporary sprinters. Carney took the silver medal in 1960, beating both his teammates who had finished ahead of him at the trials in Rome. His personal record 20.69 seconds in the Olympics, trailed the winner, Livio Berruti, by no more than a tenth of a second. Lester Carney was later drafted by the Baltimore Colts, but never played professional football. He became a purchasing agent for a major sporting goods firm in Akron, Ohio.

Sources: *Black Olympians; Guinness Book of Olympic Records; 1960 United States Sports Team, Games; Quest for Gold; United States Track and Field Olympians.*

CARR, HENRY (USA). Born November 27, 1942, in Detroit, Michigan.

1964 Gold Medal: 200-Meter Run (20.36, Olympic record)
1964 Gold Medal: 4 x 400-Meter Relay (3:00.7)

Henry Carr attended Arizona State University. A member of the Phoenix Olympic Club, he was one of the finest all-around sprinters in the world. Carr won the NCAA 220 yards in 1963 and tied for first place in the AAU (at Arizona State). In 1964 he won the AAU outright and lowered the world record for the furlong to 20.2 seconds. He had set the previous record of 20.3 in 1963. Carr also had the best times of 9.2 for 100 yards, 10.2 for 100 meters, and 45.4 for 440 yards. In 1963 he ranked in the top five in the world in all three sprints. The 4 x 400-meter relay team that clocked 3.00.7 in Tokyo, included Carr's Arizona State teammate, Ulis Williams. As a professional football player, Carr was defensive back with the New York Giants from 1965 to 1968. Following his football career, he became a devout Christian and lay preacher.

Sources: *Approved History of Olympic Games; Black Olympians;* British Virgin Islands, Olympic Committee; *Guinness Book of Olympic Records; Quest for Gold; United States Track and Field Olympians; Track and Field: The Great Ones.*

CARR, KENNETH (USA). Born August 15, 1955, in Clearwater, Florida.

1976 Gold Medal: Basketball

Kenneth Carr was a high school All-American when he was playing for DeMatha High in Hyattsville, Maryland. He graduated in 1978 from North Carolina State University. In 1976 he made 798 points (second highest ever at N.C. State), averaging 26.6 points per game. This made him the leading scorer in the Atlantic Coast Conference and fifth in the U.S. His collegiate coach was Norman Sloan. DeMatha, one of the greatest high school basketball powers in the country, gave Carr the background he needed to become an Atlantic Coast Conference star at N.C. State, an Olympic star forward in 1976, and a good professional player, first with Los Angeles, then with Cleveland and Portland.

Sources: *Guinness Book of Olympic Records; Quest for Gold; United States Olympic Team, Games.*

CARR, NATE (USA). Born June 24, 1960 in Erie, Pennsylvania.

1988 Bronze Medal: Freestyle Wrestling (149½ lbs./68 kg)

Nate Carr attended Iowa State University, where he was a three-time NCAA champion. He comes from a long line of wrestling brothers. His older brother Jimmy, made the 1972 Olympic team as a senior in high school. His brothers, Fletcher, Joe, and Michael were All-Americans in college. Carr was an alternate for the 1984 Olympic team. When he defeated Raul Cascaret of Cuba at the 1986 World Cup, he pulled off a major victory. After he moved back to the 149.5-pound class, he won the National Open in 1988. Nate Carr is currently an assistant coach at West Virginia.

Sources: "Black American Medal Winners," *Ebony* (December 1988); "Seoul Games/Medal Winners," *Los Angeles Times* (October 3, 1988); *1988 United States Olympic Team, Media Guide; Seoul '88;* "Olympics Record," *USA Today* (October 3, 1988).

CARRERAS, RICARDO LUÍS (USA). Born December 12, 1949, in New York City.

1972 Bronze Medal: Bantamweight Boxing (tied)

Ricardo Carreras first came to the attention of the world in 1966 when he won the New York Golden Gloves. He also won the bronze medal in boxing at the Pan Am Games in 1971 and the AAU Championship. Three times, in 1969, 1971, and 1972, he was inter-service champion while in the air force. Carreras took a record of 7.3 to 8 to the 1972 Munich Games, where he tied for the bantamweight boxing medal.

Sources: *Black Olympians; Guinness Book of Olympic Records; Quest for Gold; United States Olympic Team Games.*

CARTER, MICHAEL (USA). Born October 29, 1960, in Dallas, Texas.

1984 Silver Medal: Shot Put (69 ft. 2½ in./21.09 m)

While still a student at Jefferson High School in Dallas, Michael Carter threw the 12-pound shot an unbelievable 81 feet, 3½ inches, more than 10 feet past the old record. During his sophomore year at Southern Methodist University, where he earned a degree in sociology, he won the NCAA shot put title with a toss of 68 feet, 10¾ inches. Carter won the NCAA indoor shot put title four times (1980, 1981, 1983, and 1984). He became only the second four-time winner of an NCAA indoor event, the other being Suleiman Nyambui of Tanzania. Carter also won the NCAA outdoor title three times before losing, in 1984, to UCLA's John Brenner. Mike Carter threw over 70 feet (70 feet, 3 inches) for the first time in competition in the spring of 1984 at San Jose. He finished fourth in the first meet in history to see four 70-plus finishers. At the NCAAs, he put four throws past 70 feet and lost again, although he achieved his personal best performance of 21.76 meters (203 feet, 3 inches). When he won a silver medal at the Los Angeles Games, he was the first Black

athlete ever to do so in the shot put. Carter, who had been a second team All-American nose guard during his sophomore year at Southern Methodist University, signed a professional football contract with the San Francisco 49ers in 1984 and is regarded by some as the best nose guard in the NFL.

Sources: British Virgin Islands, Olympic Committee; "The Games," *Olympian* (October/November 1984); *Research Information, Games of the XXIIIrd Olympiad.*

CARUTHERS, EDWARD J., JR. (USA). Born April 13, 1945, in Troy, Alabama.

1968 Silver Medal: High Jump (7 ft. 3¼ in./2.22 m)

Edward Caruthers developed into a great high jumper while attending Arizona State University. This was after he had placed eighth in the 1964 Olympics. His only defeats in 1967 were at the NCAA and the AAU, where in each case he lost only on the countback; he was never outjumped. Although he cleared a personal best at the 1968 Olympics, he had to settle for second best behind Dick Fosbury, who was using the new "flop" style.

Sources: *Black Olympians;* British Virgin Islands, Olympic Committee; *Guinness Book of Olympic Records; Quest for Gold; Spirit Team Profiles,* Los Angeles Olympic Organizing Committee.

CASAÑAS, ALEJANDRO (Cuba). Born January 29, 1954, in Havana, Cuba.

1976 Silver Medal: 110-Meter Hurdles (13.33)
1980 Silver Medal: 110-Meter Hurdles (13.40)

Alejandro Casañas finished as follows in the 110-meter hurdles at the 1980 Olympics in Moscow: heat #1, first, with 13.44 seconds; heat #3, first, with 13.46; final, second place, after Thomas Munkelt of East Germany, with 13.40.

Sources: British Virgin Islands, Olympic Committee; *Games of the XXIInd Olympiad; Guinness Book of Olympic Records;* "Results: Track and Field," *Los Angeles Times* (July 28, 1980).

CATOR, SILVIO (Haiti). Born October 9, 1900, in Cavillon, Haiti.

1928 Silver Medal: Long Jump (24 ft. 10¼ in./7.58 m)

Silvio Cator is the only Haitian athlete to have achieved world class in the long jump. He reached this status when he won the silver medal, behind Ed Hamm of the U.S., at the 1928 Olympics in Amsterdam. Later in 1928 he became the world's first broad jumper to exceed 26 feet. Cator also captained the Haitian soccer team.

Sources: *Black College Sport*; British Virgin Islands, Olympic Committee; *Guinness Book of Olympic Records*; *Illustrated History of the Olympics*; *Ninth Olympiad, Official Report, 1928, Amsterdam*.

CHAPPÉ-GARCÍA, PEDRO (Cuba). Born August 16, 1943, in Havana, Cuba.

1972 Bronze Medal: Basketball

For a summary of Pedro Chappé-García's team's record at the 1972 Olympics in Munich, see Calderón-Gómez. Chappé-García, 6 feet, 7 inches tall and very burly, later coached his country's national team.

Sources: *Approved History of Olympic Games*; British Virgin Islands, Olympic Committee; *Die Spiele, Official Report for the Games of the XXth Olympiad*; *Guinness Book of Olympic Records*; *Munchen, 1972*; *Results of the XXth Olympiad*.

CHEESEBOROUGH, CHANDRA (USA). Born January 10, 1959, in Jacksonville, Florida.

1984 Gold Medal: 4 x 100-Meter Relay (41.65)
1984 Gold Medal: 4 x 400-Meter Relay (3:18.29, new Olympic record)
1984 Silver Medal: 400-Meter Run (49.05)

Chandra Cheeseborough attended Ribault High School in Jacksonville and Tennessee State University. The times she ran in the Pan Am Games at age 16 are still Florida sprint records. A member of Athletics West, she also won the TAC 100-meter title in 1976 and earned 10th place world ranking in the 100 that same year. A participant in the 1976, 1980, and 1984 Olympics, Cheeseborough became one of the most versatile sprinters and one of the best 400-meter runners in the world. She helped break the Eastern bloc's domination of the women's 400 (which began when that event was added to the Olympics in 1964) by winning the silver behind U.S. teammate Valerie Brisco-Hooks in 1984. The previous highest American finish was a third, by Kathy Hammond in 1972. Cheeseborough broke Rosalyn Bryant's 400-meter record of 50.62 seconds, held for 8 years, with a 50.52 on May 13, 1984 at the UCLA meet. Brisco-Hooks lowered it to 49.83 early in June 1984, but Cheeseborough took the record back from Brisco-Hooks on June 19 at the Los Angeles Coliseum with a 49.28. A child prodigy who has matured into a three-time Olympian, Cheeseborough states, "The Olympics were exciting but the most exciting thing took place in the Pan Am Games when I was 16 and won it" (*Los Angeles Times*).

Sources: British Virgin Islands, Olympic Committee; "The Black U.S. Medal Winners," *Ebony* (October 1984); "The Champions," *Los Angeles Times* (August 14, 1984); *1984 Olympic Games*; "Olympic Medal Results," *Sporting News* (August 27, 1984); *United States Olympic Team, Media Guide*.

CHIVÁS, SILVIA (Cuba). Born September 30, 1954, in Cuba.

1972 Bronze Medal: 100-Meter Run (11.24)
1972 Bronze Medal: 4 x 100-Meter Relay (43.36)

In her short career Silvia Chivás won several regional titles at both 100 and 200 meters. A bronze medalist at the age of 18 in the 100 meters at the Munich Olympics in 1972, Silvia Chivás also anchored the Cuban 4 x 100-meter relay team to a third place finish. Even though Chivás recorded the fastest time of the first two rounds (of the 100), there was never much doubt that East Germany's Renate Stecher would win. Chivás's personal bests were 11.16 seconds (in the 100 meters) and 22.85 (in the 200).

Sources: *Approved History of Olympic Games*; British Virgin Islands, Olympic Committee; *Complete Book of the Olympics*; *1972 United States Olympic Book*.

CHRISTIE, LINFORD (Great Britain). Born April 2, 1960 in St. Andrews, Jamaica.

1988 Silver Medal: 100-Meter Run (9.97)
1988 Silver Medal: 4 x 100-Meter Relay (38.28)

Before his victories in Seoul, Linford Christie won the men's 100 meters in 10.25 seconds at the International Amateur Athletic Federation Mobil Grand Prix track and field meet at London's Crystal Palace. He thus maintained his unbeaten record for the 1988 season. Christie is a youth worker and a member of the Thames Valley Harriers.

Sources: British Virgin Islands, Olympic Committee; *International Amateur Athletic Federation*; "Seoul Games/Medal Winners," *Los Angeles Times* (October 3, 1988); *Seoul '88*; "Olympics Record," *USA Today* (October 3, 1988).

COACHMAN, ALICE (DAVIS) (USA). Born November 9, 1923, in Albany, Georgia.

1948 Gold Medal: High Jump (5 ft. 6 in./1.68 m, Olympic record)

Alice Coachman attended Albany State College. She won the U.S. Indoor title in 1941-43 and also eight AAU sprint titles outdoors and two indoors. During her career she won 25 AAU Championships. Coachman won the U.S. outdoor 50-meter dash from 1943 through 1947; the 100-meter dash in 1942, 1945, and 1946; the high jump from 1939 through 1948; the indoor 50-meter dash in 1945 and 1946; and the high jump in 1941, 1945, and 1946. Coachman was the first Black woman Olympic gold medal winner, setting a record that stood until two Olympiads later. She was the only American woman to win a gold medal in the 1948 Games. She still holds the record for the most AAU outdoor high jump victories with consecutive championships between 1939 and 1948. Alice Coachman later taught school in Atlanta. She is a member of the National Hall of Fame, Black Athletes Hall of Fame, Tuskegee Hall of Fame, Georgia State Hall of Fame, and Bob Douglas Hall of Fame.

Sources: *Approved History of Olympic Games; Black Olympians; Guinness Book of Olympic Records; Hard Road to Glory; Quest for Gold; United States Track and Field Olympians; Who's Who in Track and Field.*

COAGE, ALLEN JAMES (USA). Born October 22, 1943, in New York City.

1976 Bronze Medal: Heavyweight Judo (205 lbs./102.5 kg)

Allen Coage graduated from Thomas A. Edison High School in 1961 and from the American Institute of Baking in 1963. He also attended Nikon University in Tokyo, Japan. Coage started in judo at age 22. He was the first Black to win a medal in judo at the Olympics (1976); the only American to win a gold medal in an AAU National Judo Championship (1968, 1969); the only athlete to win five heavyweight AAU National Judo Championships (1966, 1968, 1970, and 1975); the first New York native to win an AAU National Judo Championship (1966); and the only American to compete in four World Championships (1967, 1969, 1971, and 1975). In the pre-Olympic Games, Coage tied for fourth place at Montreal in 1975. In pre-World Championships in 1974 in Austria, he tied for third. He won the gold in the Pan Am Games in 1967 and 1975. He also was Pan Am champion in 1968. Allen Coage's special honors are: AAU National Grand Champion, 1970; New York Athlete of the Year, 1968; New Jersey Athlete of the Year, 1976; *Sports Illustrated* Special Achievement Award, 1968; New Jersey Athletic Hall of Fame; Black Belt Hall of Fame, 1970, 1976; Black Belt Magazine's #1 Judo Player, 1970, 1976; member, All-America Judo Team, 1968, 1969, 1970; member, International Judo Team (10 times); captain, Goodwill Tour of Europe, 1974; guest at the White House (President Ford); winner of People to People Sports Scholarship to Nikon University to train, 1970; and captain, U.S. Olympic judo team, 1976. Coage entered professional wrestling in Tokyo and continues in it. He is married and has nine children.

Sources: *Black Olympians*; Coage, Allen J. Questionnaire. 1984; *Guinness Book of Olympic Records; United States Olympic Team, Games.*

COBIAN, MIGUELINA (Cuba). Born July 28, 1947, in Santiago, Cuba.

1968 Silver Medal: 4 x 100-Meter Relay (43.36)

In the Central American and Caribbean Games Miguelina Cobian won the women's 100 meters in 1962 (12.01), 1966 (11.7) and 1970 (11.4). She also took the 200 (23.5) and sprint relay in 1970. Cobian won eight medals, including

three silvers, a record for a woman in these games. Cobian was an Olympic finalist in the 100 meters in Tokyo in 1964. She anchored the 4 x 100 team in 1968. Her career bests were 11.41 and 23.38 for the 100 and 200-meter dashes. She retired in 1970.

Sources: British Virgin Islands, Olympic Committee; *Complete Book of the Olympics; Guinness Book of Track and Field Athletics.*

COLES, VERNELL (USA). Born April 22, 1968.

1988 Bronze Medal: Basketball

Vernell Coles was a co-Player of the Year in the Metro Conference (1988). He became the first player to lead the Metro in scoring and assists in the same season. During the 1987 season he started every game, averaging 24.2 points overall and 28.2 points in 13 conference games. Coles handed out 172 assists (5.9 per game) and led the team in steals with 60. He set a school and conference record for free throws made in a season with 200. Against Southern Mississippi he scored a Metro Conference record 51 points. He also handed out 11 assists in that game. Coles was named *Sports Illustrated* Player of the Week and Windex (ESPN) National Player of the Week. He took a career high eight rebounds in a win over Memphis State. Coles hit 20 or more points 20 times during the season and had 30 points or more 7 times. He played in all 28 games as a freshman, including 18 as a starter. Coles is currently enrolled at Virginia Tech. He is majoring in hotel and restaurant management.

Sources: "Black American Medal Winners," *Ebony* (December 1988); "Seoul Games/Media Guide, *Los Angeles Times* (October 3, 1988); *1988 United States Olympic Team, Media Guide; Seoul '88*; "Olympics Record," *USA Today* (October 3, 1988).

COLLETT, WAYNE CURTIS (USA). Born October 20, 1949 in Los Angeles, California.

1972 Silver Medal: 400-Meter Run (44.80)

In high school Collett was a standout in the 200 and 400 meters, as well as in the low hurdles. At UCLA he emerged as a world-class sprinter in his freshman year, running 20.2 seconds for the 200 and 44.9 over 400 in 1968. In the longer race he had five sub-46-second marks. At the U.S. Olympic trials that year he ran 45.6 in the heats and 44.9 in the quarter-finals, where he was eliminated. A very versatile athlete, Collett also ran both relays and long-jumped for UCLA. In the event that many felt would have been his road to greatness, the 440-yard hurdles, Collett ran a personal best time of 49.2 to finish second to future silver medalist Ralph Mann at the NCAA Championships in Des Moines. However, Collett had little love for the event and gave it up after finishing college. In 1972 Collett surprisingly won the 400 at the U.S. Olympic trials, achieving his personal best of 44.1 and defeating former UCLA teammate John Smith and 1968 Olympians Lee Evans and Vince Matthews. Matthews got his revenge at the Munich Games, running 44.66 to the second-place Collett's 44.80. Collett and Matthews, however, will probably be best remembered for their banishment for life from Olympic competition by the International Olympic Committee for what was called a breach of traditional decorum at the medals presentation ceremony. Collett earned a master's degree in business administration and a doctorate in law from UCLA. He retired from all competition after 1972 and now practices law in California.

Sources: *Approved History of Olympic Games; Black Olympians*; British Virgin Islands, Olympic Committee; *Guinness Book of Olympic Records; Quest for Gold; United States Olympic Team, Games of the XXth Olympiad; United States Track and Field Olympians.*

COLÓN, MARÍA CARIDAD (Cuba). Born March 25, 1958, in Cuba.

1980 Gold Medal: Javelin (224 ft. 5 in./68.40 m, Olympic record)

María Colón was the first Cuban woman to win an Olympic gold medal. It was left to her to win the competition in the 1980 Moscow javelin throw, on her first try. This was after Ruth Fuchs, East German "queen of javelin throwing," and other women with the best records, had disappointing performances. Colón, with her victory in the javelin throw at the Moscow Olympics, also became the first non-White woman to gain an Olympic gold medal in a throwing event. Twice a Pan Am Games champion, Colón has a personal best throw of 229 feet, 6 inches (69.96 meters). A good performer in big meets, María Colón tends to "disappear" for long periods. She is a physical education teacher in Havana and is married to her coach, Angel Salcedo.

Sources: British Virgin Islands, Olympic Committee; *Complete Book of the Olympics; Encyclopaedia of Track and Field Athletics; Games of the XXIInd Olympiad, Moscow; Guinness Book of Olympic Records.*

CONLEY, MIKE (USA). Born October 5, 1962, in Chicago, Illinois.

1984 Silver Medal: Triple Jump (56 ft. 4½ in./17.18 m)

Mike Conley is one of the best horizontal jumpers in the world. In 1983 he achieved fourth place world rankings in both the long and the triple jump. In 1982 he broke onto the national scene with a second in the NCAA long jump, but he really excelled in 1983, placing in both events at the World Championships. He took third in the long jump and

fourth in the triple jump. He was also second in the NCAA long jump and third in the NCAA triple jump in 1983. While at TAC he was third in the long jump and second in the triple jump. Also in 1983 he achieved his personal record with marks of 27 feet, 2 inches and 56 feet, 6½ inches. Conley was second in the triple jump at the 1983 World University Games. Keith Connor, the 1982 NCAA champion said of Conley, "He's only become familiar with the triple jump in the last year, and already he's the best in the world right now and will be for years to come" (*Los Angeles Times*). He won both horizontal jumps indoors and outdoors in 1984 and 1985.

Sources: "The Black U.S. Medal Winners," *Ebony* (October 1984); "The Champions," *Los Angeles Times* (August 14, 1984); "The Games," *Olympian* (October/November 1984); "Mike Conley," *Track & Field News* (July 1985); *United States Olympic Team, Media Guide.*

CONNOR, KEITH (Great Britain). Born September 16, 1957, on the Caribbean island of Anguilla.

1984 Bronze Medal: Triple Jump (55 ft. 4¼ in./16.87 m)

Keith Connor was 1982 European champion in the triple jump. He was the second longest triple jumper in history, after Joao de Oliveira of Brazil. His jump of 57 feet, 7¾ inches at the 1982 NCAA Championships in Provo, Utah, was the second best leap in history—at the time. He considers his greatest rival Australian Ken Lorraway, whom he beat at the 1982 Commonwealth Games in Brisbane. Connor atoned for a disappointing World Championships performance in 1983 with the triple jump bronze medal at the Los Angeles Olympics in 1984. Connor graduated from Southern Methodist University in 1984 with a degree in sociology. He now coaches the jumpers at his alma mater.

Sources: British Virgin Islands, Olympic Committee; "The Olympics," *New York Times* (August 5, 1984); *1984 Olympic Games; Sarajevo/Los Angeles*; "The Games," *Olympian* (October/November 1984); *Research Information, Games of the XXIIIrd Olympiad.*

CONWAY, HOLLIS (USA). Born January 8, 1967.

1988 Silver Medal: High Jump (7 ft. 8¾ in./2.36 m)

Hollis Conway finished second at the Olympic trials, leaping 7 feet 7¼ inches. He was ranked second in the U.S. after Jerome Carter in 1987. His personal best was 7 feet, 8 inches. Conway attends Southwestern Louisiana University; his home is in Chicago.

Sources: British Virgin Islands, Olympic Committee; "Seoul Games/Medal Winners," *Los Angeles Times* (October 3, 1988); *1988 United States Olympic Team, Media Guide; Seoul '88*; "Olympic Record," *USA Today* (October 3, 1988).

COOPER, CYNTHIA (USA). Born April 14, 1963.

1988 Gold Medal: Basketball

Cynthia Cooper graduated in 1986 from the University of Southern California with a degree in communications. Cooper played in Parma, Italy, during the 1987-88 season. She was a member of the 1987 U.S. Pan Am Games team, which won the gold medal. She averaged 73 points per game and shot an impressive 55.6 percent from the field. She also made five of eight three-point attempts (62.5 percent). Cooper played on gold medal-winning teams at the 1986 FIBA World Championships and Goodwill Games. She played on three NCAA Final Four teams while at USC, and helped her team win the national title in 1983 and 1984. She averaged 17.2 points per game as a senior. She was a member of the 1986 Final Four All-Tournament team.

Sources: "Black American Medal Winners," *Ebony* (December 1988); "Seoul Games/Medal Winners," *Los Angeles Times* (October 3, 1988); *1988 United States Olympic Team, Media Guide; Seoul '88*; "Olympics Record," *USA Today* (October 3, 1988).

CORREA, EMILIO (Cuba). Born in Cuba.

1972 Gold Medal: Welterweight Boxing

In the welterweight boxing events at the 1972 Olympics Emilio Correa defeated: Damiano Lassandro of Italy, points 5-0; Manfred Walke of East Germany (when the referee stopped the match in the second round) in 2:02 minutes; Guenter Meier of Germany 3-2; Jesse Valdez of the U.S. 3-2; and Janos Kajdi of Hungary with 5-0 points. The final match was between the 19-year-old Pan Am champion, Correa, and the 32-year-old European title-holder, Janos Kajdi. The Cuban won the unanimous decision, even though it was close.

Sources: *Approved History of Olympic Games; Complete Book of the Olympics; Die Spiele, Official Report for the Games of the XXth Olympiad; Guinness Book of Olympic Records; Munchen 1972; Results of the Games of the XXth Olympiad.*

CRAWFORD, HASELY (Trinidad). Born August 16, 1950, in Trinidad.

1976 Gold Medal: 100-Meter run (10.06)

Hasely Crawford had been acknowledged as one of the world's best sprinters. He became the first Trinidadian to win an Olympic gold medal. (His government issued a stamp in his honor and named an airliner after him.) Early in the 1975 season Crawford was credited with the remarkable, if wind-aided, time of 9.8 seconds. His personal bests were 10.06 and 9.8 (wind-assisted) for the 100 meters, and 20.2 for the 200. He took second place in the 1975 Pan Am Games.

Sources: *Guinness Book of Olympic Records; Guinness Book of Track and Field Athletics; 1976 United States Olympic Book.*

CROCKETT, RITA LOUISE (USA). Born November 2, 1957, in San Antonio, Texas.

1984 Silver Medal: Volleyball

Rita Crockett attended John Marshall High School in San Antonio, San Antonio Junior College, North Texas State University, and the University of Houston. Crockett is recognized as one of the top four hitters in the world. She has the highest vertical jump on the U.S. team and is one of only six women in the world participating on the All-World Cup team. She jumps amazingly high and has measured 40 inches. She has been called the best American female athlete in any sport and, along with (late) teammate Flo Hyman, was considered one of the top three spikers in the world. Rita Crockett was freshman class president and was on the student council, the football and basketball drill teams, and the dance squad. Lettering 4 years in volleyball, she made All-District, and All-City for 4 years in volleyball and was All-District in basketball. In volleyball she was also Junior College All-America/National champion in 1975 and was on the All-Tournament team at Nationals. In basketball she was on the Southwest Conference team. Some special honors Crockett won are University of Houston's MVP for volleyball, 1977-78, and City League's softball home run champion, player with the highest batting average, MVP, and Best All-Around. She was named the U.S. Volleyball Association's Rookie of the Year in 1978 and MVP for the U.S. Volleyball Association's South All-Star team. Rita Crockett left the University of Houston a year early to join the U.S. National Olympic team in Colorado Springs. She planned to retire from athletics in 1984 and go into law. She would like to negotiate contracts for professional athletes. She was employed for a while with a Japanese company and divided her time between Japan and the U.S. Crockett later played volleyball with a professional women's league in the U.S.

Sources: Crockett, Rita. Questionnaire. 1984; "The 1984 Olympics," *Ebony* (October 1984); *For the Record;* "The China Factor," *Los Angeles Times* (August 7, 1984); "Volleyball," *Olympian* (October/November 1984); *United States Olympic Team, Media Guide;* "Rita Crockett," *Women's Sports* (October 1983); "Los Angeles '84," *Women's Sports* (October 1984).

CROOK, EDWARD (USA). Born April 19, 1929, in Detroit, Michigan.

1960 Gold Medal: Middleweight Boxing

Edward Crook lost in the Olympic trials finals to José Torres in 1956. However, he had vastly improved by 1960. At

Rome he knocked out three of his first four opponents before winning a 3-1-1 decision over Tadeusz Walasek of Poland. Eddie Crook won two Golden Gloves Championships and an Eastern Regional AAU title and made the Olympic team—all in 1960.

Sources: *Black Olympians; Guinness Book of Olympic Records; Quest for Gold.*

CROOKS, CHARMAINE (Canada). Born August 8, 1961, in Jamaica.

1984 Silver Medal: 4 x 400-Meter Relay (3:21.21)

Charmaine Crooks finished second at the 1984 NCAAs behind Marita Payne. She finished seventh in the 400 meters at the Los Angeles Olympics in a personal best time of 50.45 seconds. She won a silver medal leading off the Canadian 4 x 400-meter relay. Crooks has lived in Toronto for more than 18 years. She attended the University of Texas at El Paso as a child psychology student. Her brother Natty, who attended Abilene Christian, is one of Canada's leading high jumpers. Her involvement with the Royal Canadian Army Cadet leadership program in 1978 allowed her to learn German and spend two months in Germany in an exchange program as one of twenty outstanding high school students. Crooks also was chosen to accompany a reporter and photographer to Kenya in a program involving foster children in Africa. Finally, she was a member of NCAA's "Volunteers for Youth" program, which has branches in 60 universities all over Canada.

Sources: British Virgin Islands, Olympic Committee; Canadian Olympic Association; *1984 Olympic Games, Sarajevo/Los Angeles.*

JOAQUIM CARVALHO CRUZ (Photo courtesy of Rich Clarkson, Denver, Colorado.)

CRUZ, JOAQUIM CARVALHO (Brazil). Born March 12, 1963, in Tahuntinga, Brazil.

1984 Gold Medal: 800-Meter Run (1:43.00, Olympic record)
1988 Silver Medal: 800-Meter run (1:43.90)

Joaquim Cruz first came to international attention in 1981 when he set a new world junior record for 800 meters with a time of 1 minute, 44.3 seconds. In 1984 Cruz stamped his name among the all-time greats of the 800 meters. At the Los Angeles Olympics he reeled off times of 1:45.66, 1:44.84, and 1:43.82 in the preliminary rounds before taking the final in 1:43.00, half a second below the previous Olympic record set 8 years earlier by Cuba's Alberto Juantorena. Cruz's gold medal-winning performance was remarkably even-paced, with the first lap taking 51.16 seconds and the second lap 51.84. The field was probably the greatest ever assembled in the event, but after taking the lead at 600 meters the Brazilian was never really headed. In 1982 Cruz went to the U.S. where his Brazilian coach, Luiz de Oliveira, was pursuing studies for an advanced

degree at the University of Oregon. Cruz was unable to compete in his first year at Oregon, but in 1983 he won the first of two consecutive NCAA Championships in the 800. In 1984 Cruz also captured top honors in the 1,500 at the Collegiate Championships. Cruz gained his first major international honor in 1983 when he ran 1:44.27 to win the bronze medal at the World Championships in Helsinki. In 1983 he reduced his personal record in the two-lapper to 1:44.04. He also began to dabble in the 1,500 and produced a year's best of 3:39.5. In 1984 Cruz became a serious competitor in the 1,500 as well, and after running the fastest debut mile of all time (3:53.00), he set his designs on an Olympic double. Affected by a virus, Cruz won his 1,500 heat at Los Angeles, but had to withdraw from further participation. Joaquim Cruz has run 8 of the 20 fastest 800-meter races ever. As of 1986 his personal best of 1:41.77 had been surpassed only by Sebastian Coe's 1:41.73. Cruz has six times run two laps under 1:43.00. But his (1984) Olympic victory represents the fastest time ever run in a major championship. In the 1,500 he is still seeking his first major international win, but his personal best of 3:35.70, achieved in 1985, would tend to indicate vast potential in the longer race. After the Ben Johnson steroids fiasco during the Seoul Olympics, Cruz implied that both Florence Griffith-Joyner and Jackie Joyner-Kersee must be on drugs to be as muscular as they are. He so embarrassed himself with those implications that he didn't even show up to run the 1,500.

Sources: British Virgin Islands, Olympic Committee; *International Athletics Annual*; "U.S. Gets a Surprise," *Los Angeles Times* (August 8, 1984); "Unfounded Rumors," *Los Angeles Times* (September 29, 1988); "The Games," *Olympian* (October/November 1984); *Research Information, Games of the XXIIIrd Olympiad*; "Olympic Medal Results," *Sporting News* (August 27, 1984); "Cruz Joins Ranks of Elite Doublers," *Track & Field News* (July 1984); "Cruz's Sudden Speed Wins 1500," *Track & Field News* (May 1985); "Olympics Record," *USA Today* (October 3, 1988).

CULBREATH, JOSHUA (USA). Born September 14, 1932 in Norristown, Pennsylvania.

1956 Bronze Medal: 400-Meter Hurdles (51.74)

Joshua Culbreath attended Morgan State University in Baltimore. He was number 2 All-Time 400-meter hurdler and three-time National AAU 440-yard hurdles champion. He won the AAU in 1953, 1954, and 1955 and the Pan Am Games in 1955 and 1959. He set a world record for the 440 hurdles at 50.5 seconds. Culbreath became interested in hurdling while attending Morgan State. He brought his best time for the intermediate hurdles down to 50.1 in the 1956 final trials. This put him behind Glenn Davis and Eddie Southern. The Olympic final was a repeat of the U.S. trials with these three sweeping the medals. Culbreath was the first great Black intermediate hurdler.

Sources: *Black Olympians*; British Virgin Islands, Olympic Committee; *Guinness Book of Olympic Records*; *Quest for Gold*.

DABORG, ISSAKA (Niger). Born in 1940 in Danlchoandou, Niger.

1972 Bronze Medal: Light Welterweight Boxing

Issaka Daborg attended the Ecole Primaire CEZ and Collèges Suivis in Niger, and received diplomas. He was a member of Niamey Boxing Club in 1958. During his boxing career, Issaka Daborg has received the following medals: the bronze medal in the Friendship Games in Abidjan (1960); the gold medal in the Friendship Games in Dakar (1963); the silver medal in the Friendship Games in Brazzaville (1965); the gold medal in the African Championships in Lusaka (1968); and the silver medal in the African Games

in Lagos (1973). Daborg has also received special honors from his country for his athletic accomplishments. Following his own boxing career Daborg became a trainer of boxers in Agadez, Niger.

Sources: *Africa at the Olympics; Approved History of Olympic Games; Complete Book of the Olympics; Complete Handbook of Olympic Games; Die Spiele, Official Report for the Games of the XXth Olympiad; Guinness Book of Olympic Records*; Niger Embassy, Washington, District of Columbia.

DA CONCEIÇÃO, JOSÉ TELLES (Brazil). Born May 23, 1931, in Rio de Janeiro, Brazil.

1952 Bronze Medal: High Jump (6 ft. 6 in./1.98 m)

Although José da Conceição won an Olympic medal for the high jump, this lanky Brazilian was better known for his exploits in the sprints and high hurdles in the mid-1950s. In 1957 da Conceição was co-world leader in the 100 meters, with a clocking of 10.2 seconds. He also enjoyed some national success as a decathlete.

Sources: *Approved History of Olympic Games*; British Virgin Islands, Olympic Committee; *Complete Book of the Olympics; Guinness Book of Olympic Records*.

DANIELS, ISABELLE FRANCES (USA). Born July 31, 1937, in Jakin, Georgia.

1956 Bronze Medal: 4 x 100-Meter Relay (45.04)

Isabelle Daniels graduated from Tennessee State University in 1959, where she was a member of the Tigerbelles track team. Daniels finished second in the 60 meters and was on the winning relay team at the Pan Am Games. Although Mae Faggs beat her out in the 1956 AAU 100, when she went to Melbourne that same year she had reversed the decision at the final trials, and was a first-string U.S. sprinter. Daniels won seven indoor AAU sprint titles and five outdoor. At the same time she was a member of the Tennessee State team that won the AAU relay for 5 years in a row. In 1957 she established an American record (5.7 seconds) in the 50-yard dash. This wasn't broken until Wyomia Tyus broke it in 1966. Daniels was a member of the AAU All-America Track and Field Women's team each year she was in college. Daniels ran the anchor leg on the winning team in the relay that set a new U.S. record of 44.9 behind Australia and Great Britain; all three had bettered the previous world record. Isabelle Daniels lives in Atlanta with her husband, Sidney Holston. They have two sons.

Sources: *Black Olympians; Development of Negro Female Olympic Talent; Guinness Book of Olympic Records; Negro Firsts in Sports; Quest for Gold; United States Track and Field Olympics*.

DANIELS, QUINCEY (USA). Born August 4, 1941, in Biloxi, Mississippi.

1960 Bronze Medal: Light Welterweight Boxing

Quincey Daniels was a 1959 AAU lightweight champion. He also won the Golden Gloves (Western Regional) in 1959 and 1960. Daniels was third in light welterweight boxing at the 1960 Olympics in Rome. The first and second winners were Bohumil Nemecek of Czechoslovakia and Clement Quartey of Ghana.

Sources: *Black Olympians; Complete Book of the Olympics; Games of the XVIIth Olympiad, Rome 1960; Guinness Book of Olympic Records; Quest for Gold; Olympic Games, 1960.*

DANTLEY, ADRIAN (USA). Born February 28, 1955, in Washington, D.C.

1976 Gold Medal: Basketball

Adrian Dantley attended basketball powerhouse DeMatha High School in Hyattsville, Maryland and then Notre Dame University. He was a First All-American in college as a sophomore and junior. Dantley helped the U.S. team beat the taller Yugoslavs in Montreal by scoring 30 points, converting 13 of 19 shots. He beat them by more than the margin of their first meeting (112-93). "Dantley played most of the second half with a bandage over his right eye after being whacked above the eyebrow. Stitches were required to close the wound, but they failed to keep Dantley from finding the basket or from containing Yugoslavia's top player, 6 ft. 10 in. Kressmir Cosic" (*New York Times*). Adrian Dantley claimed hardship and declared himself eligible for the NBA draft, after playing on the 1976 gold medal-winning team. One of the stars of the league, he made the All-Rookie team in 1976 and was named Rookie of the Year. His best year to date was 1981 when he was an NBA All-Star second team selection and led the league in scoring. He has played in several NBA All-Star games. He was traded by the Utah Jazz to the Detroit Pistons after the 1985-86 season.

Sources: *Black Olympians*; British Virgin Islands, Olympic Committee; *Guinness Book of Olympic Records*; "Dantley Scores 30 Points in Star Role," *New York Times* (July 28, 1976); *Quest for Gold*.

DA SILVA, ADHEMAR FERREIRA (Brazil). Born September 29, 1927, in São Paulo, Brazil.

1952 Gold Medal: Triple Jump (53 ft. 2¾ in./16.22 m)
1956 Gold Medal: Triple Jump (53 ft. 7½ in./16.35 m, Olympic record)

Adhemar Ferreira da Silva was considered South America's most distinguished athlete of his time. He won every major triple jump title open to him. He was not only an Olympic champion in 1952 and 1956 but also a Pan Am titlist in 1951, 1955 and 1959. He competed in four Olympics and held the world record from 1950 to 1953 and from 1955 to 1958 and was the first man to triple jump in excess of 16 meters. Da Silva jumped 52 feet, 6 inches on December 6, 1950, in São Paulo to equal the world record after an 11th place finish in the 1948 Olympics. Although he lost the record in 1953, he leaped 54 feet, 4 inches to regain the world record in the Pan Am Games in Mexico City on March 16, 1955. After winning the gold in both the 1952 and 1956 Olympics, he placed only 14th in the 1960 Olympics. He had jumped only 53 feet, 3¾ inches in 1958. He put on an incredible show in the triple jump at Helsinki in 1952. He broke his old world record four times in six attempts in the final. Da Silva's final world record was 53 feet, 6½ inches for the triple jump. He was undefeated from 1951 through 1956. His other best marks include 21.0 seconds (wind-assisted) for a straight 220 yards and 24 feet in the long jump. He broke the world record four times in his six jumps. Da Silva, who is fluent in seven languages, acted in the internationally acclaimed film *Black Orpheus*. The multilingual, guitar-playing Brazilian was among the most popular trackmen in international competition.

Sources: British Virgin Islands, Olympic Committee; *Complete Book of the Olympics; Encyclopaedia of Track and Field Athletics; Guinness Book of Olympic Records; Official Encyclopedia of Sports; Official Report of Organizing Committee for Games of XVIth Olympiad; The Olympic Games, Melbourne, 1956; Track and Field: The Great Ones.*

DAVENPORT, WILLIE D. (USA). Born June 8, 1943, in Troy, Alabama.

1968 Gold Medal: 110-Meter Hurdles (13.33, Olympic record)
1976 Bronze Medal: 110-Meter Hurdles (13.38)

Willie Davenport attended Southern University in Baton Rouge, Louisiana, after the 1964 Games and won the AAU Outdoor title outright in 1965, 1966, and 1967; he tied for first place in 1969. One of the sensations of the 1964 Olympic final trials occurred when 19-year-old army Private Willie Davenport won the high hurdles. He finished ahead of Hayes Jones and Blaine Lindgren. He was eliminated from the Tokyo Games that year because of a thigh injury, but he took the gold medal in Mexico City 4 years later. He finished fourth in 1972 and third in 1976. Davenport competed in the four-man bobsled in the 1980 Winter Olympics. He thus became only the fourth American to compete in both the Summer and Winter Olympics. Willie Davenport has served as a youth director for the city of Baton Rouge and as an athlete's representative to the U.S. Olympic Committee.

Sources: *Approved History of Olympic Games; Black Olympians*; British Virgin Islands, Olympic Committee; *Guinness Book of Olympic Records; Quest for Gold* "Drut Takes High Hurdles Gold," *New York Times* (July 29, 1976); *Track and Field: The Great Ones; United States Track and Field Olympians.*

DAVIS, HOWARD EDWARD, JR. (USA).
Born February 14, 1956, in Glen Cove, New York.

1976 Silver Medal: Lightweight Boxing

Howard Davis won the AAU featherweight crown in 1973, the first World's Amateur Boxing Championship in 1974, and the AAU lightweight title in 1976. Davis won the Golden Gloves four times and has had a successful professional boxing career since his Olympic win in 1976. Through early 1983, his record was 22 wins and 1 loss. He had not won a World Championship. In 1986, 30-year-old Howard Davis fought Meldrick Taylor (19-year-old gold medalist from 1984) to a spirited 10-round draw in Atlantic City.

Sources: *Black Olympians; Guinness Book of Olympic Records* "5 Boxers from U.S. Hit Gold," *New York Times* (August 1, 1976); "Olympic Summaries," *New York Times* (August 2, 1976); "Olympic Winners Fight to Lively Draw," *New York Times* (August 17, 1986); *Quest for Gold.*

DAVIS, JOHN HENRY, JR. (USA).
Born January 12, 1921, in Smithtown, New York.

1948 Gold Medal: Heavyweight Weightlifting (997½ lbs./ 451.5 kg)
1952 Gold Medal: Heavyweight Weightlifting (1,014 lbs./ 460.0 kg)

John Davis was a member of a six-man weightlifting team that competed in Vienna in 1938. He secured the World Championship light heavyweight title that year to begin a 15-year reign as the titleholder. He has been considered by some to be a super heavyweight weightlifter. The fun-loving Brooklyn garageman was the only American who did not have to follow training rules in the 1952 Olympics. An avid singer, Davis once made a record which sold 71 copies. He had an ambition to sing at the Metropolitan Opera in New York, and although he never made it to the Met, he did give four concerts in Sweden. Davis retired from the New York City Department of Corrections after many years of service.

Sources: *Approved History of Olympic Games; Black Olympians; Complete Book of the Olympics; Guinness Book of Olympic Records; Negro Firsts in Sports; Official Encyclopedia of Sports; Quest for Gold; Report of the United States Olympic Team, Games of the XIVth Olympiad.*

DAVIS, OTIS CRANDELL (USA). Born July 12, 1932, in Tuscaloosa, Alabama.

1960 Gold Medal: 400-Meter Run (45.07, Olympic record/ world record)
1960 Gold Medal: 4 x 400-Meter Relay (4:2.2, Olympic record/world record)

Otis Davis attended the University of Oregon, where he played basketball; but he did not begin track and field until he was 26 years old. In 1959 he ran the 440 yards and finished third in the AAU, and in 1960 he won the AAU before going on to take the Olympic title with a new record. Davis also helped set a world record by running anchor on the gold medal-winning relay team. Davis retired after winning the 1961 AAU 440, ending a brief but brilliant track career. He coached and taught until 1980, when he was appointed director of the Sports Complex for the U.S. military in Germany.

Sources: *Black Olympians*; British Virgin Islands, Olympic Committee; *Guinness Book of Olympic Records; Quest for Gold; Track and Field: The Great Ones.*

DAVIS, WALTER PAUL (USA). Born September 9, 1954, in Pineville, North Carolina.

1976 Gold Medal: Basketball

Walter Davis began his basketball career at his high school in South Mecklenburg, North Carolina, and continued playing at the University of North Carolina, where he averaged 14 points or more all 4 years. Davis was clearly a star, despite coach Dean Smith's team approach to basketball. Davis, who continued to be coached by Smith on the 1976 Olympic team, was one of the primary reasons the U.S. regained the Olympic basketball gold medal. Davis easily made the transition into professional basketball when he was drafted by the Phoenix Suns in 1977. He was voted Rookie of the Year in 1978 and named to the All-Rookie team. He also was voted to the second team All-NBA because of his 24 points, 6 rebounds, and 4 assists per game. He repeated this feat in 1979. He has consistently been ranked among the NBA's best players, first as a forward and then as a guard.

Sources: *Black Olympians*; British Virgin Islands, Olympic Committee; *Guinness Book of Olympic Records; Quest for Gold.*

DEFRANTZ, ANITA LUCEETE (USA). Born October 4, 1952 in Philadelphia, Pennsylvania.

1976 Bronze Medal: Rowing, Eights (3:38.68)

Anita DeFrantz is a graduate of Shortridge High School, Indianapolis (1970), Connecticut College for Women and Men (1974), and the University of Pennsylvania Law

ANITA LUCEETE DEFRANTZ (Photo courtesy of Amateur Athletic Foundation.)

School (1977). She also worked toward a Ph.D. in peace science at the University of Pennsylvania. She participated in rowing and basketball in college and was affiliated with the Vesper Boat Club in Philadelphia. DeFrantz became an outspoken critic of the 1980 Olympic boycott, and because of her law background she was an eloquent spokesperson for the athletes. By supporting that Olympic movement she became only the second American athlete to receive the Bronze Medal of the Olympic Order of the International Olympic Committee. This occurred on September 24, 1981 at the IOC Congress at Baden-Baden, West Germany. The honor was awarded her "for her actions which symbolized the fight to safeguard the independence of all sports competitors from political power." While studying law, Anita DeFrantz made the Olympic Eights to become the first Afro-American to compete for the U.S. in Olympic rowing. She distinguished herself by winning six different national titles and sharing a silver medal in the Coxed Fours at the 1978 World Championships. She was a member of the 1980 U.S. Olympic team and coached the Princeton novice crew in 1980-81. Attorney DeFrantz has been a member of the President's Council on Physical Fitness, a trustee of Connecticut College, a member of the Executive Board of the U.S. Olympic Committee, and vice chair for the Athlete's Advisory Council of the USOC. She later worked as an assistant vice president for the Los Angeles Olympic Organizing Committee and was vice president in charge of the Olympic Village. Currently she is president of the Amateur Athletic Foundation of Los Angeles, which is responsible for distributing the $90 million southern California share of the 1984 Olympic surplus. In 1986 DeFrantz became the first Black woman to become a member of the International Olympic Committee, replacing the late Julian Roosevelt as one of the two U.S. representatives on the committee. On May 16, 1988 she was named winner of the Koribos Award, which is given every 4 years to an Olympian who best exemplifies the Olympic spirit.

Sources: *Approved History of Olympic Games; Black Olympians; Black Women in Sport*; British Virgin Islands, Olympic Committee; DeFrantz, Anita. Interview. 1985; *Games of the XXIst Olympiad; Guinness Book of Olympic Records*; "1976 Olympic Medalist Anita DeFrantz," *Los Angeles Times* (June 18, 1987); "Southern California Olympians Celebrate 75th Anniversary," *Olympian* (September/October 1988); *Quest for Gold; Spirit Team Profiles; Los Angeles Olympic Organizing Committee*.

AN INTERVIEW WITH ANITA DEFRANTZ

To questions about insights gained in her several roles as an Olympian, Anita DeFrantz responded as follows:

Well, I've learned ... about people and learned that (they) can care about others. It's important to meet people on their own terms.... Being in charge of Olympic Village was a huge ... responsibility and I had people ... who were older and more experienced than I who reported to me and it was a challenge to make me feel that I was ... a person to deserve their loyalty.... I was honest with people. I let them know that I expected a great deal because we were serving the most important group of guests in the world.... I was able to put together a really strong team of several *thousand* people actually who worked in the Village, who had good memories, who understood a little bit about what the Games were about—that the Games were about people, about celebration, about human excellence, about people who were willing ... to put their egos on the line and say to the world, "Yes, I believe I can be an Olympic champion and realize that the whole world will know whether I succeeded or failed."

I also feel that sports can be a real assist to Black communities. It's something that so many of our youngsters aspire to, but they aspire to play; they aspire to be on the field to play; and they should aspire, likewise, to be coaches. They should aspire likewise to be administrators, they should aspire to own the professional teams.... There is a lot of interest in sports. It is ... the third largest industry in the world.

Sports ties together the community. It's an institution of sports for the community that gives youngsters a sense of history because they come into the sports club, learn a sport or two, play in a club and then as they become older, [they] may be a manager of a younger team. As they become older, they become coaches.

It's a tradition that was lost perhaps, but the thing that Jackie Robinson did was so important but, at the same time, integration destroyed the Negro baseball groups. *Destroyed* them! All the owners, all the people who were involved in that no longer had leagues to promote and really lost that part of our community. Something that belonged to us was taken away because of integration. Now if the *league* had been integrated instead of the individual, if baseball had taken the entire league, the entire team into it, then things might be different today. But *instead* they made it only available to the athlete; which destroyed the institution. So, *I* believe it's important for us to think about rebuilding those institutions in our community.

In being asked whether Blacks are being upgraded in sports, Anita DeFrantz stated:

I think so but certainly not quickly enough. There are what, three Black men who are coaches in the NBA? K. C. Jones, and the Clippers' coach who I sense may be out of work next year, unfortunately. There is one manager. That's Elgin of the Clippers also. I don't know of any others and none in baseball. * There are none in football, and what is it?* I don't know what percentage of the players are Black. Not a single coach. It's ridiculous, just ridiculous! There are no Black people in the front office in professional baseball, a national sport. None! ... So there are a couple of boxing promoters who are Black, and of course, the vast majority of the athletes are. So it's,... to me, nowhere near where it should be. We're just at the beginning, we've got a lot of work to do!

---

*Since this interview, several Blacks have been made major professional sports managers. See "Profile of Black Management in U.S. Professional Sports" on p. 131 for a synopsis of Black involvement in professional sports administration and management.

DELIS (FOURNIER), LUIS MARIANO
(Cuba). Born December 6, 1957, in Guantánamo, Cuba.

1980 Bronze Medal: Discus Throw (217 ft. 7 in./66.32 m)

Luis Delis was the world's leading discus thrower in the 1980s. There was controversy at the 1980 Moscow Olympics because many observers felt that Delis's final throw had been marked short and that he was thus kept from a silver or even a gold medal. Delis was an excellent competitor who, in addition to winning an Olympic medal, placed second in the Helsinki World Championships and was the 1983 Pan Am champion in the shot put and discus throw. Delis holds Central American and Caribbean records in both events with personal bests of 71.06 meters (233 feet, 2 inches) and 19.89 meters (65 feet, 3 inches) in the discus and shot, respectively. Delis has also won numerous awards in World Cup competition and in the World Student and Central American Games.

Sources: British Virgin Islands, Olympic Committee; *Complete Book of the Olympics; Games of the XXIInd Olympiad, Moscow; Guinness Book of Olympic Records; Who's Who in the 1984 Olympics.*

DELOACH, JOE (USA). Born June 5, 1967.

1988 Gold Medal: 200-Meter Run (19.75, new Olympic record)

Joe DeLoach, who foiled Carl Lewis's attempt to become the first man ever to win consecutive gold medals in the 200 meters, set a new Olympic record and also tied Lewis's U.S. record. He beat Lewis's Olympic record of 19.80, set in the 1984 Games. By winning the 200-meter finals at the Olympic trials, DeLoach handed Carl Lewis his first defeat in 2 years in that event. His personal best was 19.96 in the finals. At the Olympic trials, running a wind-aided 9.90, he finished fifth in the 100. DeLoach has run a personal best of 10.03 in the 100. He won the 100-meter NCAA championship in 1988 with 10.03, the fastest in the world at that point. DeLoach makes his home in Bay City, Texas, and attends the University of Houston. He trains with Carl Lewis.

Sources: British Virgin Islands, Olympic Committee; "Black American Medal Winners," *Ebony* (December 1988); "Seoul Games/Medal Winners," *Los Angeles Times* (October 3, 1988); "DeLoach Ends Lewis' Bid for Gold Sweep," *Los*

Angeles Times (October 10, 1988); *1988 United States Olympic Team, Media Guide; Seoul '88;* "Olympics Record," *USA Today* (October 3, 1988).

DE OLIVEIRA, JOAO CARLOS (Brazil). Born May 28, 1954, in São Paulo, Brazil.

1976 Bronze Medal: Triple Jump (55 ft. 5½ in./16.90 m)
1980 Bronze Medal: Triple Jump (56 ft. 6 in./17.22 m)

In the triple jump Brazil has been exceptional. The tradition established by A.F. da Silva (1951 and 1956) and maintained by Nelson Prudencio (1968 and 1972), both world record-holders in their time, reached new heights when Joao Carlos de Oliveira achieved an astonishing exploit in the 1975 Pan Am Games. De Oliveira took full advantage of Mexico City's high altitude to hop 6.05 meters and jump 6.44 for a total distance of 17.89 meters—fully superior to the world record held by Russian Viktor Sanyeyev. De Oliveira had to settle for the bronze medal in Montreal when sciatica hampered his Olympic preparation in 1976. However, he triumphed in the World Cup in 1977 and in 1978 tied Sanyeyev's world "low altitude" best of 17.44. Although he retained his Pan Am long and triple jump titles in 1979, his Olympic hopes were dashed in Moscow when a series of mighty triple jumps were ruled fouls and he placed third again with 17.22. He is also a formidable sprinter (10.1 seconds in the 100 meters) and he has long-jumped 8.36 meters. Joao Carlos de Oliveira had a leg amputated after a car crash in 1982.

Sources: British Virgin Islands, Olympic Committee; *Encyclopaedia of Track and Field Athletics; Guinness Book of Olympic Records;* "Results of Moscow Olympics," *New York Times* (July 26, 1980); *Research Information, Games of the XXIIIrd Olympiad.*

DEVONISH, ARNOLDO (Venezuela). Born in 1933 in Venezuela.

1952 Bronze Medal: Triple Jump (50 ft. 11 in./15.52 m)

Arnoldo Devonish's win in the 1952 Helsinki Olympics made him, at the age of 19, one of the youngest field event medalists ever. He was also the first Venezuelan to win an Olympic medal. His personal best in the triple jump was 16.13 meters (52 feet, 11 inches). Devonish became a track and field administrator in Venezuela.

Sources: British Virgin Islands, Olympic Committee; *Complete Book of the Olympics; Guinness Book of Olympic Records.*

HARRISON W. DILLARD (Photo courtesy of U.S. Olympic Committee, Colorado Springs, Colorado.)

DILLARD, HARRISON W. (USA). Born July 8, 1923, in Cleveland, Ohio.

1948 Gold Medal: 100-Meter Run (10.3, Olympic record)
1948 Gold Medal: 4 x 100-Meter Relay (40.6)
1952 Gold Medal: 4 x 100-Meter Relay (40.26)
1952 Gold Medal: 110-Meter Hurdles (13.91, Olympic record)

Harrison Dillard graduated from Baldwin-Wallace College in Berea, Ohio, in 1949. While still in college he became a specialist high hurdler, and between May 1947 and June 1948 he ran 82 sprint and hurdle races without defeat. There was no doubt that he was the best high hurdler in the immediate postwar years. Track enthusiasts called him the best combination sprinter/hurdler who ever lived. (His record of 82 straight victories was only recently passed by Edwin Moses.) Dillard was inspired by Jesse Owens as a child. At an all-day military track meet, where he won four gold medals in one day, General Patton said, "He's the best ... athlete I've ever seen" (*Los Angeles Times*). At Baldwin-Wallace College, he was unbeaten. During his career "Bones" Dillard won 14 AAU titles and 6 NCAA Championships and set the world record in both the high and low hurdles. Recalling his Olympic victories, he says, "When your name is inscribed outside on the wall of the stadium in which the Olympics took place, your name is there for posterity. You're the best in the World at the moment you do it.... You have achieved excellence" (*Black Olympians*). Dillard was 61 in 1983 and business director for the Cleveland School Board, responsible for more than 3,000 employees and a budget of $80 million. He later became chief of the Business Department for Cleveland Schools (where he had been for more than 20 years). For 10 years before that he was with Bill Veeck and the Cleveland Indians baseball club.

Sources: *Approved History of Olympic Games; Black Olympians; Guinness Book of Olympic Records;* "Olympic Briefs," *Los Angeles Times* (July 25, 1984); *1980 Olympic Handbook; Quest for Gold; Tales of Gold; Who's Who in the Olympic Games; Who's Who in Track and Field.*

DIXON, DIANE (USA). Born September 23, 1964, in Brooklyn, New York.

1988 Silver Medal: 4 x 400-Meter Relay (3:15.51)

Diane Dixon won the 1988 Olympic trials in the 400 meters with a time of 50.38 seconds, just off her personal best (50.24 in 1986). The winner of five consecutive TAC indoor 400 titles, Dixon ranked fifth on the All-Time U.S. women's list and ranked third in the U.S. at the close of 1987. She finished first at the TAC in 1986 (second in 1987) and fourth at the 1987 Pan Am Games. She placed seventh at the World Championships in 1987. Dixon graduated from Ohio State University in 1983.

Sources: "Black American Medal Winners," *Ebony* (December 1988); Seoul Games/Medal Winners," *Los Angeles Times* (October 3, 1988); *1988 United States Olympic Team, Media Guide; Seoul '88;* "An Aggressive Dixon Drives Ahead," *Track & Field News* (April 1986); "Some Big Names Take a Tumble," *Track & Field News* (May 1986); "TAC Women--400," *Track & Field News* (August 1986); "Olympics Record," *USA Today* (October 3, 1988).

DOUGLAS, HERBERT P., JR. (USA). Born March 9, 1922, in Pittsburgh, Pennsylvania.

1948 Bronze Medal: Long Jump (24 ft. 9 in./7.54 m)

Herbert Douglas graduated in 1940 from Allerdice High School in Pittsburgh. There he participated in basketball, football, gymnastics, and track and field and was voted Athlete of the Year. He graduated in 1948 from the University of Pittsburgh where he participated in football and track and field. At the 1948 Olympic final trials, Douglas jumped 25 feet, 3 inches for the best mark of his career. He failed to match this at the Olympics and missed the silver medal

by 1 centimeter. He was outdoor winner at the IC4A in 1946 and won the AAU long jump title in 1947. He also won in the national AAU (three gold indoor long jump medals), and he was college All-American. Douglas is now vice president of a wine-importing company and devotes considerable time building the Jesse Owens International Amateur Award. He has two children and four grandchildren.

Sources: *Black Olympians;* Douglas, Herbert. Questionnaire. 1984; *Guinness Book of Olympic Records; Negro in Sports; Quest for Gold.*

DRAYTON, OTIS PAUL (USA). Born May 8, 1939, in Glen Cove, New York.

1964 Gold Medal: 4 x 100-Meter Relay (39.06, Olympic record/world record)
1964 Silver Medal: 200-Meter Run (20.58)

Paul Drayton won the AAU 200 meters in 1961 and 1962 and tied with Henry Carr for the 1963 220-yard title. He equaled the world record with his winning time at 20.5 seconds in 1962. Drayton was a member of the U.S. relay team at Villanova, Pennsylvania, which set a world record of 39.1 for the 400-meter relay in the 1961 U.S.-USSR dual meet. In Tokyo, 3 years later, he played a part in bringing that record down to 39.0. He was the only runner on both record-breaking teams. Although Drayton defeated Carr (who had been unbeaten that season) at the final trials, Carr took the Olympic 200 title, with Drayton finishing second.

Sources: *Black Olympians; Guinness Book of Olympic Records; Quest for Gold.*

DUMAS, CHARLES EVERETT (USA). Born February 12, 1937, in Tulsa, Oklahoma.

1956 Gold Medal: High Jump (6 ft. 11½ in./2.12 m, Olympic record)

Because he was only an 18-year-old schoolboy, Charles Dumas caused a sensation when he tied for first place in the 1955 AAU high jump. He also won the AAU high jump in 1956, 1957, and 1959. In 1956 he became the first man to break the 7-foot barrier when he cleared 7 feet, 5/8 inches at the Olympic finals trials; he went on to win the gold medal. Dumas never won the NCAA during his years at the University of Southern California. He retired in 1960 after placing sixth at the Rome Olympics. He attempted a comeback in 1964 but did not finish the season. Charles Dumas earned his Master of Arts degree at UCLA and became dean of students at Thomas Jefferson High School in Los Angeles.

Sources: *Black Olympians; Guinness Book of Olympic Records; Spirit Team Profiles, Los Angeles Olympic Organizing Committee; Track and Field: The Great Ones.*

DUVALON, RAMÓN (Cuba). Born in Cuba.

1976 Silver Medal: Flyweight Boxing

In flyweight boxing at the 1976 Olympic Games in Montreal Ramón Duvalon defeated Charlie Magri of the United Kingdom, Jo Ung Jong of North Korea, and Leo Randolph of the U.S. He lost to Virgilio Palomo Meza of Colombia in a one-sided contest.

Sources: *Approved History of Olympic Games*; British Virgin Islands, Olympic Committee; *Complete Book of the Olympics*; *Guinness Book of Olympic Records*; *Montreal 1976, Games of the XXIst Olympiad*; *Story of the Olympic Games*.

EBANGA, MARTIN NDONGO (Cameroon). Born in Cameroon.

1984 Bronze Medal: Lightweight Boxing

Martin Ebanga's record in lightweight boxing at the 1984 Los Angeles Olympics was as follows: (1/16) Ebanga defeats Shadrach Odhiambo of Sweden when the referee stops the contest 1 minute, 35 seconds into round 2; (1/8) Ebanga defeats Gordon Carew of Guyana with a knockout 2 minutes, 16 seconds into round 2; (1/4) Ebanga defeats Fahri Sumer of Turkey 4 points to 1; (1/2) Ebanga loses to Luis F. Ortiz of Puerto Rico 3 points to 2.

Sources: "The Champions," *Los Angeles Times* (August 14, 1984); *1984 Olympic Games; Sarajevo/Los Angeles; Official Report of the Games of the XXIIIrd Olympiad*.

ECHOLS, SHEILA (USA). Born October 2, 1964 in Memphis, Tennessee.

1988 Gold: 4 x 100-Meter Relay (41.98)

Sheila Echols finished fourth in the 100 meters at the Olympic trials, with a time of 11 seconds. She jumped 22 feet, 7 inches to finish second in the long jump at the trials. She tied with Carol Lewis and Yvette Bates, but Echols's second-best jump was the top mark of the three. Echols ranked second behind Jackie Joyner-Kersee in the long jump for the U.S. in 1987, jumping a personal best of 22 feet, 9¼ inches. With that mark, she also ranks fourth on the All-Time U.S. women's list. Echols won the 1988 USA/Mobil Championships in both the 100 meters and long jump and was named outstanding performer at the meet. While at Louisiana State University, Sheila Echols won the NCAA Championship. She competed at the Pan Am Games and World Championships in 1987, the same year she graduated from LSU. She ran for Athletics West for a time after 1987.

Sources: "Black American Medal Winners," *Ebony* (December 1988); "Seoul Games/Medal Winners," *Los Angeles Times* (October 3, 1988); *1988 United States Olympic Team, Media Guide; Seoul '88;* "Olympics Record," *USA Today* (October 3, 1988).

EDWARD, HARRY FRANCIS VINCENT (Great Britain). Born April 15, 1895, in British Guiana.

1920 Bronze Medal: 100-Meter Run (11.0)
1920 Bronze Medal: 200-Meter Run (22.2)

Harry Edward was Britain's first Black medalist. The high point of his career was during 2 days of the British Amateur Athletic Association Championships in 1922. He ran nine races. On the first day he ran the 220 yards (two rounds), the 440 yards (one round), and finished by taking a 220-yard relay stage. The next afternoon he ran his 100-yard heat and won his third 100-yard title, in even time. Two hours later he won the 220 yards in 22.0 seconds, and 25 minutes later he won the 440 yards, beating the 1920 Olympic silver medalist, Guy Butler. Later the same evening, he ran the 220-yard leg in the relay, in which his club finished second. Edward was coached by the Italian professional Mussabini, whose charges also included sprinters Jack London and Harry Abrahams. Harry Edward died July 8, 1973.

Sources: *Black College Sport*; British Olympic Association; British Virgin Islands, Olympic Committee; *Guinness Book of Olympic Records*; *Guinness Book of Athletic Facts and Feats*.

EDWARDS, PHILIP A. (Canada). Born August 28, 1907 in Georgetown, British Guiana.

1928 Bronze Medal: 4 x 400-Meter Relay (3:15.4)
1932 Bronze Medal: 800-Meters (1:51.5)
1932 Bronze Medal: 1,500-Meter Run (3:52.8)
1932 Bronze Medal: 4 x 400-Meter Relay (3:12.8)
1936 Bronze Medal: 800-Meter Run (1:53.6)

Philip Edwards received his undergraduate degree from New York University and his M.D. from McGill University in Montreal. When Edwards went to New York University and ran under the guidance of the famous coach Von Elling, he soon became a name in North American track circles. Edwards won the AAU 880 in 1929 and the indoor AAU 600 from 1928 through 1931. He competed as a Canadian in three Olympiads, even though he was born in British Guiana. Edwards did win a Commonwealth Games gold medal for his native land in 1934 in the 800. Until John Woodruff appeared in 1937, he held the Intercollegiate Association half-mile record of 1 minute, 52.2 seconds for New York University. He was the first winner of the Lou Marsh Trophy 1935 and a member of the Canadian Amateur Sports Hall of Fame. In 1956 he was chef de mission of the British Guianian team, and in 1966 he became the physician of the Canadian team. Philip Edwards specialized in tropical diseases and became one of the world authorities in that field. He died September 6, 1971, in Montreal.

Sources: British Virgin Islands, Olympic Committee; Canadian Olympic Association; *Games of the Xth Olympiad, Los Angeles, 1932; Guinness Book of Olympic Records;*

Negroes in Sports; Official Program, Xth Olympiad; Track and Field: The Great Ones.

EDWARDS, TERESA (USA). Born July 7, 1964, in Cairo, Georgia.

1984 Gold Medal: Basketball
1988 Gold Medal: Basketball

Teresa Edwards graduated from Cairo High School in 1982. Her basketball team had a 53-8 mark during her junior and senior years and captured the state championship. She graduated from the University of Georgia in 1986 with a major in recreation. Edwards set a school record with 189 assists in 1983. She was the Southeastern Conference (SEC) MVP as a freshman and, with 15.3 points per game, was named to several freshman All-American teams. She helped win the SEC Championship. She earned 1984 All-Tournament honors at the SEC Championship and played on a number of district and national all-star teams. Teresa Edwards scored 895 points, 154 rebounds, and 289 assists in 2 years at Georgia. In 1983-84 she set a single-season school record for assists with 189. As two-time Kodak All-American at Georgia, she scored 1,989 points, averaging nearly 20 points and 5 rebounds per game as a senior. Edwards was the 1987 ABA Player of the Year. She played in Magenta, Italy, for a year. At the 1987 Pan Am Games she helped the U.S. win the gold medal, averaging 16.8 points while shooting 60.8 percent from the field. In the 1988 Olympics the U.S. women's basketball team made amends for the defeat of the men's team by the Soviet Union. The U.S. women beat Yugoslavia 77-70 for the gold. Teresa Edwards, who had played in the gold medal-winning game in Los Angeles, scored 18 points.

Sources: "The 1984 Olympics," *Ebony* (October 1984); "Black American Medal Winners," *Ebony* (December 1988); "Seoul Games/Medal Winners," *Los Angeles Times* (October 3, 1988); *1984 Olympic Games, Sarajevo/Los Angeles; 1988 United States Olympic Team, Media Guide; Seoul '88;* "Olympics Record," *USA Today* (October 3, 1988).

EGBUNIKE, INNOCENT (Nigeria). Born November 30, 1961, in Onitsha, Nigeria.

1984 Bronze Medal: 4 x 400-Meter Relay (2:59.32)

Innocent Egbunike, who ran the anchor leg for the Nigerian squad in the 1984 Olympics, is arguably Africa's greatest-ever all-around sprinter. He has run the second fastest 400 meters by an African, clocking 44.50 seconds at Zurich in 1986; he also ranks second on the all-time African lists at both 100 meters (10.15) and 200 meters (20.42). He has won the World Student Games gold medals at both 200 and 400. An Olympic finalist in the 400 at Los Angeles,

he was also a finalist in the World Championships at half the distance. Egbunike is the youngest of six children. He attended Azusa Pacific College in California and majored in physical education and communications. He was once coached by 1968 Olympics 400-meter champion Lee Evans. Evans coached the Nigerian track team for the 1976 Olympics in Montreal.

Sources: British Virgin Islands, Olympic Committee; "Olympic Winners," *New York Times* (August 13, 1984); *1984 Olympic Games, Sarajevo/Los Angeles; Research Information, Games of the XXIIIrd Olympiad.*

ELEJARDE, MARLENE (Cuba). Born June 3, 1950, in Havana, Cuba.

1968 Silver Medal: 4 x 100-Meter Relay (43.36)
1972 Bronze Medal: 4 x 100-Meter Relay (43.36)

Marlene Elejarde led off the Cuban 4 x 100-meter bronze medal-winning relay team at the 1972 Munich Games after fulfilling the same function 4 years earlier when the Cuban women finished second at Mexico City. Primarily a hurdler, Elejarde had a best of 13.64 seconds in the 100-meter hurdles. Her best over the flat distance was 11.83. Elejarde made her international debut at the age of 16 when she competed in the Central American and Caribbean Games in the summer of 1966.

Sources: British Virgin Islands, Olympic Committee; *Complete Book of the Olympics; Guinness Book of Olympic Records; 1968 United States Olympic Book.*

ELLIS, ROMALLIS (USA). Born December 16, 1965, in Washington, D.C.

1988 Bronze Medal: Lightweight Boxing (132 lbs./60 kg)

Romallis Ellis earned a berth on the 1988 Olympic team after winning the trials and subsequently defeating Lyndon Walker in the July Olympic box-offs. He won the U.S. Amateur Championships in the lightweight division in 1988. Ellis was a silver medalist at the Goodwill Games in 1986, after losing to Orzubek Nazarov of the Soviet Union in the finals. He narrowly missed a Golden Gloves title, falling on points to Lavell Fingers in the 1986 finals. He took home the bronze medal when he competed at the 1985 Sports Festival. Romallis Ellis lives in Ellenwood, Georgia.

Sources: "Seoul Games/Medal Winners," *Los Angeles Times* (October 3, 1988); *1988 United States Olympic Team, Media Guide; Seoul '88;* "Olympics Record," *USA Today* (October 3, 1988).

PAUL ERENG (Photo courtesy of Rich Clarkson, Denver, Colorado.)

ERENG, PAUL (Kenya). Born August 22, 1968 in Kenya.

1988 Gold Medal: 800-Meter Run (1:43.45)

A member of the Turkana ethnic group, a nomadic tribe of the arid north of Kenya, Paul Ereng won a place at a school for the underprivileged in Nairobi. As a young runner, he won a place on the Kenyan team when a Nairobi newspaper spotted his results. He finished third in African Olympic trials. Ereng had never run the 800 meters until he arrived at the University of Virginia in Charlottesville in 1987. He had been a quarter-miler but the assistant track and field coach steered him toward the 800. He became the 1988 National Collegiate Athletic Association 800-meter champion in his freshman year. In the Olympic finals, Ereng was among the leaders in two-thirds of the race, then Brazil's Cruz and Great Britain's Peter Elliott pulled away. Ereng then increased his speed, passed Cruz and Elliott, and his team won with 1 minute 43.45 seconds. Ereng said of himself, "My progress was like a meteorite. It was all happening so fast. Too fast, because you can't really learn to run this kind of event in six months" (*Track & Field News*).

Sources: British Virgin Islands, Olympic Committee; *International Amateur Athletic Federation*; "Seoul Games/Medal Winners," *Los Angeles Times* (October 3, 1988); "Kingdom Repeats," *Los Angeles Times* (October 3, 1988); *Seoul '88*; "Kenya's Collegiate Connection," *Track & Field News* (December 1988); "Olympics Record," *USA Today* (October 3, 1988).

EVANS, DWAYNE (USA). Born October 13, 1958, in Phoenix, Arizona.

1976 Bronze Medal: 200-Meter Run (20.43)

Dwayne Evans attended Phoenix's South Mountain High School and the University of Arizona. He was considered an outstanding sprinter in high school, and he went on to win second place in the 1976 Olympic final trials and then finished third at the Olympics. He later won the AAU 200 meters in 1979. He attended the University of Arizona but was unable to duplicate his earlier success. However, he has shown surprising longevity, and 10 years after his Olympic prize he was still one of the world's leading half-lappers. After winning the 200-meter bronze with a 20.43 dash in Montreal, Evans won the world junior record. He was named Prep Athlete of the Year and ranked number 4 in the world. He later also won the NCAA 200 as an Arizona State senior, with the same ranking.

Sources: *Black Olympians*; British Virgin Islands, Olympic Committee; *Guinness Book of Olympic Records*; *Quest for Gold*; "Harvey Glance and Dwayne Evans," *Track & Field News* (October 1986).

EVANS, LEE EDWARD (USA). Born February 25, 1947, in Madera, California.

1968 Gold Medal: 400-Meter Run (43.86, world record)
1968 Gold Medal: 4 x 400-Meter Relay (2:56.1, Olympic record)

Lee Evans was NCAA champion while a junior at San Jose State in California in 1968. He won the 400 meters in 1967 at the Pan Am Games. He then won the Olympic final trials with a world record of 44 seconds, which he reduced to 43.86 in the Olympic final. One year out of high school Evans was undefeated and won his first AAU title. He not only won a second gold but also another world plaque in the 1600-meter relay. After placing fifth at the final trials, he went to Munich as a member of the 1600-meter relay team. However, because of various circumstances, the U.S. could not field a team in this event. Evans won the last of his five AAU titles in 1972. He joined the professional ranks after 1972. Through 1982 he still held the world record of 43.86 for the 400 meters. Lee Evans has worked as a physical fitness counselor and salesman and has coached in both Nigeria and Cameroon.

Sources: *Approved History of Olympic Games*; *Black Olympians*; British Virgin Islands, Olympic Committee; *Guinness Book of Olympic Records*; *Quest for Gold*; *Spirit Team Profiles*, Los Angeles Organizing Committee; *Track and Field: The Great Ones*; *United States Track and Field Olympians*.

EVERETT, DANNY (USA). Born November 1, 1966.

1988 Gold Medal: 4 x 400-Meter Relay (2:56.16, Olympic record)
1988 Bronze Medal: 400-Meter Run (44.09)

Danny Everett ran the fastest 400/200 double ever recorded with a 44.34 (400) and a 20.23 (200) at the Pac-10 Championships. In 1987 he ranked second in the U.S. in the 400. He also ran on the gold medal-winning U.S. 4 x 400-meter relay team at the 1987 World Championships. At the 1988 Olympic trials Everett finished second, just behind Butch Reynolds, with a time of 43.98. He won the 400 in the 1988 NCAA meet, with 44.52, and ran a leg on the 4 x 400-meter relay to help UCLA win the NCAA title and set a record fo 2:59.91. He also ran the first leg in the 4 x 400 meter relay at Seoul. Everett graduated from UCLA in 1989. His home is in Sherman, Texas.

Sources: British Virgin Islands, Olympic Committee; "Seoul Games/Medal Winners," *Los Angeles Times* (October 3, 1988); *United States Olympic Team, Media Guide*; "Olympics Record," *USA Today* (October 3, 1988).

EWELL, HENRY NORWOOD (USA). Born February 25, 1918, in Harrisburg, Pennsylvania.

1948 Gold Medal: 4 x 100-Meter Relay (40.6)
1948 Silver Medal: 100-Meter Run (10.4)
1948 Silver Medal: 200-Meter Run (21.1)

Henry "Barney" Ewell had a remarkable career as a top class sprinter, from his first AAU junior 100 meters in 1936 to his 3 medals at the 1948 Olympics 12 years later. In the interim he won 16 major outdoor titles, which included sprint doubles both in the 1940 and 1941 NCAA and IC4A meets. He was the only athlete to win 3 IC4A titles 3 years in a row: 100, 220, and long jump (1940-42). As an outstanding long jumper Ewell went on to win the AAU indoor long jump in 1944 and 1945 and the IC4A indoor long jump in 1940 and 1942. Ewell won the 100 meters at the 1948 combined AAU and final trials meet in a world record equaling 10.2 seconds, but he lost the Olympic final by inches to Harrison Dillard, and in the 200 he was beaten by Mel Patton. Barney Ewell lost his amateur status after the Olympics for accepting an excessive number of gifts from his townsfolk. Later he competed in Australia and New Zealand as a professional. He is a member of the Pennsylvania Hall of Fame, the U.S. Track and Field Hall of Fame, and the Black Hall of Fame. He was named World's Professional Champion in 1950 in Australia. A graduate of J.P. McCaskey High School in Lancaster, Pennsylvania, and Pennsylvania State University, Ewell is married to Duella Ewell and has four children: Henry Jr., Maurice, Patrick, and Denice.

Sources: *Approved History of Olympic Games; Black Olympians*; Ewell, Henry. Interview. 1984; *Guinness Book of Olympic Records; Quest for Gold; United States Track and Field Olympians*.

EWING, PATRICK (USA). Born August 5, 1962, in Kingston, Jamaica.

1984 Gold Medal: Basketball

Patrick Ewing moved from Jamaica to Cambridge, Massachusetts at the age of 12. He graduated in 1985 from Georgetown University in Washington, D.C. with a degree in fine arts. Ewing was Big East Conference Defensive Player of the Year for 3 straight years. As a freshman he was selected to All-Tournament teams at Final Four, West Regional, and Big East. He has averaged 15.5 points per game for 3 years. Pat Ewing made the All-American first team, was MVP of the 1984 Final Four, and led Georgetown to the NCAA Championship. He was also All MVP of the Big East tournament. The first pick in the NBA draft in 1985, Ewing signed with the New York Knicks. He was named NBA Rookie of the Year. His generous 10-year contract was allegedly an attempt of Knicks management to help the team relive their early 1970s glory days. Ewing's style is intense, intimidating, relentless, and tough. Basketball's $30-million man has been credited with raising the base salaries of NBA players.

Sources: British Virgin Islands, Olympic Committee; "The 1984 Olympics," *Ebony* (October 1984); "Patrick Ewing: Can This Man Save the Knicks?" *Ebony* (February 1986); "Pat Ewing Made Money," *Jet* (January 20, 1986); "The Champions," *Los Angeles Times* (August 14, 1984); *1984 Olympics Games; United States Olympic Team, Media Guide*.

FAGGS STARR, MAE HERIWENTHA (USA). Born April 10, 1932, in Mays Landing, New Jersey.

1952 Gold Medal: 4 x 100-Meter Relay (45.9)
1956 Bronze Medal: 4 x 100-Meter Relay (44.9)

Mae Faggs Starr graduated from Bayside High School, Bayside, Long Island, and from Tennessee State University. She studied toward a master's degree in special education at the University of Cincinnati. She was affiliated with the New York Police Athletic League and the Tigerbelles track team. In the summer of 1956 Faggs Starr attained the distinction of being the first U.S. woman to have participated in three different Olympics. A member of the 1954-55 and 1956 AAU All-American Women's Track and Field team, Faggs Starr won the AAU 200 meters in 1954, 1955, and 1956. She won the 100 yards in 1952 indoors and had six victories in the 220 between 1949 and 1956. She won the silver medal in the 200 and the gold medal in the relay at the 1955 Pan Am Games. Now a school teacher, married to high school principal Eddie Starr, Mae Faggs Starr is very active in promoting youth programs in Cincinnati. In 1965 she was elected to the Helms Hall of Fame.

Sources: *Black Olympians; Development of Negro Female Olympic Talent; Guinness Book of Olympic Records; Historical and Biographical Studies of Women Participants; Negro Firsts in Sports; Quest for Gold; Who's Who in Track and Field.*

FERGERSON, MABLE (USA). Born January 18, 1955, in Los Angeles, California.

1972 Silver Medal: 4 x 400-Meter Relay (3:25.2)

Mable Fergerson placed fifth in the individual 400 meters at the 1972 Olympics. However, the 17-year-old Pomona High School student ran a 51.8-second leadoff leg in the 4 x 400-meter relay. She won the AAU 400 in 1971 and both the 220 and 440 yards in 1973. Fergerson was a member of the West Coast Jets. Along with her older sister Williamae, she joined the professional International Track Association circuit in 1973.

Sources: *Black Olympians;* British Virgin Islands, Olympic Committee; *Guinness Book of Olympic Records; Quest for Gold;* United States Olympic Team; *Games of the XXth Olympiad;* United States Track and Field Olympians.

FERRELL EDMONDSON, BARBARA ANN (USA). Born July 28, 1947, in Hattiesburg, Mississippi.

1968 Gold Medal: 4 x 100-Meter Relay (42.8)
1968 Silver Medal: 100-Meter Run (11.1)

Barbara Ferrell Edmondson attended Harrison Technical High School in Chicago and Los Angeles City College. She received a B.A. in sociology with a minor in education from California State, Los Angeles, in 1969. Ferrell Edmondson was state champion for 60 meters in Illinois. She was a member of the Girls Athletic Association in Chicago and of the L.A. Mercurettes. She was coached by Fred Jones. Ferrell Edmondson set the world 100-meter record in 1968. She ran 11.1 seconds in 1967 at Santa Barbara and held the American 200-meter record with 22.8 in the 1968 Olympics. She was 1967 AAU champion in the 100 (11.1) and won the AAU 100 and 220 yards in 1969 in 10.7 and 23.8. She won the 100-meter gold medal in the 1967 Pan Am Games in 11.5. She ran fifth in the AAU 100 meters in 1972, but took first place in the same event in the Olympic trials with 11.3 and second place in the 220. In a statement on an Olympic panel, Ferrell Edmondson said, "Let kids *see* what you're doing.... What did you do?... They need to know, no I *didn't* take drugs when I was competing. Those are the things our kids need to hear.... They need to know what's important." Ferrell Edmondson is a member of the International Track Association. Her current position is area representative for the Central Area Teachers in Los Angeles. A resident of Inglewood, California, she is married to Warren Edmondson and has two children, Malika and Maya.

Sources: *Approved History of Olympic Games; Black Olympians;* Ferrell Edmondson, Barbara Ann. Questionnaire. 1984; *Guinness Book of Olympic Records; Quest for Gold; Spirit Team Profiles,* Los Angeles Olympic Organizing Committee; *United States Olympic Team, Games of the XIXth Olympiad; Who's Who in Track and Field.*

FERRER LA HERA, JUAN (Cuba). Born in Cuba.

1980 Silver Medal: Judo (172 lbs./up to 78 kg)

Juan Ferrer's placed second in the 172-pound (78-kilograms) judo at the 1980 Moscow Olympic Games. He was bested by Shota Khabareli of the USSR.

Sources: *Approved History of Olympic Games;* British Virgin Islands, Olympic Committee; *Complete Book of the Olympics; Games of the XXIInd Olympiad, Moscow, 1980; Guinness Book of Olympic Records;* "Olympic Results," *Los Angeles Times* (July 29, 1980).

FIGUEROLA CAMUE, ENRIQUE (Cuba). Born July 15, 1938, in Santiago de Cuba.

1964 Silver Medal: 100-Meter Run (10.2)
1968 Silver Medal: 4 x 100-Meter Relay (38.3)

Enrique Figuerola was a relatively late-developing sprinter. He was the first cuban to win an Olympic track and field medal. Figuerola won the 100 yards at the AAA Championships both in 1964 (9.4 seconds) and 1965 (9.6). He also won the Pan Am 100 meters in 1963 (10.3) and captured the world record in the 100 on June 17, 1967 (10.0). He won the silver medal behind Bob Hayes in the 100 in Tokyo and added another silver medal as anchor of the Cuban 4 x 100-meter relay team at Mexico City. In running the 100 at the Olympic Games in Tokyo in 1964, both Figuerola and Harry Jerome, who finished second and third, called it the best race they had run all year and had nothing but praise for the winner. Enrique Figuerola had personal bests of 10.23 in the 100 and 20.6 in the 200. He is now a sports administrator in Havana.

Sources: British Virgin Islands, Olympic Committee; *Encyclopaedia of Track and Field Athletics; Games of the XVIIIth Olympiad, Tokyo; Guinness Book of Olympic Records.*

FITZGERALD-BROWN, BENITA (USA). Born July 6, 1961, in Dale City, Virginia.

1984 Gold Medal: 100-Meter Hurdles (12.84)

Benita Fitzgerald-Brown graduated from Garfield High School, where she was a member of the National Honor Society, and from the University of Tennessee, Knoxville, with a B.S. in industrial engineering. She participated in track and field in both high school and college. Fitzgerald-Brown's special athletic achievements were many. She was state champion, 1976-79; USA Jr. National champion, 1978 and 1979; 15 times All-American; Collegiate record-holder, and Collegiate champion, 1981-83—all in the 100-meter hurdles. She won many other honors as well, both in the U.S. and abroad. Fitzgerald-Brown is excellent at both sprinting and hurdling. Her best season came in 1983 when she lowered her personal record for the hurdles to 12.84 seconds and won both national titles. She placed 8th at the World Championships and ranked 10th in the world—the same ranking she had in 1982. A member of the 1980 Olympic team and AIAW champion in 1981, she won her first NCAA title in 1982. Fitzgerald-Brown's best times in the sprints were 11.36 in the 100 (1982) and 23.0 in the 200 (1983). Fitzgerald-Brown lives in Dale City, Virginia, with her husband, Laron Brown.

Sources: Fitzgerald-Brown, Benita. Questionnaire. 1984. "The 1984 Olympics," *Ebony* (October 1984); "The Games," *Olympian* (October/November 1984); *United States Olympic Team, Media Guide*; "Benita Fitzgerald-Brown," *Women's Sports* (October 1984).

FLEMING, VERN (USA). Born February 4, 1961, in Long Island City, New York.

1984 Gold Medal: Basketball

Vern Fleming was unanimous first team All-SEC for 2 years and led the SEC in scoring in 1984 as a senior (averaging 19.8 points per game). He was career scoring leader at Georgia (1,777 points) and career leader in assists (400), games (125), steals, free throws (377), and free throw attempts (535). Fleming's career high was 44 points against Vanderbilt. He was NCAA All-District, 1984; *Sports Illustrated* National Player of the Week, March 1984 (after scoring 71 points and shooting 77.8 percent from the field in two games); and 1983 SEC tournament MVP. Vern Fleming attended the University of Georgia as a municipal recreation major. He now plays professional basketball for the Indiana Pacers of the NBA. He has a twin brother who played basketball for Xavier University (Ohio) and who was also an NBA draft choice. Fleming and his wife, Michelle, have a son, Vern, Jr.

Sources: British Virgin Islands, Olympic Committee; "The 1984 Olympics," *Ebony* (October 1984); "The Champions," *Los Angeles Times* (August 14, 1984); *Research Information, Games of the XXIIIrd Olympiad; United States Olympic Team, Media Guide.*

FORBES, JAMES (USA). Born July 18, 1952.

1972 Silver Medal: Basketball

James Forbes, a 6-foot 8-inch forward from the University of Texas at El Paso, was added to the U.S. 1972 Olympic squad after John Brown came down with an injury. The USSR defeated the U.S. in match #3 of the basketball preliminaries.

Sources: *Black Olympians*; British Virgin Islands, Olympic Committee; *Munchen 1972, Results of the Games of the XXth Olympiad; Guinness Book of Olympic Records; Quest for Gold.*

FORD, PHILIP JACKSON, JR. (USA). Born February 9, 1956, in Rocky Mount, North Carolina.

1976 Gold Medal: Basketball

Philip Jackson Ford attended the University of North Carolina and played for Dean Smith, his coach at North Carolina, in the 1976 Olympics. A college superstar, Ford made various All-American teams during his last season. Small for an NBA guard, at 6 feet, 2 inches, he was one of the quickest players to ever play on a basketball court. Although a good scorer, being a playmaker was his strong point. Phil Ford was named NBA's Rookie of the Year in 1979 while he was playing for the Kansas City Kings. He also made NBA's All-Rookie Team and was selected as second team NBA All-Star.

Sources: *Black Olympians; Guinness Book of Olympic Records; Quest for Gold.*

FOREMAN, GEORGE (USA). Born January 10, 1949, in Houston, Texas.

1968 Gold Medal: Heavyweight Boxing

George Foreman won the AAU title, the Olympic trials, and the Olympic Games, all in 1968. He is one of the most powerful punchers who has ever fought. He became famous in Mexico City after winning the final bout when he took a small American flag and waved it all over the auditorium. It was a considered significant since this was the year when Blacks—Tommie Smith and John Carlos—protested on the victory platform. Foreman, who turned professional when he fought Joe Frazier for the title on January 27, 1973, is best remembered for two fights: that savage 1973 beating of heavily favored Frazier (he floored him seven times in the second round before the fight was stopped), and his loss to Muhammad Ali in Kinshasa, Zaire, in 1974 (when he was stopped in eight rounds). Of the 47 bouts he won, 42 were by knockouts. George Foreman relates, "My greatest moment in boxing was the night I won the gold medal at the Olympics. That gold medal was then, and is today more important than anything else that ever happened to me in sports" (*Los Angeles Times*). Foreman is currently pastor of the Church of the Lord Jesus Christ in Houston.

Sources: *Black Olympians; Complete Book of the Olympics; Great Black Athletes; Guinness Book of Olympic Records;* "Foreman Ranks Gold Medal as Favorite Boxing Moment," *Los Angeles Times* (July 26, 1984); *Quest for Gold.*

FOSTER, GREG (USA). Born August 4, 1958, in Maywood, Illinois.

1984 Silver Medal: 110-Meter Hurdles (13.23)

Greg Foster, a 1980 graduate of UCLA, was considered the premier high hurdler of his time. He won the World Championship and in 1987 had been top-ranked in the world for 2 years. Foster set a personal record of 13.03 seconds in 1981 and was 1981 World Cup winner. He won the NCAA title in 1978 and 1980 and the TAC Championship in 1981 and 1983. He was World Class 200-meter runner and won the NCAA title in that event in 1979. He has a 200 best of 20.20 set in 1979. Foster beat gold medal winner Roger Kingdom in the 110-meter hurdles in Zurich (after the 1984 Olympics); Foster's 13.15, the fastest time in the world in 1984, beat Kingdom's personal best of 13.16. In Berlin he ran 13.16 to Kingdom's 13.17. Foster, at 13.39, finished second to Roger Kingdom's 13.30 in the 110-meter high hurdles at the Pepsi Invitational in June 1987. Foster, who has been called the "magnificent successor to [Renaldo] Nehemiah" by the British Virgin Islands Olympic Committee, tripped over a hurdle in a routine warm-up and broke his left arm. As a result he wasn't able to qualify for or compete in the 1988 Olympiad at Seoul.

Sources: British Virgin Islands, Olympic Committee; "The 1984 Olympics," *Ebony* (October 1984); "The Champions," *Los Angeles Times* (August 14, 1984); "Foster is Frosted at UCLA," *Los Angeles Times* (June 6, 1988); "Greg Foster's ... Olympics in Doubt," *Los Angeles Times* (July 1988); *1984 Olympic Games*; "Foster Profiting from New Outlook," *Track & Field News* (March 1987); *United States Olympic Team, Media Guide*.

FOWLER, CALVIN (USA). Born February 11, 1940, in Pittsburgh, Pennsylvania.

1968 Gold Medal: Basketball

Calvin Fowler attended St. Francis College in Loretto, Pennsylvania. He was only 5 feet, 10 inches tall, but he led his team, the Wingfoots, to the AAU Championship in 1967. He made AAU All-American that year and the next. Fowler played for the U.S. at the 1967 World's Championship and won a gold medal at the 1967 Pan Am Games. He was the spark plug of the Olympic team that won the gold medal in Mexico City in 1968. After the Olympics he returned to AAU ball and had 1 year in the NBA, playing with the Carolina Cougars in 1969-70.

Sources: *Black Olympians; Guinness Book of Olympic Records; Quest for Gold*.

FRAZIER, HERMAN RONALD (USA). Born October 29, 1954, in Philadelphia, Pennsylvania.

1976 Gold Medal: 4 x 400-Meter Relay (2:48.7)
1976 Gold Medal: 400-Meter Run (44.95)

Herman Frazier graduated from Germantown High School in 1972 and from the University of Arizona in 1977. He participated in baseball, track, basketball, and football in high school, and in track for 3 years in college. Frazier was NCAA 400-meter champion, 1977; NCAA runner-up, 1975-76; NCAA team champion, 1977; and Pan Am Games gold medalist, 1975 and 1979. He was affiliated with the Philadelphia Pioneer Club from 1974 to 1983. Frazier placed third at the Olympic final trials in 1976, then improved to become the second-best American in Montreal by taking the bronze with a career best of 44.95 seconds. He won the 500-meter World Best Indoors in 1979. After 1976 Frazier broadened his skills to train as a bobsledder in hopes of making the 1980 Winter Olympic team. His prospects for success as a sledder looked good, but his duties as assistant athletic director at Arizona State and other obligations prevented him from training for bobsledding or running. He is now associate athletic director at Arizona State and lives in Tempe, Arizona.

Sources: *Approved History of Olympic Games*; Athlete's information; *Black Olympians; Guinness Book of Olympic Records*; "Olympic Summaries," *New York Times* (August 2, 1976); *Quest for Gold; United States Track and Field Olympians*.

FRAZIER, JOSEPH (USA). Born January 12, 1944, in Beaufort, South Carolina.

1964 Gold Medal: Heavyweight Boxing

"Smokin' Joe" Frazier was one of the all-time great heavyweight champions. Winner of the New York State title in 1968, he went on to win the world championship in 1970 by stopping Jimmy Ellis in five rounds. He defended the title twice before being knocked out by former Olympian George Foreman in 1973. Frazier fought three tremendous battles with Muhammad Ali. Ali and Joe Frazier met in March 1971 and Frazier won on points over 15 rounds. Their bout in Madison Square Garden drew a crowd of 20,455 who paid a total of $1,352,000 to see it, but it grossed more than $20 million because of closed-circuit television. Each fighter was paid $2,500,000 for this undefeated world heavyweight championship. It was surprising that Frazier won the gold medal in the 1964 Olympics, because he had been beaten in the Olympic trials by Buster Mathis, a better fighter. But Mathis broke his thumb while training. Then, in the Olympic semifinals, Frazier broke his own thumb. He had the thumb taped and fought basically with one hand to win the gold medal.

Joe Frazier sang with a group called "The Knockouts" and made some television commercials. (He fought once in 1981 in a comeback attempt.) He manages his son, Marvis Frazier, a heavyweight contender.

Sources: *Approved History of Olympic Games; Black Olympians; Guinness Book of Olympic Records; Quest for Gold.*

FREEMAN, RONALD J. II (USA). Born June 12, 1947, in Elizabeth, New Jersey.

1968 Gold Medal: 4 x 400-Meter Relay (2:56.1)
1968 Bronze Medal: 400-Meter run (44.4)

The fastest 400 meters that has ever been run was Ron Freeman's 43.2 lap on the second leg of the 1,600-meter relay in Mexico City in 1968. He took over the baton 3 meters down on Nyamau of Kenya, and put the U.S. into a 20-meter lead and on their way to a new world record of 2:56.1—which stood through 1982. In the individual 400 meters, Freeman, from Arizona State University, took the bronze in 44.40, which was the fourth fastest 400 of all time. But he was never later to win a major championship in that event or match the form he had shown in Mexico City. A former dean of men at the College of the Virgin Islands, Freeman later worked for the governor of New Jersey in sports development. He has coached the national track teams of Barbados and the British Virgin Islands.

Sources: *Black Olympians*; British Virgin Islands, Olympic Committee; *Guinness Book of Olympic Records; Quest for Gold.*

GALLAGHER, KIM (USA). Born June 11, 1964, in Philadelphia, Pennsylvania.

1984 Silver Medal: 800-Meter Run (1:58.63)
1988 Bronze Medal: 800-Meter Run (1:56.91)

Kim Gallagher grew up in Fort Washington, Pennsylvania, a Philadelphia suburb. She graduated from Upper Dublin High School and attended the University of Arizona. She now lives in El Segundo, California, and is a member of the Los Angeles Track Club. Gallagher's brother Bart coached her for 5 years, until after the 1983 TAC meet when she started working with Chuck Debus. She has run the 1,500 meters but thinks the 800 record is more accessible. Gallagher finished first in the 800 at the 1984 Olympic trials, with a 1:58.50. Her best mark in the 1,500 is 4.08, recorded when she won the 1984 TAC Championships. She formerly held the U.S. high school record at 5000 meters. Gallagher's post-1984 Olympic career has been somewhat stymied by recurring difficulties with anemia, but at her best Gallagher is probably the most respected U.S. distance runner after, perhaps, Mary Dekker-Slaney.

Gallagher won the 1988 Olympic trials in the 800 meters with a time of 1:58.01, a personal best. She also finished third in the 1,500 with a time of 4:05.41.

Sources: British Virgin Islands, Olympic Committee; "The 1984 Olympics," *Ebony* (October 1984); "The Champions," *Los Angeles Times* (August 14, 1984); "Gallagher's Bronze in the 800," *Los Angeles Times* (September 26, 1988); *Research Information, Games of the XXIIIrd Olympiad; 1988 United States Olympic Team, Media Guide.*

GAMARRO, PEDRO J. (Venezuela). Born in 1955 in Venezuela.

1976 Silver Medal: Welterweight Boxing

Pedro Gamarro was the surprise of the 1976 Montreal Olympics welterweight boxing tournament. He stopped the defending Olympic and world amateur champion, Emilio Correa, in the third bout. He defeated favorite Clinton Jackson on a split decision in the quarterfinals. The 21-year-old Venezuelan went nearly all the way, but he lost a close split decision in the title match to 24-year-old Jochen Bachfeld of East Germany.

Sources: *Approved History of Olympic Games; Complete Book of the Olympics; Guinness Book of Olympic Records; Montreal 1976, Games of the XXIst Olympiad.*

GARBEY, ROLANDO (Cuba). Born November 1, 1947, in Oriente, Cuba.

1968 Silver Medal: Light Middleweight Boxing
1976 Bronze Medal: Light Middleweight Boxing (tied)

A silver medalist as a light middleweight boxer in 1968, Rolando Garbey was able to keep his skills sufficiently sharp to earn him a bronze medal at the Montreal Games 8 years later. Garbey is from a family that produced three other international athletes: long jumper Marcia, hammer thrower Pedro, and baseball player Barbaro (a former Detroit Tiger).

Sources: British Virgin Islands, Olympic Committee; *Complete Book of the Olympics; Guinness Book of Olympic Records.*

GARCÍA, VICTOR (Cuba). Born in Cuba.

1976 Bronze Medal: Volleyball

The members of the Cuban volleyball team that won the bronze at the 1976 Olympics were Leonel Marshall, Victoriano Sarmientos, Ernesto Martínez, Jesús Savigne, Lorenzo Martínez, Jorge Pérez, Raul Virches, and Victor García. To win the bronze, the Cuban players defeated Czechoslovakia (3-1), Korea (3-0), Canada (3-0), and, in the finals, Japan (3-0). They were defeated by Poland and the USSR.

Sources: *Approved History of Olympic Games*; British Virgin Islands, Olympic Committee; *Complete Book of the Olympics*; *Guinness Book of Olympic Records*; *Montreal 1976, Games of the XXIst Olympiad*.

GARDNER, KEITH A. ST. H. (British West Indies). Born June 9, 1929, in Jamaica.

1960 Bronze Medal: 4 x 400-Meter Relay (3:04.0)

Keith Gardner ran for the team representing the short-lived West Indian Federation in the 4 x 400-meter relay. He was also a world-class high hurdler. Gardner, who now resides in Florida, was a Commonwealth Games champion in the high hurdles on three occasions (1950, 1954, and 1958) and also won the 100-yard dash in 1958. Oddly enough, despite his success both as a high hurdler and quarter-miler, he was never tempted to concentrate on the intermediate hurdles.

Sources: *Approved History of Olympic Games*; British Olympic Association; British Virgin Islands, Olympic Committee; *Guinness Book of Olympic Records*.

GARRISON, ZINA (USA). Born November 16, 1963, in Houston, Texas.

1988 Gold Medal: Tennis (Doubles)
1988 Bronze Medal: Tennis (Singles)

Zina Garrison finished 1987 ranked number 9 in the world, even though she missed both the French Open and Wimbledon because of a stress fracture in her right foot. She won the Sydney, Australia, defeating Olympic teammate Pam Shriver, and the Virginia Slims of California. She was a finalist in the Canadian Open and won the Australian Open mixed doubles title with Sherwood Stewart. Garrison also won the Canadian Open and Virginia Slims of New Orleans doubles titles—with Lori McNeil—and was doubles finalist in eight other events. She won the U.S. Open and Wimbledon junior titles in 1981. Garrison has won more U.S. Tennis Association junior titles (seven) than any other black player. Pam Shriver and Zina Garrison won the women's doubles at Seoul, the first gold medal for the U.S. in Olympic tennis in 64 years. Their scores were 4-6, 6-2, 10-8. They slipped by Jana Novotna and Helena Sukova of Czechoslovakia for this victory. Garrison defeated Martina Navratilova in the U.S. Open quarterfinals at Flushing Meadow in September 1988.

Sources: "Black American Medal Winners," *Ebony* (December 1988); "Double Delight," *Los Angeles Times* (October 1, 1988); "Seoul Games/Medal Winners," *Los Angeles Times* (October 3, 1988); *1988 United States Olympic Team, Media Guide*; Seoul '88; "Olympics Record," *USA Today* (October 3, 1988).

GATHERS, JAMES (USA). Born June 17, 1930, in Sumter, South Carolina.

1952 Bronze Medal: 200-Meter Run (20.8)

Jim Gathers completed the medal sweep for the U.S. in the 1952 200 meters by finishing third in Helsinki. The first two places went to Andy Stanfield and Thane Baker. Gathers, who was in the air force, officially placed equal third in the 100 meters at the 1952 final trials. But instead of choosing him, the selectors picked Dean Smith for that event and Gathers ran only the 200 in Helsinki.

Sources: *Black Olympians*; *Guinness Book of Olympic Records*; *Quest for Gold*.

GIBSON, GREG (USA). Born November 20, 1953, in Stafford, Virginia.

1984 Silver Medal: Greco-Roman Wrestling (90-100 kg)

In the Greco-Roman heavyweight (approximately 198-220 lbs.) wrestling contest at the 1984 Olympics in Los Angeles, Greg Gibson, a member of the U.S. Marine Corps, beat Yoshihiro Fujita of Japan, 4-0, in the first round. In round two he defeated Fritz Gerdsmeier of West Germany, 7-1, and in the final he beat Jozef Tertelje of Yugoslavia, 3-1.

Sources: "The 1984 Olympics," *Ebony* (October 1984); "The Champions," *Los Angeles Times* (August 14, 1984); *Official Report of the Games of the XXIIIrd Olympiad; 1984 Olympic Games; Sarajevo/Los Angeles*.

GILLOM, JENNIFER (USA). Born June 13, 1964.

1988 Gold Medal: Basketball

Jennifer Gillom played the 1987-88 basketball season in Milan, Italy. She helped the U.S. team win the gold medal in the Pam Am Games of 1987 by averaging 95 points per game. She was also a member of the U.S. teams that earned gold medals at the FIBA World Championships and the Goodwill Games in 1986. Gillom was number 2 scorer on the 1985 U.S. World University Games team that won a silver medal. Gillom had an outstanding career at the University of Mississippi. During the 1985-86 season, she was a Kodak All-American, SEC Athlete of the Year, and NCAA Midwest Region MVP. She earned All-SEC honors three times and finished as the school's second all-time scorer with 2,186 points. She averaged 23.2 points per game as a senior. Jennifer Gillom graduated from the University of Mississippi in 1986 with a degree in education. She lives in Abbeville, Mississippi.

Sources: "Black American Medal Winners," *Ebony* (December 1988); "Seoul Games/Medal Winners," *Los Angeles Times* (October 3, 1988); *1988 United States Olympic Team, Media Guide*; Seoul '88; "Olympics Record," *USA Today* (October 3, 1988).

GLANCE, HARVEY (USA). Born March 28, 1957, in Phoenix City, Alabama.

1976 Gold Medal; 4 x 100-Meter Relay (38.33)

Harvey Glance took the 100 meters at the Olympic final trials in 1976. In 1977 he won the NCAA 100 and placed third in 1978 and 1979. He was on the team that won the 1979 Pan Am Games 400-meter relay. At Auburn University Glance scored a sprint double at the 1976 NCAA and then took the 100 at the final trials. He was the first American home (in fourth place) in the Olympic 100, the first time since 1928 the U.S. had failed to medal in the short sprint. Glance qualified for the 1980 Olympic team and was also a reserve in the sprint relay for the 1984 U.S. squad. Glance graduated from Auburn University in 1979 and continued to perform well internationally.

Sources: *Black Olympians*; British Virgin Islands, Olympic Committee; *Guinness Book of Olympic Records*; "Olympic Summaries," *New York Times* (August 2, 1976); *Quest for Gold*; "Glance Getting Older and Better," *Track & Field News* (May 1985).

GODDARD-CALLENDER, BEVERLEY (Great Britain). Born August 28, 1956, in Barbados.

1980 Bronze Medal: 4 x 100-Meter Relay (42.43)
1984 Bronze Medal: 4 x 100-Meter Relay (43.11)

Beverley Goddard-Callender represented Britain in the 1976, 1980, and 1984 Olympics. She was on the winning 4 x 100-meter relay team in the Commonwealth Games in 1982 (43.70 seconds). She won the silver medal in the 4 x 400-meter relay at the World Championships in 1983. Goddard-Callender has lifetime bests of 11.22 and 22.72 seconds in the 100 and 200.

Sources: British Virgin Islands, Olympic Committee; *Complete Book of the Olympics*; *Encyclopaedia of Track and Field Athletics*; *Guinness Book of Olympic Records*; *1984 Olympic Games, Sarajevo/Los Angeles*; "Beverley Callender," *Women's Sports* (October 1984).

GÓMEZ, JOSÉ (Cuba). Born in Cuba in 1959.

1980 Gold Medal: Middleweight Boxing

José Gómez was considered the best boxer on the Cuban team in 1980. He took the Olympic gold, even though Viktor Savchenko had won his first four fights by technical knockouts. Gómez went on to become World Cup champion in 1981 in Montreal, Canada. Colonel Hull, an International Boxing Federation official observed, "Gómez is truly a real champion. He won the World Cup in 1978, and the Russian he beat today was world champion in a weight below before moving up" (*New York Times*).

Sources: *Approved History of Olympic Games; Bruce Jenner's Guide to the Olympics; Complete Book of the Olympics; Games of the XXIInd Olympiad; Guinness Book of Olympic Records*; "Stevenson Wins 3d Boxing Gold," *New York Times* (August 3, 1980); "Olympic Winners," *New York Times* (August 4, 1980).

GORDON, BRIDGETTE (USA). Born April 27, 1967, in Deland, Florida.

1988 Gold Medal: Basketball

Bridgette Gordon was named Kodak and Naismith All-America for the 1987-88 season after leading her University of Tennessee team to a 31-3 record and a trip to the SEC Final Four. She averaged 20.8 points and 6.8 rebounds per game, shooting 54.1 percent from the field. She was sixth in steals at 2.3 a game and led the SEC in scoring. Gordon was named MVP of the 1988 SEC tournament and won a place on the NCAA East Region All-Tournament team. She averaged 10 points per game for the fifth-place U.S. team in the World University Games at Zagreb, Yugoslavia in 1987. Gordon led the South to a gold medal in the 1986 U.S. Olympic Festival and was named MVP on that occasion.

Sources: "Black American Medal Winners," *Ebony* (December 1988); "Seoul Games/Medal Winners," *Los Angeles Times* (October 3, 1988); *1988 United States Olympic Team, Media Guide; Seoul '88*; "Olympics Record," *USA Today* (October 3, 1988).

GORDON, EDWARD LANSING, JR. (USA). Born July 1, 1906, in Jackson, Mississippi.

1932 Gold Medal: Long Jump (25 ft. ¾ in./7.63 m)

Edward Gordon attended the University of Iowa where he won the AAU in 1929 and 1932 and the NCAA from 1929 to 1931. He also won the AAU indoor long jump in 1938. He displayed his career best of 25 feet, 4 3/8 inches in 1931 when he won the Kansas Relays. Gordon placed only seventh in the 1928 Olympic long jump, but he showed dramatic improvement to take the gold medal at Los Angeles in 1932. For many years Ed Gordon remained a top-flight performer. In 1938 he represented the Grand Street Boys Club of New York in the AAU. He died in September 1971 in Detroit, Michigan.

Sources: *Black Olympians; Guinness Book of Olympic Records; Quest for Gold*.

GOULD, KENNETH (USA). Born May 11, 1967, in Chicago, Illinois.

1988 Bronze Medal: Welterweight Boxing (tied)

Coached by his father, Nathaniel Gould, Kenneth Gould began boxing in 1974 at the age of 7. He earned a spot on the 1988 Olympic welterweight team by defeating Gerry Payne, 4-1, at the Olympic box-offs in July 1988. He was a silver medalist at the Pan Am Games in 1987, losing to Cuban Juan Lemus in the finals. Gould won the welterweight gold medal at the U.S. Olympic Festival in 1987. In 1985, 1986, and 1987 he captured the U.S. Amateur Welterweight crown. He defeated Cuba's Candelario Duvergel at the 1986 World Championships for the world welterweight title.

Sources: "Black American Medal Winners," *Ebony* (December 1988); "Seoul Games/Medal Winners," *Los Angeles Times* (October 3, 1988); *1988 United States Olympic Team, Media Guide; Seoul '88*; "Olympics Record," *USA Today* (October 3, 1988).

GOURDIN, EDWARD ORVAL (USA). Born August 10, 1897, in Jacksonville, Florida.

1924 Silver Medal: Long Jump (23 ft. 10¼ in./7.29 m)

Edward Gourdin was the first man in history to long-jump over 25 feet in a college international meet. He was the first of the great Black long jumpers (with the possible exception of Sol Butler). At the Harvard/Yale vs. Oxford/Cambridge meet on July 23, 1921, he set a world record of 25 feet, 3 inches. He defeated the British first string Harold Abrahams by almost 3 feet. Gourdin was also an outstanding sprinter and defeated Abrahams in the 100 yards. The AAU long jump in 1921, the pentathlon in 1921-22, and the IC4A long jump in 1921 were all won by Gourdin. A graduate of Harvard University, Gourdin was admitted to the Massachusetts Bar in 1925 and to the Federal Bar in 1931. In 1936 he became U.S. District Attorney and in 1958 was the first Black to become a member of the Massachusetts Supreme Court. He died July 21, 1966, in Quincy, Massachusetts.

Sources: *Approved History of Olympic Games; Black Olympians; Guinness Book of Olympic Records; Hard Road to Glory; Negro Firsts in Sports; Negro in Sports; Quest for Gold.*

GOURDINE, MEREDITH C. (USA). Born September 26, 1929, in Newark, New Jersey.

1952 Silver Medal: Long Jump (24 ft. 8¼ in./7.52 m)

In 1951 Meredith Gourdine won the IC4A with a career best of 25 feet, 9¾ inches. He won the 220-yard hurdles at the same meet. The following year he went on to beat Jerome Biffle to win the Olympic final trials. He had also defeated Biffle at the AAU but had finished second to George Brown. Biffle finished just 4 centimeters ahead of Gourdine to win the gold in the Olympic final. Gourdine graduated from Cornell University with a B.S. degree in engineering physics. He later earned a Ph.D. from the California Institute of Technology. The inventor of electro-gas

dynamics, an industrial cleaning technology, Gourdine founded the firm Energy Innovations in Houston in 1974. A subsidiary of that firm will work in the areas of fog removal over airports and the application of paint particles to industrial machinery.

Sources: *Black Olympians;* Gourdine, Meredith C. Questionnaire. 1984; *Guinness Book of Olympic Records; Quest for Gold.*

GRADDY, SAM (USA). Born February 10, 1964 in Gaffney, South Carolina.

1984 Gold Medal: 4 x 100-Meter Relay (37.83, Olympic record and world record)
1984 Silver Medal: 100-Meter Run (10.19)

As a student at Northside High School in Atlanta, Sam Graddy owned the Georgia high school state record in the 100-yard dash (9.61 seconds), breaking the 9.71 time of Stanley Floyd in the state finals his senior year. Graddy was fifth in the NCAA 100 meters in 1983 and ranked 10th in the world in the 100 in 1983. He was twice NCAA Track and Field All-American at the University of Tennessee and was 1984 NCAA 100-meter champion. Graddy finished second, after Carl Lewis, in the 100 meters at the 1984 U.S. Olympic trials, with 10.21. He was a formidable competitor of Lewis and said he was going to do everything he could to stop Lewis from getting gold medals. Graddy won the bronze medal in the 100 meters at the Pan Am Games (10.18) and the gold in the 400-meter relay in Caracas (38.49). He has personal best performances of 10.09 for the 100 (1984) and 20.30 for the 200 (1985). Graddy attended the University of Tennessee where he majored in marketing. His father was the first Black pilot to fly for Delta Airlines.

Sources: British Virgin Islands, Olympic Committee; "The 1984 Olympics," *Ebony* (October 1984); *Games of the XXIIIrd Olympiad, Los Angeles;* "The Champions," *Los Angeles Times* (August 14, 1984); "The Games," *Olympian* (October/November 1984); *Research Information, Games of the XXIIIrd Olympiad; United States Olympic Team, Media Guide.*

GRAHAM, WINTHROP (Jamaica). Born November 17, 1965, in Jamaica.

1988 Silver Medal: 4 x 400-Meter Relay (3:00.30)

In addition to his membership on the silver-winning Jamaican team in Seoul, Winthrop Graham has participated in World Championships and Pan Am Games. He was holder of two Jamaican records in the 400-meter hurdles in 1987. His progression in that event is 1986-50.03, 1987-48.49, 1988-49.04. His personal best is 45.81 (1987).

Sources: British Virgin Islands, Olympic Committee; *International Amateur Athletic Federation*; "Seoul Games/Medal Winners," *Los Angeles Times* (October 3, 1988); *Seoul '88*; "Olympics Record," *USA Today* (October 3, 1988).

GRAYER, JEFF (USA). Born December 17, 1965.

1988 Bronze Medal: Basketball

Jeff Grayer was named to the second team All-America 1988 by the Associated Press. He was first team All-Big Eight three consecutive seasons and he was on the All-Big Eight Defensive team for four consecutive seasons. Then he was three-time All-District Five. Grayer was Honorable Mention All-America in 1985-86 and 1986-87. He was MVP at the 1985-86 Music City Invitational (Nashville) and at the 1987-88 Blade City Classic (Toledo). He was Iowa State team MVP for three consecutive seasons and the 1987 Big Apple All-Tournament's leading scorer, averaging 32.2 points per game. He was invited to the 1986 and 1987 U.S. National Team trials. Grayer graduated from Iowa State University in 1988.

Sources: "Black American Medal Winners," *Ebony* (December 1988); Seoul Games/Medal Winners," *Los Angeles Times* (October 3, 1988); *1988 United States Olympic Team, Media Guide; Seoul '88*; "Olympics Record," *USA Today* (October 3, 1988).

GREENE, CHARLES EDWARD (USA). Born March 21, 1944, in Pine Bluff, Arkansas.

1968 Gold Medal: 4 x 100-Meter Relay (38.24, Olympic record/world record)
1968 Bronze Medal: 100-Meter Run (10.07)

Charlie Greene graduated from O'Dea High School in 1963 and from the University of Nebraska in 1967. He participated in track and football in high school and was an All-American in track. Greene tied the world record in the indoor 60-yard dash in 1966 (5.9 seconds), and in the 100-meter dash in 1968 (9.9). He had set the world record for the 100-yard dash in 1967 (9.21). Greene, as a freshman at University of Nebraska, was hampered by a muscle injury and finished sixth in the 100 meters at the 1964 Olympic final trials. He placed second in the trials 4 years later at Tokyo and won a gold medal in the relay and a bronze in the 100. After graduating from Nebraska, Greene entered the U.S. Army. Captain Greene now coaches the army's track and field squad. He and his wife, Linda, have two daughters, Mercedes and Sybil.

Sources: *Black Olympians*; British Virgin Islands, Greene, Charles E. Questionnaire. 1984; Olympic Committee; *Guinness Book of Olympic Records; Quest for Gold; Track and Field: The Great Ones*.

FLORENCE GRIFFITH-JOYNER (Photo courtesy of Rich Clarkson, Denver, Colorado.)

GRIFFITH-JOYNER, FLORENCE (USA). Born December 21, 1959, in Los Angeles, California.

1984 Silver Medal: 200-Meter Run (22.04)
1988 Gold Medal: 100-Meter Run (10.54, Olympic record)
1988 Gold Medal: 200-Meter Run (21.34)
1988 Gold Medal: 4 x 100-Meter Relay (41.98)
1988 Silver Medal: 4 x 400-Meter Relay (3:15.51, American record)

Florence Griffith-Joyner graduated from Jordan High School in Los Angeles, attended California State University, Northridge, and graduated from UCLA. In college she participated in the 100 meters, 200 meters, 400 meters, 4 x 100-meter relay, and 4 x 400-meter relay. She married triple jump gold medal champion Al Joyner in October 1987. Griffith-Joyner is a member of the World Class Athletic Club. She was second in the 200 meters at the NCAA and third at TAC in 1983. She won the NCAA 400-meter title in 1983 with a career best of 50.94 seconds. She won the NCAA 200 and was second at TAC in the same race in 1982. She also placed fourth in the 200 in the World Championships at Helsinki in 1983. In the 1988 Olympics, Griffith-Joyner won the women's 100 meters in a wind-assisted 10.54 seconds, faster than any woman had run the race in the Olympics. She had won the world record of 10.49 seconds at the U.S. Olympic trials in July. In the 200 meters at Seoul, she set an American and Olympic record by qualifying with 21.76 seconds. She beat her own American record of 21.77 and Valerie Brisco-Hooks's record of 21.81. Her actual gold-winning time was 21.34, wind-aided. She won her third gold medal in 1988 for running the third leg of the 400-meter relay, which her team ran in 41.98. Her final medal, silver, was for the 1600-meter relay when she anchored the U.S. team to a 3:15.51 American record win. Florence Griffith-Joyner ("FloJo") has emerged as the world's fastest woman, as well as the most celebrated U.S. track and field athlete. She models her start in the 100 after Ben Johnson, when she explodes with her arms and upper body before her legs even leave the blocks. Her coach-husband, Al, got a videocassette tape of Johnson's start after Johnson's world record performance in Rome in September 1987. FloJo made headlines for the 6-inch fingernails on her left hand, and for running in a skin-tight one-legged suit. "The woman who could be fairly called the 'greatest sprinter of all time,' announced her retirement" in February 1989 (*Runner's World*, June 1989). She planned to go into writing and acting. Griffith-Joyner had won a succession of awards in 1989: Associated Press Female Athlete of the Year, United States Olympic Committee Sportswoman of the Year, Jesse Owens International Trophy, and the Sullivan Award. She was particularly pleased with the Sullivan Award, stating that "it's the highest award you can get for your accomplishments."

Sources: British Virgin Islands, Olympic Committee; "The 1984 Olympics," *Ebony* (October 1984); *Guinness Book of Olympic Records*; "Joyner Pulls Fast One," *Los Angeles Times* (September 25, 1988); "Hingsen Fouls Out," *Los Angeles Times* (September 28, 1988); "Women Win Gold, Silver for U.S.," *Los Angeles Times* (October 1, 1988); "What's Griffith's Best Race?" *Track & Field News* (December 1984); "Griffith Moving to Center Stage," *Track & Field News* (December 1987); *United States Olympic Team, Media Guide*; "No Mo Flo Jo," *Runner's World* (June 1989).

HALL, ERVIN (USA). Born July 2, 1947, in Philadelphia, Pennsylvania.

1968 Silver Medal: 110-Meter Hurdles (13.42)

Ervin Hall graduated from Overbrook High School in 1966 and from Villanova University in 1970. He was a member of the Philadelphia Pioneer Club. Hall won the IC4A title in 1968 while attending Villanova. He set an Olympic record of 13.38 seconds in winning the first semifinal in Mexico City, but in the final he could not match Willie Davenport's superb start; Davenport went on to take the gold medal. Ervin Hall was also a sprinter of consequence with a best 100-yard clocking of 9.4 seconds in 1967.

Sources: *Black Olympians*; British Virgin Islands, Olympic Committee; *Guinness Book of Olympic Records*; *Quest for Gold*; *United States Team, Games of the XIXth Olympiad*.

HAMPTON, MILLARD FRANK (USA). Born July 8, 1956 in Fresno, California.

1976 Gold Medal: 4 x 100-Meter Relay (38.33)
1976 Silver Medal: 200-Meter Run (20.29)

Millard Hampton attended UCLA and was a member of the Bay Area Striders. He won the 1976 Olympic final trials by setting a career best of 20.10 seconds. He also took the AAU title in 1976. His second place to Don Quarrie of Jamaica at the Olympics was his only defeat of the season. Hampton placed second at the TAC Championships in 1980.

Sources: *Black Olympians*; *Guinness Book of Olympic Records*; "Olympic Summaries," *New York Times* (August 2, 1976); *United States Olympic Team, Games of XXIst Olympiad, Montreal*; *United States Track and Field Olympians*.

HARDY, CATHERINE (USA). Born February 8, 1930, in Carrollton, Georgia.

1952 Gold Medal: 4 x 100-Meter Relay (46.14, Olympic record)

The winner of the AAU outdoor double in 1952 and the AAU indoor 50 yards in 1951, Cathy Hardy scored a sprint double at the 1952 AAU, and at the final trials she ran 24.3 for 200 meters to break Helen Stephens's long-standing U.S. record. She failed to reach the final of either of the individual sprints at the Helsinki Olympics, but she anchored the relay team that took the gold medal with a new world record. Hardy attended Fort Valley State College in Georgia.

Sources: *Black Olympians*; *Guinness Book of Olympic Records*; *Lexikon der 12000 Olympianikens*; *Quest for Gold*; *United States Olympic Team, United States Track and Field Olympians*.

HARRIS, DANNY (USA). Born September 7, 1965, in Torrance, California.

1984 Silver Medal: 400-Meter Hurdles (48.13)

Danny Harris set a national high school record in the 300-meter low hurdles at 35.32 seconds. As a freshman at Iowa State University in 1984, he also played football—he was a top defensive back and punt and kickoff returner. Harris was a member of the Cyclone Track Club and Athletics West. Early in 1984, 18-year-old Harris lowered the world junior record for the 400-meter hurdles. His was one of the real surprises of the Olympic trials with his second place finish behind Edwin Moses in 48.02, which was a world junior record for this star. In 1985 Harris won the Weltklasse meet in Zurich by breaking the 48-second barrier in the 400-meter hurdles with a time of 47.63. Extremely fast on the flat, he ran 100 meters in 9.9 (wind-aided) at the Drake Relays in 1985. Harris broke Edwin Moses's 107-race winning streak in the 400-meter intermediate hurdles when he ran 47.56 to Moses's 47.69 in the international meet at Madrid in 1987. His time was the best of his career. During 3 years at Iowa State Harris competed in 17 finals and won them all, under coach Steve Lynn. He won the NCAA 400 hurdles title each year. In 1984 he was named Most Outstanding Performer and winner of the Omaha World-Herald's Henry Shuttle Award at the Big Eight Championships.

Sources: British Virgin Islands, Olympic Committee; "The 1984 Olympics," *Ebony* (October 1984); *Games of the XXIIIrd Olympiad, Los Angeles*; "The Champions," *Los Angeles Times* (August 14, 1984); *1984 Olympic Games*; "Danny Harris a Deadly Double Threat," *Track & Field News* (June 1985); "Harris Enjoys Sameness of Change," *Track & Field News* (May 1987); *United States Olympic Team, Media Guide*.

HARRIS, LUSIA MAE (USA). Born February 10, 1955, in Minter City, Mississippi.

1976 Silver Medal: Basketball

Lusia Harris attended Amanda Elzy High School in Greenwood, Mississippi, and graduated from Delta State University in Cleveland, Mississippi, in 1977. Harris was consensus All-American in her junior and senior years, 1975-76. She led the team to three straight AIAW National Championships and was Broderick Cup Winner in 1977. She was Regional Basketball champion for 3 years (1975-77), Kodak All-American (1975-77), State Basketball champion (1974-77), and MVP, Delta State University (1974-77). Harris was one of the first great female centers in this country. In college she averaged 31 points and 15 rebounds per game, including a high of 58 points (against Tennessee Tech) in her senior year. She was named Homecoming Queen at Delta State in 1975, the first Black to be so honored. In addition to the 1976 Olympic team, Harris played in the 1975 Pan Am and World University Games.

Although she was drafted by the New Orleans Jazz, she did not make a serious effort to make the team. Lusia Harris has since become admissions counselor and assistant basketball coach at Delta State and has worked toward a master's degree in health, recreation, and physical education. She and her husband, George Steward, have a son, George "Eddie" Steward, Jr.

Sources: *Black Olympians; Black Women in Sport; Guinness Book of Olympic Records; Quest for Gold; United States Olympic Team, Games of the XXIst Olympiad.*

HARRIS, RONALD W. (USA). Born September 3, 1948, in Canton, Ohio.

1964 Bronze Medal: Lightweight Boxing
1968 Gold Medal: Lightweight Boxing

Ronnie Harris attended Kent State University. He achieved the rare feat of winning the National AAU title for 3 consecutive years: 1966-68. He twice won the Golden Gloves title and was a bronze medalist at the 1967 Pan Am Games. Harris turned professional in 1968 and fought until 1976. He had a good record, but did not fight against well-known fighters.

Sources: *Black Olympians*; British Virgin Islands, Olympic Committee; *Guinness Book of Olympic Records; Quest for Gold.*

HART, EDDIE JAMES (USA). Born April 24, 1948, in Martinez, California.

1972 Gold Medal: 4 x 100-Meter Relay (38.19, Olympic record/world record)

Eddie Hart graduated from Pittsburgh High School in 1967 and from the University of California, Berkeley, in 1971. He was affiliated with the Bay Area Striders. Even though Hart won the 1970 NCAA 100 yards at Berkeley, he never finished prominently at AAU meets. After winning his heat in the 1972 Olympics 100 meters, Hart, along with Rey Robinson, failed to arrive at the start in time to compete for the second round. This was tragic, for Hart had equaled the world record of 9.9 in winning the final trials and was considered a sure prospect for further honors. Later in the Games, Hart gained some consolation when he ran the anchor leg (holding off 100-meter champion Valery Borzov of the USSR) on the relay team that set a new world record. Although Hart retired in 1972, he made a comeback in 1978 and was ranked again among the top U.S. sprinters.

Sources: *Black Olympians; Guinness Book of Olympic Records; Quest for Gold; United States Olympic Team, Games of the XXth Olympiad; United States Track and Field Olympians.*

HAWKINS, HERSEY (USA). Born September 29, 1965.

1988 Bronze Medal: Basketball

Hersey Hawkins was named National Player of the Year for 1987-88 by the Associated Press, UPI, the U.S. Basketball Writers Association, *The Sporting News*, and ESPN. He was consensus All-American and the nation's leading scorer with 36.3 points per game average. Hawkins was the unanimous Player of the Year selection (for the second season in a row) in the Missouri Valley Conference. He was number 1 scorer in the history of Bradley, and number 4 all-time scorer in the history of the NCAA, with 3,008 points. Hawkins started all 125 collegiate games for Bradley University and had per game averages of 24.1 points, 6.5 rebounds, and 3.2 assists. He had high games of 51 and 63 points the winter of 1987-88, scoring at least 40 points 9 times. Hersey Hawkins had an NCAA tournament's high game of 44 points (against Auburn). He was invited to the 1986 and 1987 U.S. National Team trials. Hersey Hawkins graduated in 1988 from Bradley University in Peoria, Illinois, with a degree in communications.

Sources: "Black American Medal Winners," *Ebony* (December 1988); "Seoul Games/Medal Winners," *Los Angeles Times* (October 3, 1988); *1988 United States Olympic Team, Media Guide; Seoul '88*; "Olympics Record," *USA Today* (October 3, 1988).

HAYES, ROBERT L. (USA). Born December 20, 1942, in Jacksonville, Florida.

1964 Gold Medal: 100-Meter Run (10.06, Olympic record/ world record)
1964 Gold Medal: 4 x 100-Meter Relay (39.06, Olympic record/world record)

Bob Hayes attended Florida A & M University where his track coach was Robert P. Griffin. At the National AAU Championships in 1963 he became the first man to run 100 yards in 9.1 seconds and the first to break 6.6 in the indoor 60-yard dash. During the 1963 and 1964 seasons he was undefeated in the finals at 100 yards and 100 meters. In 1964 Hayes won by 7 feet, the biggest margin in Olympic 100-meter history. This equaled the world record and broke the Olympic record. He was reportedly timed at 8.4 to 8.6 seconds for his 100-meter leg. He was considered "The Fastest Human in the World" (*Black Olympians*). A panel of track experts unanimously elected Bob Hayes as the greatest 100-meter sprinter of all time. He had an unorthodox rolling, lumbering style that relied on strength. Hayes played professional football with the Dallas Cowboys for 10 years starting in 1966, plus a final one with the San Francisco 49ers. He set records for most yards receiving (7,295), average per catch (20.0), most touchdowns (7.1), and highest punt return average (11.1). He also won a Super Bowl ring. In later years Hayes was convicted of drug

charges and spent several months in prison. He has since been rehabilitated and his reputation is being restored. Bob Hayes cherishes his moments on the victory stand and says, "When you're standing there to get the gold medal and the national anthem is playing, there isn't a greater feeling you can have as an individual" (*Los Angeles Times*).

Sources: *Black Olympians; Guinness Book of Olympic Records*; "And Then There Was Bob Hayes," *Los Angeles Times* (July 25, 1984); *1980 Olympic Handbook; Quest for Gold; Track & Field: The Great Ones; United States Olympic Team, Games of the XVIIIth Olympiad; United States Track and Field Olympians*.

HAYWOOD, SPENCER (USA). Born April 22, 1949, in Silver City, Mississippi.

1968 Gold Medal: Basketball

Spencer Haywood attended the University of Detroit. He could play either center or forward, and in the Olympics he completely dominated the big men from other countries to win the gold. Haywood joined the Denver Rockets of the ABA in 1969 and began an outstanding career. During his first year he was Rookie of the Year and MVP and made first team ABA. He next joined the Seattle SuperSonics and became one of the great forwards in the NBA. For 3 years in succession he made first team NBA and then was named to the second team for 2 years after that. Traded to the New York Knicks in 1975, Haywood played 4 seasons and finished his career with the Los Angeles Lakers in 1980. Spencer Haywood acquired a cocaine habit, which devastated him. However, he overcame it and currently is lecturing young people on drug abuse.

Sources: *Black Olympians; Guinness Book of Olympic Records*; "Golden Boy," *Newsweek* (January 6, 1969); *Quest for Gold; United States Olympic Team, Games of the XIXth Olympiad*.

HAZZARD, WALTER RAPHAEL (Mahdi Abdul-Rahman) (USA). Born April 15, 1942, in Wilmington, Delaware.

1964 Gold Medal: Basketball

Walter Hazzard attended Overbrook High School and UCLA. He was the star of the UCLA team when they won their first NCAA title in 1964. He helped win another NCAA title and was twice All-American. After the 1964 Olympics Hazzard made his professional debut with Seattle. He later joined the Los Angeles Lakers and played with them for three seasons. He was then traded back to the Seattle SuperSonics and had his best year, averaging 23.9 points per game. He also played in the NBA All-Star Game that year. After several seasons with Atlanta, Buffalo, and Golden State, Hazzard returned to Seattle where he continued to play through the 1974 season, when he retired. Hazzard coached at Compton College in California for two seasons. Later, while coaching at Chapman College in Orange County, California, he became the California Collegiate Athletic Association's Coach of the Year for the 1982-83 season. Walt embraced the Muslim faith during his career and played his last seasons under his Muslim name. When he became head coach at UCLA (March 1984), he once again became known as Walt Hazzard. At UCLA he led his Bruins to the National Invitation Tournament Championship in 1985. He left UCLA after 4 years.

Sources: *Black Olympians*; British Virgin Islands, Olympic Committee; "A Boon in Black Coaches," *Ebony* (April 1986); *Guinness Book of Olympic Records*; "UCLA Decides 4 Years Is Enough," *Los Angeles Times* (March 31, 1988); "Hazzard May Get Laker Job in Front Office," *Los Angeles Times* (May 19, 1988); *Quest for Gold; United States Olympic Team, Games of XVIIIth Olympiad*.

HENDERSON, THOMAS EDWARD (USA).
Born January 26, 1952, in Newberry, South Carolina.

1972 Silver Medal: Basketball

Thomas Henderson attended DeWitt Clinton High School in the Bronx, San Jacinto College in Pasadena, Texas, and the University of Hawaii. At Hawaii, he made first team All-American in 1974. Henderson scored 24.6 points in 1970-71 and 24.5 in 1971-72. He scored 20 or more points in 70 of 82 college games. In 1971-72 he was Junior College All-American and All-Texas Junior College Conference. Drafted in the first round of the NBA draft by the Atlanta Hawks in 1974, Henderson later played for the Washington Bullets and the Houston Rockets. In 1978 he helped the Bullets win the NBA Championship.

Sources: *Black Olympians; Guinness Book of Olympic Records; Quest for Gold; United States Olympic Team, Games of the XXth Olympiad*.

HERNÁNDEZ, JORGE (Cuba). Born in Cuba.

1976 Gold Medal: Light Flyweight Boxing

Jorge Hernández was the winner of the 48-kilogram light flyweight class of the 1974 World Championships in Havana. He was reigning world amateur and Pan Am champion in light flyweight boxing. In the 1976 Olympics Hernández defeated Beyhan Foujedjiev of Bulgaria when the referee stopped the match 59 seconds into the third round. Hernández won on points over Orlando Maldonado of Puerto Rico and defeated Zoffa Yarawi of Papua, New Guinea, with a knockout 1 minute, 45 seconds into the third round. He went on to defeat Chan-Hee Park of Korea, 3-2, and to win in the final, 4-1, over Byong Uk Li of North Korea.

Sources: *Approved History of Olympic Games; Bruce Jenner's Guide to the Olympics; Complete Book of the Olympics; Guinness Book of Olympic Records; Montreal 1976; Games of the XXIst Olympiad*; "Olympic Gold Medal Winners, Boxing," *New York Times* (August 2, 1976).

HERNÁNDEZ, JUAN (Cuba). Born in Cuba.

1980 Gold Medal: Bantamweight Boxing

The second youngest boxer at the Moscow Summer Olympics, 17-year-old Juan Hernández defeated five opponents, including two Africans. He began by defeating Sandor Farkas of Hungary on points, 4-1. In the 1/8 final, Hernández defeated Ayele Mohammed of Ethiopia when the referee stopped the match 2 minutes, 59 seconds into the second round. He went on to defeat Geraldi Issaick of Tanzania when the referee stopped the match in the first round and then Michael Anthony of Guyana on points, 5-0. In the final, Hernández defeated Bernardo José Pinango on points, 5-0.

Sources: *Approved History of Olympic Games; Complete Book of the Olympics; Games of the XXIInd Olympiad, Moscow 1980; Guinness Book of Olympic Records*; "Olympic Games, Boxing," *New York Times* (August 3, 1980); "Olympic Winners," *New York Times* (August 4, 1980).

ANGEL HERRERA (Photo courtesy of Amateur Athletic Foundation, Los Angeles, California.)

HERRERA, ANGEL (Cuba). Born August 2, 1952, in Guantánamo, Cuba.

1976 Gold Medal: Featherweight Boxing
1980 Gold Medal: Lightweight Boxing

In world championships Angel Herrera won the gold for featherweight boxing in 1978 and the gold for lightweight boxing in 1982. In the 1981 World Cup, he took the gold for lightweight boxing. His victories in the Pan Am Games were gold in 1979 and silver in 1983. Had Cuba participated in the 1984 Olympics, Herrera would have become Sagarra-Gron's junior national coach and a lieutenant in Cuba's 50-strong full-time coaching team. Herrera is retired and coaches in Cuba's junior boxing program.

Sources: *Approved History of Olympic Games*; British Virgin Islands, Olympic Committee; *Bruce Jenner's Guide to the Olympics*; *Complete Book of the Olympics*; *Guinness Book of Olympic Records*; "Cuban Gold Rush Is Under Way," *Los Angeles Times* (August 23, 1987); "Olympic Summaries," *New York Times* (August 2, 1976); "Olympic Winners," *New York Times* (August 4, 1980); *Who's Who in the 1984 Olympics*.

HERRERA, RUPERTO (Cuba). Born in Cuba.

1972 Bronze Medal: Basketball

A 6-foot 7-inch forward with outstanding shooting range, Ruperto Herrera was one of the world's leading amateur players in the 1970s. His international career lasted until the Central American and Caribbean Games in his home country of Cuba in 1982. For a summary of the Cuban team's record at the 1972 Munich Games, see Calderón-Gómez.

Sources: *Approved History of Olympic Games*; British Virgin Islands, Olympic Committee; *Die Spiele, Official Report for the Games of the XXth Olympiad*; *Guinness Book of Olympic Records*.

HERRERA, TOMÁS (Cuba). Born in Cuba.

1972 Bronze Medal: Basketball

Tomás Herrera was a stocky guard (6 feet, 1 inch) with a fiery temper. "El Jabato" (young, wild boar), whose international career spanned over 20 years, was considered the key playmaker on the Cuban teams that, along with Puerto Rico, dominated competition in the Central American and Caribbean region between the late 1960s and the early 1980s. For a summary of the Cuban team's record at the 1972 Munich Games, see Calderón-Gómez.

Sources: *Approved History of Olympic Games*; British Virgin Islands, Olympic Committee; *Die Spiele, Official Report for the Games of the XXth Olympiad*.

HILL, CLARENCE (Bermuda). Born in Bermuda.

1976 Bronze Medal: Heavyweight Boxing

Clarence Hill began at the 1976 Montreal Olympics by defeating Parviz Badpa of Iran with a knockout in the second round. He went on to defeat Rudy Gauwe of Belgium, 5-0, and to lose to Mircea Simon of Romania, 5-0. Hill lost in the semifinals to American John Tate; Teófilo Stevenson of Cuba took the gold and Simon the silver.

Sources: *Approved History of Olympic Games*; British Virgin Islands, Olympic Committee; *Complete Book of the Olympics*; *Guinness Book of Olympic Records*; *Montreal 1976*; *Games of the XXIst Olympiad*.

HILL, THOMAS LIONEL (USA). Born November 17, 1949, in New Orleans, Louisiana.

1972 Bronze Medal: 110-Meter Hurdles (13.48)

Tom Hill graduated from Walter L. Cohen High School in New Orleans in 1967 and from Arkansas State University in 1972. He has an M.S. degree in education from C. W. Post-Long Island University and is a Ph.D. candidate in counselor education at the University of Florida. In high school Hill participated in basketball, high jump, and long jump. In his senior year, he placed third in high jump at a state track meet. His later accomplishments included becoming Southland Conferences hurdles and 100-yard dash champion, NCAA 60-yard high hurdles winner, and AAU 120-yard hurdles champion. He tied the world record for the 120-yard high hurdles at Arkansas State and in 1974 ran 7.3 in the 60-meter high hurdles in Moscow to establish new world record. His best auto-timed performance in the 110 hurdles was 13.42 seconds, recorded at Bakersfield, California in 1970. Tom Hill became a U.S. Army captain, assigned to the adjutant general's office, and assistant track coach at West Point (1972-76); a counselor at Arkansas State (1976-79); assistant academic advisor in the athletic department at the University of Florida (1979-81); and coordinator, University College, and instructor in education and psychology at Arkansas State University (1982 to present). Hill was inducted into the Arkansas State Hall of Honor in 1982 and into the Arkansas Sports Hall of Fame in 1984. He is married to Billye Hill and has two sons, Lionel and Lamont.

Sources: British Virgin Islands, Olympic Committee; *Die Spiele, Official Report of XXth Olympiad*; *Guinness Book of Olympic Records*; Hill, Thomas. Interview; *United States Olympic Team, Games of the XXth Olympiad*; *United States Track and Field Olympians*.

HILL, VIRGIL (USA). Born January 8, 1964, in Missouri.

1984 Silver Medal: Middleweight Boxing

Virgil Hill, whose mother was the first female licensed boxing judge in North Dakota and whose father was a boxer, began boxing as a youngster and went on to win the National Golden Gloves and a silver medal in the 1984 Olympics. He had won the silver in the USA/American Boxing Federation Championships in 1982 and soon exploded on the international scene. In East Germany he completely outboxed two veterans and stunned officials. His final points victim was Bernardo Comas, Cuban world champion, whom he defeated at the North American Championships in 1983. He took second at the Pan Am trials and third in the 1983 World Cup. Virgil was a member of the Good Sam Club and was coached by Bruce Wiegley. He lives in Williston, North Dakota, where he graduated from Williston High School in 1983. He studied business administration.

Sources: "The 1984 Olympics," *Ebony* (October 1984); *United States Olympic Team, Media Guide; Who's Who in the 1984 Olympics.*

HINDS, STERLING (Canada). Born October 31, 1961, in Toronto, Canada.

1984 Bronze Medal: 4 x 100-Meter Relay (38.70)

Sterling Hinds attended the University of Washington and majored in computer science. He followed his older brothers Doug and Jerry onto Canada's international track teams. A sprinter good enough to run 10.27 and 20.61 in the 100 and 200 meters, Hinds was surprisingly not selected for the individual sprints but was chosen instead to anchor Canada's 4 x 100-meter relay team at Los Angeles. His bronze medal there marked the end of his track career. Sterling Hinds now plays in the Canadian Football League, after a successful career in both football and track at the University of Washington where he played some spectacular games at tailback for the Huskies in 1983.

Sources: British Virgin Islands, Olympic Committee; Canadian Olympic Association; *1984 Olympic Games, Sarajevo/Los Angeles;* "The Games," *Olympian* (October/ November 1984).

HINES, JAMES R. (USA). Born September 10, 1946, in Dumas, Arkansas.

1968 Gold Medal: 4 x 100-Meter Relay (38.24, Olympic world record)
1968 Gold Medal: 4 x 100 Meter Relay (38.24, Olympic record/world record)

James Hines graduated from McClymonds High School in Oakland, California, in 1964 and from Texas Southern University in 1969. He competed for the Houston Striders. Hines was the first athlete to better 10 seconds for 100 meters. The occasion was the American AAU Championships at Sacramento in June 1968 where, after a wind-assisted 9.8-second semifinal heat, he established a new world record of 9.9 seconds. At Mexico City he won the Olympic crown by a full meter in an electrically-timed 9.95 seconds, which remained the world record on fully-automatic

timing through 1976. He also ran a dynamic anchor leg in the 4 x 100-meter relay, taking his team to both a victory and a world record of 38.2 seconds. Hines, who was coached by 1956 Olympic sprint hero Bobby Morrow, also equaled world records of 5.9 for the indoor 60 yards and 9.1 for 100 yards. After the 1968 Olympic season, Hines went into professional football and had a brief career with the Miami Dolphins. Coach Stan Wright of Texas Southern considered Jim Hines the best sprinter he ever coached.

Sources: *Approved History of Olympic Games; Black Olympians; Guinness Book of Olympic Records; Quest for Gold;* "Inefficient but Fast," *Time* (June 9, 1967); *Track and Field: The Great Ones; United States Olympic Team, Games of the XIXth Olympiad; United States Track and Field Olympians.*

HOLYFIELD, EVANDER (USA). Born October 19, 1962, in Atmore, Alabama.

1984 Bronze Medal: Light Heavyweight Boxing

Evander Holyfield graduated from Fulton High School in 1980. He was on the football team, was commended for excellence in physical education, and received certificates for outstanding service. He is a lifetime member of Warren Memorial Boys Club in Atlanta and has been honored by the governor of Georgia, the mayors of Dallas and Atlanta, the Georgia Boxing Association, the 100% Wrong Club, and the Georgia Hall of Fame. Holyfield was the first Georgia boxer to knock out five opponents and to win the National Golden Gloves Championship (Knoxville, 1984). He was the first Georgia boxer to participate in the Olympics. At the 1984 Olympics Holyfield was disqualified on the grounds that he knocked down Kevin Barry of New Zealand after the Yugoslavian referee called "stop." Yugoslavia's Anton Josipovic got the gold. Other medals Holyfield has won are: gold at the 1983 Sports Festival; silver at the 1983 Pan Am Games; bronze at the 1983 ABF; gold at the 1984 Golden Gloves Southeastern tournament; and gold at the 1984 National Golden Gloves Championship. Holyfield's professional debut was on November 15, 1984 in Madison Square Garden. It was a six-round decision over Lionel Bryam. His second professional fight was on January 20, 1985 in Atlantic City, where he won in a six-round decision over Eric Winbush. Holyfield outclassed Ricky Parkey in May 1987, stopping him in three rounds at Caesar's Palace. He thus added the IBF title to his WBC crown. He had become a cruiserweight, a new designation, that might finally win public acceptance. Holyfield and his wife, Paulette, have a son, Evander Holyfield, Jr.

Sources: "The 1984 Olympics," *Ebony* (October 1984); Holyfield, Evander. Questionnaire. 1984; *Illustrated History of Boxing;* "Breland and Whitaker Turn Pro," *Los Angeles Times* (September 11, 1984); *United States Olympic Team, Media Guide.*

HORTA, ADOLFO (Cuba). Born March 10, 1957, in Camaguey, Cuba.

1980 Silver Medal: Featherweight Boxing

Adolfo Horta has been ranked as the leading amateur in his weight class for most of the decade of the 1980s and is generally considered Cuba's leading boxer. Horta won gold in 1982 and bantam gold in 1978 in the World Championships. He has also won World Championship challenge matches (1983). Finally, he took the Pan Am Games gold in 1981 and 1983. Horta has been the most consistent of the Cuban boxers and has firmly ruled the world of featherweights. He is retired and coaches Cuba's junior boxing program.

Sources: *Approved History of Olympic Games*; British Virgin Islands, Olympic Committee; *Bruce Jenner's Guide to the Olympics; Complete Book of the Olympics; Games of the XXIInd Olympiad, Moscow, 1980; Guinness Book of Olympic Records*; "Cuban Gold Rush Is Under Way," *Los Angeles Times* (August 23, 1987); *Who's Who in the 1984 Olympics*.

HOWARD, DENEAN (USA). Born October 5, 1964, in Sherman, Texas.

1988 Silver Medal: 4 x 400-Meter Relay (3:15.51)

Denean Howard graduated from Kennedy High School, Granada Hills, California, in 1982 and from California State University, Los Angeles, in 1986. Howard finished second in the 400 meters at the Olympic trials with a time of 50.40 seconds. In 1987 she ranked fourth in the U.S. in the 400 with a personal best of 50.72. She won the 1987 World University Games title and three straight TAC Championships (1981-83). Sherri, her sister, won the 1985 NCAA 400 title. Denean Howard ran the first leg in the women's 4 x 400-meter relay (49.8), leading to the silver medal. Her teammates were Diane Dixon, second leg (49.3), Valerie Brisco-Hooks, third leg (48.5), and Florence Griffith-Joyner, anchor (47.9). The Soviets won the gold.

Sources: "Black American Medal Winners," *Ebony* (December 1988); "Seoul Games/Medal Winners," *Los Angeles Times* (October 3, 1988); *1988 United States Olympic Team, Media Guide; Seoul '88*; "Olympics Record," *USA Today* (October 3, 1988).

HOWARD, RICHARD W. (USA). Born August 22, 1935, in Oklahoma City, Oklahoma.

1960 Bronze Medal: 400-Meter Hurdles (49.7)

Dick Howard attended Compton College in California and the University of New Mexico. He began running track in the service and ran low hurdles for Compton College in 1957. He placed fourth in the AAU 400-yard hurdles in

1958, after sustaining a serious back injury in an automobile accident. His record was AAU 400-meter hurdles and NCAA 400-meter hurdles, both in 1959. At the 1960 Olympics, the defending champion, Glenn Davis, came on like a whirlwind in the homestretch of the 400-meter hurdles. He overcame Howard at the head of the stretch, and Kansan Cliff Cushman was pulled with him. Howard came in third for the bronze. Howard died at age 32 of a heroin overdose.

Sources: *Complete Book of the Olympics; Games of the XVIIth Olympics, Rome; Guinness Book of Olympic Records; 1960 United States Sports Teams, Games; Story of the Olympic Games; United States 1960 Olympic Book; United States Track and Field Olympians*.

HOWARD, SHERRI (USA). Born June 1, 1962, in Sherman, Texas.

1984 Gold Medal: 4 x 400-Meter Relay (3:18.29, Olympic record)

Sherri Howard, who lives in Granada Hills, California, attended UCLA for 2 years, then transferred to California State University, Los Angeles. She majored in electrical engineering and received two engineering scholarships. Howard became a candidate for the U.S. Olympic 4 x 400-meter relay team after finishing fourth in the 400-meter (4 x 100-meter) relay trials. She is the second of four sisters, who as a relay team, set a national 4 x 400 interscholastic high school record (1979), with a 3:42.8. Sherri anchored the 1979 U.S. World Cup 4 x 400 relay squad. Sherri, Tina, and Denean Howard all attended California State, Los Angeles, where their sister Artra had been a student and where their father, Eugene Howard, is assistant track coach. They set another 4 x 400-meter national mark of 3:37.98, and a new 4 x 100-meter relay mark of 45.81. Sherri's best event is the 400-meter run, but she has also done well in the 100 and 200, with bests of 11.24 and 22.97.

Sources: "The 1984 Olympics," *Ebony* (October 1984); "The Champions," *Los Angeles Times* (August 14, 1984); "The Games," *Olympian* (October/November 1984; *Research Information, Games of the XXIIIrd Olympiad; United States Olympic Team, Media Guide*.

HOYTE-SMITH, JOSLYN Y. (Great Britain). Born December 16, 1954, in Barbados.

1980 Bronze Medal: 4 x 400-Meter Relay (3:27.5)

Joslyn Hoyte-Smith, a former 100 and 200-meter sprinter, not only won a bronze medal as a member of the British 1,600-meter relay team, in the Moscow Olympics in 1980, but she also anchored the fourth-place team in Los Angeles 4 years later. Hoyte-Smith was on the winning team in the

Commonwealth Games 1,600-meter relay in 1978, with a 3:27.2. In the United Kingdom Championships, women's events, she won the 400-meter run in 1979 with a 52.24. At the Women's Amateur Athletic Association, she won the 400 meters in 1978 with a 52.66 and in 1979 with a 51.90. Hoyte-Smith had a personal best performance in 1980 of 51.06 in the 400 and also ran 23.28 over 200 meters.

Sources: British Olympic Association; British Virgin Islands, Olympic Committee; *Complete Book of the Olympics; Encyclopaedia of Track and Field Athletics; Guinness Book of Olympic Records*.

HUBBARD, PHILLIP GREGORY (USA).
Born December 13, 1956, in Canton, Ohio.

1976 Gold Medal: Basketball

Phillip Hubbard graduated from McKinley High School in Canton, Ohio, in 1975 and attended the University of Michigan. His special achievements were: 1975 Ohio High School Player of the Year, 1976 All-College Freshman Basketball Weekly, and High School All-American. His coach was Johnny Orr. Hubbard made the Olympic basketball team as its youngest member while only a freshman at Michigan. He played center for the Wolverines, but he was better at forward. He left school after his junior year when he missed a year of college basketball because of a knee injury. Hubbard joined NBA's Detroit Pistons and as a forward averaged 10-15 points per game. He was later traded to the Cleveland Cavaliers.

Sources: *Black Olympians; Guinness Book of Olympic Records; Quest for Gold; United States Team, Games of the XXIst Olympiad*.

HUBBARD, WILLIAM DEHART (USA). Born
November 25, 1903 in Cincinnati, Ohio.

1924 Gold Medal: Long Jump (24 ft. 5 1/8 in./7.44 m)

William DeHart Hubbard graduated from the University of Michigan. During his college years he held the national and collegiate titles in the long jump and the hop, skip, and jump. Hubbard had the best mark of his career in 1927 when he jumped 26 feet, 2¼ inches, but the mark was not recognized as a world record because the takeoff board was 1 inch higher than the landing pit. Altogether he beat 25 feet on 11 occasions and was undoubtedly the greatest jumper of the pre-Owens era. His long jump at the University of Michigan has stood for more than 50 years! In 1922 Hubbard won the first six straight AAU long jump titles. He won the AAU triple jump in 1922 and 1923. At the NCAA he won the 100 yards in 1925 and the long jump in 1923. In jumping 24 feet, 5 1/8 inches, as he did in the Olympics, he became the first Black in Olympic history to win an

individual medal. He set a world record of 25 feet, 10 2/8 inches in 1925 when he took the NCAA title for the second time. He equaled the world record of 9.6 for 100 yards. National broad jump champion from 1922 through 1927, Hubbard was best known for his broad-jumping feats. His style was imitated by other track men. William DeHart Hubbard, a housing administrator following his track career, died June 23, 1976, in Cleveland, Ohio.

Sources: *Black Olympians; Guinness Book of Olympic Records; Hard Road to Glory; Negro Firsts in Sports; Negro in Sports; Olympic Gold; Quest for Gold; Track and Field: The Great Ones; United States Track and Field Olympians; Who's Who in Track and Field*.

HUDSON, MARTHA (USA). Born March 21, 1939,
in Eastman, Georgia.

1960 Gold Medal: 4 x 100-Meter Relay (44.72)

Martha Hudson attended Twin City High School and graduated in 1957 as salutatorian of her class. She received medals in basketball and track and a work-aid scholarship to Tennessee State University, where she had attended three summer track and field clinics. She graduated from Tennessee State in 1962. Hudson participated in national and international competition for 6 years and in 20 meets. She was listed by the AAU as the holder of American girls' championships and noteworthy performance records in 50- and 75-yard dashes and in 50- and 75-meter runs. She earned a position on the AAU All-American women's track and field team in 1959 and won the indoor 100 yards that same year. After her team's victory at the Rome Olympics a Martha Hudson Day was held at her hometown in her honor. Hudson lives in Thomaston, Georgia, where she has taught elementary school since 1963. She has also been basketball coach for elementary school girls.

Sources: *Black Olympians*; British Virgin Islands, Olympic Committee; *Development of Negro Female Olympic Talent; Historical and Biographical Studies of Women Participants; 1960 United States Sports Team, Games; Quest for Gold; United States Track and Field Olympians*.

HYMAN, FLO (USA). Born July 31, 1954, in Los
Angeles, California.

1984 Silver Medal: Volleyball

Flo Hyman attended the University of Houston. She became a member of the U.S. National Volleyball team in 1975 and stayed on the team longer than any other member. Hyman was named Tournament MVP at the 1979 NORCECA Championship. Selected to the All-World Cup team at the 1981 World Cup Games in Tokyo, she was honored as best hitter of that competition. The All-World Cup team consists of the top six women in the world. After the 1984

Olympics Hyman had planned to pursue teaching, coaching, or a business career, but she chose instead to do public relations for the national team. She died suddenly on January 24, 1986, in Matsue City, Japan, while playing volleyball for a Japanese club. Her death was attributed to an ailment known as Marfan's syndrome. Flo Hyman might have been the best-known women's volleyball player in the world. Moreover, her former national coach, Pat Zartman, stated that Hyman was a major force in turning the U.S. women's team "from recreational into an internationally competitive program." An overpowering spiker, Hyman was respected throughout the world. Cliff McPeak, associate director of the U.S. Volleyball Association, stated that Hyman "meant a lot to the sport of volleyball, not only in the U.S., but all over the world. She was a real force in the growth of the sport in this country." Flo Hyman had planned to pursue an acting career and had played a guerrilla warrior in a movie, *Order of the Black Eagle*. On February 4, 1987, National Women in Sports Day, the first annual Flo Hyman Memorial Award—for commitment to excellence—was presented to a friend of Hyman's, Martina Navratilova.

Sources: British Virgin Islands, Olympic Committee; "The 1984 Olympics," *Ebony* (October 1984); *For the Record*; "Olympic Briefs," *Los Angeles Times* (July 27, 1984); "U.S. Olympic Volleyball Star Dies in Match," *Los Angeles Times* (January 25, 1986); "Volleyball," *Olympian* (October/November 1984); "Olympic Medal Results," *Sporting News* (August 13, 1984); *United States Olympic Team, Media Guide*; "Player's Passion for Sport Lives On," *USA Today* (September 22, 1988); "Flo Hyman," *Women's Sports* (October 1984).

IKHOURIA, ISAAC (Nigeria). Born in Nigeria.

1972 Bronze Medal: Light Heavyweight Boxing

At the 1972 Olympics in Munich Ikhouria defeated Anton Schaer of Switzerland on points, 3-2; Valdemar Oliveira of Brazil on points, 5-0; and Nikolay Anfimov of the USSR on points, 3-2.

Sources: *Approved History of Olympic Games; Complete Book of the Olympics; Die Spiele, Official Report for the Games of the XXth Olympiad; Guinness Book of Olympic Records; Munchen 1972; Results of the Games of the XXth Olympiad.*

INGRAM, SHEILA RENA (USA). Born March 23, 1957, in Washington, D.C.

1976 Silver Medal: 4 x 400-Meter Relay (3:22.81)

As a 17-year-old in 1974, Sheila Ingram set a U.S. junior record of 53.0 seconds in the 400-meter run while attending Coolidge High School in Washington, D.C. As her talent developed she finished second in the AAU 400 meters in

1976, won the Olympic final trials, and went to Montreal where she added the U.S. senior record to the junior record, which she still held. Ingram set a new U.S. record of 51.31 at the Olympics in the quarterfinals only to lose it to Debra Sapenter (51.23) later in the same round. She recaptured the record in the first semifinal with 50.90 but lost it again when Rosalyn Bryant ran 50.62 in the second semifinal. In the final, Ingram finished sixth and was later clocked in 50.0 when she ran the second stage for the silver medal-winning relay team. Ingram delayed her entry into collegiate athletics for several years but ran for the University of the District of Columbia in the NCAA Division II competition in the early 1980s. She was a member of the Pioneer Track Club.

Sources: *Black Olympians*; British Virgin Islands, Olympic Committee; *Guinness Book of Olympic Records*; "Olympic Summaries," *New York Times* (August 2, 1976); *Quest for Gold; United States Olympic Team, Games of the XXIst Olympiad; United States Track and Field Olympians.*

ISSAJENKO, ANGELLA (TAYLOR) (Canada). Born September 28, 1958, in St. Andrew, Jamaica.

1984 Silver Medal: 4 x 100-Meter Relay (42.77)

Angella Taylor Issajenko went to high school in Manchester, Jamaica but now lives in Downsview, Ontario. She was a member of the 1980 Canadian Olympic team. Issajenko held the Commonwealth record for 100 meters with an 11.00 clocking in 1982 and has run 22.25 for 200 meters. An Olympic finalist in the 200 in Los Angeles, Issajenko had made the 100 final at the 1983 World Championships. She won a bronze in the 100 in 1983 at the World Student Games. Issajenko's silver medal in the Los Angeles Olympics, added one more victory to a long list of international honors in both short sprints and the relays. She has a 400 best time of 51.81 seconds. Issajenko, whose career has been hampered somewhat by a series of minor injuries, did not compete in 1985, the year she gave birth to her first child. Married to sprinter Tony Issajenko, she returned to world-class competition in 1986 and won a gold in the 200 and a bronze in the 100 meters at the Commonwealth Games in Edinburgh, Scotland.

Sources: British Virgin Islands, Olympic Committee; Canadian Olympic Association; *1984 Olympic Games; Sarajevo/Los Angeles*; "The Games," *Olympian* (October/November 1984); *Research Information, Games of the XXIIIrd Olympiad; Who's Who in the 1984 Olympics.*

JACKSON, COLIN (Great Britain). Born February 18, 1967, in Cardiff, England.

1988 Silver Medal: 110-Meter Hurdles (13.28)

Colin Jackson finished second in Seoul in the 110-meter hurdles, after Roger Kingdom, with 13.28 seconds. Tonie

Campbell of the U.S. won the bronze. Among Jackson's other wins in the 110-meter hurdles were: World Championships, 1987 (third); Commonwealth Games, 1986 (second); World Jr. Championships, 1986 (first); European Jr. Championships, 1985 (second); and European Cup, 1987 (second). He has also excelled in the 60-meter hurdles. Jackson's progression in the 110-meter hurdles was from 13.92 seconds in 1984 to 13.11 (auto-timed) in 1988. Colin Jackson is a student and a member of Cardiff Amateur Athletic Club.

Sources: British Virgin Islands, Olympic Committee; *International Amateur Athletic Federation*; "Seoul Games/Medal Winners," *Los Angeles Times* (October 3, 1988); *Seoul '88*; "Olympics Record," *USA Today* (October 3, 1988).

JACKSON, GRACE (Jamaica). Born June 14, 1961, at St. Ann, Jamaica.

1988 Silver Medal: 200-Meter Run (21.72)

Grace Jackson won the women's 200-meter run with a time of 22.40 seconds at the International Amateur Athletic Federation Mobil Grand Prix track and field meet at London's Crystal Palace. At the same meet, she beat Ana Quirot of Cuba in the women's 400 meters with a time of 49.57. It was the second best time in the world in 1988. Grace Jackson is a member of Atoms Track Club, USA.

Sources: *International Amateur Athletic Federation*; "Bile Beats Cram," *Los Angeles Times* (July 9, 1988); "Bubka Leaps to Pole Vault Mark," *Los Angeles Times* (July 11, 1988); "Seoul Games/Medal Winners," *Los Angeles Times* (October 3, 1988); "Olympics Record," *USA Today* (October 3, 1988).

JACKSON, LUCIUS BROWN (USA). Born October 31, 1941, in San Marcos, Texas.

1964 Gold Medal: Basketball

Luke Jackson, at 6 feet, 9 inches and 240 pounds, was one of the strongest forwards to ever play basketball. While attending Pan American University in Edinburg, Texas, he became a first-round draft pick of the Philadelphia 76ers in 1964. He made the NBA All-Rookie team in his first year and later played in two NBA All-Star games. Jackson was an outstanding defensive player and strong rebounder who was never asked to score a lot of points. His role as a team player culminated when, in 1966-67, his team won 68 games and lost only 13. During his 8 years with Philadelphia Luke Jackson was an indispensable cog in the machine of what was considered to be the greatest NBA team ever.

Sources: *Black Olympians; Guinness Book of Olympic Records; Quest for Gold; United States Olympic Team, Games of the XVIIIth Olympiad*.

JACOBS, SIMONE (Great Britain). Born September 5, 1966, in England.

1984 Bronze Medal: 4 x 100-Meter Relay (43.11)

Simone Jacobs showed little sign of nerves as she led off Britain's bronze medal-winning sprint relay quartette. At 17, she was one of the youngest Olympic medalists. She has personal bests of 11.45 seconds for 100 meters and 23.28 for 200. She was third in the European Jr. 200 in 1983. Simone Jacobs has not maintained a strong record since the 1984 Games, probably because of a combination of injuries and waning interest.

Sources: British Virgin Islands, Olympic Committee; *1984 Olympic Games*; "The Games," *Olympian* (October/November 1984).

JAMES, GEORGE LAWRENCE (USA). Born November 6, 1947, in Mount Pleasant, New Jersey.

1968 Gold Medal: 4 x 400-Meter Relay (2:56.16, Olympic record/world record)
1968 Silver Medal: 400-Meter Run (43.97)

Before 1968 Larry James was known primarily as a hurdler and triple jumper; but in the 1968 Olympic year he concentrated on the one-lap event with amazing success. He was beaten in the 400-meter run at the final trials and the Olympics by Lee Evans, but later in the same Games, he ran a 43.8 relay leg for a team gold medal when the U.S. bettered the world record by more than 3 seconds. James's 1968 record of 43.9 ranked as second fastest in the 400 meters through 1982. He won the IC4A outdoor 440 yards and the NCAA indoor 440 yards for 3 straight years from 1968 and the NCAA outdoor 440 yards in 1970. He had a best 400-meter hurdles time of 50.2 seconds. Larry James graduated from Villanova University in 1970.

Sources: *Black Olympians; Guinness Book of Olympic Records; Quest for Gold; United States Olympic Team, Games of the XIXth Olympiad; United States Track and Field Olympians*.

JEFFERSON, THOMAS (USA). Born August 6, 1962, in Cleveland, Ohio.

1984 Bronze Medal: 200-Meter Run (20.26)

Thomas Jefferson ran the 200 meters in 20.73 seconds in heats at the NCAA in 1984, but he didn't run the final. His personal best going into the Olympic trials was 20.43, but he caught two other members of the 1983 World Championships 200-meter team—Larry Myricks and Elliott Quow—and made the last spot on the team. Jefferson finished third in the 200 meters at the Olympic trials, with a 20.37. Jefferson lives in Kent, Ohio, where he attended Kent State University.

Sources: "The 1984 Olympics," *Ebony* (October 1984); "The Champions," *Los Angeles Times* (August 14, 1984); "The Games," *Olympian* (October/November 1984); "Olympic Games," *New York Times* (August 9, 1984); "Olympic Winners," *New York Times* (August 13, 1984); *Research Information, Games of the XXIIIrd Olympiad.*

JENKINS, CHARLES LAMONT (USA). Born January 7, 1934, in New York City.

1956 Gold Medal: 400-Meter Run (46.85, Olympic record)
1956 Gold Medal: 4 x 400-Meter Relay (3:04.81)

Charlie Jenkins was a surprise winner of the Olympic gold medal in the 400 meters; he had placed second in the 1956 IC4A, NCAA, and Olympic trials. Even though his winning time of 46.85 at the Olympics was the slowest since 1928, he showed a truer indication of his abilities with a 45.5 relay leg, which gave him a second gold medal. Jenkins won the AAU in 1955 and the IC4A in 1955 and 1957 while at Villanova University. He won the AAU 60 yards three times indoors and set a world record for the 500 yards in 1956. Jenkins became a track and field coach at Villanova in 1961 and eventually succeeded the legendary Jumbo Elliott as head coach there. After earning a doctorate in education, Charlie Jenkins worked for the State Department.

Sources: "More about Winning," *American Visions* (1988); *Black Olympians; Guinness Book of Olympic Records; Quest for Gold.*

JEROME, HARRY WINSTON (Canada). Born September 30, 1940, in Prince Albert, Saskatchewan, Canada.

1964 Bronze Medal: 100-Meter Run (10.2)

"[Harry Jerome] was probably Canada's most maligned athlete, always it seemed the centre of controversy, all because at the young immature age of 19 he became a world record holder and always strove to be the best" (Canadian Olympic Association). Jerome set a world record in the 100 meters at the Canadian Olympic trials in 1960 (10.0 seconds), was Pan Am 100-meter champion in 1960 (10.0) and 1967 (10.2), won the 100 (10.5) and 200 (21.3) at the British Columbia Championships in 1964, and finished first in the 100 meters at the Commonwealth Games in 1966 (9.4). In 1970 he and five other athletes toured the country on a sports demonstration campaign on behalf of the Canadian government. According to Jerome, the objective was "to motivate young people and get them interested in sports" (Cecil Smith, Canadian Olympic Association). Harry Jerome became the first native Canadian to hold a world record and the first Canadian athlete to hold the record for both the 100 meters and 100 yards at the same time. He was elected to the Canadian Sports Hall of Fame in May 1971. Jerome graduated from the University of Oregon with an M.A. in physical education. In later years he became a teacher at Templeton High School in Vancouver and undertook special studies for the Federal Health Department. He died in Vancouver in 1982.

Sources: British Virgin Islands, Olympic Committee; "The Career of One of Canada's Greatest Sprinters," Canadian Olympic Association; *Guinness Book of Olympic Records; Lexikon der 12000 Olympioniken; Track and Field: The Great Ones; Who's Who in Track and Field.*

JILES, PAMELA THERESA (USA). Born July 10, 1955, in New Orleans, Louisiana.

1976 Silver Medal: 4 x 400-Meter Relay (3:22.81)

In 1975 Pamela Jiles was Louisiana's AAU Female Athlete of the Year. During that and the following year she competed successfully at national and international meets. She ran fourth in the 1976 Olympic trials 100 and 200 meters. Her selection for the 1,600-meter relay was somewhat surprising in that her mark had been made in the shorter sprints. Jiles graduated in 1977 from Dillard University in New Orleans with a degree in mathematics. She was a member of the New Orleans Superdames.

Sources: *Black Olympians*; British Virgin Islands, Olympic Committee; *Guinness Book of Olympic Records*; "Olympic Summaries," *New York Times* (August 2, 1976); *Quest for Gold; United States Track and Field Olympians.*

JIPCHO, BENJAMIN W. (Kenya). Born March 1, 1943, in Mt. Elgon, Kenya.

1972 Silver Medal: 3,000-Meter Steeplechase (8:24.62)

Benjamin Jipcho ripped the world steeplechase record twice in 1973. He ran 8:19.8 at Helsinki on June 18 and a fantastic 8:13.91 9 days later at the same spot. Jipcho ran the fastest mile in history with 3:52.17 on July 3, 1973, in Stockholm. On the following day he ran 8:18.2 in the steeplechase. Jipcho was one of the world's leading middle distance runners of the early 1970s. His best performances included a 1,500-meter clocking of 3:33.16 in finishing third to Tanzania's Filbert Bayi in a fantastic Commonwealth Games final in 1974; 8:16.38 in running 2 miles in 1973; 13:14.4 in winning the 5,000-meter run at the Commonwealth Games in 1974, and 8:20.8 in taking the steeplechase at the same games. Jipcho's honors also included African Games victories in the 5,000 meters and in the 3,000-meter steeplechase in 1973. Jipcho competed professionally in 1974 with the International Track Association and retired when that organization folded.

Sources: British Virgin Islands, Olympic Committee; *Guinness Book of Olympic Records; Lexikon der 12000 Olympioniken; Who's Who in Track and Field.*

JOHNSON, BENJAMINE SINCLAIR, JR.

(Canada). Born December 30, 1961, at Falmouth, Jamaica.

1984 Bronze Medal: 100-Meter Run (10.22)
1984 Bronze Medal: 4 x 100-meter Relay (38.70)

Benjamine Johnson emigrated to Canada in 1976 and settled in Toronto. A member of the York University Optimist Athletic Club, he was coached by former Canadian sprint champion Charlie Francis. In 1985-86 Ben Johnson laid claim to the title of "World's Fastest Human." Once more his super start proved too much for his indoor rivals and he captured the season's major championship 60 meters in winning at the World Indoor Games. Outdoors in 1985 he won his national championships in both sprints, clocking 10.02 seconds (wind-aided) and 20.41 for personal best in the 200. At the America's Cup meet in San Juan, Puerto Rico, he equaled Lennox Miller's Commonwealth record by clocking 10.04. Two weeks later he broke the record with an impressive win in the World Cup at Canberra, Australia; his time of 10.00 seconds was the sixth-fastest ever. In 1986 Johnson continued to reign as the scourge of the indoor tracks at 50 and 60 meters. Outdoors he won the 100 at both the Commonwealth Games and Goodwill Games. Three times he defeated Olympic champion Carl Lewis. He recorded an unprecedented 10 sub-10 performances and lost only once at 100 meters. His best time of 9.95 was equal of the second fastest of all time and the fastest at sea level. Johnson's championship record was further enhanced by a bronze at 200 meters and another gold in the sprint relay at the Commonwealth Games. Johnson's first major impact on the international scene came at the 1980 Commonwealth Games in Brisbane, Australia, where he clocked a windy 10.05, finishing second to 1980 Olympic champion Allan Wells. Johnson won another silver medal in the 1,600-meter relay. Earlier that year Johnson had surprisingly won the 200 at a dual meet against the U.S. at Colorado Springs where the Canadians set a national mark of 38.43 in the 400-meter relay with Johnson running the leadoff leg. If 1980 was a year of promise for Johnson, 1983 was a nightmare. He failed to win medals in the year's three major championships: the World University Games, World Championships, and Pan Am Games. He did, however, manage to reduce his personal best in the 100 to 10.19. After a very successful indoor season Johnson finally established himself as one of the world's best sprinters in 1984. After winning his national championships in a windy 10.01 seconds, he went to the Los Angeles Olympics tipped as the sprinter most likely to prevent a 1-2-3 American sweep. He did not disappoint. Ben Johnson became the first winner of the IAAF Indoor World Championships 60 meters, setting a world record of 6.41 at Indianapolis in March 1987. He also set a world record of 5.55 over 55 meters. Johnson shattered the previous record of 9.93, set by Calvin Smith in 1983, when he scored 9.83 in the 100-meter dash at the World Track and Field Championships in Rome in August 1987. Johnson bested a field of elite sprinters, including his chief rival, Carl Lewis. At the age of 26, Johnson set a world record of 5.20 seconds in the indoor 50-yard dash, when he opened his 1988 track season in Canada. He went on to break it 2 weeks later with a blazing 5.15. Ben Johnson broke the world record by running a remarkable 9.79 in the 100 at Seoul to win the gold. Carl Lewis finished second in 9.92. Johnson's margin of victory was the largest in the 100 meters since the introduction of automatic timing. Lewis believed he was beaten by Johnson's legendary start. Johnson's start in the summer of 1988 at the World Championships at Rome had been a point of contention; there he ran 9.83 and beat Lewis. Two days after winning the gold, the steroid stanozolol was discovered in Johnson's urine. He was stripped of the medal and record. He emphatically denied the charge, following the advice of Drew Mearns, his adviser, who stated that Johnson needed to make a "tough, strong statement," in the aftermath of the furor. Mearns said that Johnson's future would be ruined if he did not refute it (*Los Angeles Times*). The Canadian Center for Doping Control's Dr. Robert Masse stated that Johnson's unnaturally low testosterone levels would suggest a heavy use of steroids. According to one of his teammates, sprinter Angella Issajenko, Ben knowingly took steroids. "Ben takes steroids. I take steroids. [Dr.] Jamie [Astaphan] gives them to us, and [coach] Charlie isn't a scientist but he knows what's happening" (*Los Angeles Times*). Ben Johnson was suspended from competition for 2 years by the Canadian Track and Field Association. His personal coach, Charlie Francis, was also suspended. Francis's suspension was handed down by the International Amateur Athletic Foundation.

Sources: Johnson, Benjamine. Questionnaire. 1984; British Virgin Islands, Olympic Committee; Canadian Olympic Association; "The World's Fastest Human," *Ebony* (May 1988); "Johnson Runs Off," *Los Angeles Times* (September 24, 1988); "Johnson's Adviser Calls for Honesty," *Los Angeles Times* (September 29, 1988); "Teammate Says Johnson Took Steroids," *Los Angeles Times* (October 10, 1988); "Johnson Suspended 2 Years," *Los Angeles Times* (October 25, 1988).

JOHNSON, CORNELIUS (USA). Born August 21, 1913, in Los Angeles, California.

1936 Gold Medal: High Jump (6 ft. 8 in./2.03 m, Olympic record)

Cornelius Johnson competed as a high school student in the 1932 Olympics. He later attended Compton Junior College in California. Johnson won or shared the AAU title five times and was AAU indoor champion three times, twice tied. In 1934 Johnson tied with Walter Marty at 6 feet, 8 5/8 inches. Johnson set a world indoor record of 6 feet, 8 15/16 inches in 1936 and an Interscholastic world record of 6 feet, 6 5/8 inches (after not winning a medal in the 1932 Games). In the final tryouts for the 1936

Games, he jumped to a new world record of 6 feet, 9¾ inches, tying Dave Albritton. At the Olympics, although Johnson took the title, he unsuccessfully attempted a new world record of 6 feet, 10 inches. In 1939 Cornelius Johnson became the first Black high jumper to clear the bar at 6 feet, 9 inches.

Sources: *Black Olympians; Compton's Gift to the Olympic Games; Guinness Book of Olympic Records; Quest for Gold; Track and Field: The Great Ones; Who's Who in Track and Field.*

JOHNSON, MARVIN L. (USA). Born August 12, 1954, in Indianapolis, Indiana.

1972 Bronze Medal: Middleweight Boxing (tied)

Marvin Johnson won the 1971 and 1972 AAU Championships and the 1971 Golden Gloves crown. In 1972 he took the Olympic trials before losing in the semifinals at Munich. After the Olympics, Johnson turned professional and has done a better job than he did as an amateur. He has fought mostly as a light heavyweight and has won both the World Boxing Council title (1978-79) and the World Boxing Association title (1979-80).

Sources: *Black Olympians; Guinness Book of Olympic Records; Lexikon der 12000 Olympioniken; Quest for Gold.*

JOHNSON, R. EARL (USA). Born in Baltimore, Maryland.

1924 Bronze Medal: 10,000-Meter Cross-Country (35:21.0)

Earl Johnson was National Five Miler in 1921, 1922, and 1923. His best five-mile time was 25 minutes, 23 seconds. He was National Senior Cross-Country champion in 1921 and also captured the National Ten Mile title in 1924. Johnson's time in the 10,000-meter cross-country in 1924 won the U.S. team the silver medal. The cross-country race was never again included in Olympic competition allegedly because it was "too strenuous." Johnson was a member of the Thomas Steel Works Athletics Club near Pittsburgh.

Sources: *Approved History of Olympic Games; Black Olympians*; British Virgin Islands, Olympic Committee; *Negro in Sports.*

JOHNSON, RAFER LEWIS (USA). Born August 18, 1934, in Hillsboro, Texas.

1956 Silver Medal: Decathlon (7,587 points)
1960 Gold Medal: Decathlon (8,392 points)

For the 1984 Olympics, Rafer Johnson's challenge was to open the Games—dramatically. "The fact that I was this

RAFER LEWIS JOHNSON (Photo courtesy of Amateur Athletic Foundation, Los Angeles, California, and Michael Yada AAF/LPI 1984.)

final torch bearer, completing the relay, the whole thing was very inspiring." Johnson said. "So my approach to it was like it was the 11th event [in a decathlon]." When it was time, Johnson waited on the track and took the torch from Gina Hemphill, granddaughter of Jesse Owens. "It [the rising stairway] was like a piece of artwork, it was so beautiful and worked so well. It was beautiful with the sun hitting it, like a painting." As he reached the top, Johnson turned, held the torch aloft, and saluted the stadium. He then lifted the torch to the huge gas jets above his head, sending the flame toward the Olympic rings and finally to the Coliseum torch (*Los Angeles Times*). Twenty-four years earlier, on the occasion of the Olympic opening ceremonies in Rome, Johnson had become the first Black to carry the American flag. Johnson excelled in track events, football, basketball, and baseball while in high school, concentrating at age 16 on the decathlon. He won two state meets and earned a scholarship to UCLA. He came onto the stage of international competition at age

19 and broke Bob Mathias's world record at the National AAU Championship. Johnson won the gold Olympic medal in 1960 with 8,392 points. His statistics for the individual events were as follows: 100 meters, 10.9 seconds; long jump, 24 feet, 3/8 inches; shotput, 51 feet, 10¾ inches; high jump, 6 feet, 7/8 inches; 400 meters, 48.3; 110-meter hurdles, 15.3; discus, 159 feet, 1 inch; pole vault, 13 feet, 5 3/8 inches; javelin, 229 feet, 10 3/8 inches; 1,500 meters, 4:48.5. He won the silver in the decathlon in 1956 with 7,587 points. Johnson, with size, speed, and ability, was near perfection in the 10-event decathlon feat. His duels with fellow decathletes Russian Kuznyetsov and Yang of Formosa captured the interest of the world. He regained his world status by defeating Kuznyetsov 8,302 to 7,897 in 1958. The Russian recaptured the world record in 1959 after Johnson was injured in an automobile accident. Johnson made a remarkable recovery in 1960 and defeated Yang in a record 8,683 performance in Eugene, Oregon. UCLA teammates Johnson and Yang staged a dramatic duel at the Rome Olympics. In the final event, Johnson held onto the lead to beat both Yang (by only 58 points) and Kuznyetsov (by almost 600 points). Rafer Johnson has been an executive with Continental Telephone, served as director of the Kennedy Foundation, acted in films, and worked in public service. He has remained intimately involved in the Olympic movement, at one time serving as chairman of the Olympian Citizens Advisory Commission. In 1960 he was honored as the Associated Press's Athlete of the Year. Johnson has devoted innumerable hours to the mentally and physically handicapped and has served as president of the board of directors of the California Special Olympics. He is also national head coach for Special Olympics, Inc. of Washington, D.C. In addition, Johnson served on the board of directors of the Los Angeles Olympic Organizing Committee and on the board of the Amateur Athletic Foundation. One of six children, Johnson grew up in Kingsburg, California, and graduated from UCLA. He is the father of two children, Jenny and Josh.

Sources: *Black Olympians; Guinness Book of Olympic Records; Lincoln Library of Sports Champions*; "R. Johnson President of CSO," *Los Angeles Sentinel* (August 2, 1984); "L.A. Coliseum," *Los Angeles Times* (July 29, 1984); *Negro Firsts in Sports; Spirit Team Profiles; Who's Who in Track and Field*.

JONES, ALFRED (USA). Born October 1, 1946, in Grace, Mississippi.

1968 Bronze Medal: Middleweight Boxing

Alfred Jones graduated in 1965 from Western High School in Detroit, where he was president of his class. He also graduated, in 1985, from Wayne County Community College with an associate of arts degree. In high school

Jones participated in the pole vault, hurdles, broad jump, and swimming. In college he played intramural basketball. Jones was 1965 National Golden Gloves champion (Kansas City, Missouri), 1968 New England Golden Gloves champion, and 1968 National AAU boxing champion. He was also Michigan Fighter of the Year in 1970. Between 1969 and 1971, as a professional, he had 15 straight wins and 1 loss, with 10 knockouts. In 1978 Alfred Jones was chairman of the Kercheval Street Olympic Games. He owned a liquor store from 1971 to 1983 and is now a job development specialist for a major U.S. car manufacturer. He has also been chairman of Kercheval McCellan Citizens District Council. He lives in Detroit, is married to Jacqueline Jones, and has a son, Alexander D.

Sources: *Approved History of Olympic Games; Black Olympians; Guinness Book of Olympic Records*; Jones, Alfred. Questionnaire.; *Quest for Gold; United States Olympic Team, Games of the XIXth Olympiad*.

JONES, BARBARA PEARL (USA). Born March 26, 1937, in Chicago, Illinois.

1952 Gold Medal: 4 x 100-Meter Relay (46.14, Olympic record)
1960 Gold Medal: 4 x 100-Meter Relay (44.72)

After Barbara Jones graduated from St. Elizabeth High School in 1955, she attended Marquette University for one year and then transferred to Tennessee State University. Tennessee State awarded her a work-aid scholarship and she graduated from there in 1961. She was a member of the Tigerbelles track team. The youngest woman in Olympic history to win a track and field event, Barbara Jones was only 15 years old when she won her first Olympic gold, in 1952. She missed the 1956 Games, but in 1960, while attending Tennessee State, she won a second Olympic gold medal in the relay. All the members of this team were Tigerbelles. In fact, these were the Games in which all six of the gold medals in U.S. track and field went to Tigerbelles. Jones won the AAU 100 meters in 1953 and 1954, and the 100 yards in 1957—between her two Olympic successes. She earned a position on four AAU All-American women's track and field teams and over an 8-year period won 335 medals (9 gold) and 56 trophies. Jones married Marcellus Slater, also a student at Tennessee State. She now lives with her two daughters in Chicago, where she is a physical education teacher in the city schools.

Sources: *Approved History of Olympic Games; Black Olympians; Development of Negro Female Olympic Talent; 1960 United States Sports Teams; Historical and Biographical Studies of Women Participants; Quest for Gold; United States Olympic Team, 1952; United States Track and Field Olympians*.

JONES, DWIGHT ELMO (USA). Born February 27, 1952, in Houston, Texas.

1972 Silver Medal: Basketball

Dwight Jones attended Wheatley High School in Houston and the University of Houston. He was All-State High School for 3 years and All-American High School for 2 years. As a center on the Houston basketball team, Jones averaged 16.5 points and 13.3 rebounds in 1971-72. He had averaged 21.7 points and 20.3 rebounds as a freshman in 1970-71. His college coach was Guy Lewis. Jones won the gold medal for the 1971 Pan Am team and then, after the Olympics, played another season for Houston before becoming eligible for the NBA hardship draft. In the 1973 NBA draft, Jones was selected by the Atlanta Hawks; he was the ninth pick overall. Since becoming a professional, Jones has played either power forward or back-up center. He left Atlanta in 1976 and has since played for the Houston Rockets, the Chicago Bulls, and the Los Angeles Lakers. He was released in 1981.

Sources: *Black Olympians; Guinness Book of Olympic Records; Quest for Gold; United States Olympic Team, Games of the XXth Olympiad.*

JONES, EARL (USA). Born July 11, 1964, in Inkster, Michigan.

1984 Bronze Medal: 800-Meter Run (1:43.83)

Earl Jones attended Eastern Michigan University, which he represented for 2 years before moving to the West Coast to join fellow internationals Johnny Gray, David Mack, and James Robinson as members of the Santa Monica Track Club. In 1986 they accounted for four of the top five places on the U.S. performance list in the 800 meters. Jones first made an impression on the national scene with a 1:44.5 relay leg in the 1,600-meter relay at the Frake Relays in 1983. At the NCAA Championships that year he placed second in the 1,500 meters with a 3:40.64 clocking. His best open 800 that year was 1:48.6. In 1984 he concentrated primarily on the 800, placing second at the NCAA Championships. He stamped his name firmly among the leading Olympic medal contenders by winning the Olympic trials 800 in 1:43.74, in a virtual dead heat with Gray. At the Games in Los Angeles he had no answer for the majestic Joaquim Cruz and the determined Sebastian Coe, but he ranked third in the world for 1984. In 1985 Earl Jones won the NCAA 800 handily, in a time of 1:45.12, and added a third-place finish in the TAC Championships. He was ranked eighth by *Track & Field News*. In 1986 the front-running Jones faded to fifth place in the 800 at the TAC Championships after leading to 600 meters. He had a fairly successful European summer campaign, establishing personal bests in both the 800, at Zurich, and the 1,500, at Hengelo (Netherlands). He placed third in a pedestrian 800 at the IAAF Grand Prix final, finishing in 1:47.16.

Sources: British Virgin Islands, Olympic Committee; "The 1984 Olympics," *Ebony* (October 1984); "The Champions," *Los Angeles Times* (August 14, 1984); "The Games," *Olympian* (October 1, 1984); *United States Olympic Team, Media Guide.*

JONES, HAYES WENDELL (USA). Born August 4, 1938, in Starksville, Mississippi.

1960 Bronze Medal: 110-Meter Hurdles (14.17)
1964 Gold Medal: 110-Meter Hurdles (13.67, Olympic record)

Hayes Jones attended Eastern Michigan University. He won the 1958 AAU indoor and outdoor high hurdles with a meet record of 7.1 seconds indoors and a fine 13.8 outdoors. He won the 1958 NCAA for Eastern Michigan in 13.6. Jones was AAU indoor champion in 1960-62, setting a meet record with a time of 7.0. He took the AAU outdoor crowns in 1960-61 with a record-tying 13.6 both years. Jones shaved time off his own record with his two Olympic medals. As a world-class hurdler, he had an explosive start and blazing speed on the flat, which seemingly made up for his being only 5 feet, 11. His exceptional starting ability on the indoor circuit put him on his way to 6 AAU titles, and he won 55 consecutive indoor races from March 1959 through his retirement in 1964. He led off several U.S. 400-meter relay teams in international competition. Jones was director of recreation in New York City for 2 years after retirement. He then returned to private business, where he was a sales executive for a major U.S. airlines and head of the urban market development program for a large brewing company.

Sources: *Black Olympians*; British Virgin Islands, Olympic Committee; *History of the Olympics; Quest for Gold; Track and Field: The Great Ones; Who's Who in Track and Field.*

JONES, JOHN WESLEY (USA). Born April 4, 1958, in Lawton, Oklahoma.

1976 Gold Medal: 4 x 100-Meter Relay (38.33)

John W. Jones was first in the 1976 Texas High School 100 and 200 yards, first in the 1975 Texas High School 440 yards, and first in the 100, third in the 200, and third in the 400 of the 1976 Prefontaine Classic. He earned 10 athletic awards in high school: 4 in track, 3 in football, and 3 in basketball. He scored 45 touchdowns in his last 2 years at Lampasas High. Jones had placed fourth in the 100 meters at the 1976 Olympic final trials before starting college, but he was nominated for the individual event in Montreal when Houston McTear withdrew because of injury. He finished sixth in the Olympic 100 but won a gold medal in the relay after running an outstanding second leg. He never won a national title in either collegiate or open competition. "Lam" Jones graduated from the University of Texas where he was a wide receiver for the Longhorns in the late 1970s. It was there he earned his nickname. He was a wide receiver with the New York Jets from 1981 to 1987.

Sources: *Black Olympians; Guinness Book of Olympic Records; History of the Olympic Games*; "Olympic Summaries," *New York Times* (August 2, 1976); *Quest for Gold; United States Olympic Team, Games of the XXIst Olympiad*.

JONES, K. C. (USA). Born May 25, 1932, in Taylor, Texas.

1956 Gold Medal: Basketball

K. C. Jones attended the University of San Francisco where he helped win the NCAA titles in 1955 and 1956. As a professional, he was with the Boston Celtics for 9 years, the first 8 of which were NBA Championship years for the Celtics. Jones is one of four men to have played as an Olympic, NCAA, and NBA champion. He is one of the most titled men in basketball history, an honor he shares with Bill Russell with whom he spent his entire collegiate and professional career. A defensive stalwart who always guarded the opposition's leading guard, Jones, like Russell, was the ultimate team player. Jones began a career as a professional coach after retiring as a player. He was assistant coach with the Celtics, then head coach with the San Diego Conquistadors in 1972. He was head coach with the Washington Bullets in the mid-1970s for 3 successful years. He returned to the Celtics as head coach in 1983 and remained with that club until his retirement at the end of the 1988 season. During his coaching career, he led the Celtics to the NBA finals for 4 straight years, and won 2 of those championships. After retiring from his coaching position, Jones became a Celtics vice president and director of player personnel. He was replaced as head coach by assistant coach Jimmy Rodgers.

Sources: *Approved History of Olympic Games; Black Olympians; Guinness Book of Olympic Records*; "Jones to Retire as Celtics Coach," *Los Angeles Times* (May 4, 1988); *Quest for Gold; United States 1956 Olympic Book*.

JONES, LOUIS WOODARD (USA). Born January 15, 1932, in New Rochelle, New York.

1956 Gold Medal: 4 x 400-Meter Relay (3:04.81)

Louis Jones graduated from New Rochelle High School and from Manhattan College in the Bronx, New York, in 1954. He received an M.A. from Columbia University. In high school he participated in track and field and football and was state 440 yards champion in 1949-50. In college he was IC4A 440 and 600 yards champion. Jones won the

Pennsylvania Relay Championships and set a world record at the Indoor Mile Relay Championships. He was national 600 yards champion in 1956 at Madison Square Garden and broke the world record in winning the 400 meters at the Pan Am Games in Mexico City in 1955, with a 45.4 seconds clocking. At the final U.S. Olympic trials in 1956 Jones improved the world 400-meter mark to 45.2 but failed to show his true form in Melbourne. He ran no better than 48.1 for sixth place in the individual 400, and in the relay he was clocked at a modest 47.1 as leadoff man in the final. Lou Jones is a member of the Black International Sports Hall of Fame, Westchester County Sports Hall of Fame, and Manhattan College Sports Hall of Fame. He was a member of the New York Pioneer Club. Jones did some high school coaching in track and field, football, soccer, and cross-country and was assistant to the Westchester county executive. He lives in White Plains, New York, with his wife, Vivian. His children are Louis IV, Steven, and Carla.

Sources: *Approved History of Olympic Games; Black Olympians*; British Virgin Islands, Olympic Committee; *Guinness Book of Olympic Records; Hard Road to Glory*; Jones, Louis. Questionnaire. 1984; *Quest for Gold; United States Track and Field Olympians*.

JONES, ROY (USA). Born January 16, 1969, in Pensacola, Florida.

1988 Silver Medal: Light Middleweight Boxing

Roy Jones, who began boxing at age 10, was coached by his father, Roy Jones, Sr. Roy, Jr. was the light welterweight junior Olympics champion in 1984. Jones won the 1988 Olympic trials and defeated Frank Liles (3-2) at the July box-offs, which determined who was to be included on the Olympic team. Jones had been beaten by Liles at the 1988 U.S. Amateur Championships earlier in the year. Even though Jones was a two-time National Golden Gloves champion, in 1986-87, he took only the bronze medal at the Goodwill Games. He lost to Igor Ruzhnikov of the USSR.

Sources: "Black American Medal Winners," *Ebony* (December 1988); "Seoul Games/Medal Winners," *Los Angeles Times* (October 3, 1988); *1988 United States Olympic Team, Media Guide; Seoul '88*; "Olympics Record," *USA Today* (October 3, 1988).

JORDAN, MICHAEL JEFFERY (USA). Born February 17, 1963, in Wilmington, North Carolina.

1984 Gold Medal: Basketball

During his college basketball career, at the University of North Carolina, Michael Jordan was chosen National Player of the Year by the U.S. Basketball Writers Association,

United Press International, and *Sporting News* and was winner of the Wooden Award, the Naismith Trophy, and the Eastman Award. Jordan received All-American honors after the 1982-83 and 1983-84 seasons and was named National Player of the Year in 1982-83 by *The Sports News*. Jordan led the AAC in scoring in 1984. He did this with a 19.6 points per game average, shooting 55.1 percent from the field. In 3 years at North Carolina he hit 54 percent from the field, 74.8 percent from the line, and averaged 17.7 points and more than 5 rebounds a game. He hit a 16-foot jump shot to win the 1982 NCAA Championship. Jordan was the leading scorer for the gold medal-winning U.S. team at the 1983 Pan Am Games, and he toured Europe with the All-Star team in 1982. Jordan signed professionally with the Chicago Bulls of the NBA in 1984. He is a 6-foot, 6-inch guard who is generally considered the league's most exciting player. The Bulls signed the 22-year-old star to a 7-year, $6 million contract. Clipper Coach Gene Shue, said of Jordan, "Michael is an unbelievable player.... Not only is he a winning player, but he's one of the very best one-on-one players we've ever had in the NBA and probably before it's all over he'll be the very best" (*Los Angeles Times*).

Sources: *Biographical Dictionary of American Sports: Basketball*; British Virgin Islands, Olympic Committee; "The 1984 Olympics," *Ebony* (October 1984); "The Incredible Michael Jordan," *Ebony* (March 1988); "The Champions," *Los Angeles Times* (August 14, 1984); "Clippers Can't Slow Air Jordan," *Los Angeles Times* (March 31, 1988); "Names in the News," *Los Angeles Times* (May 18, 1988); *United States Olympic Team, Media Guide*.

JOYNER, ALFREDERICK (USA). Born January 19, 1960, in East St. Louis, Illinois.

1984 Gold Medal: Triple Jump (56 ft. 7½ in./17.26 m, Olympic record)

Al Joyner attended Arkansas State University and was a member of the Bud Light Track America Club. Joyner reached his peak in 1983 by placing second at the NCAA meet and third at the TAC meet. He took eighth place at the World Championships that same year and also set a personal record of 56 feet, 2¾ inches in 1983, a performance that helped him to be ranked 10th in the world. He won the Modesto Relays on May 11, 1984, and finished third at the UCLA/Pepsi meet the next day. Al and his sister Jackie are called the "first family of track and field," and are the first brother and sister team to win Olympic track and field medals on the same day. Joyner was a decided underdog in competing for the 1984 gold medal. Al calls sister Jackie his inspiration (he has been a much slower starter than she). The 1984 Olympics were the 14th time the brother and sister competed together. Al Joyner is also a national-class high hurdler with a best time of

ALFREDERICK JOYNER (Photo courtesy of Rich Clarkson, Denver, Colorado.)

13.51 seconds, recorded in Zurich in 1985. In October 1987 Joyner married sprinter and Olympic champion Florence Griffith, one of the superstars of the 1988 Summer Olympics. He became his wife's coach in 1988 after she stopped training with Bob Kersee.

Sources: British Virgin Islands, Olympic Committee; "The 1984 Olympics," *Ebony* (October 1984); "Track's First Family," *Los Angeles Times* (July 26, 1984); "The Champions," *Los Angeles Times* (August 14, 1984); "Kersee Says a Split Was Inevitable," *Los Angeles Times* (August 4, 1988); "Winners of the Summer Games," *New York Times* (August 13, 1984); "The Joyners," *Track & Field News* (July 1985); *United States Olympic Team, Media Guide*.

JOYNER-KERSEE, JACQUELINE (USA). Born March 3, 1962, in East St. Louis, Illinois.

1984 Silver Medal: Heptathlon (6,385 points)
1988 Gold Medal: Heptathlon (7,291 points Olympic record/world record)
1988 Gold Medal: Long Jump (24 ft. 3½ in./7.40 m, Olympic record)

Jackie Joyner-Kersee graduated from Lincoln High School in East St. Louis and from UCLA, where she played basketball under the sponsorship of the World Athletic Club. In 1984 Joyner-Kersee set an American record of 6,520 points when she won the heptathlon at the U.S. Olympic trials. In the

JACQUELINE JOYNER-KERSEE (Photo courtesy of Rich Clarkson, Denver, Colorado.)

1988 trials she scored 7,215 points in the heptathlon for her third world record since 1986. She won the Olympics heptathlon with 7,291 points, a world record that beat the old record and her own by 76 points. Her performance in the individual events was: 100-meter hurdles (12.69); high jump (6 feet, 1¼ inches); shot put (51 feet, 10 inches); 200 meters (21.56, world record); 100 meters (10.54, Olympic record); 800 meters (2 minutes, 8.51 seconds, career best); and the long jump (24 feet, 3½ inches, Olympic record—the old Olympic record was her own, 23 feet, 10 inches). Joyner-Kersee was the first U.S. woman to win the Olympic long jump and the first athlete in 64 years to win both a multi-event competition and an individual event in one Olympics. Jackie Joyner-Kersee was called the greatest athlete in high school history. In volleyball she was captain of her team and an All-Metro selection. In track she was the state champion in the 400 meters and long jump. She set a long jump record of 22 feet, 4¼ inches. In basketball she averaged 21 points and 14 rebounds per game. She was a three-time All-State selection and a two-time high school All-American.

As a senior she led the Lincoln High Tigerettes to the state basketball title. In college she was TAC and NCAA heptathlon champion in 1982. Prior to the 1984 Olympics she had a second-best-ever point total by an American. Joyner-Kersee's sprint coach, Bob Kersee (whom she married in January 1986), calls her "the best woman athlete I've ever been associated with" (*Los Angeles Times*). She scores consistently well in all the running and jumping events. Winning four individual events, she contributed 53½ points as the UCLA Bruins claimed the WCAA title on May 10 and 11, 1985, scoring 55.87 seconds in the 400-meter hurdles, she became the seventh fastest American ever. She competed at the WCAA in the 100-meter hurdles (13.31 seconds), the long jump (21 feet 11 inches), the triple jump (42 feet 6¾ inches), and a 1,600-meter relay leg (44.75). Jackie Joyner-Kersee is considered by *Ebony* Magazine to be the best female athlete in the world. In 1986 she set her second world heptathlon record in less than a month, scoring 7,161 points at the Olympic Festival in Houston, where she went to test her endurance in heat and humidity. A few weeks earlier, at the Goodwill Games in Moscow, she had become the first woman to break the 7,000-point barrier, scoring 7,148 and breaking the existing world record by 202 points. These games were especially noteworthy for her because all the outstanding heptathletes participated. This was not true in 1984 when many Eastern European nations boycotted. She set personal bests in the shot put (49 feet, 10½ inches) and in the 200 meters (22.85 seconds, also a world record), and matched her personal best in the high jump (6 feet, 2 inches). The next day in Houston, she became the first person to score more than 3,000 points in the second day's events. She set personal bests in the javelin (164 feet 5 inches) and the long jump (23 feet, ¾ inch, a heptathlon world record) and became the first American athlete to hold the world's multi-event record, male or female. Joyner-Kersee's husband and coach, Bob Kersee, said, "I don't think we've seen the best of Jackie yet." She said, "I don't mean to sound ungrateful, but I set high standards for myself, and I believe if I think positive, good things will happen" (*USA Today*). In 1986 Jackie Joyner-Kersee was awarded the Broderick Cup as America's top female collegiate athlete. In 1987 she won the Sullivan Award as the nation's outstanding amateur athlete and was named the U.S. Olympic Committee's Sportswoman of the Year. In 1988 she was named Amateur Sportswoman of the Year by the Women's Sports Foundation (for the heptathlon and long jump at Seoul, the World Championships, and the Pan Am Games). During a February 1989 awards luncheon in New York City, Joyner-Kersee received *The Sporting News'* Waterford Trophy, a custom-designed piece of Irish crystal valued at $15,000. "We reserve our award for that special person in sports, the one who makes the biggest impact and the most important contribution during the year," said TSN editor Tom Barnidge. She is the first woman to earn this prestigious annual honor.

Sources: "The 1984 Olympics," *Ebony* (October 1984); "The World's Greatest Woman Athlete," *Ebony* (October 1986); "Track's First Family," *Los Angeles Times* (July 16, 1984); "Even If She Doesn't Do It Right," *Los Angeles Times* (July 30, 1984); "Joyner-Kersee Leaps to Her Second Gold," *Los Angeles Times* (September 29, 1988); "Joyner-Kersee Leads," *Los Angeles Times* (September 23, 1988); "Woman of the Year," *Sporting News* (January 2, 1989); "Olympics Record," *USA Today* (October 3, 1988).

JUANTORENA, DANGER ALBERTO (Cuba).
Born December 3, 1951, in Santiago, Cuba.

1976 Gold Medal: 400-Meter Run (44.26)
1976 Gold Medal: 800-Meter Run (1:43.5, Olympic record/ world record)

Alberto Juantorena was called "El Caballo" (the horse). He began his sports career as a basketball player, but switched to track and field at age 19. He won the World Student Games title in 1973 and the following year led the world 400-meter rankings with a time of 44.7 seconds. He barely had any experience in the 800 meters before the Olympic year but dashed to victory in the final in a world record of 1 minute, 43.5 seconds. He became the first man to win both the 400 and the 800 at one Olympics. Many believe that Juantorena was the foremost athlete at the Montreal Games. He was named Athlete of the Year twice in his home country. Juantorena defeated Britain's David Jenkins in the 400 meters for the 1973 World Student Games title and in 1974 topped the world rankings with 44.7 seconds. His best marks were 20.7 for the 200, 44.26 for 400, and 1:43.5 for 800. Alberto Juantorena's 44.26 in the 400 at the 1976 Olympics was the fastest non-altitude time on record. The art of the 400 and 800 has never been more majestically demonstrated. Juantorena is currently president of the Cuban Track and Field Federation.

Sources: *Approved History of Olympic Games; Guinness Book of Olympic Records; International Athletics Annual; Montreal 1976; Games of the XXIst Olympiad; 1980 Olympic Handbook; The Olympic Challenge 88*; "Juantorena Remembered," *Track & Field News* (September 1986); *Who's Who in the Olympic Games.*

KARIUKI, JULIUS (Kenya). Born April 12, 1961, in Kenya.

1988 Gold Medal: 3,000-Meter Steeplechase (8:05.51, Olympic record)

Julius Kariuki set a new Olympic record of 8:05.51, the fastest ever run although only a 10th of a second faster than the 10-year-old record of Henry Rono (also Kenya). Kariuki won the 3,000-meter steeplechase at the International

JULIUS KARIUKI (Photo courtesy of Emmett Jordan, Rich Clarkson and Associates, Denver, Colorado.)

Amateur Athletic Federation Mobil Grand Prix track and field meet at the Crystal Palace in London. His time was 8:15.71. Julius Kariuki's chance came after he placed sixth in the World Indoor 3,000-meter in Indianapolis in 1987. When he came to the U.S., he went first to Blinn Community College in Texas, invited by Coach Steve Silvey. He became a major cog in Blinn's cross-country team, placing eighth at the Junior College Nationals. Next he was called to Riverside Community College by Ted Banks. Kariuki became the 1985 World Cup champion and competed in his first 10,000-meter run. He won the Kenyan trials in the 3,000-meter steeplechase in an altitude-slowed 8:23.3 and knew he was ready. Both coaches agree that Kariuki is the man who has what it takes to go under the 8-minute barrier.

Sources: British Virgin Islands, Olympic Committee; *International Amateur Athletic Federation*; "Bile Beats Cram," *Los Angeles Times* (July 9, 1988); "Seoul Games/Medal Winners," *Los Angeles Times* (October 3, 1988); "Exhilarating Kenyan Runners," *Seoul '88*; "Kenya's Collegiate Connection," *Track & Field News* (December 1988); "Olympics Record," *USA Today* (October 3, 1988).

KEASOR, LLOYD WELDON (USA). Born February 9, 1950, in Pumphrey, Maryland.

1976 Silver Medal: Freestyle Lightweight Wrestling

Lloyd Keasor graduated from Brooklyn Park High School in Baltimore in 1968 and from the U.S. Naval Academy in 1972. His club coach was Jim Jackson. "Butch" Keasor first came to national prominence with his AAU Championship in 1973. In 1975 he performed the unusual feat of winning both the national Greco-Roman title and the Pan Am Games freestyle title. He won the AAU title again and was thought to be a favorite for the gold medal in Montreal. Keasor was the 1975 UCB freestyle Classic and 1976 national AAU senior freestyle champion. He was on the U.S. AAU senior World Cup freestyle team and was 1973 national AAU All-American. Keasor established himself early as the best wrestler in the freestyle lightweight category at the Olympics. He was leading the competition going into his final match with archrival Pavel Pinigan of the Soviet Union. Keasor and his coaches determined that he could lose to Pinigan and still win the title going into the final match. He just needed to avoid being pinned. He wrestled with that in mind and was beaten decisively on points. (In the demerit system, when a wrestler receives six penalty points, he is eliminated.) The American coaches had miscalculated in their determination that Keasor could lose to Pinigan and still win the gold, and Pinigan's victory by "majority decision" handed him the gold. Keasor is currently a lieutenant in the U.S. Air Force.

Sources: *Approved History of Olympic Games*; *Black Olympians*; *Guinness Book of Olympic Records*; *Quest for Gold*; *United States Olympic Team, Games of the XXIst Olympiad*.

KEDIR, MOHAMMED (Ethiopia). Born September 6, 1953, in Ethiopia.

1980 Bronze Medal: 10,000-Meter Run (27:44.7)

The slightly built Mohammed Kedir gave no quarter to his opponents. In the 1980 Olympics at Moscow, there was a duel between Finland and Ethiopia in the 10,000 meters. The Ethiopians were dominant. Miruts Yifter and Mohammed Kedir changed the pace and exchanged the lead every few hundred meters, and Yifter sprinted into the lead in the final 300 meters. He covered the last 200 in 26.8 seconds and won by 10 meters. Although Maaninka finished in second place, Kedir went ahead of Finland's Viren for third place. Kedir's 1980 bronze medal in the 10,000 meters highlighted a brilliant career that also saw him place first and second in world cross-country championships and set a world best in the half marathon. Mohammed Kedir recorded bests of 13 minutes, 17.5 seconds for 5,000 meters in 1980 and 27:39.44 in the 10,000, in 1981. He is still active.

Sources: *Approved History of Olympic Games*; British Virgin Islands, Olympic Committee; *Complete Book of the Olympics*; *Games of the XXIInd Olympiad, Moscow*; *Guinness Book of Olympic Records*; "Results of Yesterday's Competition at the Olympic Games," *New York Times* (July 28, 1980).

KEINO, KIPCHOGE (Kenya). Born January 17, 1940, in Kipsamo, Kenya.

1968 Gold Medal: 1,500-Meter Run (3:34.91, Olympic record)
1968 Silver Medal: 5,000-Meter Run (14:05.16)
1972 Gold Medal: 3,000-Meter Steeplechase (8:23.64, Olympic record)
1972 Silver Medal: 1,500-Meter Run (3:36.81)

With four Olympic medals Kipchoge Keino has been Africa's most successful athlete in Olympic competition. Keino made his Olympic debut at Tokyo in 1964, finishing fifth in the 5,000 meters but going unplaced in the 1,500. He showed obvious promise, however, and the following year he set new world records at 3,000 and 5,000 meters with times of 7:39.5 and 13:24.2. In 1966 he won titles at both 1 and 3 miles at the Commonwealth Games in Kingston, Jamaica. At the Mexico City Games in 1968 Keino astonished the pundits by entering the 1,500, 5,000, and 10,000 races. He failed to finish the 10,000 but won a silver medal in the 5,000, clocking 14:05.2, behind Mohammed Gammoudi of Tunisia who ran 14:05.0. In the 1,500 he ran an Olympic record time of 3:34.91 to easily defeat co-favorite Jim Ryun of the U.S. and win the gold. Four years later, in Munich, Keino failed in his attempt to defend his 1,500 title, but won the silver in a creditable 3:36.8, five-tenths of a second slower than Finland's Pekka Vasala. Surprisingly, he bypassed the 5,000 in favor of the 3,000-meter steeplechase. Although he was not particularly adept at hurdling the heavy wooden barriers, Keino upset teammate Ben Jipcho to capture the gold medal with a clocking of 8:23.64. Keino's personal bests included times of 3:34.91 at 1,500 meters, 3:53.1 for the mile, 7:39.5 for the 3,000, 12:24.2 for the 5,000, 8:23.64 for the 3,000-meter steeplechase, and 28:06.4 for the 10,000-meter run. Top-ranked in the world at one time or another in the 1,500, 5,000, and steeplechase, Keino had an excellent record in major competitions. Besides two Olympic gold and two Olympic silver medals, Keino also boasted two gold medals at the

THE ATHLETES—King / 67

African Games and three Commonwealth Games victories. A policeman by profession, Kip Keino ran the short-lived ITA professional track circuit in 1973-74. He returned to Kenya where he became involved in a number of business ventures. In 1984 he was named head coach of the Kenya athletic team for the Los Angeles Games.

Sources: *Approved History of Olympic Games*; British Virgin Islands, Olympic Committee; *Encyclopaedia of Athletics; Guinness Book of Olympic Records; Lexikon der 12000 Olympioniken; 1980 Olympic Handbook; Track and Field: The Great Ones; Who's Who in the Olympic Games; Who's Who in Track and Field.*

KERR, GEORGE E. (British West Indies). Born in 1937, in Kingston, Jamaica.

1960 Bronze Medal: 800-Meter Run (1:47.25)
1960 Bronze Medal: 4 x 400-Meter Relay (3:04.13)

George Kerr, a graduate of the University of Illinois, had bests of 45.7 seconds for the 400 meters and 1:45.8 for the 800. He consistently ranked among world leaders in both events in the late 1950s and early 1960s. The 800 meters was expected to be a great duel between 30-year-old world-record holder Roger Moens of Belgium and George Kerr of Jamaica in 1960. Although Kerr won the first semifinal, the second semi produced a surprise when Peter Snell beat Moens. Snell, a little-known New Zealander, had not been taken seriously, but he went on to finish first in the final, with Moens second and Kerr third. Kerr scored 46.1 in the Pan Am 400 in 1959 and took the AAA 880 yards in 1:51.5 in 1961. In the 1962 Commonwealth Games he took the 440 yards in 46.7 and helped his team achieve a score of 3:10.2 in the 4 x 400-yard relay.

Sources: *Approved History of Olympic Games*; British Virgin Islands, Olympic Committee; *Complete Book of the Olympics; Encyclopaedia of Track and Field Athletics; Games of the XVIIth Olympiad, Rome; Guinness Book of Olympic Records; Lexikon der 12000 Olympioniken.*

KILGOUR, LENNOX (Trinidad). Born in Trinidad-Tobago.

1952 Bronze Medal: Middle Heavyweight Weightlifting (887¼ lbs./402.5 kg)

In 1952 at the Helsinki Olympics, Norbert Schemansky of the U.S. won the gold in the middle heavyweight weightlifting event. Gregory Nowak of the Soviet Union took the silver and Lennox Kilgour the bronze.

Sources: *Approved History of Olympic Games*; British Virgin Islands, Olympic Committee; *Complete Book of the Olympics; Guinness Book of Olympic Records; Olympic Games: The Records.*

KILLINGBECK, MOLLY (Canada). Born February 3, 1959, in Jamaica.

1984 Silver Medal: 4 x 400-Meter Relay (3:21.21)

Molly Killingbeck for several years was one of Canada's top all-around sprinters. Her bests for the 100, 200, and 400 meters are 11.25, 22.79, and 51.08 seconds. She was a member of the second-place 1,600-meter relay squad that set a Canadian record at the Los Angeles Games. A former physical education student at York University in Toronto, Killingbeck lives in Scarborough, Ontario.

Sources: British Virgin Islands, Olympic Committee; Canadian Olympic Association; *1984 Olympic Games; Sarajevo/Los Angeles; Research Information, Games of the XXIIIrd Olympiad.*

KIMELI, KIPKEMBOI (Kenya). Born in Kenya.

1988 Bronze Medal: 10,000-Meter Run (27:25.16)

Kipkemboi Kimeli won the bronze in the 10,000 meters in Seoul, behind Salvatore Antibo of Italy, who finished second. Brahim Boutaib, by passing them both to win the gold, stole the Moroccan limelight in that event from compatriot Saïd Aouita.

Sources: British Virgin Islands, Olympic Committee; "Seoul Games/Medal Winners," *Los Angeles Times* (October 3, 1988); *Seoul '88*; "Olympics Record," *USA Today* (October 3, 1988).

KING, JAMES (USA). Born February 9, 1943, in New Orleans, Louisiana.

1968 Gold Medal: Basketball

James King graduated from Oklahoma State University in 1966. A forward at Oklahoma State, he was named to the All-Big Eight Conference in 1966. King played for several years for the AAU with the Goodyear Wingfoots and later (1967-68) played with the Inter-Continental Cup Champions.

Sources: *Approved History of Olympic Games; Guinness Book of Olympic Records; Lexikon der 12000 Olympioniken; Quest for Gold; United States Olympic Team, Games of the XIXth Olympiad.*

KING, LEAMON (USA). Born February 13, 1936, in Tulare, California.

1956 Gold Medal: 4 x 100-Meter Relay (39.60, Olympic record/world record)

Leamon King of the University of California placed only fourth at the Olympic final trials, after he had set the world record of 9.3 seconds for the 100 yards in May 1956. However, he made the Olympic team as a member of the relay squad. King twice equaled the world record of 10.1 for the 100 meters after the Melbourne team had been chosen. On both occasions he beat Bobby Morrow who later won the Olympic title. King's major championship was the AAU 100 yards in 1957. His gold medal-winning 400-meter relay team broke the world record and Olympic record with 39.5. After the Olympics, he ran on the world record U.S. 800-meter (880-yard) relay team that ran 1:23.8 in Sydney, Australia, in December 1956.

Sources: *Black Olympians; Guinness Book of Olympic Records; Hard Road to Glory; Olympic Games, Melbourne, 1956; Quest for Gold; Track and Field: The Great Ones; Who's Who in Track and Field*.

KINGDOM, ROGER (USA). Born October 26, 1962, in Vienna, Georgia.

1984 Gold Medal: 110-Meter Hurdles (13.20, Olympic record)
1988 Gold Medal: 110-Meter Hurdles (12.98, Olympic record)

At the Michelob Invitational in San Diego on June 24, 1988, Roger Kingdom easily beat Greg Foster in the 110-meter hurdles in 13.17 seconds, while running into a head wind of 2.76 meters per second. Kingdom became the second man ever to crack the 13-second barrier in the 110. He won the event in 12.97 (high altitude), and came within .04 of the world record (12.93) set by Renaldo Nehemiah in 1981. Kingdom had developed very rapidly in 1983. He won both the NCAA and the Pan Am Games titles and achieved a world ranking of eighth. Early in the 1984 season he set a personal record of 13.44 and lowered that to 13.43. He also won the NCAA indoor high hurdles title in 1983. Kingdom's time of 13.20 in the 110-meter hurdles at the 1984 Olympics was both an Olympic record and a personal best. He improved his personal record to 13.14 in 1985. In Seoul he ran the third-fastest time ever (12.98). An excellent all-around athlete, Kingdom is a former Georgia high school discus champion and has high-jumped 7 feet. A 1983 graduate of the University of Pittsburgh, he was affiliated with the New Image Track Club.

Sources: British Virgin Islands, Olympic Committee; "The 1984 Olympics," *Ebony* (October 1984); "The Champions," *Los Angeles Times* (August 14, 1984); "Over the Hump," *Los Angeles Times* (June 24, 1988); "Kingdom 13.17 Into Wind, Routs Foster," *Los Angeles Times* (June 26, 1988) "Kingdom Takes 110 Hurdles," *Los Angeles Times* (August 12, 1988); "Kingdom Overcomes Favored Foster," *Track & Field News* (September 1984); *United States Olympic Team, Media Guide*.

KIPRUGUT CHUMA, WILSON (Kenya). Born in 1938 in Kericho, Kenya.

1964 Bronze Medal: 800-Meter Run (1:45.9)
1968 Silver Medal: 800-Meter Run (1:44.57)

Wilson Kiprugut Chuma won the 400 meters in the African Games in 1965 with a 46.9 clocking and the 800 meters in 1:47.4. The final in the 800 at Tokyo the year before saw Kiprugut lead the field for 550 meters. Snell, the New Zealander, swung outside and went on to win. Kiprugut tripped on George Kerr's heel 50 yards from the finish but still gained a bronze medal. This was the first Olympic medal ever won by a Kenyan. William Crothers of Canada won the silver. Although Kiprugut Chuma, half-miler, won two Olympic medals and rarely finished a meet under third, he was never quite able to shake his "bridesmaid" reputation, as his only major championship victory came in the African Games. As a fairly good quarter-miler, he was a frontrunner rather than a "kicker."

Sources: *Africa at the Olympics; Approved History of Olympic Games*; British Virgin Islands, Olympic Committee; *Complete Book of the Olympics; Encyclopaedia of Track and Field Athletics; The Games, Organizing Committee of the XIXth Olympiad; Guinness Book of Olympic Records; Lexikon der 12000 Olympioniken*.

KOECH, PETER (Kenya). Born February 18, 1958, in Kiliburani, Kenya.

1988 Silver Medal: 3,000-Meter Steeplechase (8:06.79)

In 1988, for the first time in Olympic history, Kenya took first and second place in the 3,000-meter steeplechase. Julius Kariuki and Peter Koech dominated the race. Winning it in 8:11.61, Koech bettered the previous best for the season (set at the Nikai Grand Prix track and field meet) by almost 4 seconds.

Sources: *International Amateur Athletic Federation*; "Bubka Leaps to Pole Vault World Mark," *Los Angeles Times* (July 11, 1988); "Seoul Games/Medal Winners," *Los Angeles Times* (October 3, 1988); "Exhilarating Kenyan Runners," *Seoul '88*; "Olympics Record," *USA Today* (October 3, 1988).

KOGO, BENJAMIN (Kenya). Born in 1946, in Kapsumb, Kenya.

1968 Silver Medal: 3,000-Meter Steeplechase (8:51.56)

A versatile steeplechaser, Benjamin Kogo once won a national title in the 400-meter hurdles. He first made an impact with a third-place finish in the 3,000-meter steeplechase at the 1966 British Empire Games. Winner of the 3,000-meter steeplechase in the 1965 African Games (with 8:47.4) he went into the 1968 Olympics as co-favorite in the steeple but was surprisingly beaten by unorthodox fellow Kenyan Amos Biwott. During the 3,000-meter steeplechase at the Mexico City Olympics, there was great curiosity as to how well neophyte Amos Biwott would stand up in the final 2 days. He had to compete with favorites Ben Kogo, Victor Kudinsky, and George Young. Biwott let Kogo do most of the pace-setting. Kogo took the lead from Belgian Gaston Roelants, but with 300 meters left, Young made his move, passing Kogo on the backstretch. Kogo fought him off, only to be passed by Biwott. Although Kogo was still in front as they cleared the last hurdle, 60 meters from the finish, Biwott passed him and won by 3 meters.

Sources: *Approved History of Olympic Games*; British Virgin Islands, Olympic Committee; *Complete Book of the Olympics; Encyclopaedia of Track and Field Athletics; The Games, Organizing Committee of the XIXth Olympiad; Guinness Book of Olympic Records; Lexikon der 12000 Olympioniken*.

KONYEGWACKIE, PETER (Nigeria). Born in Nigeria.

1984 Silver Medal: Featherweight Boxing

To win the silver medal featherweight boxing in the 1984 Olympics, Peter Konyegwackie defeated Ali Faki of Malawi, points 5-0; Rafael Zuniga Medrano of Colombia, 2-3, reversed by the jury, 4-1; and Charles Lubuiwa of Uganda, 5-0. (final) He lost in the final to Meldrick Taylor of the U.S.

Sources: "The Champions," *Los Angeles Times* (August 14, 1984); *Official Report of the Games of the XXIIIrd Olympiad*; "Olympic Medal Results, *Sporting News* (August 3, 1984).

KORIR, JULIUS (Kenya). Born April 21, 1960, in Kenya.

1984 Gold Medal: 3,000-Meter Steeplechase (8:11.80)

Julius Korir won a scholarship to Washington State University following his upset victory in the 3,000-meter steeplechase at the 1982 Commonwealth Games in Brisbane, Australia. His time was 8 minutes, 23.94 seconds. Korir won the NCAA Championship in the 5,000-meter run in 1984 and twice placed second in the NCAA steeplechase before winning his first NCAA title in his specialty in 1986. Julius Korir's seventh-place finish at the World Championships was a major disappointment, but he atoned for that loss with a gold medal at the Los Angeles Olympics, which gained for him *Track & Field News'* number 1 ranking for 1984. Injured in 1985, the affable Korir made a successful return to international competition in 1986, adding several impressive performances in Europe to his NCAA triumph. Korir's

best performance in the 3,000-meter steeplechase is 7:48.90; he has also clocked 12:38.7 in the 5,000-meter run and 3:40.31 in the 1,500.

Sources: British Virgin Islands, Olympic Committee; "The Champions," *Los Angeles Times* (August 14, 1984); *The 1984 Games*; "Olympic Medal Results," *Sporting News* (August 27, 1984); "Korir Defuses Marsh's Kick," *Track & Field News* (September 1984).

LABEACH, LLOYD (Panama). Born June 28, 1923, in Panama City, Panama (of Jamaican parentage).

1948 Bronze Medal: 100-Meter Run (10.4)
1948 Bronze Medal: 200-Meter Run (21.2)

Lloyd LaBeach, who spent most of his running career in the U.S., attended UCLA. With Olympic bronzes at both 100 and 200 meters in 1948, LaBeach ranked among the world's best in the late 1940s, although his best year was 1950 when he ranked first in the world in the 200. His personal best performance of 10.1 in the 100 broke a 100-meter record in 1950. LaBeach was the archrival of USC's Mel Patton. They faced stiff competition in the 1948 100 meters in London from Harrison Dillard and Barney Ewell. Dillard flashed into the lead and held it the entire way. Ewell caught him at the tape and mistakingly thought he had won. LaBeach had to settle for third place. He is the only Panamanian to have won an Olympic medal. LaBeach's brother Sam joined him on Panamanian teams that won several medals in both the 400 and 1,600 relays in regional competition. Another LaBeach, Byron, ran for Jamaica, also in the later 1940s and early 1950s. More recently Lloyd LaBeach has been in the dairy business.

Sources: *Approved History of Olympic Games*; British Virgin Islands, Olympic Committee; *Complete Book of the Olympics; Encyclopaedia of Track and Field Athletics; Guinness Book of Olympic Records; Official Report of the Organizing Committee for the XIVth Olympiad*.

LAING, LESLIE (Jamaica). Born February 19, 1925, in Linstead, Jamaica.

1952 Gold Medal: 4 x 400-Meter Relay (3:04.04, Olympic record/world record)

Leslie Laing won six medals during 1950-54. A quarter-miler, he ran the second leg in the 1,600-meter relay at the 1952 Olympics, pinned against American Gene Cole. Jamaica won the gold in that event, with the U.S. taking the silver, and Germany the bronze.

Sources: *Approved History of Olympic Games*; British Virgin Islands, Olympic Committee; *Guinness Book of Olympic Records; Incredible Olympic Feats; 1984 Olympic Handbook; Official Report of the Organizing Committee, XVth Olympiad; Olympic Games: The Records*.

LANNAMAN, SONIA M. (Great Britain). Born March 24, 1956, in England (of Jamaican parentage).

1980 Bronze Medal: 4 x 100-Meter Relay (42.43)

Sonia Lannaman was a 100-meter champion in the Commonwealth Games in 1978 with a 11.27. She also was a member of the 4 x 100-meter relay team in 1978 with a 43.70. She won the European Indoor Championships in the 60 meters in 1976, and in 1973 she took the European Jr. Championships in the 100 meters and the 4 x 100-meter relay. In the United Kingdom Championships she won the following women's events: 100 in 1977 (11.30) and 1978 (11.24); 200 in 1977 (23.16) and 1978 (23.16). Her personal bests over the years were 11.20 and 22.58. Lannaman competed at the Munich, Montreal, and Moscow Olympics. Her only medal came at Moscow in 1980 where she anchored the British 4 x 100-meter relay team.

Sources: British Virgin Islands, Olympic Committee; *Complete Book of the Olympics; Encyclopaedia of Track and Field Athletics; Guinness Book of Olympic Records*.

LAWRENCE, ALBERT (Jamaica). Born April 26, 1961, in Jamaica.

1984 Silver Medal: 4 x 100-Meter Relay (38.62)

Albert Lawrence, who attended Abilene Christian College in Abilene, Texas, led off Jamaica's silver medal-winning foursome at the Los Angeles Games. Known for an explosive start, Lawrence has enjoyed most of his major success indoors. His best 100-meter time is 10.34 seconds.

Sources: British Virgin Islands, Olympic Committee; *1984 Olympic Games*; "The Games," *Olympian* (October/ November 1984).

LAWRENCE, JANICE (USA). Born June 7, 1962, in Lucedale, Mississippi.

1984 Gold Medal: Basketball

Janice Lawrence graduated in 1984 from Louisiana Tech University where she was a member of two National Championship teams and the 1983 NCAA runner-up team. She scored 20.7 points per game during the 1982-83 season, averaged nine rebounds, and led the team in steals. She was MVP of the 1982 NCAA Championships and unanimous MVP of the 1984 NCAA Midwest Regional Tournament. During her years at Louisiana Tech, the women's team compiled an incredible 130-6 mark. Janice Lawrence completed her collegiate career in 1984 with 2,403 points, 1,097 rebounds, and 194 assists, missing just one of 136 games in that time. She was a member of the 1983 Pan Am Games and World Championship teams, the 1982 U.S. National team, and the 1981 USA Jr. National team. She was also MVP and all-tournament selection at the 1981

National Sports Festival. Lawrence was the first college senior picked by the Professional Women's American Basketball Association in 1984, and she signed with the New York franchise. She was 1984 Wade Trophy winner (averaging 20.7 points and 9.1 rebounds) and 1984 Champion Player of the Year. Lawrence was also twice selected as Kodak All-American and three times chosen for the NCAA All-Tournament team.

Sources: "The 1984 Olympics," *Ebony* (October 1984); *For the Record*; "Aussie Coach Calls U.S. Best Ever," *Los Angeles Times* (August 1, 1984); "The Champions," *Los Angeles Times* (August 14, 1984); "Basketball," *Olympian* (October/November 1984); "Olympic Medal Results," *Sporting News* (August 13, 1984); *United States Olympic Team, Media Guide*; "Best Bets from the U.S." *Women's Sports* (November 1983).

LEATHERWOOD, LILLIE (USA). Born July 6, 1964, in Northport, Alabama.

1984 Gold Medal: 4 x 400-Meter Relay (3:18.29, Olympic record)

Lillie Leatherwood graduated from Tuscaloosa County High School in 1982 and attended the University of Alabama. New on the scene, Leatherwood posted a personal record of 50.98 early in the 1984 season. She later won the SEC Conference 400 title. She came in second in the NCAA Indoor 400 and ran on Alabama's seventh-place 4 x 100-meter relay team at the NCAA Outdoor meet in 1983. Leatherwood's previous personal record was 53.2 in 1983. Leatherwood held the American collegiate record in the 400 at 50.18 in 1986, and thus became the second-fastest collegian and fourth-fastest American ever. She held 9 of the 10 fastest times ever recorded in the 400 by American collegians. She finished 1986 ranked number 3 in the U.S. and number 6 in the world in the 400. Her coach, Wayne Williams, felt that she was talented enough to become the best in the country by 1988. Leatherwood finished fourth in the 400 meters in the 1984 Olympic trials with a time of 50.68. The year 1987 was outstanding for her: she won the NCAA Championships for the second straight year, won the TAC title, and broke the 50-second barrier for the first time, running a personal best of 49.95. She was first in the U.S. (1987) and third on the all-time U.S. Women's list. She also finished the year fifth in world ranking.

Sources: "The 1984 Olympics," *Ebony* (October 1984); "The Champions," *Los Angeles Times* (August 14, 1984); *1988 United States Olympic Team, Media Guide*; "Olympic Medal Results," *Sporting News* (August 17, 1988); "National 400 Meter Champions," *Track & Field News* (August 1985); "Leatherwood Ready for School," *Track & Field News* (May 1987); *United States Olympic Team, Media Guide*.

LEE, NORVEL LA FOLLETTE RAY (USA). Born September 22, 1924.

1952 Gold Medal: Light Heavyweight Boxing

Norvel Lee won the AAU Championship in 1950 and 1951 and was awarded the Val Barker trophy (as the best boxer in any division) in 1952. Lee came to the fore as a light heavyweight when he lost in the 1948 Olympic trials in the heavyweight class to Jay Lambert. By losing weight and outshining Charles Spiesen in training, Lee entered and became successful in the light heavyweight division. Norvel Lee earned a master's degree from Howard University.

Sources: *Approved History of Olympic Games; Black Olympians; Complete Book of the Olympics; Guinness Book of Olympic Records; Quest for Gold; United States Team for 1952 Olympic Games.*

LEONARD, SILVIO (Cuba). Born September 20, 1955, in Cienguegos, Cuba.

1980 Silver Medal: 100-Meter Run (10.25)

Silvio Leonard's world-class records in the 100 meters were 9.9 (June 5, 1975) and 9.9 (March 27, 1977). He won in the Pan Am Games in the 100 in 1975 (10.15) and in 1979 (10.3). His win in the 200 in the same games was in 1979 (20.37). When the U.S. athletes boycotted the 1980 Olympics, the mantle of favorite in the 100 fell to Silvio Leonard. His 100-meter race in 1980 with Allan Wells was one of the closest in Olympic history as the two crossed the line simultaneously. Neither was sure who had won. It was so close that they could not be separated even by 1/100th of a second at 10.25 seconds. Wells won on the basis of the photo of the finish. Despite his silver medal, Silvio Leonard left his countrymen wondering what might have been. Twice a Pan Am champion at 100 meters and once at 200, Leonard had best times of 9.98 and 20.6 to his credit. However, an apparent lack of dedication often caused him to perform at less than his best in important meets, and this was most evident in the sprint relay. He was possibly the world's best all-around sprinter of the 1970s.

Sources: British Virgin Islands, Olympic Committee; *Complete Book of the Olympics; Encyclopaedia of Track and Field Athletics; Games of the XXIInd Olympiad, Moscow; Guinness Book of Olympic Records;* "Results of Moscow Olympics," *New York Times* (July 26, 1980).

LEONARD, "SUGAR" RAY CHARLES (USA). Born April 17, 1956, in Wilmington, Delaware.

1976 Gold Medal: Light Welterweight Boxing

Sugar Ray Leonard was Golden Gloves champion twice (1974-75), North American Amateur champion twice (1974-75), and AAU champion twice (1974-75). He won the gold medal at the 1975 Pan Am Games. Leonard turned professional in 1977 and became a top welterweight and a media favorite. After winning the light welterweight Olympic gold he later became world welterweight champion. He won the first title in 1979 by defeating Wilfred Benitez for the World Boxing Association's version of the welterweight championship. His only loss was to Roberto Duran in 1980. Leonard regained the title from Duran in 1981 by a technical knockout in the eighth round. In 1981, Leonard fought Tommy Hearns for the World Boxing Championship version of the welterweight crown and to unify the title. He won the fight and collected $10 million, the largest paycheck ever taken home by a boxer (to that point). Leonard later also won the light middleweight title in 1981 by defeating Ayub Kabule. Leonard's presumed last fight was in early 1982, when he was diagnosed as having a detached retina. Although it was repaired, he retired from the ring and later worked as a boxing commentator for television. Sugar Ray made a successful comeback against "Marvelous" Marvin Hagler in 1987, defeating him soundly. In Las Vegas on November 7, 1988, Leonard knocked out Canadian Donny Lalonde. By so doing, he won the World Boxing Council's light heavyweight championship, as well as the newly created super middleweight division title. That made five championships for Leonard.

Sources: *Approved History of Olympic Games; Black Olympians;* British Virgin Islands, Olympic Committee; *Guinness Book of Olympic Records;* "Sugar Ray Rises," *Los Angeles Times* (November 8, 1988); *Montreal 1976, Games of the XXIst Olympiad;* "Olympic Summaries," *New York Times* (August 2, 1976); *Quest for Gold; Olympic Team, Games of the Olympiad.*

LEWIS, CHARLOTTE (USA). Born September 10, 1955, in Chicago, Illinois.

1976 Silver Medal: Basketball

Charlotte Lewis graduated from Woodruff High School in Peoria, Illinois, in 1973 and from Illinois State University in 1977. In high school Lewis participated in volleyball, track and field, and softball. In college she was in volleyball, track and field, and basketball. Her club affiliation was with Taft for softball, basketball, volleyball and with Don Musicland for softball. Lewis won a record in rebounding at Illinois State, with 1,700 points over 4 years. She was in the nationals in the 1973-74 season and during her college athletics career won medals in the javelin, high jump, long jump, open 220, and basketball. She participated and won medals in major national and international basketball contests. Lewis was elected to the Illinois State Basketball Hall of Fame and was named Tri-County Athlete of the Year (Kodak All-American), Pre Street and Smith All-American, and Philadelphia Classic All-American. As a professional, Lewis played for France (La Gerbe), where she won a gold medal in 1978-79 and was named Sportsman of the Year;

for the Iowa Cornets, who were second in the world for the 1979-80 season; for Nebraska who were first in the world for the 1980-81 season; and for Chicago Spirit (1984 season). Lewis has coached men's teams (Warner All-Stars and 505 Jannos in basketball) and women's teams (Taft softball and volleyball). She was also player coach assistant for Chicago Spirit.

Sources: Lewis, Charlotte. Questionnaire. 1984; *Black Olympians; Guinness Book of Olympic Records; Montreal 1976, Games of the XXIst Olympiad; Quest for Gold*.

FREDERICK CARLTON LEWIS (Photo courtesy of Amateur Athletic Foundation, Los Angeles, California, and Robert Long AAF/LPI 1984.)

LEWIS, FREDERICK CARLTON (USA). Born
July 1, 1961, in Birmingham, Alabama.

1984 Gold Medal: 100-Meter Run (9.99)
1984 Gold Medal: 200-Meter Run (19.8, Olympic record)
1984 Gold Medal: Long Jump (28 ft. ½ in./8.54 m)
1984 Gold Medal: 4 x 100-Meter Relay (37.83, Olympic record/world record)
1988 Gold Medal: 100-Meter Run (9.92)
1988 Gold Medal: Long Jump (28 ft. 7½ in./8.72 m)
1988 Silver Medal: 200-Meter Run (19.79, Olympic record)

Carl Lewis attended the University of Houston where he was coached by Tom Tellez. He is a member of the Santa Monica Track Club. Lewis was the first winner of four gold medals in a single Olympics since Jesse Owens. These four wins were all world-class performances. In addition, Lewis has set many other records and won numerous other honors. He was named Athlete of the Year by *Track & Field News* in 1982, 1983, and 1984 and was first in the world in 1987 in the 200 meters (he finished behind Ben Johnson in the 100 in 1987). At the 1987 World Championships he equaled the previous world record of Calvin Smith (9.93) but was outrun by Johnson, who won with 9.83. Johnson defeated Lewis three times in 1987. Lewis grew up in an unusual environment. His sports-oriented parents were high school teachers. Both his father, Bill, a track coach, and his mother, Evelyn, an international hurdler, encouraged their children in sports. Their daughter, Carol, is one of the world's leading women long jumpers, and their eldest son is a soccer coach. Lewis's only coach in the long jump before college had been his mother, and still he was jumping 26 feet, 8 inches his senior year. The long jump has been his first love. Lewis actually met Jesse Owens at a school awards ceremony, and Owens gave him the same advice he himself had received, "Dedication will bring its rewards." Lewis had two main ambitions: to equal Jesse Owens's four gold medals and to become the first man to break the 30-foot barrier in the long jump. In 1988 Carl Lewis won the 100 meters at the Olympic trials, running a wind-aided 9.78, which was the fastest 100 ever recorded. He also won the long jump with a leap of 28 feet, 9 inches. The dominant long jumper in the world over the past few years, Lewis broke the 28-foot barrier 17 times in 1987. That same year, he won the Mount San Antonio relays, TAC, the Pan Am Games, and the World Championships. Lewis has threatened Bob Beamon's unbelievable record of 29 feet, 2½ inches. At the 30th Annual Mount San Antonio College Relays in Walnut, California (1988), Lewis placed only fifth in the 100 meters. This unaccustomed position for America's premier sprinter placed him behind first-place winner Texas Christian University's Raymond Stewart of Jamaica. At Seoul in the 100 Lewis's worst fears were realized. He was defeated by his archrival, Canadian Ben Johnson. Johnson's incredible time for the event was 9.79 (Lewis finished at 9.92). This was the greatest margin of victory in the 100 since the introduction of automatic timing. Johnson's legendary fast start was credited for the victory. Two days after winning the gold, the steroid stanzolol was discovered in Johnson's urine and he was stripped of his medal and record. Thus Lewis was named winner of the gold in what became one of the most highly publicized contests in the history of the Olympic Games. During the 1988 Olympics Lewis ran an American record in the 100 of 9.92 (bettered only by Ben Johnson's run in Rome in 1987 and by Johnson's disqualified time of 9.79 in Seoul). Lewis also leaped the sixth farthest jump ever with 8.72 meters (28 feet, 6 inches), and ran the fourth fastest 200 with 19.79. All this was done with a tight schedule between long jump and 200 heats. Tom Tellez, his coach, stated: "He is phenomenal." Carl Lewis is considered to have star personality. He is loved by some fans and envied by many fellow athletes. He has great self-confidence and dedication, but also is considered self-important. However, his winning four gold medals in 1984 and his many other achievements cannot be underrated. At top speed, he seems to have a high gear that no one else can equal.

Sources: "The 1984 Olympics," *Ebony* (October 1984); "The World's Fastest Human," *Ebony* (May 1988); "Lewis," *Los Angeles Times* (July 1984); "Lewis Continues Gold Rush with Long Jumping," *Los Angeles Times* (August 7, 1984); "Lewis Slips All the Way to Fifth," *Los Angeles Times* (April 25, 1988); "Lewis Wins 100," *Los Angeles Times* (June 28, 1988); "Johnson Suspended Two Years," *Los Angeles Times* (October 25, 1988); *Seoul '88*; "Olympic Medal Results," *Sporting News* (August 13, 1984); "Triumph and Tragedy in L.A.," *Sports Illustrated* (August 20, 1984); "Lewis Again," *Track & Field News* (January 1985).

LEWIS, LENNOX (Canada). Born February 9, 1965, in London, England.

1988 Gold Medal: Super Heavyweight Boxing

Lennox Lewis attended school in Kitchener, Ontario, where he still lives. He was named Athlete of the Year of Canada in 1983. His coaches were Arnie Boehm and Adrian Teodorescu. Lewis's medal-winning performances include: gold, February 1983, Canada Winter Games; gold, November 1983, World Jr. Championships, Dominican Republic; gold, January 1984, Stockholm Box-Open International Tournament; gold, March 1984, National Senior Championships; gold, March 1985, National Senior Championships; gold, June 1985, Albena Tournament, Bulgaria; gold, August 1985, North American Championships, Beaumont, Texas; silver, November 1985, World Cup, Seoul; gold, March 1986, National Senior Championships; gold, July 1986, Commonwealth Games, Edinburgh; gold, December 1986, Quebec Cup, Montreal; gold, January 1987, Box Open Tournament, Stockholm; gold, March 1987, National Senior Championships; gold, April 1987, French International Tournament, St. Nazaire; silver, August 1987, Pan Am Games, Indianapolis; gold, August 1987, North American Championships, Toronto; gold, November 1987, Felix Stamm Tournament, Warsaw; silver, April 1988, Intercup, Karlsruhe, West Germany; gold, June 1988, Canada Cup, Ottawa; gold, September 1988, Olympic Games, Seoul.

Sources: Lewis, Lennox. Questionnaire; "Seoul Games/Medal Winners," *Los Angeles Times* (October 3, 1988); *Seoul '88*; "Olympic Record," *USA Today* (October 3, 1988).

LEWIS, RAYMOND GRAY (Canada). Born October 8, 1910, in Hamilton, Ontario.

1932 Bronze Medal: 4 x 400-Meter Relay (3:12.8)

Ray Lewis was the leadoff runner in the 4 x 400 race at the 1932 Olympics in Los Angeles, and Guyanese-born Phil Edwards ran the third leg. During his career Lewis won titles in 100, 220, and 440-yard runs and in the mile relay. He twice won the national 440-yard title. He also took the silver in the mile relay and won the 600-yard indoor title. Lewis is married to Vivienne Lewis and has a son, Larry.

Sources: *Approved History of Olympic Games*; Canadian Olympic Association; *Complete Book of the Olympics*; *Guinness Book of Olympic Records*.

LEWIS, STEVE (USA). Born May 16, 1969.

1988 Gold Medal: 400-Meter Run (43.87)
1988 Gold Medal: 4 x 400-Meter Relay (2:56.16, Olympic record)

Steve Lewis set the World Jr. mark in the 400 meters at the U.S. Olympic track and field trials in Indianapolis in July 1988. His time was 44.11. He won the gold in the 4 x 400-meter relay when he ran the second leg at Seoul. Danny Everett ran first, Kevin Robinzine third, and Butch Reynolds anchor. Reynolds won by at least 40 meters. By finishing first in the 400 meters at Seoul, Steve Lewis won the World Jr. record. At 19, he was the least experienced of the three Americans. He finished third in Olympic trials. In the finals he ran a 44.37. In the semifinals he set a World Jr. record of 44.11. Lewis had an outstanding freshman year at UCLA, finishing second behind teammate Danny Everett at the NCAA meet. He repeated this position behind Everett at the PAC-10 Championships. In addition, Lewis ran on UCLA's 4 x 400-meter relay championship team, setting an NCAA record of 2:59.91.

Sources: "Seoul Games/Medal Winners," *Los Angeles Times* (October 3, 1988); *1988 United States Olympic Team, Media Guide*; *Seoul '88*; "Olympics Record," *USA Today* (October 3, 1988).

LIDDIE, EDWARD (USA). Born July 24, 1959, in Union, Georgia.

1984 Bronze Medal: Extra Lightweight Judo

Edward Liddie graduated from New York Prep School in New York City in 1977 and earned a degree in physical education from Cumberland College (Kentucky) in 1983. As a student he participated in track and baseball as well as judo. Liddie won the judo Collegiate Championships in 1981 and 1982 and was third in 1979. He won the 1983 Senior National title and was fourth at both the World

Championships in Moscow and the Pan Am Games. He finished second at the National Sports Festival and won a silver medal at the 1984 Belgium Open. Edward Liddie is a former teacher who now works in the hotel and restaurant industry in Colorado Springs.

Sources: "The 1984 Olympics," *Ebony* (October 1984); "The Champions," *Los Angeles Times* (August 14, 1984); "Judo," *Olympian* (October/November 1984); *United States Olympic Team, Media Guide*.

LONDON, JACK E. (Great Britain). Born in 1905, in British Guiana.

1928 Silver Medal: 100-Meter Run (10.9)
1928 Bronze Medal: 4 x 100-Meter Relay (41.8)

Jack London, a medical student at London University, was called "Mr. London of London." Many thought he might have beaten Percy Williams if he had been entered in the 200 meters as well as the 100. Williams, a 19-year-old high school student from Vancouver, British Columbia, beat London and George Lammers of Germany to the tape, scoring the first stunning surprise at the Amsterdam Olympics. London finished second. London was trained by the Italian professional coach Mussabini, as was fellow Guianese Harry Edward.

Sources: *Approved History of Olympic Games; Black College Sport;* British Olympic Association; British Virgin Islands, Olympic Committee; *Guinness Book of Olympic Records.*

LUVALLE, JAMES ELLIS (USA). Born November 10, 1912, in San Antonio, Texas.

1936 Bronze Medal: 400-Meter Run (46.84)

James LuValle proved himself to be a great furlong runner while at UCLA. He ran 20.8 for 220 yards on a straightaway in 1934. The only sprinters in the world who matched his time that year were Bob Kiesel and Foy Draper. In 1935 Jimmy LuValle took the big NCAA 440 yards in 47.7 and moved up to the quarter-mile. He brought his best 440-yard time down to 47.1 at the Princeton Invitational in the Olympic year. Two weeks later he would attain the best mark of his career—46.3 in the 400 at the western Olympic trials. A Phi Beta Kappa scholar, LuValle went on to earn his doctorate in chemistry. He later became a college professor at Stanford University.

Sources: *Black Olympians; Guinness Book of Olympic Records; Hard Road to Glory; Illustrated History of the Olympics; Quest for Gold; United States Track and Field Olympians.*

MAGERS, ROSE (USA). Born June 25, 1960, in Big Spring, Texas.

1984 Silver Medal: Volleyball

Rose Magers attended the University of Houston where she was named MVP for 3 years (1978-80). She also won the Best Hitter award at the 1979 National Sports Festival. Magers joined the National team in 1982 and participated on the 1982 World Championship team that won the bronze medal.

Sources: "The 1984 Olympics," *Ebony* (October 1984); "The Champions," *Los Angeles Times* (August 14, 1984); *United States Olympic Team, Media Guide*.

MAIYEGUN, NOJIM (Nigeria). Born in Nigeria.

1964 Bronze Medal: Light Middleweight Boxing

During the 1964 Olympics in Tokyo, Nojim Maiyegun competed in light middleweight boxing as follows: (series 2) he defeated William Robinson of Britain when the referee stopped the match because of a head blow, in the first round, 1 minute, 59 seconds; (series 3) he won by defeating Tom Frank Bogs of Denmark, when the referee stopped the match in the first round, 58 seconds. Maiyegun was the first Nigerian to win an Olympic medal.

Sources: *Approved History of Olympic Games; Complete Book of the Olympics; Games of the XVIIIth Olympiad, Tokyo 1964; Guinness Book of Olympic Records.*

MANNING, DANNY (USA). Born May 17, 1966.

1988 Bronze Medal: Basketball

Danny Manning graduated from the University of Kansas in 1988 with a degree in communications. As a college basketball player, he was unanimously selected for three years in a row as both AP's and UPI's Big Eight Conference Player of the Year and was named first team All-America by *Basketball Weekly*, UPI, AP, *Sporting News*, Naismith, Kodak, and *Basketball Times*. He was also *Basketball Weekly*, Naismith, Wooden, Joe Lapchick, Red Auerbach, ABAUSA, and CBS/Chevrolet Player of the Year. Manning was all-time leading scorer at Kansas, with 2,951 points, and all-time rebounder, with 1,197. He completed his career as the sixth all-time leading scorer in NCAA history. He is the first player since David Thompson of North Carolina State in 1974 to win both the Collegiate Player of the Year and the NCAA Tournament MVP award in the same year. Manning finished his career as second all-time leading scorer in NCAA tournament history with 328 points, second only to Elvin Hayes's 358 points. In the 1988 NCAA title game, against Oklahoma, he had 31 points, a career-high 18 rebounds, 2 blocks, and 5 steals. He was a member of the 1987 U.S. Pan Am team. The

Los Angeles Clippers 1989 number 1 draft pick, 23-year-old Manning emerged as the leading candidate for Rookie of the Year. He quickly became an integral part of the team and was regarded as a major part of the team's future foundation. During the first quarter of a January 4, 1989, game at Milwaukee, Manning badly damaged the anterior cruciate ligament in his right knee. This injury had the potential of sidelining him for the rest of the current season and possibly all of the next.

Sources: "Black American Medal Winners," *Ebony* (December 1988); "Seoul Games/Medal Winners," *Los Angeles Times* (October 3, 1988); "Manning Is Out for Rest of Season," *Los Angeles Times* (January 12, 1989); *1988 United States Olympic Team, Media Guide; Seoul '88;* "Olympics Record," *USA Today* (October 3, 1988).

MARBLEY, HARLAN J. (USA). Born October 11, 1943, in White Oak, Maryland.

1968 Bronze Medal: Light Flyweight Boxing (tied)

Harlan Marbley had finished third at the 1967 Pan Am Games prior to the Mexico City Olympics, where he lost in the semifinals to eventual champion Francisco Rodriguez of Venezuela. Marbley followed Yong-ju Jee of Korea, who won the silver, and tied with Hubert Skrzypczak of Poland. Marbley won the National AAU title in 1968.

Sources: *Black Olympians; Guinness Book of Olympic Records; 1968 United States Olympic Book; Olympic Games: The Record; Quest for Gold.*

MARCUS, EGERTON (Canada). Born of Guyanese parents.

1988 Silver Medal: Middleweight Boxing

Henry Moshe of East Germany defeated Egerton Marcus of Canada in the 165-pound category, 5-0.

Sources: British Virgin Islands, Olympic Committee; "Seoul Games/Medal Winners," *Los Angeles Times* (October 3, 1988).

MARQUIS, GAIL ANNETTE (USA). Born November 18, 1954, in New York City.

1976 Silver Medal: Basketball

Gail Marquis graduated from Andrew Jackson High School in New York City in 1972 and from Queens College, City University of New York, in 1980. In high school Marquis won varsity letters in three sports: basketball, track and field, and softball. She was City champion in the girl's shotput, and was a Division champion in basketball in 1970. She was also in the Police Athletic League for

track and field and the Catholic Youth Organization, and played for a French basketball organization in Antibes in the south of France. In college, Marquis was on the varsity basketball team for 4 years and participated in track and field for 2. She was co-captain of her basketball team and All-American for 2 years. In 1975 and 1976 she was Eastern Region Player of the Year. Marquis averaged 19.9 points per game in 1976, 110 in 1974, and 40 in 1975. One of her coaches was Lucille Kyvallos. Marquis was on the President's Council for Physical Fitness and on the 1977 U.S. Women's World University basketball team, which won a silver medal. As a professional, she was with the New York Stars Women's Basketball League in 1979-80 and with the New Jersey Gems Women's Basketball League in 1980-81. Gail Marquis is a lecturer, clinician, and guest speaker at various basketball camps in the U.S. and Europe. She is a transfer agent for a major U.S. financial investment firm and lives in St. Albans, New York.

Sources: *Black Olympians; Guinness Book of Olympic Records;* Marquis, Gail. Questionnaire. 1984; *United States Olympic Team, Games of the XXIst Olympiad.*

MARSHALL, LEONEL (Cuba). Born in Cuba.

1976 Bronze Medal: Volleyball

For a summary of the Cuban team's record at the 1976 Olympics in Montreal, see García.

Sources: *Approved History of Olympic Games;* British Virgin Islands, Olympic Committee; *Complete Book of the Olympics; Guinness Book of Olympic Records; Montreal 1976; Games of the XXth Olympiad.*

MARTIN, LOUIS (Great Britain). Born November 11, 1936, in Jamaica.

1960 Bronze Medal: Middle Heavyweight Weightlifting (981 lbs./445 kg)
1964 Silver Medal: Middle Heavyweight Weightlifting (1,047 lbs./475 kg)

Considered the British Commonwealth's greatest weightlifter, Louis Martin won four world and three Commonwealth Games titles. He possessed tremendous zest for competition, amazing dedication, a keen and sensitive brain, and massive strength. In 1959, after winning his first British title, Martin sprang one of the biggest shocks ever in weightlifting. In Warsaw, at the World Championships, he defeated Arcady Vorobyev, the Russian holder of the title. Although both men totaled 980¾ pounds, Martin was awarded the title on the lighter bodyweight rule. To round off his career, Louis Martin entered the 1970 British Commonwealth Games in Edinburgh, an important contest. There he was awarded his third successive gold medal. He retired soon thereafter.

Sources: *Approved History of Olympic Games*; British Virgin Islands, Olympic Committee; *Complete Book of the Olympics; Guinness Book of Olympic Records; The Super Athletes*.

MARTÍNEZ, ARMANDO (Cuba). Born August 29, 1961, in Ciego de Avila, Cuba.

1980 Gold Medal: Light Middleweight Boxing

Armando Martínez had an unusually arduous early career. He fought mighty battles with two other light middleweight boxing stars, Aleksander Koshkin of the USSR and Shawn O'Sullivan of Canada. These battles left him so drained that he was given a year to recuperate for the Olympics. As an underdog Martínez first beat Koshkin in the 1980 Olympic final to emerge a clear winner, and then did much the same in the World Championships final. Martínez fared less well with O'Sullivan in 1981, when O'Sullivan beat him. Martínez lost fewer than 20 of the 300 bouts he fought. He won silver medals in the 1981 World Cup and 1982 World Championships and was Cuban champion in 1982.

Sources: *Approved History of Olympic Games; Complete Book of the Olympics; Games of the XXIInd Olympiad, Moscow, 1980; Guinness Book of Olympic Records*; "Summer Games, Boxing," *New York Times* (August 3, 1980); "Olympic Winners," *New York Times* (August 4, 1980); *Who's Who in the 1984 Olympics*.

MARTÍNEZ, ERNESTO (Cuba). Born in Cuba.

1976 Bronze Medal: Volleyball

For a summary of the Cuban team's record at the 1976 Olympics in Montreal, see García.

Sources: *Approved History of Olympic Games*; British Virgin Islands, Olympic Committee; *Complete Book of the Olympics; Guinness Book of Olympic Records; Montreal 1976; Games of the XXIst Olympiad*.

MARTÍNEZ, LORENZO (Cuba). Born in Cuba.

1976 Bronze Medal: Volleyball

For a summary of the Cuban team's record at the 1976 Olympics in Montreal, see García.

Sources: *Approved History of Olympic Games*; British Virgin Islands, Olympic Committee; *Complete Book of the Olympics; Guinness Book of Olympic Records; Montreal 1976; Games of the XXIst Olympiad*.

MARTÍNEZ, LUIS (Cuba). Born in Cuba.

1976 Bronze Medal: Middleweight Boxing

Luis Martínez's progression to the bronze medal in middleweight boxing at the Montreal Olympics in 1976 was as follows: lost to Bernd Wittenburg of East Germany, 5; lost to David Odwell of Great Britain, 0; defeated Rufat Riskiev of the USSR, knockout in the second round, 2:02 minutes; lost to Michael Spinks of the U.S., 2.

Sources: *Approved History of Olympic Games*; British Virgin Islands, Olympic Committee; *Complete Book of the Olympics; Guinness Book of Olympic Records; Montreal 1976; Games of the XXIst Olympiad*.

MARTÍNEZ, ORLANDO (Cuba). Born September 2, 1944, in Havana, Cuba.

1972 Gold Medal: Bantamweight Boxing

Orlando Martínez was the first Cuban to win an Olympic gold medal since 1904, when Ramón Forst, the fencer, won. Martínez defeated the following boxers at the 1972 Olympics to win the gold: Maung Win of Burma, points 4-1; Michael Dowling of Ireland, 3-2; Ferry Egberty Moniaga of Indonesia, 5-0; George Turpin of Great Britain, 3-2; and Alfonso Zamora of Mexico, 5-0.

Sources: *Approved History of Olympic Games; Complete Book of the Olympics; Die Spiele, Official Report for the Games of the XXth Olympiad; Guinness Book of Olympic Records; Munchen 1972; Results of the Games of the XXth Olympiad*.

MATSON, OLLIE ADRIAN (USA). Born May 1, 1930, in Trinity, Texas.

1952 Silver Medal: 4 x 400-Meter Relay (3:04.0)
1952 Bronze Medal: 400-Meter Run (46.8)

Ollie Matson attended San Francisco City College and the University of San Francisco. An All-American junior college halfback at San Francisco City College, Matson scored 21 touchdowns and gained 1,566 yards to lead the nation. As a senior at the University of San Francisco, he was again selected as an All-American. Matson was the first draft choice of the Chicago Cardinals of the NFL in 1952, for which he received Rookie-of-the-Year honors. He was traded from the Cardinals to the Los Angeles Rams for nine players in 1959. In 1956 and 1959, his best years, he gained 924 yards and 863 yards, respectively. He finished his career in 1966 after playing with the Detroit Lions and Philadelphia Eagles. In his 14 years with the NFL, Ollie Matson was second only to the legendary Jim Brown in combined rushing yardage. He was selected to the Professional Football Hall of Fame in 1972 and became a football coach.

Sources: *Black Olympians; Guinness Book of Olympic Records; Lincoln Library of Sports Champions; Quest for Gold; Spirit Team Profiles*, Los Angeles Olympic Organizing Committee.

MATTHEWS, MARGARET REJEAN (USA).
Born August 5, 1935, in Griffin, Georgia.

1956 Bronze Medal: 4 x 100-Meter Relay (44.9)

Margaret Matthews graduated from D.T. Howard High School in Atlanta in 1953. She held the state record in the 50-, 75- and 100-yard dashes and in the broad jump. She also was an honor student and belonged to the All-State basketball team. She graduated from Tennessee State University, after first attending Bethune-Cookman and Lewis College in Chicago. She was a member of the Tigerbelles track team. In 1958 Matthews became the first American woman to broad-jump 20 feet. She failed to qualify for the Olympic finals in her specialty, the long jump, but she picked up a bronze medal in the 4 x 100-meter relay race. In the long jump, she set a record of 19 feet, 4 inches at the 1956 AAU, and improved to 19 feet, 9¼ inches at the final trials, even though she did not repeat this form in Melbourne. She won the AAU in 1957-59. Matthews achieved a position on the 1957-58 and 1959 AAU All-American women's track and field teams. (In retrospect, she feels that she quit track and field too early and wonders if she ever reached her peak.) Matthews married Jesse Wilburn, a physical education major at Tennessee State. The parents of two sons, they now live and teach in Memphis, Tennessee.

Sources: *Black Olympians; Development of Negro Female Olympic Talent; Guinness Book of Olympic Records; Historical and Biographical Studies of Women Participants; Quest for Gold.*

MATTHEWS, VINCENT EDWARD (USA).
Born December 16, 1947, in Queens, New York.

1968 Gold Medal: 4 x 400-Meter Relay (2:56.1, world record)
1972 Gold Medal: 400-Meter Run (44.66)

In 1968 Vince Matthews ran 440 yards in 44.4 seconds to better the world record. He took the silver medal in the 1967 Pan Am Games 400 meters in 45.11 and won the NAIA 440 yards for Johnson C. Smith University that same year. He won the AAU in 45.0 in 1968 and bested the world record in the 1968 U.S. preliminary Olympic trials meet at South Lake Tahoe by running his 44.4. However, IAAF disallowed the mark because of the "brush" spiked shoes he wore during the race. Matthews missed a place in the 400 meters but ran on the U.S. 4 x 400-meter relay team, which set a world record at Mexico City. He ran a 45.0 leadoff leg in the 2:56.1 run. Vince Matthews retired in 1970-71 but he returned to competition in 1972. He finished second with 45.1 at the 1972 AAU Championships and made the Olympic Team with 44.9 for third place. On the victory stand after winning the gold medal, he and Wayne Collett allegedly failed to display the proper decorum and both men were banned from further Olympic competition. It is thought that they behaved disrespectfully to protest treatment of Blacks in the U.S. A former student at Johnson C. Smith University in Charlotte, North Carolina, Matthews is now a youth worker.

Sources: *Black Olympians; Guinness Book of Olympic Records; Quest for Gold; Who's Who in Track and Field.*

MAY, SCOTT (USA). Born March 19, 1954, in Waynesboro, Mississippi.

1976 Gold Medal: Basketball

Scott May attended high school in Sandusky, Ohio, and graduated in 1976 from Indiana University. He was high school All-American; 1975 and 1976 All-Big Ten; 1976 Consensus All-American; and 1976 AP and UPI, *Sporting News*, and *Basketball Weekly* College Player of the Year. His coach was Bob Knight. May won the most points in one season at Indiana (752 in 1976) and averaged 12.5 points per game in 1974, 16.3 points per game with 199 rebounds in 1975, and 23.5 points per game with 245 rebounds in 1976. May played on two of the greatest collegiate teams ever at Indiana University, in 1975 and 1976. The 1976 team succeeded in winning the NCAA Championship. He was the acknowledged leader of that team and in 1976 was the backbone of the Olympic team. A great professional career was expected of this 6-foot 7-inch forward, but it did not quite materialize. When he was released by the Detroit Pistons in the middle of the 1982-83 season, he retired and devoted himself to a real estate business.

Sources: *Black Olympians; Quest for Gold; United States Olympic Team, Games of the XXIst Olympiad.*

MAY, WILLIAM LEE (USA). Born November 11, 1936, in Knoxville, Alabama.

1960 Silver Medal: 110-Meter Hurdles (13.4)

Willie May attended Indiana University and was a member of the University of Chicago Track Club. In 1960, when he was a senior at Indiana, May placed second to Lee Calhoun at the Olympic final trials. Calhoun again defeated May in the Olympic finals. May has an impressive record of fast clockings, with a career best of 13.4, although he never won a major title.

Sources: *Black Olympians; Guinness Book of Olympic Records; Quest for Gold; United States 1960 Olympic Book, Games of the XVIIth Olympiad; United States Track and Field Olympians.*

MAYNARD, ANDREW (USA). Born April 8, 1964, in Cheverly, Maryland.

1988 Gold Medal: Light Heavyweight Boxing

Andrew Maynard began boxing in 1985. He won the light heavyweight gold medal at the U.S. Olympic Festival both in 1986 and 1987 and was the 1987 U.S. Army and U.S. Armed Forces light heavyweight champion. He was a bronze medalist at the Pan Gam Games in 1987, losing to Pablo Romer of Cuba. Maynard was the U.S. Amateur champion in the light heavyweight division in both 1987 and 1988. He took back-to-back victories over Olympic trials champion Alfred Cole (4-1, 4-1) at the July 1988 Box-offs to gain a spot on the Olympic team. Maynard is a member of the U.S. Army and is stationed at Fort Carson, Colorado. He is married and has one child.

Sources: "Black American Medal Winners," *Ebony* (December 1988); "Seoul Games/Medal Winners," *Los Angeles Times* (October 3, 1988); *1988 United States Olympic Team, Media Guide; Seoul '88*; "Olympics Record," *USA Today* (October 3, 1988).

MBUGUA, SAMUEL (Kenya). Born January 1, 1946, in Nairobi, Kenya.

1972 Bronze Medal: Lightweight Boxing

Samuel Mbugua won his bronze medal in lightweight boxing at the 1972 Olympic Games in Munich by defeating Girmaye Gabre of Ethiopia, points 5-0, and Muniswamy Hav Venu of India, points 5-0.

Sources: *Approved History of Olympic Games; Complete Book of the Olympics; Die Spiele, Official Report for the Games of the XXth Olympiad; Guinness Book of Olympic Records; Munchen 1972; Results of the Games of the XXth Olympiad.*

MCCLAIN, KATRINA (USA). Born September 19, 1965, in Washington, D.C.

1988 Gold Medal: Basketball

Katrina McClain studied political science at the University of Georgia and graduated in 1987. When Georgia finished second in the 1985 NCAA Championships, she earned All-Final Four honors. She led the nation in field goal percentage as a freshman, shooting 69.5 percent from the field. McClain was the leading scorer and rebounder for the U.S. at the 1985 World University Games, when the U.S. team won the silver medal, and she helped the U.S. win gold medals at the 1986 FIBA World Championships and Goodwill Games. As a junior, she averaged 21.3 points and 10.3 rebounds, shooting 66.2 percent from the field, and was named a Kodak All-American. McClain played the 1987 season in Chiba, Japan, for Kyoseki. She sparked the U.S. team to a gold medal at the 1987 Pan Am Games by scoring 30 points and pulling down 11 rebounds in the gold medal game against Brazil. She led the team in scoring (17.8) and rebounding (10.0) while shooting 57.5 percent from the field. She averaged 24.9 points and 12.2 rebounds as a Kodak All-American during her senior year at Georgia (1986-87), helping her team finish with a 27-5 record.

Sources: "Black American Medal Winners," *Ebony* (December 1988) "Seoul Games/Medal Winners," *Los Angeles Times* (October 3, 1988); *1988 United States Olympic Team, Media Guide; Seoul '88*; "Olympics Record," *USA Today* (October 3, 1988).

MCCLURE, WILBERT JAMES (USA). Born October 29, 1938, in Toledo, Ohio.

1960 Gold Medal: Light Middleweight Boxing

Wilbert McClure graduated from Scott High School in Toledo in 1956 and attended the University of Toledo and Wayne State University, Detroit. He received his Ph.D. in 1973. By the time "Skeeter" McClure went to Rome in 1960, he had won the 1959 Pan Am Games gold medal, as well as the 1959 and 1960 National AAU Championships. In Rome he won four straight decisions but was never seriously challenged. McClure was in professional boxing from 1961 to 1969. He ranked third in the world as a middleweight in 1963-64. During his 7 years as a professional, he compiled a lifetime record of 23 wins, 7 losses, and 1 draw. He seemed to stand on the edge of greatness but never quite broke through. McClure was a professor at Northeastern University in Boston from 1973 to 1980 and is now president of his own consulting firm in Boston. He has an 18-year-old daughter, Karen.

Sources: *Black Olympians; Games of the XVIIth Olympiad, Rome, 1960; Guinness Book of Olympic Records;* McClure, Wilbert. Questionnaire.

MCCRORY, STEVE (USA). Born April 13, 1964, in Detroit, Michigan.

1984 Gold Medal: Flyweight Boxing

Steve McCrory graduated from Pershing High School, Detroit, in 1982. He is the younger brother of professional boxer Milt McCrory, the former World Boxing Council welterweight champion. Having started boxing very young, Steve McCrory won the 1984 Olympic trials, the 1983 U.S. Amateur title, and the 1982 and 1983 U.S. title. In 1984, before the Olympics, he lost to Pedro Reyes of Cuba the world title he had won in 1983 by defeating Yuri Alexandrov of the USSR at the World Championships challenge. A boxer with extensive international experience, McCrory took third at the Pan Am Games. At the Los Angeles Olympics, it took McCrory only 1 minute, 46 seconds to dispose of Mexican southpaw, Fausto García. Twice down from rights to the head, García, a 28-year-old medical doctor with 13 losses in 104 bouts, was never a threat.

Sources: "The 1984 Olympics" *Ebony* (October 1984); "Boxing," *Olympian* (October/November 1984); *United States Olympic Team, Media Guide; Who's Who in the 1984 Olympics.*

MCDANIEL, MILDRED LOUISE (USA). Born November 4, 1933, in Atlanta, Georgia.

1956 Gold Medal: High Jump (5 ft. 9¼ in./1.76 m, Olympic record/world record)

Mildred McDaniel attended Tuskegee Institute in Alabama. She won the AAU outdoor high jump in 1953 and both the outdoor and indoor titles in 1955 and 1956. She achieved the ultimate in track and field by winning an Olympic gold with a new world record performance. She also beat the future world record holder, Iolanda Balas of Romania. McDaniel later won the high jump at the 1959 Pan Am Games.

Sources: *Black Olympians; Hard Road to Glory; Negro Firsts in Sports; Quest for Gold; United States Track and Field Olympians; Who's Who in Track and Field.*

MCGEE, PAMELA DENISE (USA). Born December 1, 1962, in Flint, Michigan.

1984 Gold Medal: Basketball

Pamela McGee graduated from Northern High School in Flint, Michigan, and from the University of Southern California. She and her twin sister, Paula, led their high school team to two championships. Paula did not make the Olympic team but Pam publicly presented her gold medal to her twin sister. Pam McGee capped her career at USC with back-to-back NCAA titles. She was named to the NCAA All-Tournament team, the Kodak All-American team, the *ABA USA* All-American team, the 1983 and 1984 Western Region All-Tournament team, and the 1982-84 All-WCAA Conference teams. She was 1981 YMCA Silver Achievement Award recipient and CBS-Television's Player of the Game in the 1984 NCAA Championships. McGee completed her USC career with 2,214 points, 1,255 rebounds and 158 assists; she played all 127 games in her 4 years. She was a 1983 Pan Am Games and World Championships U.S. team member and a 1981 National Sports Festival participant. With her twin sister, Paula, and superstar Cheryl Miller, they led the women of USC to the NCAA championships in 1983 and 1984. These three probably formed the most formidable front line in the history of college basketball for women. Pam was the all-time leading rebounder at USC.

Sources: *Black Olympians*; "The Champions," *Los Angeles Times* (August 14, 1984); *Research Information, Games of the XXIIIrd Olympiad; United States Olympic Team, Media Guide.*

MCGUIRE, EDITH MARIE (USA). Born June 3, 1944, in Atlanta, Georgia.

1964 Gold Medal: 200-Meter Run (23.05, Olympic record)
1964 Silver Medal: 4 x 100-Meter Relay (43.92)
1964 Silver Medal: 100-Meter Run (11.62)

EDITH MARIE MCGUIRE (Photo courtesy of U.S. Olympic Committee, Colorado Springs, Colorado.)

In high school Edith McGuire was an honor student and was named best all-around student in her class. She received awards in basketball and track and a scholarship to Tennessee State University, where she became a Tigerbelle. She graduated from Tennessee State in 1966. McGuire was a better prospect at the shorter sprint and the long jump, until she won her Olympic title at 200 meters. She won the 100 meters and long jump at both the AAU indoor and outdoor meets in 1963. She established herself as a sprinter by winning the 100-meter run in São Paulo, Brazil, setting a Pan Am record of 11.5 seconds and equaling Wilma Rudolph's record in the 100. McGuire established six records in 1964: 70-yard dash (world), 100-meter run (American), 100-meter run (senior champion in California), 200-meter run (Olympic tryouts and Olympics), and 220-yard dash (American outdoor record). McGuire specialized in the longer sprint to good effect in the Olympic year and was undefeated in major races over 200 meters throughout the season. McGuire won the AAU 200 in 1964 prior to her Olympic victory and defended her title at 220 yards in 1965. She won the AAU 220 yards in 1965 and 1966. McGuire participated in over 50 meets during her 7 years of national and international competition. She held world, Olympic, Canadian, AAU American, and AAU champion records in the 200-meter run and 220-yard dash. McGuire was a place on six AAU All-American women's track and field teams. Following her running career, Edith McGuire taught school and worked with underprivileged children in a federal program in Detroit.

Sources: *American Women in Sport, 1887-1987; Black Olympians; Development of Negro Female Olympic Talent; Guinness Book of Olympic Records; Historical and Biographical Studies of Women Olympic Participants; Quest for Gold; United States Olympic Team, Games; United States Track and Field Olympians.*

MCKAY, ANTONIO RICARDO (USA). Born February 9, 1964, in Atlanta, Georgia.

1984 Gold Medal: 4 x 400-Meter Relay (2:57.91)
1984 Bronze Medal: 400-Meter Run (44.71)

Antonio McKay shocked the track world in February 1983 when he ran 45.79 to set a world indoor best in the 400 meters. He later won the NCAA indoor 400 title and ran just as well outdoors, clocking a 45.1 early in the season. He had run 45.9 while still in high school in 1982 but sat out the 1983 season, his freshman year at Georgia Tech, because of injury. In 1984 McKay won the NCAA indoor and outdoor championships in the 400-meter dash, and after an impressive win at the U.S. Olympic trials, he was widely tipped to win the event at the Olympics. This was not to be, however, and McKay had to settle for a bronze medal. His time of 44.71 seconds, good enough for victory at the trials, was not good enough to beat his teammate Alonzo Babers and Gabriel Tiacoh of the Ivory Coast in Los Angeles. He ran the anchor leg for the victorious U.S. squad in the 4 x 400. McKay set an indoor 300-meter best at the Stuttgard International in 1987. He led all the way to clock 32.51. Indoors, the winter of 1987, he claimed the World Championships in the 400. McKay finished fifth in the 400 at the 1988 Olympic trials (44.79). He had the fourth-fastest U.S. time in 1987 with 44.69, his personal best. A 1987 graduate of Georgia Tech, McKay competed for the Mazda Track Club.

Sources: "The 1984 Olympics," *Ebony* (October 1984); "McKay is a Swift Talking Runner," *Los Angeles Times* (July 29, 1984); *United States Olympic Team, Media Guide; 1984 Olympic Games; Seoul '88;* "Record 300 m for McKay," *Track & Field News* (March 1987); "McKay Knows What He's Doing," *Track & Field News* (July 1987); *United States Olympic Teams, Media Guide.*

HERBERT MCKENLEY (Photo courtesy of U.S. Olympic Committee, Colorado Springs, Colorado, and the Jamaica Information Service, Jamaican Embassy, Washington, D.C.)

MCKENLEY, HERBERT (Jamaica). Born July 10, 1922, in Clarendon, Jamaica.

1948 Silver Medal: 400-Meter Run (46.4)
1952 Gold Medal: 4 x 400-Meter Relay (3:03.9, world record)
1952 Silver Medal: 100-Meter Run (10.4)
1952 Silver Medal: 400-Meter Run (45.9, Olympic record)

Herb McKenley attended the University of Illinois after an impressive career at Calabar High School, Jamaica. While at Illinois McKenley was a double winner in the 200 and 400 meters in both 1946 and 1947 and won two AAU titles at 400 meters, in 1947 and 1948. He ran for New York's Grand Street Boys Track Club. Although McKenley never won an Olympic gold medal in an individual event, he was arguably the best sprinter ever developed by a Caribbean country. He won one Olympic gold medal in the 4 x 400-meter relay at Helsinki in 1952, when he joined Arthur Wint, Leslie Laing, and George Rhoden to shatter the existing Olympic record by 5.1 seconds in a 3:03.9 victory. McKenley ran the third leg. He twice finished second in the Olympic 400-meter dash (silver), losing each time to a fellow Jamaican. In 1948 in London he was overtaken by Arthur Wint (46.4 to 46.2) and, in an exceptionally close finish, George Rhoden beat him in 1952 when both ran 45.9. McKenley added another silver medal in 1952 by finishing second in the 100 to American Lindy Remigino in another nailbiter; the three medalists were clocked in 10.4 seconds. McKenley figured prominently in *Track & Field News* world rankings from 1947 to 1953. He ranked third in the 100 in 1952; second in the 200 in 1947, 1950 and 1952; and fifth in the same event in 1948, 1949 and 1952. In the 400 he ranked first in 1947 and 1948, second from 1950 to 1952, third in 1949, and sixth in 1953. Surprisingly, for all McKenley's prowess in the 200, he won only one major international title in that event—at the 1950 Central American and Caribbean Games in Guatemala, where he also won the 400. Herb McKenley five times broke the world record for 440 yards and had lifetime bests of 10.3 for the 100, 20.8 for the 200, and 45.7 for the 400. His relay leg in the Helsinki victory (44.6 seconds) was the fastest ever recorded to that time. McKenley later became a track coach and president of the Jamaica Amateur Athletic Association and also managed the American track and field team at the 1979 World Cup in Montreal. He is an executive with an insurance company in Kingston. His twin sons have represented Jamaica in junior competition.

Sources: British Virgin Islands, Olympic Committee; *Complete Book of the Olympics; Guinness Book of Olympic Records; 1980 Olympics Handbook; Official Report of Organizing Committee, XIVth Olympiad; Track and Field: The Great Ones; United States 1952 Olympic Book; World's All Sports Who's Who*.

MCKINNEY, KENNEDY (USA). Born January 10, 1966, in Memphis, Tennessee.

1988 Gold Medal: Bantamweight Boxing

Kennedy McKinney graduated from high school in 1984 and competed for the U.S. Army until 1988. McKinney began boxing in 1979. He was a gold medalist as a flyweight at the 1986 U.S. Olympic Festival and was the U.S. Army flyweight champion in 1985 and 1986. He took the title again in 1987 as a bantamweight. McKinney finished second in 1986, third in 1987, and second in 1988 at the U.S. Amateur Championships. He was Olympic trials bantamweight champion and defeated Michael Collins (4-1) at the July Box-offs to earn a place on the Olympic team.

Sources: "Black American Medal Winners," *Ebony* (December 1988); "U.S. Wins Two Golds in Boxing," *Los Angeles Times* (October 1, 1988); "Seoul Games/Medal Winners," *Los Angeles Times* (October 3, 1988); *1988 United States Olympic Team, Media Guide; Seoul '88*; "Olympics Record," *USA Today* (October 3, 1988).

MCMILLAN, KATHY LAVERNE (USA). Born November 7, 1957, in Raeford, North Carolina.

1976 Silver Medal: Long Jump (21 ft. 10¼ in./6.66 m)

Kathy McMillan graduated from Hoke County High School, Raeford, North Carolina, in 1976 and from Tennessee State University in 1980. As a recent high school graduate, she set a new U.S. record of 22 feet, 3 inches in winning the 1976 AAU long jump. She jumped 22 feet, 4½ inches at the Montreal Olympics, which would have won the gold had a marginal foul not been called. This matched Willye White's performance of 20 years earlier as the best ever by a U.S. woman in the Olympic long jump. As a student at Tennessee State, McMillan placed second in the AAU in 1977 and 1978. She won the AAU with a 21-foot 3¼-inch jump, and was the Pan Am Games champion in 1979, leaping to 21 feet, 2¼ inches to win her eighth Pan Am gold medal. She placed second in the Olympic trials in 1980 but could not participate in the Games because of the U.S. boycott.

Sources: *Black Olympians; Guinness Book of Olympic Records; Historical and Biographical Studies of Women Participants; Quest for Gold; United States Olympic Team Games; United States Olympic Team, Media Guide; United States Track and Field Olympians*.

MEGHOO, GREGORY (Jamaica). Born August 11, 1965, in Jamaica.

1984 Silver Medal: 4 x 100-Meter Relay (38.62)

Gregory Meghoo celebrated his 19th birthday by winning an Olympic silver medal. Meghoo's best 100-meter time remains his 10.36 clocking from 1984. He later had wind-aided times of 10.24 and 20.6 while competing for Abilene Christian University in 1985.

Sources: British Virgin Islands, Olympic Committee; *1984 Olympic Games*; "The Games," *Olympian* (October/November 1984).

MERCER, RAY (USA). Born April 4, 1961, in Jacksonville, Florida.

1988 Gold Medal: Heavyweight Boxing

Ray Mercer, who never boxed a round until he was 22, was the Olympic trials heavyweight champion and winner of the

July Box-offs over Michael Bent (3-2). He was also the U.S. Amateur, U.S. Army, and U.S. Armed Forces champion. In Seoul, Mercer defeated Arnold Van der Lidje of the Netherlands by a knockout in the second round, after delivering two standing eight counts. He went on to defeat South Korean Baik Hyun Man with a left hook to the jaw for a gold.

Sources: "Black American Medal Winners," *Ebony* (December 1988); "Mercer Just May Be Sowing the Seeds," *Los Angeles Times* (September 29, 1988); "Seoul Games/Medal Winners," *Los Angeles Times* (October 3, 1988); *1988 United States Olympic Team, Media Guide; Seoul '88*; "Olympics Record," *USA Today* (October 3, 1988).

RALPH HAROLD METCALFE
(Photo courtesy of Amateur Athletic Foundation, Los Angeles, California.)

METCALFE, RALPH HAROLD (USA). Born May 29, 1910, in Atlanta, Georgia.

1932 Silver Medal: 100-Meter Run (10.38, Olympic record)
1932 Bronze Medal: 200-Meter Run (21.51)
1936 Gold Medal: 4 x 100-Meter Relay (39.8, Olympic record/world record)
1936 Silver Medal: 100-Meter Run (10.4)

Ralph Metcalfe, one of the most sensational individual performers in track history, was called the "world's fastest human" in 1934-35. Metcalfe began his running career in high school, where he won a sprint double in the Illinois State Meet three times. In 1932 as a student at Marquette University, he won both metric sprints in the NCAA in 10.2 and 20.3. He also won both sprints in the AAU. Metcalfe tied the world 100-meter record of 10.3 three times and the 200 record of 20.6 once. In 1933 and 1934 he won the NCAA 100 and 220 yards for Marquette, and he took the AAU 100 yards in 1932-34 and the 200 meters in 1932-36. Metcalfe defeated rival Eddie Tolan in the 100 and 200 in the 1932 Olympic trials. (Tolan won both the 100 and 200 in the 1932 Olympics.) In 1933 Metcalfe won doubles again in the NCAA and the AAU. He also added the indoor AAU title. In Budapest, in August of that year, he ran a 10.3 in the 100 meters and a 20.6 in the 200. In 1934 he became the only man to win the NCAA doubles three times. Metcalfe again doubled in the AAU and won his second indoor title. In Japan he ran a wind-assisted 200 meters in 20.2. In 1935 Metcalfe won the 200, and in 1936 he won the indoor AAU for the third time and the AAU 200 for the fifth time. He became the only sprinter to win five times in one event. He made the Olympic team behind Jesse Owens in the 100 but failed in the 200. He then ran second to Owens in the 100 meters at the 1936 Games in Berlin. Metcalfe finally won his gold medal in the 400-meter relay. Metcalfe tied the World 100-meter record of 10.3 seconds 10 times and broke it once. He lost only 5 times in the 100 and 3 times in the 200 in his 5 years of competition. Metcalfe's son Ralph, Jr., was one of the best-ever U.S. high school hammer throwers while a student at the prestigious Choate Academy in Connecticut in 1966. However, he never competed in the event as a collegian. Ralph Metcalfe became a coach and political science instructor, a Chicago city councilman, and a member of the U.S. House of Representatives. He became well known in Chicago politics in his late years, serving under Mayor Richard Daley on the City Council for many years. He was elected to Congress from Illinois' First District, serving until his death. He was also elected to the Board of Directors of the U.S. Olympic Committee in 1969. He died October 10, 1978, in Chicago.

Sources: *Black Olympians; Famous American Athletes of Today; Guinness Book of Olympic Records; Quest for Gold; Track and Field: The Great Ones; United States Track and Field Olympians; Who's Who in Track and Field.*

MIGUEL, AURELIO (Brazil). Born in Brazil.

1988 Gold Medal: Heavyweight Judo (209 lbs./95 kg)

Aurelio Miguel won Brazil's first gold medal in Seoul, and Brazil's first-ever gold medal in judo, when he defeated Marc Meiling of East Germany by a half point.

Sources: "Seoul Games/Medal Winners," *Los Angeles Times* (October 3, 1988); *Seoul '88*; "Olympics Record," *USA Today* (October 3, 1988).

MILBURN, RODNEY, JR. (USA). Born May 18, 1950, in Opelousas, Louisiana.

1972 Gold Medal: 110-Meter Hurdles (13.24, Olympic record/equaled world record)

Rodney Milburn attended Southern University in Baton Rouge, Louisiana and was affiliated with the Tiger International Track Club. Milburn held the world record in the 120 yards and was named World Athlete of the Year in 1971 by *Track & Field News*. As a college freshman, in 1970, he won the NAIA Championships in the 120-yard hurdles and was a gold medalist at the 1971 Pan Am Games in 13.4. Milburn had a fine 1972 indoor season with a 7.0 win in a 60-high hurdle in the U.S./USSR indoor meet. He won the NCAA in 13.5 in 1972 and the AAU in 13.4; in 1973 he won the NCAA but lost in the AAU. In 1971 Milburn went through 28 races unbeaten, two of which were sensational. On June 4, he was timed at 13.0, with wind assistance over the limit, and 3 weeks later—at the AAU Championships—he clocked 13 seconds flat again for the 120-yard hurdles, his legal time. In Munich in 1972 he won the gold medal in 13.2, equaling the world record for the 110-meter event. Milburn competed professionally in track with the International Track Association in 1973-74 and also had a brief unsuccessful professional football career. He was reinstated as an amateur, except in international competition, in 1977 and continued to be a force in the high hurdles until 1982. He returned to Southern University as a coach in 1984.

Sources: *Black Olympians*; British Virgin Islands, Olympic Committee; *Guinness Book of Olympic Records*; *Quest for Gold*; *United States Track and Field Olympians*; *Who's Who in Track and Field*.

CHERYL DE ANN MILLER (Photo courtesy of Amateur Athletic Foundation, Los Angeles, California, and Joe DiMaggio AAF/LPI 1984.)

MILLER, CHERYL DE ANN (USA). Born January 3, 1964, in Riverside, California.

1984 Gold Medal: Women's Basketball

Cheryl Miller graduated from Riverside Polytechnic High School and in 1986 was awarded a B.A. degree in broadcast journalism from the University of Southern California. On the occasion of the Olympic round-robin tournament in 1984, Don McCrae, coach of the Canadian team, described Miller as the greatest player in women's basketball. Winner of more than 1,140 trophies and 125 plaques, she has had the most illustrious basketball career, male or female, in USC women's basketball history (*Los Angeles Times*). At 6 feet, 3 inches she combines athletic grace with exuberance and flamboyance. She is a good student and is at ease behind a microphone, fielding questions with intelligence and wit. Miller says she feels "cheated that women don't have the same opportunities as men" to play professionally after college (*Women's Sports*). While attending high school, Miller scored 105 points in a single game. During her senior year she led the team to a CIF state championship.

She was perhaps the most highly recruited high school athlete in women's basketball history, receiving approximately 250 scholarship offers. At Riverside Polytechnic, the team went 132-4, and she set records for points scored in a career (3,405), season (1,156), and single game (105). Miller proved more than ready to adapt her style of play to the USC team concept, though she is known for her flair on the court and skills as an individual player. In the first 2 years Miller played for USC, the team compiled a 60-6 record and two NCAA titles. She was leading scorer at the 1983 Pan Am Games (19.8 points per game); a member of the 1983 World Championship team; MVP of the NCAA's Final Four tournament in her freshman and sophomore years (she helped propel USC to the National Championships both years); and a member of almost every All-American team. Miller was a member of the 1981 Jr. National team and a 1981 National Sports Festival participant. She was the only prep athlete selected to play on the 1982 U.S. National team to Europe. She holds the season record for most points scored in one game for USC (39) and in 1983-84 set a single-season scoring average record with 22.2 points per game. Miller had a total of 1,399 points, 670 rebounds, and 235 assists in just two seasons at USC. She was the first player, male or female, to be named to the Parade All-American team 4 years in a row. She was 1984 Naismith Player of the Year, a member of the J.C. Penney All-American Five team, and was *Sports Illustrated* Player of the Week in December 1983. Miller was the ABA/USA Female Athlete of the Year in 1986. This was after leading the U.S. to gold medals at the FIBA World Championships and the Goodwill Games. She was the Naismith Player of the Year for 3 years in a row and Kodak All-American for 4 consecutive seasons. When the U.S. defeated South Korea 85-55 at the 1984 Olympics, this was the first gold in women's basketball for the Americans. Miller finished as the leading scorer in the tournament with 99 points. She was to have been one of the outstanding players on the gold-winning U.S. team in Seoul in 1988, but surgery on her right knee in April 1987 prevented her from participating. She has not played competitively since. Miller's older brother Darrell has played major league baseball as a catcher and outfielder with the California Angels, and her younger brother Reggie, a student at UCLA, is considered one of the top collegiate basketball players in the U.S. Since graduating from USC, Miller has worked as a commentator for ABC Sports.

Sources: "The 1984 Olympics," *Ebony* (October 1984); *For the Record*; "Miller Sounds Alarm," *Los Angeles Times* (July 31, 1984); "It's Miller Time Again," *Los Angeles Times* (August 1, 1984); "The Champions," *Los Angeles Times* (August 14, 1984); "A Mother's Day Sampler," *Los Angeles Times* (May 11, 1986); *1988 United States Olympic Team, Media Guide; Research Information, Games of the XXIIIrd Olympiad*; "Cheryl Miller," *Women's Sports* (November 1983).

MILLER, LENNOX V. (Jamaica). Born October 8, 1946, in Kingston, Jamaica.

1968 Silver Medal: 100-Meter Run (10.0)
1972 Bronze Medal: 100-Meter Run (10.33)

Lennox Miller graduated from the University of Southern California with a B.S. degree in psychology in 1969. He went on to earn a doctorate in dental surgery in 1973 and a certificate in advanced prosthodontics in 1980. Miller set the world record for the 4 x 100-yard relay in 1967 and the world record for the indoor 100-yard dash in 1969. He was captain of the USC track and field team in 1969. He was gold and silver medalist in the British Commonwealth Games at Edinburgh in 1970 and gold and silver medalist in the

Pan Am Games at Cali, Colombia in 1971. He was named Jamaican Sportsman of the Year in 1972. Miller has been ambassador to the International Olympic Attaché Council, 1982-84; Jamaican attaché to the Los Angeles Olympic Organizing Committee, 1982-84; Jesse Owens games official, 1983; and coach and administrator of numerous sporting events, 1965-83. In addition to his private dental practice, Miller has taught dentistry at USC and has been a dental consultant to numerous health-care facilities. A resident of Altadena, California, he is married to Avril Zoe and has two children: Inger Zoe and Heather Lauren.

Sources: *The Games, Organizing Committee of XIXth Olympiad; Guinness Book of Olympic Records; Die Spiele, Official Report of Organizing Committee for Games of XXth Olympiad*; Miller, Lennox. Questionnaire. 1984.

MILLER, WILLIAM PRESTON (USA). Born February 22, 1930, in Lawnside, New Jersey.

1952 Silver Medal: Javelin Throw (237 ft. 8½ in./72.46 m)

William Miller graduated from the Naval Academy at Annapolis, Maryland. Even though Bill Miller beat Cy Young three times in Olympic meets, it was Young who took the gold medal in Helsinki. Yet, Miller's second-place win was the best showing ever made by the U.S. in Olympic javelin competition. Miller won the AAU in 1952, and in 1954 a technicality denied his becoming the only Black athlete to ever hold the world javelin record. His mark of 266 feet, 8½ inches was made with a javelin that had been broken then repaired in such a way that its center of gravity was moved out of the specified limits. After he retired from competition, Miller spent a number of years in the Far East as coach to various national teams.

Sources: *Black Olympians; Guinness Book of Olympic Records; Quest for Gold; United States Olympic Team, Helsinki, Finland, 1952.*

MIMS, MADELINE (MANNING) (USA). Born 11, 1948, in Cleveland, Ohio.

1968 Gold Medal: 800-Meter Run (2:00.9, Olympic record)
1972 Silver Medal: 4 x 400-Meter Relay (3:25.2)

The first U.S. 800-meter runner of truly world class, Madeline Mims was the first American woman to win the 800-meter event in the Olympics. During the 14-year span of her career, she won, in addition to Olympic titles, a Pan Am title, (gold, 1967); seven AAU championships outdoors and five indoors, and the 1966 World University Games. She failed to make the 800 finals in 1972 and 1976 but won the Olympic trials in 1980 in 1:58.3, which was the second best mark of her life. She was then a 32-year-old graduate student at Oral Roberts University. Mims was a member of four Olympic teams (1968-80), set a new American record in the 1967 Pan Am Games, was the first American woman to break a time of 2 minutes in the 800-meter run, was ranked first in the world by *Track & Field News* (1967-69), was four times Olympic trials champion (1968-80), and was captain of her 1972, 1976, and 1980 Olympic teams. Mims held the American record for the 800-meter run (1:57.9) until June 1983. She had set that record at College Park, Maryland, during a U.S. vs. USSR meet on August 7, 1976. She has held the Olympic, American, and world records for the 800. Mims was once described as "easily the best female 800-meter runner the United States had ever produced" (*Hard Road to Glory*). Mims is a member of the U.S. Track and Field Hall of Fame, the Ohio Track and Field Hall of Fame, the National Track and Field Hall of Fame, and the Olympic Track and Field Hall of Fame. She was named to the All-Time, All-Star Indoor Track and Field Team in 1983. She gives clinics on running and is a motivational and public speaker as well as an ordained minister. She is president of Madeline Manning Mims Ministries, Inc. and lives in Tulsa, Oklahoma.

Sources: *Black Olympians; Black Women in Sport; Guinness Book of Olympic Records; Hard Road to Glory; Historical and Biographical Studies of Women Participants*; Mims, Madeline Manning. Questionnaire. 1984; *Quest for Gold; United States Olympic Team, Games; United States Track and Field Olympians*.

MONDAY, KENNY (USA). Born November 25, 1961, in Tulsa, Oklahoma.

1988 Gold Medal: Freestyle Wrestling

Kenny Monday attended Oklahoma State University after posting a record of 140-0-1 as a four-time state high school champion. Monday was four-time All-American at Oklahoma State and was the NCAA champion at 150 pounds in 1984. He was the 1985 and 1988 Senior Open Freestyle champion and runner-up in 1986. He won the Hall of Fame Classic tournament in 1986 and was the U.S. Olympic Festival runner-up. Monday was the only non-Russian to reach the finals at the Soviet National tournament in Tbilisi in 1988 and was voted the meet's Outstanding Wrestler after winning the 163-pound title.

Sources: "Black American Medal Winners," *Ebony* (December 1988); "Seoul Games/Medal Winners," *Los Angeles Times* (October 3, 1988); *1988 United States Olympic Team, Media Guide; Seoul '88*; "Olympics Record," *USA Today* (October 3, 1988).

MONTES, PABLO (Cuba). Born November 11, 1944, in Havana, Cuba.

1968 Silver Medal: 4 x 100-meter Relay (38.3)

Pablo Montes first represented his country as a 400-meter runner in the 1967 Pan Am Games. However, this tall

Cuban's greatest moments of glory came in Mexico City in 1968 when he followed a fourth-place finish in the 100 meters with a silver medal, running the second leg on Cuba's sprint relay team. Five feet behind Enrique Figuerola at the exchange, American James Hines ripped into the lead after 30 yards and won by a yard. The Cubans mailed their silver medals to activist Stokely Carmichael as a symbol of support for U.S. Blacks. In a long career Pablo Montes recorded best times of 10.14, 20.7, and 46.7 seconds in the three sprints.

Sources: British Virgin Islands, Olympic Committee; *Complete Book of the Olympics; Guinness Book of Olympic Records*.

MOONEY, CHARLES MICHAEL (USA). Born January 27, 1951, in Washington, D.C.

1976 Silver Medal: Bantamweight Boxing

Charles Mooney compiled most of his amateur record while in the army. When he made the Olympic team in 1976, he was an Army and Interservice champion. His record was 55 wins, 1 loss.

Sources: *Black Olympians; Guinness Book of Olympic Records*; "Summer Games, Boxing," *New York Times* (July 28, 1976); *Quest for Gold; United States Olympic Team, Games of the XXIst Olympiad*.

MORALES, JUAN (Cuba). Born July 12, 1948, in Santiago, Cuba.

1968 Silver Medal: 4 x 100-Meter Relay (38.3)

Juan Morales had a relatively short, though fairly successful, career. Primarily a hurdler, with a personal best of 13.70 seconds over 110 meters, Morales also boasted a career best of 10.2 for 100 meters flat. He was considered one of the best leadoff runners in the world in the sprint relay and in that capacity won a silver medal at Mexico City. After being narrowly beaten by the U.S. in the 1968 Olympics, the Cubans mailed their silver medals to Stokely Carmichael, activist, to demonstrate their support for U.S. Blacks. Morales is now a coach of junior athletes in Havana.

Sources: British Virgin Islands, Olympic Committee; *Complete Book of the Olympics; Guinness Book of Olympic Records*.

MOSES, EDWIN CORLEY (USA). Born August 31, 1955, in Dayton, Ohio.

1976 Gold Medal: 400-Meter Hurdles (47.63, world record/ Olympic record)
1984 Gold Medal: 400-Meter Hurdles (47.75)
1988 Bronze Medal: 400-Meter Hurdles (47.20)

EDWIN CORLEY MOSES (Photo courtesy of Rich Clarkson, Denver, Colorado.)

Edwin Moses participated in track and field and gymnastics in high school and in track and field in college. He graduated from Morehouse College in Atlanta in 1978. A dedicated, highly intelligent sportsman, Moses has won over 100 consecutive finals. Of the 20 fastest times in the 400-meter hurdles, he has 17 of them. Since Moses lost in West Berlin to West Germany's Harold Schmid in 1982, he has beaten Schmid eight straight times. Few runners in history have

dominated their event like Edwin Moses. He is the only man to have perfected the astonishing technique of taking 13 strides between the hurdles. The tremendous respect that Moses has garnered was evidenced by his being chosen as one of the three representatives of the U.S. to the International Amateur Athletic Federation. After breaking the world record and the Olympic record in 1976, Edwin Moses again broke the world record at UCLA in 1977, with a 47.45 clocking, and then 3 years later in Milan, Italy, with a 47.13 performance. In 1983 he set the still-standing world record (as of January 1990) of 47.02 seconds at Koblenz, West Germany. Moses won his 19th consecutive final when he claimed his second Olympic gold in 1984. (The Olympic record of 47.63 he set in Montreal survived the Los Angeles race.) Moses stated, "It was very important to win this race.... I had a sense of total, absolute relief at the end, especially after having to wait eight years for this" (Track & Field News). In 1984 Edwin Moses won the Sullivan Award, which goes annually to the nation's top amateur athlete. He has other personal records of 13.64 for the high hurdles, set in 1978, and 45.60 for the flat 400, set in 1977. He was three times voted Athlete of the Year. He also won the Sports Illustrated Victor Award for 1985 and was inducted into the Olympics Hall of Fame that same year. Moses won his 100th straight 400-meter hurdles final at the Budapest Grand Prix track and field meet. He beat a strong international field in 47.76 seconds, his second best time in 1986. Earlier in the year he had clocked at 47.66. Moses began his winning streak in the 400-meter intermediate hurdles on September 2, 1977, in Dusseldorf, West Germany. A crowd of 35,000 enthusiastic fans cheered the Californian as he outdistanced runner-up Toma Tomov of Bulgaria (Los Angeles Times). This winning streak ended when 21-year-old Danny Harris outdistanced the 31-year-old Moses in 47.56 at the International Meet in Madrid June 4, 1987. Moses' time was 47.69. It was his first defeat in 10 years. His 107-race winning streak was the longest ever for a track event. Even though Edwin Moses won the gold in the 400-meter intermediate hurdles at Rome in the 1977 World Championships, his competition and his 32 years were catching up with him. American Danny Harris and West German Harald Schmid were only two-hundredths of a second behind. At the 1988 Seoul Games Moses was overshadowed by both teammate Andre Phillips and Elhadjdia Ba of Senegal, but he nevertheless won the bronze. Moses is an aeronautical engineer for a major aerospace corporation. He is married to Myrella Moses, a West German.

Sources: Black Olympians; British Virgin Islands, Olympic Committee; "The 1984 Olympics," Ebony (October 1984); Guinness Book of Olympic Records; International Athletics Annual; "Edwin Moses," Los Angeles Times (July 26, 1984); "Edwin Moses," Los Angeles Times (June 5, 1987); Moses, Edwin. Questionnaire. 1984; "Moses Still on Top," Los Angeles Times (September 2,1 987); Quest for Gold; "Moses Streak Reaches 90," Track & Field News (September 1984); "Olympics Record," USA Today (October 3, 1988).

MOTTLEY, WENDELL (Trinidad). Born in 1941, in Trinidad.

1964 Silver Medal: 400-Meter Run (45.2)
1964 Bronze Medal: 4 x 400-Meter Relay (3:01.7)

An outstanding student, Wendell Mottley graduated from Yale University and did graduate work at Cambridge University. In running the 400 meters at Tokyo in 1964, the bespectacled Mottley was overtaken by Michael Larrabee 10 meters from the finish. Larrabee won by 2 feet, and Mottley finished second. While studying at Cambridge in 1966, Mottley won the British AAA indoor 440-yards title with a time of 47.3 seconds and added the outdoor 440 title that same year with a time of 45.9. He won the Commonwealth Games Championships in the 440 yards in 1966, with 45.0, and in the 4 x 400-yard relay in 1966. In that relay, he and his teammates, Kent Bernard, Ed Skinner, and Ed Roberts, set a world record with a time of 3:02.8. A former minister of industry in his home country, Wendell Mottley had a best 400-meter time of 44.99 seconds.

Sources: British Virgin Islands, Olympic Committee; *Complete Book of the Olympics; Encyclopaedia of Track and Field Athletics; Games of the XVIIIth Olympiad, Tokyo; Guinness Book of Olympic Records.*

MUGABI, JOHN (Uganda). Born in Uganda.

1980 Silver Medal: Welterweight Boxing

John Mugabi needed a total of only 9 minutes to knock out his first 3 opponents. Even though he got by Kazimierz Szczerba on a split decision, he was defeated by Andrés Aldama. Known as "The Beast," Mugabi has enjoyed a fairly successful professional career as a junior middleweight, although he has twice lost in bids for world titles.

Sources: *Approved History of Olympic Games;* British Virgin Islands, Olympic Committee; *Complete Book of the Olympics; Games of the XXIInd Olympiad, Moscow, 1980; Guinness Book of Olympic Records;* Uganda Olympic Committee.

MUKWANGA, ERIDARI (Uganda). Born July 12, 1943, in Kawanda, Uganda.

1968 Silver Medal: Bantamweight Boxing

In the bantamweight boxing division of the 1968 Mexico City Olympic Games, Eridari Mukwanga finished second to Valery Sokolov of the USSR; Eiji Morioka of Japan won the bronze.

Sources: *Approved History of Olympic Games; Complete Book of the Olympics; Guinness Book of Olympic Records; Mexico 68; Participants in the XIXth Olympiad;* Uganda Olympic Committee.

MURCHISON, IRA (USA). Born February 6, 1933, in Chicago, Illinois.

1956 Gold Medal: 4 x 100-Meter Relay (39.50, Olympic record/world record)

Ira Murchison competed for Western Michigan University and the University of Iowa. He first ran 10.2 in the 100 meters at Compton, California on June 10, 1956. Both he and Bobby Morrow ran 10.2 at Los Angeles on June 29, 1956, and they jointly held the World 100-meter record. In Berlin, at the International Armed Services meet on August 4, 1956, Murchison ran 10.1 to tie the day-old record of Willie Williams. In 1956 he cost the U.S. a sweep when he finished fourth behind Hector Hogan of Australia, but returned to favor when he started the U.S. 400-meter relay that won the gold medal and set the world record of 39.5. Murchison put the U.S. on record pace with his great start. Ira Murchison was one of the shortest great sprinters at 5 feet, 4 inches. He was AAU's indoor 60-yard dash champion, in 6.2 seconds. He also was 1958 NCAA 100-yard champion for Western Michigan with 9.5. He won 36 consecutive indoor races without being beaten.

Sources: *Black Olympians; Guinness Book of Olympic Records; Hard Road to Glory; The Olympic Games, Melbourne, 1956; Quest for Gold; Who's Who in Track and Field.*

MURUNGA, DICK "TIGER" (Kenya). Born in Kenya.

1972 Bronze Medal: Welterweight Boxing

Dick "Tiger" Murunga, fighting in the welterweight boxing division at the 1972 Olympics in Munich, won the bronze when he defeated Vartex Porsanian of Iran. The referee stopped the contest 2 minutes into the third round.

Sources: *Approved History of Olympic Games; Complete Book of the Olympics; Die Spiele, Official Report for the Games of the XXth Olympiad; Guinness Book of Olympic Records; Munchen 1972, Results of the Games of the XXth Olympiad.*

MUSYOKI, MICHAEL (Kenya). Born May 28, 1956, in Machakos, Kenya.

1984 Bronze Medal: 10,000-Meter Run (28:06.46)

Michael Musyoki attended the University of Texas at El Paso and still lives there. He has made quite a name for himself as a competitor on the North American road-racing circuit. He is married to an American and has a daughter. Mike Musyoki, fourth in the 1980 Olympics 10,000-meter run, won the bronze medal when Finn Marti Vainio was disqualified. He was NCAA 10,000-meter champion at UTEP in 1978, runner-up in 1979 and 1981. Musyoki's appearances in Kenyan colors internationally have been rare. Musyoki has personal bests of 27:41.92 for 10,000 meters, 13:24.89 for 5,000 and 2:17.37 for the marathon.

Sources: British Virgin Islands, Olympic Committee; *1984 Olympic Games; Sarajevo/Los Angeles*; "The Games," *Olympian* (October/November 1984).

MYRICKS, LARRY (USA). Born March 10, 1956, in Jackson, Mississippi.

1988 Bronze Medal: Long Jump (27 ft. 1¾ in./8.27 m)

Larry Myricks graduated from Mississippi College in Clinton, Mississippi, in 1979. Myricks finished second to Carl Lewis at the 1988 Olympic trials, and qualified for his third Olympic team, with a jump of 28 feet, 8¼ inches. He finished second at the 1976 Olympic trials, even though he broke his right ankle during qualifying. He then finished fourth at the Los Angeles 1984 Games. He won the NCAA and TAC titles as well as the World Cup in 1979. Larry Myricks won the 1980 Olympics trials, the last year he ranked number 1 in the world. Four times he has jumped more than 28 feet, with a personal best of 28 feet, 8¼ inches. Myricks finished second at TAC and the Pan Am Games, in 1987, losing to Carl Lewis each time. He also ran the 200 at the 1983 TAC meet, finishing second to Lewis, with a personal best of 20.03. He finished third at the World Championships in 1987. Myricks won the long jump in the Hungalu Grand Prix track and field meet in July 1988 (28 feet, 3 inches).

Sources: "Black American Medal Winners," *Ebony* (December 1988); "Seoul Games/Medal Winners," *Los Angeles Times* (October 3, 1988); "Myricks Wins Long Jump at Budapest," *Los Angeles Times* (August 13, 1988); *1988 United States Olympic Team, Media Guide*; "Heart & Soul," *Sports Illustrated* (August 1, 1988); "Jumping for Joy," *Sports Illustrated* (June 18, 1988); "Larry Myricks," *Track & Field News* (April 1987); "Olympics Record," *USA Today* (October 3, 1988).

NESTY, ANTHONY (Surinam). Born in Surinam.

1988 Gold Medal: 100-Meter Butterfly Swimming (53.00, new Olympic record)

The medal Anthony Nesty won in Seoul was the first-ever medal for Surinam. It was a major upset for American favorite Matt Biondi. Anthony Nesty performed a sprint to the finish. So great was this victory for Surinam that the government released a stamp and a gold coin in Nesty's honor. "There is only one pool in the whole of Surinam, the former Dutch colony in Latin America. In defeating Matt Biondi, the famed American, by the smallest possible margin of one hundredth of a second, Nesty set four records" (*Seoul '88*): He was the first Black swimming champion of the Olympic Games,

the first swimming champion from South America, his country's first medalist, and the swimmer who set a new Olympic record in the 100-meter butterfly. Anthony Nesty was Surinam's only competitor in the Games. Nesty attends the University of Florida.

Sources: "Seoul Games/Medal Winners," *Los Angeles Times* (October 3, 1988); *Seoul '88*; "Olympics Record," *USA Today* (October 3, 1988).

NETTER, MILDRETTE (USA). Born June 16, 1948, in Gunnison, Mississippi.

1968 Gold Medal: 4 x 100-Meter Relay (42.8, world record)

Mildrette Netter graduated from Alcorn Agricultural and Manual University in 1971. Before winning fourth place in both the 100 and 200 meters at the 1968 U.S. final Olympic trials, Mildrette Netter had been virtually unknown. She thus won a place on the 1968 Olympic relay team. She confirmed her form after the trials by taking third place in both sprints at the AAU Championships and then in Mexico City by winning an Olympic gold medal and two world record plaques as the U.S. relay team beat the previous global best in both heats and the final.

Sources: *Black Olympians; Guinness Book of Olympic Records; Quest for Gold; United States Olympic Team, Games; United States Track and Field Olympians*.

NEWHOUSE, FREDERICK VAUGHN (USA). Born October 8, 1948, in Haney Grove, Texas.

1976 Gold Medal: 4 x 400-Meter Relay (2:58.7)
1976 Silver Medal: 400-Meter Run (44.40)

Fred Newhouse attended Galilee High School in Hallsville, Texas, and graduated from Prairie View Agricultural and Manual College with an engineering degree. His college coach was Hoover Wright. He was affiliated with the Baton Rouge Track club. He earned a master's in business from the University of Washington. Newhouse was ranked ninth in the world by *Track & Field News* for 1975. In 1975 he was second in the AAU and in 1976 third. After running 44.2 in the semifinals at the 1972 Olympic final trials, Newhouse faded badly in the final and failed to make the team for Munich. In the 1976 trials, representing the Baton Rouge Track Club, he qualified for the Montreal team by finishing second to Maxie Parks. Newhouse beat Parks at the Olympics but lost first place to Alberto Juantorena, the Cuban. In the relay Newhouse ran 43.8 on the third leg and lengthened the considerable lead of the U.S. team. An outstanding relay runner, Newhouse had a 200-meter best of 20.5 seconds. Today Fred Newhouse is an engineer with a major oil company in Baton Rouge and is an athletes' liaison with both the U.S. Olympic Committee and the TAC.

Sources: *Black Olympians*; British Virgin Islands, Olympic Committee; *Guinness Book of Olympic Records*; "Olympic Summaries," *New York Times* (August 2, 1976); *Quest for Gold; Tales of Gold; United States Olympic Team, Games of the XXIst Olympiad; United States Track and Field Olympians*.

JOHN NGUGI (Photo courtesy of Rich Clarkson, Denver, Colorado.)

NGUGI, JOHN (Kenya). Born May 10, 1962, in Myahururu, Kenya.

1988 Gold Medal: 5,000-Meter Run (13:11.70)

John Ngugi runs with a powerful loping action. He has a remarkable track speed of 3:37 (1,500 meters); 7:49 (3,000), and 13.11 (5,000). He literally runs away from the other runners, with a devastating display of power and speed. Ngugi was the winner of one medal in the Kenyan gold sweeps in the distance events at the 1988 Olympics and is a three-time world cross-country champion. He had previously finished only 12th after fading in the World Championships. (He subsequently had a cyst removed from behind his knee.) The week after his third world cross-country title early in 1988, he won the Bali road 10-kilometer race in 27.29, in April 1988. Ngugi is a member of Club Namyuki and is a civil servant in Nairobi.

Sources: "Super Marathon-Man," *Cheza Kenya Factbook 34; International Amateur Athletic Federation*; "Kenyans Rono and Ngugi Sweep to Victories," *Los Angeles Times* (October 1, 1988); "Seoul Games/Medal Winners," *Los Angeles Times* (October 3, 1988); *Seoul '88*; "Olympics Record," *USA Today* (October 3, 1988).

NIX, SUNDER (USA). Born December 2, 1961, in Chicago, Illinois.

1984 Gold Medal: 4 x 400-Meter Relay (2:57.91)

Sunder Nix finished third in the 400 meters in the World Championships in 1983 to achieve a number 2 ranking in the world in the 400 that year. His personal record of 44.68 was set in 1982, but his greatest accomplishments came in 1983 when he was ranked second in the world, after a third place finish at the NCAA meet. He won the TAC title and was third at the World Championships. He was ranked seventh in the world in 1982 and fourth at TAC. Nix's 44.68 in the 400 was the fastest time in the world in 1982. The 4 x 400 relay time of 2:57.91 at the 1984 Olympics was the fastest ever recorded at sea level. Nix attended Indiana University.

Sources: British Virgin Islands, Olympic Committee; "The 1984 Olympics;" *Ebony* (October 1984); "The Champions," *Los Angeles Times* (August 14, 1984); "The Games," *Olympian* (October/November 1984); *United States Olympic Team, Media Guide; Who's Who in 1984 Olympics*.

NUÑEZ, AGUILAR DANIEL (Cuba). Born September 12, 1958, in Havana, Cuba.

1980 Gold Medal: Bantamweight Weightlifting (606¼ lbs./ 275 kg, world record)

Daniel Nuñez, the little Cuban, first gained world weightlifting recognition when he took the 1978 World Championships 56-kilogram title. In 1982 he moved to the heavier 60-kilogram class, and in Copenhagen that year he set the world snatch record with a lift of 137.5 kilograms (303 pounds). Nuñez's score in the bantamweight weightlifting category was snatch-125.0, world record; jerk-150.0; and total kilograms-275.0, world record. Nuñez won the Pan Am Games title in 1983 as a bantamweight but was later disqualified for use of prohibited drugs.

Sources: *Approved History of Olympic Games*; British Virgin Islands, Olympic Committee; *Complete Book of the Olympics*; *Guinness Book of Olympic Records*; *Who's Who in 1984 Olympics*.

NYAMAU, HEZEKIAH MUNYORO (Kenya).
Born December 5, 1946, in Kisii, Kenya.

1968 Silver Medal: 4 x 400-Meter Relay (2:59.6)
1972 Gold Medal: 4 x 400-Meter Relay (2:59.83)

Hezekiah Nyamau's silver medal in the 4 x 400-meter relay in 1968 was followed by a gold in the same event in 1972; on each occasion he ran the second leg for the Kenyan squad. Nyamau was one of the members of the Kenyan 4 x 400 relay team at the 1970 Commonwealth Games; Kenya won with a 3:03.6. The West Germans were in first place for most of the way in the 4 x 400-meter relay in the 1972 Munich Games. But Kenyan Julius Sang, running a 43.5 anchor leg, passed Karl Honz 75 meters from the finish and went on to give Kenya a 3-meter victory. Hezekiah Nyamau was a member of that relay team. Nyamau, whose best open 400-meter performance was 45.91 seconds, enjoyed modest international success in events other than the relays.

Sources: British Virgin Islands, Olympic Committee; *Complete Book of the Olympics*; *Die Spiele, Official Report of the Games of the XXth Olympiad*; *Encyclopaedia of Track and Field Athletics*; *Guinness Book of Olympic Records*.

NYAMBUI, SULEIMAN (Tanzania).
Born February 13, 1953, in Tanzania.

1980 Silver Medal: 5,000-Meter Run (13:21.6)

"The 1976 African boycott robbed Suleiman Nyambui of his first chance of Olympic gold. Miruts Yifter stopped him the second time" (*Who's Who in the 1984 Olympics*). Nyambui was the dominant middle-distance runner on the American collegiate scene in the late 1970s and early 1980s. Very versatile, Nyambui had times of 3:35.8 for 1,500 meters, 3:51.94 for the mile, 7:40.3 for the 3,000, 27:51.73 for the 10,000, and 13:12.29 for the 5,000. He ran second to phenomenal Miruts Yifter of Ethiopia in the 5,000 meters at the Moscow Olympics in 1980. Nyambui finished fifth in the 5,000 at the Commonwealth Games in 1978, fourth in 1974, and fifth in the 10,000 in 1978.

Sources: British Virgin Islands, Olympic Committee; *Complete Book of the Olympics*; *Games of the XXIInd Olympiad, Moscow*; *Guinness Book of Olympic Records*; "Yifter Takes 5,000 for Double," *New York Times* (August 2, 1980); *Who's Who in the 1984 Olympics*.

OAKES, HEATHER R. (HUNTE) (Great Britain).
Born August 14, 1959, in England, of Guyanese parentage.

1980 Bronze Medal: 4 x 100-Meter Relay (42.43)
1984 Bronze Medal: 4 x 100-Meter Relay (43.11)

Heather Oakes won the European Jr. Championships in the 4 x 100-meter relay in 1977 and the WAAA Championships in 1978 with a 7.39 in the 60 meters. Her United Kingdom Championships win in the 200 was in 1979 with 23.15. She won the 100 at the 1979 WAAA Championships with 11.58. Oakes earned bronze medals in the 4 x 100-meter relay at both Moscow and Los Angeles, leading off at the 1980 Games and anchoring 4 years later. She was also a finalist in the 100 in 1984. Oakes has personal bests of 11.20 for 100 meters and 22.97 for 200. She enjoyed a very successful year in 1986, placing second in the Commonwealth Games 100 and dipping under 23 seconds in the 200 for the first time in European Championships semifinals. Oakes is married to Olympic bronze medalist Gary Oakes.

Sources: British Virgin Islands, Olympic Committee; *Complete Book of the Olympics*; *Encyclopaedia of Track and Field Athletics*; *Guinness Book of Olympic Records*; *1984 Olympic Games*; *Sarajevo/Los Angeles*; "Heather Hunte," *Women's Sports* (October 1984).

ORTEGA, JUAN (Cuba). Born in Cuba.

1972 Bronze Medal: Basketball

A forward with the Cuban Olympic team, Juan Ortega did not enjoy as long a career on the national team as did most of his teammates. For a summary of the team's record at the Munich Games, see Calderón-Gómez.

Sources: *Approved History of Olympic Games*; British Virgin Islands, Olympic Committee; *Guinness Book of Olympic Records*; *Munchen 1972*; *Results of the Games of the XXth Olympiad*.

OTTEY-PAGE, MERLENE (Jamaica). Born May 10, 1960, in Jamaica.

1980 Bronze Medal: 200-Meter Run (22.20)
1984 Bronze Medal: 100-Meter Run (11.16)
1984 Bronze Medal: 200-Meter Run (22.09)

Merlene Ottey-Page was 1982 NCAA champion in the 100-meter sprint and finished second in the 200. She was one of the world's leading sprinters in the 1980s. Her Olympic bronze medals in the 200 at both Moscow and Los Angeles, as well as her silver in the same event at the World Championships and a bronze in the 100 in Los Angeles, attest to that fact. Ottey-Page has personal bests of 10.92, 21.93, and 51.12 for the 100, 200, and 400 meters. Ottey-Page's international honors also include a Commonwealth Games gold medal in the 200 (22.19 seconds) in 1982 and a silver medal in the 200 at the 1983 World Championships. Ottey-Page rocketed a 10.87 in the 100, which was the fastest time in the world for the 1987 season; it was also a personal best by 0.05. That Jamaican-record dash moved her to fourth all-time. She also took over the global lead in the 200 with 22.22. Merlene Ottey-Page lives in Lincoln, Nebraska, where she was an art student at the University of Nebraska. She married American high jumper-hurdler Nat Page in 1984, but she wants to keep competing for Jamaica. The couple met in 1982 on a track trip to Czechoslovakia.

Sources: British Virgin Islands, Olympic Committee; *Guinness Book of Olympic Records*; "The Champions," *Olympian* (October/November 1984); *Research Information, Games of the XXIIIrd Olympiad*; "Two World Leaders for Ottey," *Track & Field News* (July 1987); "Merlene Ottey," *Women's Sports* (October 1984).

OUKO, ROBERT (Kenya). Born October 24, 1948, in Manga Kisii, Kenya.

1972 Gold Medal: 4 x 400-Meter Relay (2:59.83)

Robert Ouko attended North Carolina Central University. An outstanding college runner, he was best known for his blazing first laps in the 800 meters. Ouko won the 800 meters in the Commonwealth Games in 1970 at 1:46.8. He also was a member of the Kenyan 4 x 400-meter relay team, which finished with a 3:03.6. The 4 x 400-meter relay at the 1972 Munich Olympics was an exciting race. The West Germans were in first place most of the way. But Julius Sang of Kenya, running a 43.5 anchor leg, passed the fading Karl Honz 75 meters from the finish and went on to give Kenya a victory by 3 meters. Ouko ran the third leg of that gold-winning team. Ouko placed fifth in the 1972 Olympics 800 meters. He had bests of 46.0 for 400 meters and 1:46.0 at double the distance. He is now a track and field administrator in Nairobi.

Sources: British Virgin Islands, Olympic Committee; *Complete Book of the Olympics; Die Spiele, Official Report of the Games of the XXth Olympiad; Encyclopaedia of Track and Field Athletics; Guinness Book of Olympic Records*.

OWENS, JAMES CLEVELAND (JESSE) (USA). Born September 12, 1913, in Danville, Alabama.

1936 Gold Medal: 100-Meter Run (10.3, tied Olympic record)
1936 Gold Medal: 200-Meter Run (20.7, Olympic record)
1936 Gold Medal: Long Jump (26 ft. 5½ in./8.06 m, Olympic record)
1936 Gold Medal: 4 x 100-Meter Relay (39.8, Olympic record/world record)

JESSE OWENS (Photo courtesy of Amateur Athletic Foundation, Los Angeles, California.)

Jesse Owens attended East Technical High School in Cleveland, Ohio, and Ohio State University. His university coach was Larry Snyder, who once said that Owens had a "high-tension nervous system." He worked up such great tension before competing, that he had great strength under pressure. He was, at the same time, graceful, and he always appeared relaxed. Jesse Owens is remembered for record breaking, and especially for his feat on May 25, 1935, at Ann Arbor, Michigan, when he beat or equaled six world records within 45 minutes. His single long jump of 8.13 meters (26 feet, 8¼ inches) was to last for 25 years. Owens scored 9.4 in 100 meters in 1933, a record that was not broken until 1967. His 220 straightaway mark, 20.7, didn't fall until 1953. His national prep long jump mark, 24 feet, 11¼ inches, lasted until George Brown jumped 25 feet, 2½ inches in 1949. Owens, a courageous and humble man, was one of the greatest of all track and field atheltes. At the peak of his career he won nine world records in seven events. At one time he held 11 world records. His name remained in the record book for 40 years. One of his world marks, the indoor 60-meter dash (6.6), was set in 1935 and wasn't broken until 1975. He equaled or broke 12 Olympic records on his way to gold medals. His 200 meters in 20.7 seconds at the 1936 Olympics was the fastest ever at that time around a full turn. The nine Black Americans on the U.S. track and field team collected a total eight gold, three silver, and two bronze medals. (Black Americans won every track event from 100 to 800 meters in 1936.) It was claimed, with some evidence, that Adolph Hitler snubbed Jesse Owens by refusing to acknowledge the medals he had won at the 1936 Berlin Olympics. Hitler had been profuse in his praise of German and Nordic winners before Blacks began to take medals in track and field events. Jesse turned professional at age 23, shortly after the Berlin Olympics, and he experienced many years of financial hardship and racial discrimination. But, always a fighter, he eventually became a successful businessman and inspirational speaker and youth worker. He was named a member of the United States Olympic Committee and in 1976 was awarded the Presidential Medal of Freedom. In 1950 the Associated Press selected Owens as the greatest track and field athlete of the half century. Jim Thorpe (an American Indian) finished second in that poll and Paavo Nurmi (a Finn) finished third. Owens was awarded an honorary doctorate by his alma mater in 1972 and in 1974 the NCAA presented him with the Theodore Roosevelt Award for his collegiate contributions. Owens died March 30, 1980. Someone once said of this great athlete, "If you knew him, you loved him" (*Los Angeles Times*). That is how he is best remembered.

Sources: *Black Olympians; Guinness Book of Olympic Records; Hard Road to Glory; Illustrated History of the Olympics*; "The Greatest Day Ever," *Los Angeles Times* (July 22, 1984); *Negro Almanac; Negro Firsts in Sports; Quest for Gold; Who's Who in Track and Field*.

PAGE, JERRY (USA). Born January 15, 1961, in Columbus, Ohio.

1984 Gold Medal: Light Welterweight Boxing

Jerry Page graduated from Linden McKinley High School in Columbus, Ohio, in 1979 and attended Ohio State University, where he majored in business. He trained under Edward Williams at Sawyer Parks and Recreation Club. Page came to national prominence in 1980. A few years later, in 1983 at the U.S.-USSR contest in Las Vegas, he meted out an awful drubbing to prominent Vassily Shiskov. In Reno, at the World Championship Challenges, he came desperately close to outpointing world champion Cuban fighter Carlos García—but faded. Page who had been boxing for 14 years, took third at Pan Am trials in 1983 but won the box-off to go to the Pan Am Games, where he took second. However, knee surgery sidelined him until the 1984 Olympic trials, where he finished third. Other medals Page won during his career include: USA/American Boxing Federation, silver, 1982; Ohio State Fair, gold, 1981; Sports Festival, gold, 1982; and National Golden Gloves, bronze, 1981.

Sources: "The 1984 Olympics," *Ebony* (October 1984); "The Champions," *Los Angeles Times* (August 14, 1984); "Boxing," *Olympian* (October/November 1984); *United States Olympic Team, Media Guide; Who's Who in the 1984 Olympics*.

PANZO, HERMANN (France). Born February 8, 1958, in Martinique.

1980 Bronze Medal: 4 x 100-Meter Relay (38.53)

Hermann Panzo was a winner in the European Jr. Championships 100 meters in 1977, with a 10.40. However, the colorful Panzo's chief claim to fame was a victory in the 100 meters at the IAAF Golden Sprints in 1981, after having anchored a rather ordinary French 400-meter relay team to a bronze medal in the 1980 Moscow Olympics. He was the first French-based Antillean to make an impact internationally. With best performances of 10.24 for the 100 meters and 21.01 for the 200, Panzo began to be troubled by injuries in 1982.

Sources: British Virgin Islands, Olympic Committee; *Complete Book of the Olympics; Encyclopaedia of Track and Field Athletics; Guinness Book of Olympic Records*.

PARKS, MAXIE LANDER (USA). Born July 9, 1951, in Arkansas City, Arkansas.

1976 Gold Medal: 4 x 400-Meter Relay (2:58.65)

Maxie Parks graduated from Union High School, Fresno, California, and, in 1976, from UCLA. Parks won the Jr. College State Championship in the 440 yards in 1971 and was first in the AAU and in the Olympic trials in 1976. Although Parks attended UCLA, he was never a major force in the NCAA Championships, his highest placing in the 440 yards being third in 1974. He was anchoring the U.S. 1,600-meter relay team to an astounding victory at the World Cup in 1979 when he collapsed with a severely pulled hamstring. Maxie Parks placed no better than fifth in the individual 400 at the 1976 Olympics, despite winning both the AAU and final trials in that event. However, as anchor leg in the 4 x 400, he helped the U.S. relay team clinch the gold medal.

Sources: *Black Olympians; Guinness Book of Olympic Records*; "Olympic Summaries," *New York Times* (August 2, 1976); *Quest for Gold; United States Olympic Team, Games of the XXIst Olympiad*.

PATTERSON, AUDREY (USA). Born September 27, 1926, in New Orleans, Louisiana.

1948 Bronze Medal: 200-Meter Run (25.2)

Audrey Patterson graduated from high school in 1947 and attended Tennessee State University. "Mickey" Patterson was inspired by hearing Jesse Owens speak when she was 15. Several years later, in London, she became the first American woman to compete in the 200 meters and the first Black woman medalist in the history of the Olympic Games. It was shown 25 years later, in an examination of a photo-finish picture, that her bronze medal should have gone to Australian Shirley Strickland. Patterson finished second in the 100 meters and won the 200 at the 1948 Olympic final trials. In London she was a surprise winner of the bronze medal in the longer sprint but failed to make the 100. When Patterson was at her best, the AAU sprints were dominated by Stella Walsh, but Patterson did win the indoor 200 in 1948. Audrey Patterson has in more recent years become a coach in southern California.

Sources: Patterson, Audrey. Panelist. 1984; *Black Olympians*; British Virgin Islands, Olympic Committee; *Guinness Book of Olympic Records; Negro Firsts in Sports; Quest for Gold; United States Track and Field Olympians*.

PATTERSON, FLOYD P. (USA). Born January 4, 1935, in Waco, North Carolina.

1952 Gold Medal: Middleweight Boxing

Floyd Patterson took an excellent amateur record to the 1952 Olympics. In 1951-52 he won six major amateur titles, including the National AAU and New York Golden Gloves Championships. He won his gold medal easily when he knocked out Romania's Vasile Trita in the first round. Less than a month after the Olympics, Patterson fought Eddie Godbold and knocked him out in four rounds. Patterson outgrew the middleweight class and defeated light heavyweight champion Archie Moore for the vacant heavyweight title. In the next 2 years he defended the title 4 times and fought for several exhibitions. At 21 Patterson became the youngest world heavyweight champion ever and the first man to twice win and lose the heavyweight title in the ring. He was the first to regain the world heavyweight championship when he knocked out Ingemar Johannsson, after being defeated by earlier (June 20, 1960). Patterson defended the title twice before losing to Sonny Liston by a knockout. He fought twice more—against Liston and Muhammad Ali—and was knocked out both times. He retired in 1967 with a career record of 44 wins and 5 losses.

Sources: *Black Olympians; Guinness Book of Olympic Records; 1980 Olympians Handbook*; Patterson, Floyd. Questionnaire. 1984; *Quest for Gold; United States Olympic Team, 1952*.

PAYNE, MARITA (Canada). Born October 7, 1960, in Barbados.

1984 Silver Medal: 4 x 100-Meter Relay (42.77)
1984 Silver Medal: 4 x 400-Meter Relay (3:21.21)

Marita Payne in 1984 became one of only two athletes (Chandra Cheeseborough being the other) to gain medals in both the 400- and 1,600-meter relays in the same Olympic Games. An excellent all-around sprinter, she competed with distinction at Florida State while representing Canada

internationally. Her personal bests are 11.43, 22.62, and 49.91 seconds in the three sprints. Payne attended Florida State University, where she majored in elementary education. She now resides in Houston and competes for the Puma Track Club.

Sources: British Virgin Islands, Olympic Committee; Canadian Olympic Association; *1984 Olympic Games; Sarajevo/Los Angeles*; "The Games," *Olympian* (October/November 1984); *Research Information, Games of the XXIIIrd Olympiad*.

PENDER, MELVIN (USA). Born October 31, 1937, in Atlanta, Georgia.

1968 Gold Medal: 4 x 100-Meter Relay (38.24, Olympic record/world record)

Melvin Pender graduated from Lynwood High School in Atlanta and from Adelphi University, Long Island, New York. He is married to Christina Pender and has three children: Javier, Mazana, and Germaine. He was a member of the Philadelphia Pioneers track club. In the Tokyo 100-meter final in 1964, the diminutive (5-foot, 4-inch) Pender ran 10.4, but finished sixth. After getting off to a usual fast start, he was leading with 20 meters to go. However, a rib injury slowed him. In Mexico City, in 1968, the same bad luck held, despite his 10.1 time. He was the only U.S. sprinter to compete in both the 1964 and 1968 Olympics. Mel Pender ran 6.8 in 70 yards for a world record in 1965; he matched the time in 1971. He ran 5.9 to tie the indoor record in 1972. Pender became a captain in the U.S. Army and assistant track coach at West Point. He has also worked as a track shoe designer and marketing specialist and has been director of the Youth Development Program of the NFL Players Association.

Sources: Pender, Melvin. Questionnaire. 1984; *Guinness Book of Olympic Records; Quest for Gold; Who's Who in Track and Field*.

PÉREZ, JORGE (Cuba). Born in Cuba.

1976 Bronze Medal: Volleyball

For a summary of the Cuban team's record at the 1976 Olympics in Montreal, see García.

Sources: *Approved History of Olympic Games*; British Virgin Islands, Olympic Committee; *Complete Book of the Olympics; Guinness Book of Olympic Records; Montreal 1976; Games of the XXIst Olympiad*.

PÉREZ ARMENTEROS, CONRADO (Cuba). Born December 21, 1950, in S.C. Villas, Cuba.

1972 Bronze Medal: Basketball

For a summary of the Cuban team's record at the 1972 Munich Games, see Calderón-Gómez.

Sources: *Approved History of Olympic Games*; British Virgin Islands, Olympic Committee; *Die Spiele, Official Report for the XXth Olympiad*; *Guinness Book of Olympic Records*; *Munchen 1972, Results of the Games of the XXth Olympiad*.

PERKINS, SAMUEL BRUCE (USA). Born June 14, 1961, in Latham, New York.

1984 Gold Medal: Basketball

Sam Perkins, a forward at the University of North Carolina, was first team All-American for 1982, 1983, and 1984. He was the third person in North Carolina history to achieve that distinction. He was in the All-Atlantic Coast Conference for 3 years and was second leading scorer in Carolina history, with 2,145 points. He is also the career rebounding leader with 1,167. He played in 15 NCAA tournament games, and scored in double figures in all 15. In 4 years he shot 57.6 percent from the field and 79.6 percent from the line, averaging 8.6 rebounds and 15.9 points per game. He hit 85.6 percent of his free throws as a senior. Perkins played on North Carolina's 1982 NCAA Championship team along with Olympic teammate Michael Jordan. He was a member of the U.S. Gold Medal team of the 1983 Pan Am Games and played in the 1979 National Sports Festival and on the 1979 U.S. Select team at the World Championships for junior men. Perkins joined the Dallas Mavericks of the NBA following the Olympics, and the 6-foot 9-inch forward has developed into one of the NBA's leading players.

Sources: "The 1984 Olympics," *Ebony* (October 1984); "The Champions," *Los Angeles Times* (August 14, 1984); "Basketball," *Olympian* (November/December 1984); *United States Olympic Team, Media Guide*.

PETERS, (ULO) ROTIMI (Nigeria). Born December 18, 1955, in Nigeria.

1984 Bronze Medal: 4 x 400-Meter Relay (2:59.32)

Rotimi Peters, a graduate of the University of Illinois, has been a steady if unspectacular performer for several years. His personal best time in the individual 400 meters is 45.6 seconds, but he has been a dependable relay runner for Nigeria. Peters's third leg at the Los Angeles Games helped his country win a bronze medal.

Sources: British Virgin Islands, Olympic Committee; *The 1984 Games, Sarajevo/Los Angeles*; "The Games," *Olympian* (October/November 1984); "Olympic Winners," *New York Times* (August 13, 1984).

PHILLIPS, ANDRE (USA). Born September 5, 1959, in Milwaukee, Wisconsin.

1988 Gold Medal: 400-Meter Hurdles (47.19, Olympic record)

Andre Phillips graduated from UCLA in 1981, the year he became NCAA champion. He was a member of the World Class Athletic Club. Phillips was a triple winner at the Tucson Elite track and field meet at the University of Arizona. He won the 200 meters in 20.51 seconds, the 400 in 45.10, and the 110-meter hurdles in 13.65. He ranked number 1 in the world in both 1985 and 1986, with Moses out of the running in 1986. He won the 1985 TAC Championship. Phillips, with a 47.58, finished second after Edwin Moses at the 1988 Olympic trials. In 1987 he had ranked seventh in the U.S. in the 400 hurdles with a best time of 49.02. He had ranked fourth on the all-time world list with a time of 47.51, run in 1986, and third on the all-time U.S. list. Phillips won the 1988 400-meter hurdles in an Olympic record time of 47.19 seconds, a personal best and the fastest time since Edwin Moses set the world record of 47.02 in 1963. Phillips said, "I've been chasing Edwin since 1979.... He was my motivation, my inspiration, my idol. I don't think I'd have made it this far if he hadn't been out there in the last 15 years" (*Los Angeles Times*).

Sources: "Black American Medal Winners," *Ebony* (December 1988); "World Records Are Broken," *Los Angeles Times* (June 12, 1988); "Seoul Games/Medal Winners," *Los Angeles Times* (October 3, 1988); *1988 United States Olympic Team, Media Guide*; *Seoul '88*; "Olympics Record," *USA Today* (October 3, 1988).

POAGE, GEORGE COLEMAN (USA). Born November 6, 1880, in Hannibal, Missouri.

1904 Bronze Medal: 400-Meter Hurdles (54.8)
1904 Bronze Medal: 200-Meter Hurdles (25.2)

George Poage was the first Black student to graduate from La Crosse, Wisconsin, High School and the first Black athlete to become a member of the Milwaukee Athletic Club. More importantly, he was the first Black Olympian medalist. A superb hurdler and quarter-miler, Poage was a star on his high school track team. He established a collegiate record of 49.0 for the 440-yard sprint and 25 seconds for the low hurdles. He also set the collegiate record for the 220-yard hurdles of 25.0. Poage was also an orator and a scholar, who earned a pre-law degree in 1903 and did graduate work in history and political science at the University of Wisconsin. After the 1904 Games, he became a teacher at Charles Sumner High School in St. Louis, where he remained until 1914. He then returned to Wisconsin and purchased a quarter section, which he farmed until 1920. Finally, he moved to Chicago and worked for 27 years for the U.S. Postal Service before retiring. George Poage died in 1962.

Sources: *Approved History of Olympic Games; Black Olympians; Negro Firsts in Sports; Negro in Sports; Quest for Gold.*

POLLARD, FREDERICK DOUGLAS, JR.

(USA). Born February 18, 1915, in Springfield, Massachusetts.

1936 Bronze Medal: 110-Meter Hurdles (14.4)

"Fritz" Pollard, the son of Brown University's All-American football player of the same name, attended the University of North Dakota and played football, ran track, and was on the school boxing team. He was considered the greatest all-around athlete that the University of North Dakota ever had. Pollard later attended law school before beginning a career as a physical educator in Chicago. Later, he was appointed director of the U.S. State Department's Office of Equal Employment Opportunity.

Sources: *Approved History of Olympic Games; Black Olympians; Guinness Book of Olympic Records; Negro in Sports; Quest for Gold.*

POWELL, MIKE (USA). Born November 20, 1963, in Philadelphia, Pennsylvania.

1988 Silver Medal: Long Jump (27 ft. 10¼ in./8.49 m)

Mike Powell graduated from West Covina High School in southern California in 1981 and from UCLA in 1986. In the 1988 Olympic trials, Powell finished third in the long jump, behind Carl Lewis and Larry Myricks, with a jump of 27 feet, 5 inches. In 1987 he ranked fourth in the U.S. in the long jump. His personal best in 1987 was 27 feet, 1¾ inches. Also a high jumper, Powell has high-jumped more than 7 feet.

Sources: "Black American Medal Winners," *Ebony* (December 1988); "A New Lewis (Steve)," *Los Angeles Times* (July 19, 1988); "Seoul Games/Medal Winners," *Los Angeles* (October 3, 1988); *1988 United States Olympic Teams, Media Guide; Seoul '88;* "Olympics Record," *USA Today* (October 3, 1988).

PRUDENCIO, NELSON (Brazil). Born April 4, 1944, in São Paulo, Brazil.

1968 Silver Medal: Triple Jump (56 ft. 8 in./17.27 m)
1972 Bronze Medal: Triple Jump (55 ft. 11¼ in./17.05 m)

Nelson Prudencio proved a worthy successor to two-time Olympic gold medalist Ferreira da Silva. Brazilians Prudencio, Joao Carlos de Oliveira, and A. F. da Silva were all exceptional triple jump champions. Prudencio won a silver medal in Mexico City in 1968 and a bronze at Munich in 1972, although he had originally been left off the Brazilian squad for the Olympic Games in Germany. During the 1968 Mexico City triple jump competition, Prudencio, who never jumped beyond 53 feet, 5¾ inches before, leaped an ominous 55 feet, 11¼ inches in the second round. (This was after Giuseppe Gentile had leaped 56 feet, 6 inches in the first round.) Several jumps later, Prudencio exploded with another world record of 56 feet, 8 inches. Then, with his last jump, he again broke Józef Schmidt's old record with a jump of 56 feet, 3¼ inches. (Schmidt had dominated the event for 6 years.)

Sources: *Approved History of Olympic Games*; British Virgin Islands, Olympic Committee; *Complete Book of the Olympics; Encyclopaedia of Track and Field Athletics; The Games, Organizing Committee of the XIXth Olympiad; Guinness Book of Olympic Records.*

DONALD QUARRIE (Photo courtesy of Jamaica Information Service.)

QUARRIE, DONALD (Jamaica). Born February 25, 1951, in Kingston, Jamaica.

1976 Gold Medal: 200-Meter Run (20.23)
1976 Silver Medal: 100-Meter Run (10.08)
1980 Bronze Medal: 200-Meter Run (20.29)
1984 Silver Medal: 4 x 100-Meter Relay (38.62)

Don Quarrie graduated from the University of Southern California with a B.A. in public administration in 1973. Quarrie is one of the greatest sprinters in history. He had won six important gold medals by the time he was 20. He won the 100 and 200 meters and was a member of the victorious Jamaican 4 x 100-meter relay team at both the 1970 Commonwealth and the 1971 Pan Am Games. Notable in the Pan Am Games at Cali (Colombia) was his time in the 200—then the second-ever electrically-timed race—of 19.86 seconds. Quarrie's second-place time in the 100 meters in the 1976 Olympics was a mere .02 seconds behind Jamaican Hasely Crawford. Quarrie has won more Commonwealth Games medals than any other track and field competitor, emerging victorious in the 100 in 1970, 1974, and 1978 and in the 200 in 1970 and 1974. He gained another gold medal in the 4 x 100-meter relay in 1970. From 1968, when he was a 17-year-old reserve on Jamaica's 4 x 100-meter Olympic squad, to 1984, when he concluded his career with his customary blazing third leg in the 4 x 100 relay at Los Angeles to play a large part in Jamaica's second-place finish, the popular "D.Q." represented his country with honor all around the world. A statue in his honor stands outside the National Stadium in Kingston. Quarrie is currently coaching track at USC.

Sources: *Approved History of Olympic Games*; British Virgin Islands, Olympic Committee; *Games of the XXIInd Olympiad, Moscow 1980*; *Guinness Book of Olympic Records*; *Montreal 1976, Games of the XXIst Olympiad*; *Research Information, Games of the XXIIIrd Olympiad*.

QUARTEY, CLEMENT (Ghana). Born in Ghana.

1960 Silver Medal: Light Welterweight Boxing

"Ike" Quartey, in taking second place in light welterweight boxing in the 1960 Rome Olympics, won the distinction of becoming the first Black African to win an Olympic medal. He was considered quite inexperienced as compared with gold medal winner Bohumil Nemeček of Czechoslovakia.

Sources: *Approved History of Olympic Games*; *Complete Book of the Olympics*; *Games of the XVIIth Olympiad, Rome 1960*; *Guinness Book of Olympic Records*.

QUESADA, VIOLETA (Cuba). Born July 11, 1947, in Santa Clara, Cuba.

1968 Silver Medal: 4 x 100-Meter Relay (43.36)

Violeta Quesada never quite made it to the top echelon of Cuban sprinting, but she was a very valuable member of several good sprint relay teams. She was on Cuba's 400-meter relay team in the 1968 Mexico City Olympics, which also included Marlene Elejarde, Fulgencia Romay, and Miguelina Cobian. Winning a silver medal as a member of this team was the high point of Quesada's career. Her personal bests included 11.5 (100 meters) and 23.6 (200 meters).

Sources: British Virgin Islands, Olympic Committee; *Complete Book of the Olympics*; *Guinness Book of Olympic Record*.

RAMBO, JOHN (USA). Born August 9, 1944, in Rambo, Texas.

1964 Bronze Medal: High Jump (7 ft. 1 in./2.16 m)

"Twig" Rambo was NCAA high jump champion, College and University Division, 1964-65; Germany's Foreign Athlete of the Year, 1966; AAU outdoor high jump champion, 1964; AAU indoor high jump champion, 1966, 1967, and 1970; College Division basketball All-American, 1964-65; College Division track and field All-American, 1964; Athlete of the Year, Long Beach City College (basketball, track and field), 1963; All-Coast first team basketball tournament MVP for 7 years; and College Athlete of the Year, 1964. He was ranked among the top 10 high jumpers in the world in 1964, 1966, 1967, and 1968. Rambo graduated from Long Beach Polytechnic High School and, in 1966, from Utah State University. He has conducted a summer tutorial program for youths whose reading skills are below grade level. For this experiment, he raised funds from a number of major companies and from the Henry Salvatore Foundation. In 1974 a Long Beach newspaper talked about Rambo's work in the community: "Rambo himself is an interesting guy.... He has the ideal job, community relations specialist for General Telephone, which allows him to pursue such projects as the tutorial program and to coach a neighborhood girls basketball team that managed to come in 13th in the nation this year" (*Press Telegram*).

Sources: *Black Olympians*; *Guinness Book of Olympic Records*; "Building for Tomorrow with Minority Children," *Long Beach Press Telegram* (September 24, 1984); *Quest for Gold*; Rambo, John. Interview. 1984.

RAMÍREZ, HERMES (Cuba). Born June 7, 1948, in Guantánamo, Cuba.

1968 Silver Medal: 4 x 100-Meter Relay (38.40)

Hermes Ramírez was an outstanding curve runner who enjoyed considerably more success in the 100 than the 200 meters. He was one of the world's best sprinters between 1968 and 1973. He was the leadoff runner for the silver-winning Cuban relay team at the 1968 Olympics and helped Cuba win another silver in leading off the relay at the 1975 Pan Am Games. His career best performances were 10.10 seconds for the 100 and 20.6 for the 200. In the 1968 Mexico City 4 x 100-meter relays, Cuba beat the U.S. in both the opening round and the semifinals. But in the finals, 5 feet behind Enrique Figuerola at the exchange, American James Hines ripped into the lead after 30 yards and won by a yard. The other members of the Cuban team were Juan Morales and Pablo Montes.

Sources: British Virgin Islands, Olympic Committee; *Complete Book of the Olympics; Guinness Book of Olympic Records*.

RAMOS, HIPOLITO (Cuba). Born in Cuba.

1980 Silver Medal: Light Flyweight Boxing

To win the silver medal in the 1980 Moscow Olympics light flyweight boxing events, Hipolito Ramos defeated Farid Salman Mahdi of Iraq, points 5-0; Gyorgy Gedes of Hungary, 5-0; and Shamil Sabirov of USSR, 3-2.

Sources: *Approved History of Olympic Games; Complete Book of the Olympics; Games of the XXIInd Olympiad, Moscow 1980; Guinness Book of Olympic Records*.

RANDOLPH, LEO (USA). Born February 27, 1958, in Mississippi.

1976 Gold Medal: Flyweight Boxing

Leo Randolph won the Golden Gloves Association of America title, the National AAU, and the 1976 final Olympic trials. He was named Youth of the Year and was awarded the Key to the City. Randolph was also junior featherweight champion of the world in 1980. He turned professional after the Olympics but has had only moderate success. Randolph later became program director for a boys' and girls' club. A resident of Tacoma, Washington, he is married to Lee Dora and has a son, Leo, Jr.

Sources: Randolph, Leo. Questionnaire. 1984; *Guinness Book of Olympic Records; Montreal 1976, Games of the XXIst Olympiad; Quest for Gold; United States Olympic Team*.

RATLEFF, EDWARD (USA). Born March 29, 1950, in Bellefontaine, Ohio.

1972 Silver Medal: Basketball

Ed Ratleff attended East High School in Columbus, Ohio, and graduated from California State University, Long Beach. His college coach was Jerry Tarkanian. Ratleff, one of the top guards in the nation at Long Beach State in the early 1970s, earned several All-American honors. He averaged 40 points per game in freshman ball and over 20 points per game as a 3-year varsity starter, including an amazing high game of 68 against San Diego State in 1970. In 1972 he was selected for 12 out of 12 All-American teams and was named MVP in the Pacific Coast Athletic Association. After the Olympics and his senior year of

college, Ratleff was drafted by the Houston Rockets. He played only 5 years in the NBA and never reached the level of stardom he had attained as a collegian.

Sources: *Black Olympians; Quest for Gold; United States Olympic Team, Games of the XXth Olympiad*.

REGUEIFEROS, ENRIQUE (Cuba). Born July 15, 1948, in Oriente, Cuba.

1968 Silver Medal: Light Welterweight Boxing

Enrique Regueiferos had to settle for a silver medal when he was beat in 1968 by policeman Jerzy Kulej of Poland, a strong puncher 8 years his junior. Kulej had also won the Olympic title in 1964.

Sources: *Approved History of Olympic Games*; British Virgin Islands, Olympic Committee; *Complete Book of the Olympics; Guinness Book of Olympic Records; Olympic Games 1980, Moscow and Lake Placid*.

REID, J. R. (USA). Born March 31, 1968.

1988 Bronze Medal: Basketball

J. R. Reid was a first team All-America selection and a first team All-Atlantic Coast Conference selection in 1988. He led the University of North Carolina as a sophomore in scoring (18.0) and rebounds (8.9), hitting at .607 clip from the field and .680 from the lines. Reid helped North Carolina build up a 59-11 record over two seasons, win two straight AAC regular season championships, set a 25-3 league record, and earn a spot in two NCAA finals. Reid collected 1,000 points faster than any player in Carolina history, with one exception. He netted 1,123 points and grabbed 561 rebounds over his first 2 seasons. His career highs are 31 points and 15 rebounds. He played the past 2 years for the South team at the U.S. Olympic Festival.

Sources: "Black American Medal Winners," *Ebony* (December 1988); "Seoul Games/Medal Winners," *Los Angeles Times* (October 3, 1988); *1988 United States Olympic Team, Media Guide; Seoul '88*; "Olympics Record," *USA Today* (October 3, 1988).

REYNOLDS, HARRY (BUTCH) (USA). Born June 8, 1964, in Akron, Ohio.

1988 Gold Medal: 4 x 400-Meter Relay (2:56.16, Olympic record)
1988 Silver Medal: 400-Meter run (43.93)

"Butch" Reynolds set the world record in the 400 meters at 43.29 seconds at the Grand Prix track meet in Zurich, Switzerland, August 17, 1988. He shattered Lee Evans's mark of 43.86, which had stood for 20 years. Reynolds won the Olympic trials with a 44.93, the second-fastest 400 meters in history. The only faster time was that of Lee Evans (43.86) at the 1968 Olympic Games. Reynolds is third on the all-time world list. He won both the 1987 TAC and NCAA Championships. Americans Lee Evans and Larry James ran the only times better than Reynolds's, in 1968, both at altitude. Reynolds ran under 44.50 eight times in 1987, amazing in that no one had broken that mark even three times in a career. Reynolds became the first sub-44 quarter-miler in 20 years by winning the 1988 Olympics 400 in 43.93 seconds. A 1987 graduate of Ohio State University, he competes for Athletics West.

Sources: "Black American Medal Winners," *Ebony* (December 1988); "Reynolds Shatters 400 Record," *Los Angeles Times* (August 8, 1988); "Seoul Games/Medal Winners," *Los Angeles Times* (October 3, 1988); *1988 United States Olympic Team, Media Guide; Seoul '88*; "Reynolds' Olympic Task," *Sport Magazine* (July 1988); "Reynolds Changes with His Times," *Track & Field News* (June 1987); "Reynolds Scorches Track," *Track & Field News* (June 1987); "Reynolds Faster Than McGrady," *Track & Field News* (July 1986); "Olympics Record," *USA Today* (October 3, 1988).

RHODEN, GEORGE VINCENT (Jamaica). Born December 13, 1926, in Kingston, Jamaica.

1952 Gold Medal: 400-Meter Run (45.09, Olympic record)
1952 Bold Medal: 4 x 400-Meter Relay (3:03.09, Olympic record/world record)

During the 4-year period from 1949 to 1952, George Rhoden was the world's dominant 400-meter runner. In the U.S. he won three consecutive AAU titles in the 400 (1949-51) and duplicated the feat in NCAA competition between 1950 and 1952. He also added a 200-meter title at the collegiate level in 1951. At the Central American and Caribbean Games George Rhoden won more medals than any other male competitor (10). These included four golds—in the 4 x 100 relay, in the 4 x 400 (two), and in the 800-meter run. Oddly, he was never to win the 400-meter run in this competition, in which he participated in 1946, 1950, and 1954. In 1950 Rhoden set a world record for the 400-meter dash with a clocking of 45.8 seconds at a competition in Finland. Returning to that country 2 years later he ran an Olympic record time of 45.9, edging teammate Herb McKenley. Later in the Games they combined with Arthur Wint, 400-meter winner 4 years earlier, and sprinter Les Laing to eclipse the previous Olympic 1,600-meter relay record with a win in 3:03.9. With two Olympic gold medals under his belt, Rhoden continued competing at the highest international level until 1954. He made a brief return to the track in the early 1970s and was one of the early stars of Masters competitions—as a 100- and 200-meter sprinter. Rhoden attended Morgan State College in Baltimore, where he pursued

premedical studies. He is now a podiatrist in southern California.

Sources: *Approved History of Olympic Games*; British Virgin Islands, Olympic Committee; *Complete Book of the Olympics*; *XVth Olympiad, Helsinki 1952*; *Guinness Book of Olympic Records*; *The Sackville Illustrated Dictionary of Athletics*; *Track and Field: The Great Ones*.

RICHARDSON, JILLIAN (Canada). Born March 10, 1965, in Trinidad.

1984 Silver Medal: 4 x 400-Meter Relay (3:21.21)

Jillian Richardson has represented Canada internationally since 1981. A silver medalist in the 4 x 400-meter relay at Los Angeles, her first international honors came in the same event at the 1983 World University Games, where the Canadians also finished second. She has a best time of 51.58 seconds for 400 meters. Richardson attended the University of Toronto, where she majored in physical education. She lives in Calgary, Alberta.

Sources: British Virgin Islands, Olympic Committee; *1984 Olympic Games; Sarajevo/Los Angeles; Research Information, Games of the XXIIIrd Olympiad*; "Jillian Richardson," *Women's Sports* (October 1984).

RICHMOND, MITCH (USA). Born June 30, 1965.

1988 Bronze Medal: Basketball

Mitch Richmond broke Bob Boozer's single-season scoring record at Kansas State in 1988 by netting 768 points. Richmond ranked fifth on the school's career scoring list with 1,327 points, the most ever by a two-year player at KSU. He was second team All-America pick by the USBWA, *Basketball Weekly, Sporting News*, and United Press International. Richmond was a Consensus All Big Eight selection. He scored in double figures in 63 of the 64 games he played at Kansas State, including the last 50 in a row. His single game best was 41 at Oklahoma. Richmond was the leading scorer in the U.S. silver medal-winning squad at the World University Games in Yugoslavia. He averaged 160 points per game. Richmond graduated in 1988 from Kansas State University with a social sciences degree.

Sources: "Black American Medal Winners," *Ebony* (December 1988); "Seoul Games/Medal Winners," *Los Angeles Times* (October 3, 1988); *1988 United States Olympic Team, Media Guide; Seoul '88*; "Olympics Record," *USA Today* (October 3, 1988).

RIDDICK, STEVEN EARL (USA). Born September 18, 1951, in Newport News, Virginia.

1976 Gold Medal: 4 x 100-Meter Relay (38.33)

In high school Steven Riddick lettered in track and won MVP for 2 years. In college track, he was a 4-year letterman and was for 3 years NCAA division champion in the 100 meters (1972-74). He was also 200-meter champion in 1973. Riddick competed in the World University Games and was a member of the Philadelphia Pioneers. In 1975 Riddick had the fastest automatically-timed 100 meters in the world, 10.05 seconds. He was ranked in the top 10 in the world in the 100 from 1974 to 1979 and in the 200 from 1975 to 1977. His personal best in the 200 was 20.31 seconds (1985). Riddick graduated from Hampton High School, Virginia, in 1970 and from Norfolk State University in 1975. He has worked as assistant coach at LaSalle College in Philadelphia, and in corporate sales and marketing. He is married to Martinique Riddick and lives in Philadelphia.

Sources: *Approved History of Olympic Games*; Riddick, Steven. Questionnaire. 1984; *Black Olympians*; British Virgin Islands, Olympic Committee; *Guinness Book of Olympic Records*; "Olympic Summaries," *New York Times* (August 2, 1976); *Quest for Gold; United States Olympic Team, Games of the XXIst Olympiad*.

ROBERSON, IRVIN (USA). Born July 23, 1935, in Blakely, Georgia.

1960 Silver Medal: Long Jump (26 ft. 7¼ in./8.11 m)

"Bo" Roberson attended Cornell University. When competing for the Cornell/Pennsylvania team against Oxford/Cambridge in 1958, he was ranked only 25th in the world as a long jumper, with a mark of 24 feet, 10½ inches. Roberson showed dramatic improvement in 1959 when he won the Pan Am Games with a legitimate mark of 26 feet. In 1960 he pushed the defending champion, Greg Bell, back into fourth place when Roberson qualified for the Olympic team. In Rome he came within 1 centimeter of matching Ralph Boston's winning jump. Bo Roberson signed a professional football contract with the San Diego Chargers in 1961. For 6 years he played defensive back in the AFL with the Chargers, the Oakland Raiders, the Buffalo Bills, and the Miami Dolphins. He later became the track coach at the University of California, Irvine.

Sources: *Approved History of Olympic Games; Guinness Book of Olympic Records; 1960 United States Sports Teams; Quest for Gold*.

ROBERTS, EDWIN (Trinidad). Born August 12, 1941, in Trinidad.

1964 Bronze Medal: 4 x 400-Meter Relay (3:01.7)
1964 Bronze Medal: 200-Meter Run (20.63)

Edwin Roberts attended North Carolina Central University and, in a distinguished collegiate career spanning the years 1963-66, won one 200-meter title in NAIA competition and three in NCAA Division II Championships. In the sixties

and early seventies Roberts was one of the world's most durable and versatile sprinters. Primarily a 200-meter runner, with a best time of 20.33, Roberts also ran 10.1 for 100 meters and 45.6 in the 400. Roberts ran in the 1964, 1968, and 1972 Olympics and on the first two occasions made the final in both the 200 and the 4 x 400-meter relay. At Tokyo in 1964 he claimed the bronze medal in the half-lapper and added another bronze in the relay, teaming with Ed Skinner, Kent Bernard, and Wendell Mottley to bring the baton home in 3:01.7. His time in the 200 was 20.6, which he bettered 4 years later in Mexico City, but on that occasion his 20.33 clocking was good enough for only fourth place. Roberts was one of the few athletes to win medals at the Central American and Caribbean Games, Pan Am Games, British Empire Games, *and* Olympics. His most outstanding achievement came at the British Empire Games in Kingston, Jamaica, in 1966, where he teamed with Bernard, Mottley, and Lennox Yearwood to establish a new world record in the 4 x 440-yard relay, with a time of 3:02.8. After graduating from college Roberts settled in Philadelphia and became a track coach at Temple University.

Sources: British Virgin Islands, Olympic Committee; *Complete Book of the Olympics; Encyclopaedia of Track and Field Athletics; Games of the XVIIIth Olympiad, Tokyo; Guinness Book of Olympic Records*.

ROBERTS, PATRICIA (USA). Born June 14, 1955, in Monroe, Georgia.

1976 Silver Medal: Basketball

Patricia Roberts graduated from Monroe High School and from Kansas State University at Emporia in 1977. Her college coach was Linda K. Caruthers. Roberts averaged 23 points and 15 rebounds per game in 1974, 22 points and 12 rebounds per game in 1975, and 20 points and 13 rebounds per game in 1976. She made 20 or more points in all the 24 games she played in 1976.

Sources: *Black Olympians; Guinness Book of Olympic Records; Montreal 1976, Games of the XXIst Olympiad; United States Olympic Team, Games of the XXIst Olympiad*.

ROBERTSON, ALVIN CYRRALE (USA). Born July 22, 1962, in Barberton, Ohio.

1984 Gold Medal: Basketball

"Dog" Robertson was first team All-Southwest Conference, second team United Press International All-American, and Associated Press third team All-American. He was also named to the Southwest Conference defensive team. Robertson played 3 years at the University of Arkansas after transferring from Crowder (Missouri) Junior College. He finished 10th on the Arkansas All-Time scoring list with 1,097 points. In 3 years he hit 52.2 percent from the field and 65.6 percent from the line and averaged 12.5 points per game. Now a member of the San Antonio Spurs of the NBA, Robertson has made the NBA All-Star second team and the All-Defensive team and has played well in All-Star games. He hosts a reggae music show on a San Antonio radio station. A former criminal justice major at Arkansas, Robertson eventually wants to work for the Federal Bureau of Investigation.

Sources: British Virgin Islands, Olympic Committee; "The 1984 Olympics," Ebony (October 1984); "The Champions," Los Angeles Times (August 14, 1984); "Basketball," Olympian (October/November 1984); United States Olympic Team, Media Guide.

ROBERTSON, OSCAR PALMER (USA). Born November 24, 1938, in Charlotte, Tennessee.

1960 Gold Medal: Basketball

Oscar Robertson is thought by some to be the greatest guard ever to play basketball. "The Big O" began at Crispus Attucks High School in Indianapolis and went on to the University of Cincinnati. For 3 straight years he led the NCAA in scoring, made first team All-American, and became collegiate Player of the Year. He broke the NCAA scoring mark in his junior year, which had been set in a 4-year college career. Robertson averaged 17 points per game during a U.S. 8-game sweep of 1960 competition. He had an outstanding career and captained the U.S. gold medal-winning team in 1960. When he graduated from the University of Cincinnati in 1960, he was the third-highest scorer in college history. Robertson turned professional with the Cincinnati Royals in 1961 and was voted MVP at two consecutive All-Star games. He moved to the Milwaukee Bucks in 1970 and helped them win the NBA championship the following season. Robertson rewrote the record book in his 14-year career. He was 10 times named to first team NBA and twice, near the end of his career, was named to the second team. He was Rookie of the Year in 1961 and MVP in 1964. Probably his greatest honor came in 1980 when he was named to NBA's 35th Anniversary All-Time team. Robertson's career averages did not fall below a triple-double standard (where a player scores in double figures in points, rebounds, and assists) until his seventh year.

Sources: Approved History of Olympic Games; Black Olympians; Guinness Book of Olympic Records; Negro Firsts in Sports; 1960 United States Sports Team, Games; Quest for Gold.

ROBINSON, ALBERT (USA). Born June 18, 1947, in Paris, Texas.

1968 Silver Medal: Featherweight Boxing

Albert Robinson graduated from Phoenix Union High School in Arizona in 1964. He joined the U.S. Navy and was stationed at the U.S. Naval Air Station, Alameda, California. Of his 142 bouts Robinson had 123 victories (42 knockouts, 61 decisions) and 19 defeats. In the 1967 Pan Am Games he took third place. He was 1968 All-Navy and won first place in the Interservice CISM (international military games). Robinson was the victim of ill luck. In the 1968 Olympic finals against Antonio Roldan of Mexico, the bout was stopped in the second round. Although Robinson appeared to be in complete control, the referee gave the verdict to Roldan, disqualifying Robinson for head butts. Robinson was allowed to keep the silver medal when films of the fight failed to show the infraction. Al Robinson began a promising professional career shortly after the Olympics. However, on April 30, 1971, he collapsed during a workout, never to regain consciousness. He died 3 years later, on January 25, 1974.

Sources: Black Olympians; Guinness Book of Olympic Records; Quest for Gold; United States Olympic Team, Games of the XIXth Olympiad.

ROBINSON, ARNIE, JR. (USA). Born April 7, 1948, in San Diego, California.

1972 Bronze Medal: Long Jump (26 ft. 4 in./8.03 m)
1976 Gold Medal: Long Jump (27 ft. 4¾ in./8.35 m)

Arnie Robinson graduated from Morse High School, San Diego, in 1966 and from San Diego State University in 1971. He was a member of the U.S. Army and belonged to the Macabi Track Club. In the long jump Robinson was AAU first in both 1971 and 1972, Pan Am first in 1971, NCAA fourth in 1971, U.S.-USSR first in 1971, and Olympic trials first in 1972. Robinson was the top-rated long jumper in the world in 1971. In the U.S.-USSR World All-Star meet, he won with 25 feet, 10¾ inches. He was Pan Am champion with a leap of 26 feet, 3¾ inches. In 1972, while in the army, he won the AAU with a jump of 26 feet, 5¾ inches. Robinson surpassed the 27-foot (8.23-meter) mark for the first time in 1974. He jumped to a lifetime, though wind-assisted, best of 8.27 meters (plus a narrow foul of 8.53 meters) to win the U.S. Olympic trials. In the Games themselves he won with his opening leap of 8.35 meters. His best career marks were: 100-yard run, 9.5 seconds; high jump, 2.08 meters and long jump, 8.35 meters (8.37 wind-assisted).

Sources: Black Olympians; Guinness Book of Olympic Records; United States Olympic Team, Games of the XXth Olympiad; United States Track and Field Olympians; Who's Who in Track and Field.

ROBINSON, DAVID (USA). Born August 6, 1965.

1988 Bronze Medal: Basketball

David Robinson graduated from the U.S. Naval Academy in 1987 with a major in mathematics. Robinson was the first Division I player in NCAA history to score 2,500 points, (he scored 2,669), grab 1,300 rebounds, and shoot better than 60 percent from the field (.613). He was the greatest player in Naval Academy history and one of the top centers in NCAA history. He ranked 10th on the NCAA all-time scoring list with 2,669 career points at the close of his career. Robinson was also NCAA career leader in blocked shots (516), and he set the record in 1985-86 for blocks in a season (207) and games (14). He was winner of the 1987 Naismith, Rupp, and Wooden awards as the nation's Player of the Year. He holds or shares 33 Navy records. Robinson scored in double figures in 98 of his last 99 games. He played on the 1987 U.S. Pan Am team and was a member of the 1986 U.S. World Championship team.

Sources: "Black American Medal Winners," Ebony (December 1988); "Seoul Games/Medal Winners," Los Angeles Times (October 3, 1988); 1988 United States Olympic Team, Media Guide; Seoul '88; "Back to Olympian Heights," Sports Illustrated (June 4, 1988); "Olympics Record," USA Today (October 3, 1988).

ROBINSON, MATTHEW (USA). Born July 18, 1914, in Cairo, Georgia.

1936 Silver Medal: 200-Meter Run (21.1)

Mack Robinson graduated from John Muir High School in Pasadena, California, and attended Pasadena City College and the University of Oregon. Robinson set a broad jump record of 25 feet and was National Jr. College long jump champion. He also set a record of 20.7 seconds in the 220-yard dash (later broken by Jesse Owens). He was literally a one-man track team during a brief career at the University of Oregon. Robinson's time of 21.1 in the 200 at Berlin was second only to Jesse Owens's. Robinson held the record in the long jump from 1944 to 1946. He won the NCAA 220 yards in 1938 and also the 200 meters. His best marks were: 9.5 (100 yards), 20.8 (200-meter run), and 25 feet, 5½ inches (long jump). In a panel discussion on the Olympics, Robinson said: "I feel great because I made Jesse Owens greater. Had he not been there I would have been number one. However, that did not affect me, my outlook, my attitude in life … because I did the best I could" (panel discussion, California Afro-American Museum). Robinson was elected to the Hall of Fame of the University of Oregon and of the Pasadena City College, and has been honored by the Advancement of Civil Rights, and the American Civil Liberties Union. Robinson took the lead in having a bronze statue erected to Jackie Robinson (his brother) at UCLA's baseball stadium. He felt that he himself has had bad breaks and would have progressed further as an athlete had he not been Black. He had apparently returned to Pasadena after the Olympics only to be snubbed and given a hard time. For the past several years Matthew Robinson has worked with young people, dealing primarily with drug problems.

Sources: Robinson, Matthew. Panelist. 1984; Black Olympians; "Mack Robinson," Los Angeles Times (July 22, 1984); Negro Firsts in Sports; Quest for Gold; Spirit Team Profiles, Los Angeles Olympiad Organizing Committee.

ROBINZINE, KEVIN (USA). Born April 12, 1966, in Fort Worth, Texas.

1988 Gold Medal: 4 x 400-Meter Relay (2:56.16, Olympic record)

Kevin Robinzine graduated from Southern Methodist University in 1987. He runs with the Accusplit Track Club. Robinzine finished fourth at the Olympic trials with 44.61, which is his personal best. In 1987 he was ranked eighth in the U.S., and at the 1987 NCAA Championships he finished fourth.

Sources: "Black American Medal Winners," Ebony (December 1988); "Seoul Games/Medal Winners," Los Angeles Times (October 3, 1988); 1988 United States Olympic Team, Media Guide; Seoul '88; "Olympics Record," USA Today (October 3, 1988).

RODRÍGUEZ, DOUGLAS LUÍS (Cuba). Born in Cuba.

1972 Bronze Medal: Flyweight Boxing

The Cubans led the boxing world in Munich, winning three golds, a silver, and a bronze. The bronze winner in flyweight boxing, Luís Rodríguez, defeated Jorge Mejia of Ecuador on points, 5-0; Fujio Nagai of Japan, 5-0; and Constantin Gruescu of Romania, 3-2.

Sources: Approved History of Olympic Games; British Virgin Islands, Olympic Committee; Complete Book of the Olympics; Die Spiele, Official Report for the Games of the XXth Olympiad; Guinness Book of Olympic Records; Munchen 1972; Results of the Games of the XXth Olympiad.

RODRÍGUEZ, RAFAEL (Cuba). Born in Cuba.

1980 Silver Medal: Judo (up to 60 kg/132¼ lbs.)

In his weight category in Judo at the 1980 Moscow Olympics, Rafael Rodríguez of Cuba finished behind gold-winner Thierry Rey of France and took the silver medal.

Sources: Approved History of Olympic Games; British Virgin Islands, Olympic Committee; Complete Book of the Olympics; Guinness Book of Olympic Records; "Olympic Results," Los Angeles Times (August 1, 1980).

ROJAS, RICARDO (Cuba). Born in Cuba.

1980 Bronze Medal: Light Heavyweight Boxing

At the 1980 Moscow Olympic Games in the light heavyweight (179 pounds) boxing semifinals, silver-winning

Parvel Skrzecz of Poland decisioned Ricardo Rojas, who finished with the bronze.

Sources: *Approved History of Olympic Games*; British Virgin Islands, Olympic Committee; *Complete Book of the Olympics*; *Guinness Book of Olympic Records*; "Olympic Games, Boxing," *Los Angeles Times* (August 1, 1980).

ROMAY, FULGENCIA (Cuba). Born January 16, 1944, in Havana, Cuba.

1968 Silver Medal: 4 x 100-Meter Relay (43.36)
1972 Bronze Medal: 4 x 100-Meter Relay (43.36)

Fulgencia Romay was one of the Caribbean's leading sprinters from the mid-sixties to the mid-seventies. Her best 100-meter time (11.2) was recorded in 1968; she had run her fastest 200 meters (23.4) 4 years earlier. Her consistency and durability was rewarded by a 4 x 100-meter relay silver medal in 1968 and a bronze in the same event in 1972. Her teammates on the Cuban relay team at the 1968 Olympics, were Marlene Elejarde, Violeta Quesada, and Miguelina Cobian.

Sources: *Approved History of Olympic Games*; British Virgin Islands, Olympic Committee; *Complete Book of the Olympics*; *The Games, Organizing Committee of the XIXth Olympiad*; *Guinness Book of Olympic Records*.

RONO, PETER (Kenya). Born July 31, 1967, in Nandi District, Kenya.

1988 Gold Medal: 1,500-Meter Run (3:35.96)

Peter Rono took the gold in the 1,500 meters in Seoul, continuing the domination of the distance events by Africans during that era. His coach, Jim Deegan, wasn't surprised when Rono took the lead with 800 to go and held on. Rono led all but the first lap. He bested Peter Elliott of Great Britain, who finished second, and Jens-Peter Herold of East Germany, who finished third. Saïd Aouita had pulled out of the race with an injured hamstring. "It's a psychological advantage, you know, if you believe you are good," said Rono. "In the Rift Valley, people believe" (*Track & Field News*). Rono attended St. Patrick's High School in Iten, Kenya and Mount St. Mary's College in western Maryland.

Sources: *International Amateur Athletic Federation*; "Kenyans Rono and Ngugi Sweep to Victories," *Los Angeles Times* (October 1, 1988); "Seoul Games/Medal Winners," *Los Angeles Times* (October 3, 1988); *Seoul '88*; "Kenya's Collegiate Connection," *Track & Field News* (December 1988); "Olympics Record," *USA Today* (October 3, 1988).

RUDISHA, DANIEL MATESI (Kenya). Born in August, 1946, in Kilgoris, Kenya.

1968 Silver Medal: 4 x 400-Meter Relay (2:59.64)

Daniel Rudisha was a member of the Kenyan 4 x 400-meter relay team in Mexico City in 1968. That silver medal-winning team consisted of Charles Asati, Munyoro Nyamau, Naftali Bon, and Rudisha. Rudisha's 44.6-second opening leg played no small part in his team's outstanding performance. He was unable, however, to realize his potential in the open 400 meters. Rudisha's best time ever of 45.5 seconds in the 400 in 1967 gained him his only world ranking.

Sources: *Approved History of Olympic Games*; British Virgin Islands, Olympic Committee; *Complete Book of the Olympics*; *The Games, Organizing Committee of the XIXth Olympiad, Mexico City*; *Guinness Book of Olympic Records*.

WILMA GLODEAN RUDOLPH (Photo courtesy of U.S. Olympic Committee, Colorado Springs, Colorado.)

RUDOLPH, WILMA GLODEAN (USA). Born June 23, 1940, in St. Bethlehem, Tennessee.

1956 Bronze Medal: 4 x 100-Meter Relay (45.04)
1960 Gold Medal: 100-Meter Run (11.18, Olympic record)
1960 Gold Medal: 200-Meter Run (24.12)
1960 Gold Medal: 4 x 100-Meter Relay (44.72)

Wilma Rudolph, the 20th of 22 children, became paralyzed in the left leg by scarlet fever and pneumonia and was unable to walk normally until age 10. She graduated from Burt High School in Clarksville, Tennessee, and from Tennessee State University. As a basketball star in high school, she set a single game scoring record of 49 points that stood for a long time. At 16, Wilma was a member of the women's 4 x 100-meter relay team that won a bronze medal at the Melbourne Olympics in 1956. Four years later she was the outstanding athletics champion of the 1960 Olympics in Rome. No other American woman had won three track gold medals in the Olympics. (Valerie Brisco-Hooks would be the next to win three, in 1984.) After the Rome Games, coach Ed Temple of Tennessee State took his track team (the Tigerbelles) on a triumphant tour of Europe. They competed in Athens, Amsterdam, Cologne, Wuppertal, Frankfurt, Berlin, and London. Rudolph was known as *la gazelle noire* (the black gazelle) by Europeans. Her autobiography, *Wilma*, was made into a highly acclaimed television film in 1977. Among Rudolph's many honors are: First Place, James E. Sullivan Award (top amateur athlete in U.S.), 1961; Helms World Trophy for the North American Continent, 1960; *Los Angeles Times* Award for Women's Track and Field, 1960; *Mademoiselle* award, 1960; *New York Times* selection as one of the 10 most outstanding women in the U.S., 1960; European Sportswriters Association award for Most Outstanding Athlete of the Year, 1960; *Sports Magazine* award for top performance in track and field, 1960; Eagle Frederic C. Miller Trophy (Associated Press award for world's top female athlete), 1960; *Nashville Banner* outstanding athlete, 1960; National Newspaper Publisher Association's Russwurm Award, 1960; Babe Didrickson Zakaris Trophy for Outstanding Female Athlete in U.S., 1960; Christopher Columbus Prize for Outstanding Sports Achievement (in Genoa, Italy), 1961; personal citation by the governor of Tennessee for outstanding achievement. Herself the mother of four, Rudolph established the Indianapolis-based Wilma Rudolph Foundation, which benefits youngsters both athletically and academically. Within the structure of the foundation is the Wilma Rudolph Track Club and 10 educational components, such as social behavior, self-esteem, respect for adult decision-making, and personal grooming. The foundation, which also includes a reading program, works hand in hand with the Indiana public school system. Over 1,000 people are involved in the foundation. Rudolph is also a lecturer, talk-show host, author and good-will ambassador.

Sources: *Black Olympians; Golden Girls; Guinness Book of Olympic Records;* "Rudolph Not Fading Away," *Los Angeles Times* (July 25, 1984); *Negro Almanac; Negro Firsts in Sports; 1980 Olympic Handbook; Quest for Gold; Who's Who in Track and Field;* "Wilma Rudolph," *Women's Sports* (October 1984).

WILLIAM FENTON RUSSELL (Photo courtesy of Rich Clarkson, Denver, Colorado.)

RUSSELL, WILLIAM FENTON (USA). Born February 12, 1934, in Monroe, Louisiana.

1956 Gold Medal: Basketball

Bill Russell graduated from the University of San Francisco in 1956. He was coached by George Powles. With K. C. Jones, Russell led the San Francisco Dons to 55 consecutive victories and to national championships in 1955 and 1956. He was consensus All-American in his junior and senior years and won two NCAA championships. Russell turned professional after the 1956 Melbourne Olympics. He grabbed over 20 rebounds per game in 10 of his 13 seasons with the Boston Celtics and dominated the game as a defensive standout. He helped Boston win 11 NBA championships in 13 seasons. He played on 2 NCAA and 10 NBA championship teams with the Celtics—8 of those in succession. In the 11 NBA crowns led by Russell's playoff performance, he was selected to the All-NBA team 11 times; he was

NBA's MVP in 1958, 1961-63, and 1965. He has a reputation as the greatest defensive player in the history of the games. Russell was named *The Sporting News* Athlete of the Decade in 1970 and Sportsman of the Year by *Sports Illustrated*. After retirement he was named to NBA's 25th and 35th Anniversary All-Time teams and elected to the Basketball Hall of Fame (1974). His greatest honor was to be elected NBA's greatest player ever in a poll of basketball writers. Bill Russell forever changed the shape of professional basketball, whether he is considered the greatest star ever or simply its greatest champion. Russell turned the game into a consumate team game, where defensive ability, rebounding, and hustle were as important as great offensive skills. He was virtually always first or second team All-NBA, often alternating the honor with his archrival Wilt Chamberlain. That rivalry began when Chamberlain joined the professional ranks in 1959-60. Chamberlain shot and shot, while Russell blocked and stole. Russell seemed to save his greatest feats for playoffs. In the 1965 playoffs, he made 428 rebounds in 17 games, averaging 25 per contest. Russell was the dominant figure in the Boston Celtics' basketball dynasty. As a player-coach, the first Black coach in NBA history, he led the Celtics to the 1969 championship. He was able to excel at rebounding and created a record with 51 rebounds in a single game. On his retirement, he had a 21,721 career total for rebounds—the highest in basketball history. He had averaged more than 20 rebounds per game for 10 of his 13 seasons. Bill Russell retired from playing in 1969 and became a basketball commentator for CBS Sports. He was later coach and general manager of the Seattle SuperSonics. He also served as spokesman for several companies in television commercials.

Sources: *Approved History of Olympic Games*; *Black Olympians*; *Guinness Book of Olympic Records*; *Lincoln Library of Sports Champions*; "American Basketball," *Los Angeles Times* (July 27, 1984); *Official Report of the Organizing Committee of the XVIth Olympics*; *Quest for Gold*.

RWABWOGO, LEO (Uganda). Born in Uganda.

1972 Silver Medal: Flyweight Boxing

In flyweight boxing in the 1972 Olympic Games at Munich Leo Rwabwogo defeated Jorge Acuna of Uruguay when the referee stopped the contest in the third round in 2:12. He then went on to beat Maurice Sullivan of Great Britain when the referee stopped the fight in the first round (time 1:30). Finally, he defeated Orn-chin Chawalit of Thailand, with points, 4-1.

Sources: *Africa at the Olympics*; *Approved History of Olympic Games*; British Virgin Islands, Olympic Committee; *Complete Book of the Olympics*; *Die Spiele, Official Report for the Games of the XXth Olympiad*; *Guinness Book of Olympic Records*; *Munchen 1972*; *Results of the Games of the XXth Olympiad*; Uganda Olympic Committee.

SALEH HOUSSAIN, AHMED (Djibouti). Born in 1956, in Ali Sabreh, Djibouti.

1988 Bronze Medal: Marathon (2 hrs. 10:59.0)

Saleh Houssain is the fastest marathoner in the field by 44 seconds. A threat to the Japanese, he has beaten Nakayama but lost to Seko. Saleh, an army officer, won the IAAF World Marathon Cup race in 1985 in Hiroshima and in 1987 in Seoul and finished second at the 1987 World Championships in Rome. He won the Paris Marathon in 1984 and 1986 and the African Championships in 1985.

Sources: British Virgin Islands, Olympic Committee; *International Amateur Athletic Federation*; "Seoul Games/Medal Winners," *Los Angeles Times* (October 3, 1988); "Dutch Feat," *Runner's World* (July 1988); "For the Record," *Runner's World* (July 1988); *The Olympic Games; Seoul '88*.

HAYES EDWARD SANDERS (Photo courtesy of Amateur Athletic Foundation, Los Angeles, California.)

SANDERS, HAYES EDWARD (USA). Born March 24, 1930, in Los Angeles, California.

1952 Gold Medal: Heavyweight Boxing

Ed Sanders attended Jordan High School, Los Angeles, Compton Junior College, and Idaho State University. In high school he was class and student body president. In college he participated in football, track and boxing, and won NCAA championships for boxing at Compton in 1952 and at Idaho State in 1950 and 1951. (His brother Don joined him on the same boxing team at Idaho State in 1951.) An Idaho All-State wide receiver in football, Ed Sanders competed in the decathlon under former Olympian and coach Ken Carpenter. Sanders also took up boxing, learned quickly, and knocked out several opponents on his way to the 1952 Helsinki Olympics. There, his final opponent, Ingemar Johansson, was so terrified of Sanders's knockout punch that he was disqualified. Johansson was later awarded the silver medal that had earlier been denied him. Sanders's gold medal marked the first time the Olympian heavyweight crown had been won by an American since 1904. Sanders was also the first and only athlete from Compton schools to win a gold medal in boxing. After winning the gold medal, Sanders served 2 years in the navy and then turned professional. He won seven of his first eight fights, avenging his one loss with a later knockout. His career—and life—ended, however, when he fought Willie James for the New England heavyweight title on December 11, 1954 in Boston. James knocked him out in the 11th round and Sanders had to be carried from the ring. In this his ninth professional fight, he sustained a blood clot on the brain and died. Edward Sanders was married to Mary Larue and was the father of Russell Sanders, who later played basketball at Washington State.

Sources: *Compton's Gift to the Olympic Games; Guinness Book of Olympic Records; Quest for Gold*; Sanders, Don. Interview. 1984.

SANDERSON, TESSA (Great Britain). Born March 14, 1956, in St. Elizabeth, Jamaica.

1984 Gold Medal: Javelin (228 ft. 2 in./69.56 m, new Olympic record)

Tessa Sanderson began throwing the javelin when she was 14 years old. Amazingly, between 1976 and 1977 she improved 30 feet. She came within a foot of the world record in 1980 when she threw 69.70 meters (228 feet, 8 inches). Favored to win a medal at the Moscow Games, she surprisingly seemed overwhelmed by the occasion and failed to qualify for the final. That remains the only blot on her record, as she twice won the event at the Commonwealth Games (1978, 1986) and also placed second at the European Championships in 1978. Sanderson also placed fourth at the World Championships in Helsinki in 1983 and rebounded to win the javelin throw at the Los Angeles Olympics, defeating her Helsinki conquerors, Tiina Lillak of Finland and Patima Whitbread of Britain. Tessa Sanderson, an excellent all-around athlete, scored another Commonwealth record, 6,114 points, in the heptathlon in 1981 and planned

to finish her career in that event. She now lives in Leeds, England, where she is a sports promotion assistant.

Sources: British Virgin Islands, Olympic Committee; "Javelin," *Los Angeles Times* (August 7, 1984); "The Champions," *Los Angeles Times* (August 14, 1984); "Los Angeles '84," *Women's Sports* (October 1984).

SANG, JULIUS (Kenya). Born September 19, 1948, in Kapabet, Kenya.

1972 Gold Medal: 4 x 400-Meter Relay (2:59.83)
1972 Bronze Medal: 400-Meter run (44.92)

Julius Sang attended North Carolina Central University, where he had an outstanding career in the 200 and 400 meters. Sang's Olympic bronze in the 400 in Munich was the first medal ever won in an individual sprint by someone representing a Black African nation. Sang, inspired by fellow countryman Kipchoge Keino's performances in the metric mile, ran a 43.5 anchor leg in the Munich 4 x 400-meter relay. He passed West Germany's Karl Honz 75 meters from the finish line to take the Kenyan team to victory. Sang was a member of the winning relay team at the Commonwealth Games in the 4 x 400-meter relay in 1970 (3:03.6). He had personal bests of 20.3 for the 200 and 44.92 for the 400.

Sources: *Africa at the Olympics*; British Virgin Islands, Olympic Committee; *Complete Book of the Olympics; Die Spiele, Official Report for the Games of the XXth Olympiad; Guinness Book of Olympic Records*.

SAPENTER, DEBRA (USA). Born February 27, 1952, in Indianapolis, Indiana.

1976 Silver Medal: 4 x 400-Meter Relay (3:22.81)

Debra Sapenter attended George C. Marshall High School in Ankara, Turkey, and in 1974 graduated from Prairie View (Texas) Agricultural and Mechanical University. She did graduate work in English at Northwestern University. Sapenter won the AAU 440 yards in 1974 and the 400 meters in 1975, and finished second in the 400 meters at the 1975 Pan Am Games. Although she finished in eighth place in the 400-meter run at the 1976 Olympics, she won a well-deserved medal in the 4 x 400 relay after a 51.8 leadoff stage.

Sources: *Black Olympians; Guinness Book of Olympic Records*; "Olympic Summaries," *New York Times* (August 2, 1976); *Quest for Gold; United States Olympic Team, Games; United States Track and Field Olympians*.

SARMIENTOS, VICTORIANO (Cuba). Born in Cuba.

1976 Bronze Medal: Volleyball

For a summary of the Cuban team's record at the 1976 Montreal Olympics, see García.

Sources: *Approved History of Olympic Games*; British Virgin Islands, Olympic Committee; *Complete Book of the Olympics*; *Guinness Book of Olympic Records*; *Montreal 1976*; *Games of the XXIst Olympiad*.

SAVIGNE, JESÚS (Cuba). Born in Cuba.

1976 Bronze Medal: Volleyball

For a summary of the Cuban team's record at the 1976 Olympics in Montreal, see García.

Sources: *Approved History of Olympic Games*; British Virgin Islands, Olympic Committee; *Complete Book of the Olympics*; *Guinness Book of Olympic Records*; *Montreal 1976*; *Games of the XXIst Olympiad*.

SCOTT, CHARLES THOMAS (USA). Born December 15, 1948, in New York City.

1968 Gold Medal: Basketball

Charles Scott graduated from Laurinburg Institute in North Carolina in 1966 and the University of North Carolina in 1970. He was in the 1968 All-Atlantic Coast Conference with an average of 18 points per game; his high was 34 points against North Carolina State. He helped North Carolina make the NCAA finals that year. Although lightly regarded before the 1968 Olympics, Scott, Spencer Haywood, and JoJo White were the stars of the gold medal-winning team. Scott signed with the Virginia Squires of the ABA, where he had two brilliant years. He was Rookie of the Year in 1971 and led the league in scoring to 1972. He then signed with the Phoenix Suns of the NBA and went on to a successful career in that league.

Sources: *Black Olympians*; *Guinness Book of Olympic Records*; *Quest for Gold*; *United States Olympic Team, Games of the XIXth Olympiad*.

SEALES, CHARLES AUGUSTUS (USA). Born September 4, 1952, in St. Croix, U.S. Virgin Islands.

1972 Gold Medal: Light Welterweight Boxing

Before winning the gold at the 1972 Olympics, "Sugar Ray" Seales had already won 115 fights as an amateur, against 12 losses. He won the 1972 Western Hemisphere and Olympic trials and the 1971 North American and National AAU. He also came in first four times in the Tacoma and Seattle Golden Gloves Championships. His coach was Joe Clough. At the Olympics he had to win five fights by decision to earn his gold medal. After he turned professional, Seales fought mostly as a middleweight. He won his first 20 fights but was defeated by Marvin Hagler in August 1974. Seales later fought a draw with Hagler and

started winning again. Then he was knocked out by Alan Minter in 1976. Seales subsequently retired after becoming almost blind in both eyes, the result of fight-caused detached retinae.

Sources: *Black Olympians*; *Guinness Book of Olympic Records*; *Quest for Gold*; *United States Olympic Team, Games of the XXth Olympiad*.

SEYE, ABDOULAYE (France). Born July 30, 1934, in Saint Louis, Senegal.

1960 Bronze Medal: 200-Meter Run (20.70)

A superb all-around sprinter, Abdoulaye Seye was the first Black African to win an Olympic medal. He won his bronze in the 200 meters in Rome with a time of 20.7 seconds, after winning the semifinal in 20.8. Seye's major accomplishments in international athletics occurred while he was wearing the colors of France. His personal bests were 10.32 for the 100, 20.82 for the 200, and 45.82 for the 400.

Sources: *Approved History of Olympic Games*; British Virgin Islands, Olympic Committee; *Complete Book of the Olympics*; *Games of the XVIIth Olympiad, Rome*; *Guinness Book of Olympic Records*.

SHARPE, ANTHONY (Canada). Born June 28, 1961, in Jamaica.

1984 Bronze Medal: 4 x 100-Meter Relay (38.70)

Tony Sharpe, who attended York University and Clemson University, is best known for his ability to make the most of helpful atmospheric conditions. In Los Angeles he ran the second leg in the 400-meter relay, his usual duty, and helped his team win a bronze medal. Sharpe has competed widely, both nationally and internationally. A very good year for him was 1982, when he finished first in the 200 meters in Celje, Yugoslavia (20.99); in Venice, Italy (20.92); and in Colorado Springs (20.22). He was also first in the 100 in Colorado Springs (10.19) and in Ottawa (10.31). Sharpe is a member of Scarborough Optimists Track Club.

Sources: British Virgin Islands, Olympic Committee; Canadian Olympic Association; *1984 Olympic Games, Sarajevo/Los Angeles*.

SHEPPARD, STEVEN (USA). Born March 21, 1954, in New York City.

1976 Gold Medal: Basketball

Steve Sheppard attended DeWitt Clinton High School in New York City and the University of Maryland. Named New York City Player of the Year in 1973, Sheppard led the Maryland team to victory over the Soviet Union by scoring 22 points and pulling down 15 rebounds. Sheppard averaged 14.3 points per game in 1975 and 17.6 in 1976. Also in 1976 he scored 28 points against Long Island University and East Carolina. His coach was Lefty Driesell. After leaving Maryland in 1977, he played 2 years of basketball in the NBA, first with Chicago, then with Detroit.

Sources: *Black Olympians; Guinness Book of Olympic Records; Quest for Gold; United States Olympic Team, Games of the XXIst Olympiad*.

SKINNER, EDWIN (Trinidad). Born in 1940, in Trinidad.

1964 Bronze Medal: 4 x 400-Meter Relay (3:01.7)

Ed Skinner made his mark as a relay runner at the Tokyo Olympics in 1964 when he ran the first leg on his country's bronze medal-winning 1,600-meter squad. In addition to Skinner, the following Trinidadians were on the relay team: Kent Bernard, Edwin Roberts, and Wendell Mottley. Skinner had a 400-meter best of 46.5 seconds. A graduate of Maryland State University, he now resides in Port-of-Spain.

Sources: *Approved History of Olympic Games*; British Virgin Islands, Olympic Committee; *Complete Book of the Olympics; Games of the XVIIIth Olympiad, Tokyo; Guinness Book of Olympic Records*.

SMITH, CALVIN (USA). Born January 8, 1961, in Bolton, Mississippi.

1984 Gold Medal: 4 x 100-Meter Relay (37.83, new Olympic record/world record)
1988 Bronze Medal: 100-Meter Run (9.99)

Calvin Smith and Carl Lewis are the only athletes to have broken 10.00 in the 100 and 20.00 in the 200. Smith won the 1987 World Championship in the 200 and ranked fifth in the world in the 100. In the Seoul Olympics in 1988 he ran third in the 100 meters, after Ben Johnson and Carl Lewis (before Johnson's disqualification). At an earlier Olympiad (1984) he had won a gold in the 4 x 100-meter relay, along with his teammates Ron Brown, Sam Graddy, and Carl Lewis. They set a new Olympic record and a world record with a time of 37.83 seconds. Smith became world record holder in the 100 meters at 9.93 at the National Sports Festival. His greatest success was in the 200 when he set a personal record of 19.99, won the World Championships, and was ranked first in the world. His first national title was the TAC 200 in 1982. In 1983, the year he graduated from the University of Alabama, he was second in the NCAA 100 and 200 and third in the TAC 100 and 200. That same year he shared a world record when he ran on the U.S. 4 x 100-meter relay team that clocked 37.86. In 1985 Smith became the IAAF's first Grand Prix

champion in the 200 meters. He has continued to perform well in both short sprints.

Sources: British Virgin Islands, Olympic Committee; "The 1984 Olympics," *Ebony* (October 1984); *Games of the XXIIIrd Olympiad, Los Angeles*; "The Champions," *Los Angeles Times* (August 14, 1984); *1988 United States Olympic Team, Media Guide*; "The Games," *Olympian* (October/November 1984); "Calvin Smith," *Track & Field News* (December 1987); *United States Olympic Team, Media Guide*; "Olympics Record," *USA Today* (October 3, 1988).

SMITH, CHARLES D. (USA). Born July 16, 1965.

1988 Bronze Medal: Basketball

Charles D. Smith graduated from the University of Pittsburg in 1988 with a liberal arts degree. A basketball standout, he was named Big East Player of the Year and was the only unanimous selection for first team All-Big East honors. He led the Pittsburgh Panthers in scoring, field goal percentage, field goal attempts, free throws and attempts, and blocked shots. Smith also played for the East team at the 1985 National Sports Festival and was a member of the 1986 U.S. World Championship team. He was named Scripps-Howard first team All-America and he graduated in 1988 the Panthers' all-time leading scorer. Holder of the record for career blocked shots, Smith blocked at least one shot in his last 51 games and in 111 of his last 113 games.

Sources: "Black American Medal Winners," *Ebony* (December 1988); "Seoul Games/Medal Winners," *Los Angeles Times* (October 3, 1988); *1988 United States Olympic Team, Media Guide; Seoul '88*; "Olympics Record," *USA Today* (October 3, 1988).

SMITH, CHARLES E. IV (USA). Born November 29, 1967.

1988 Bronze Medal: Basketball

Charles Smith, playing for Georgetown University, was a *Basketball Weekly* second team All-East selection. In 1988 he led his team in scoring (averaging 15.7 points per game), steals (averaging 2.36 per game) and free throw percentage (he hit 77 out of 100). Smith set career highs in 1988 with 28 points against Seton Hall and 8 rebounds against Syracuse. He was twice selected as Big East Player of the Week. Smith saw international action the summer of 1987 with the Big East All-Stars in Australia, where he led in scoring, assists, and steals, shooting .875 from the free-throw line.

Sources: "Black American Medal Winners," *Ebony* (December 1988); "Seoul Games/Medal Winners," *Los Angeles Times* (October 3, 1988); *1988 United States Olympic Team, Media Guide; Seoul '88*; "Olympics Record," *USA Today* (October 3, 1988).

SMITH, RONNIE RAY (USA). Born March 28, 1949, in Los Angeles, California.

1968 Gold Medal: 4 x 100-Meter Relay (38.24, Olympic record/world record)

Ronnie Ray Smith graduated from Manual Arts High School in Los Angeles in 1967 and from San Jose State College in 1971. He was a member of the Southern California Striders. Smith set a new world record along with Jim Hines in the semifinals of 1968 AAU 100 meters. They both ran 9.9. At the Olympic final trials Smith placed fourth in the 100 and ran only in the relay in Mexico City, where the U.S. set a world record in the 4 x 100. Smith's best performances in the 100 meters were 9.9 at sea level and 10.0 at 7,400 feet. He was fifth in this event at the 1968 AAU and third at the Los Angeles Olympic trials. His best electronic time in the 100 was 10.14 seconds in 1968. Smith never repeated his success as a junior competitor and had an undistinguished collegiate career.

Sources: *Black Olympians*; British Virgin Islands, Olympic Committee; *Guinness Book of Olympic Records; Quest for Gold; United States Olympic Team, Games of the XIXth Olympiad; United States Track and Field Olympians*.

SMITH, TOMMIE C. (USA). Born June 4, 1944, in Clarksville, Texas.

1968 Gold Medal: 200-Meter Run (19.83, Olympic record/world record)

Tommie Smith graduated in 1969 from Lemore High School in Lemore, California, where he competed in basketball, football, and track. He completed his studies at San Jose State College in 1969 and went on to earn an M.A. from Cambridge-Goddard University in Plainfield, Vermont, in 1974. Smith was voted Most Valuable Athlete for 3 years and Outstanding High School Athlete of the West Coast Relays Track and Field meet in 1963. He was *Sun Reporter* Athlete of the Year (1966), U.S. Track and Field Federation Athlete of the Year (1963), European Press Athlete of the Year (1967-68), and MVP in basketball (1963). Smith made a sensational debut as a record-breaker in 1966 when he was timed at 19.5 seconds for 220 yards and 200 meters on a straight track, thus reducing the previous world record by half a second, the biggest single advance in the history of the events. The same year, he set a world record for 220 yards and 200 meters on a turn in 20.0. In 1967 he held the world record for 400 meters at 44.5 seconds. Smith won the AAU and NCAA 220 yards in 1967 and the AAU 200 meters in 1968. He was top-ranked 200-meter, 220-yard man in the world in 1967-68 (*Track & Field News*). Smith held 11 world records indoors and outdoors at distances up to 440 yards. He was one of the best all-around sprinters ever and gained world rankings in the 100, 200, and 400 meters, as well as in the long jump. He had a best time in the 100 yards of 9.35 and ran 10.1 seconds in the 100 meters. When Tommie Smith and John Carlos refused to recognize the American flag and national anthem at the 1968 Olympics in Mexico City, they made a very strong political statement. Head lowered, each raised a fist, encased in a black glove. (See photo with John Carlos entry.) This culmination of a decade of Blacks' civil rights protests in the U.S. could have resulted in the expulsion of the whole U.S. team from the Games, but only Smith and Carlos were expelled. The movement was headed by Harry Edwards, academic and former athlete. Smith was a professor and athletic director at Oberlin College and later, in 1968, became physical education professor and coach at Santa Monica City College.

Sources: *Approved History of Olympic Games; Black Olympians*; British Virgin Islands, Olympic Committee; *Guinness Book of Olympic Records; Hard Road to Glory; Quest for Gold*; Smith, Tommie C. Questionnaire. 1984; Smith, Tommie. Panelist. 1985; *Spirit Team Profiles*, Los Angeles Olympic Organizing Committee; *Track and Field: The Great Ones; United States Olympic Team, Games of the XIXth Olympiad*.

SORIA, SIXTO (Cuba). Born in Cuba.

1976 Silver Medal: Light Heavyweight Boxing

Sixto Soria, Cuban light heavyweight boxer in the 1976 Olympics competition, required only 9 minutes, 5 seconds to dispose of his first three opponents. However, he met his match in Leon Spinks, who knocked him down in the first round and battered him until the fight was stopped. Soria had reigned as world amateur light heavyweight champion prior to the 1976 Olympic Games.

Sources: *Approved History of Olympic Games*; British Virgin Islands, Olympic Committee; *Complete Book of the Olympics; Guinness Book of Olympic Records; Montreal 1976; Games of the XXIst Olympiad; Story of the Olympic Games*.

SPENCE, MALCOLM (British West Indies). Born January 2, 1936, in Kingston, Jamaica.

1960 Bronze Medal: 4 x 400-meter Relay (3:04.0)

Not to be confused with a South African runner of the same name, Jamaica's Mal Spence formed one of the greatest-ever twin combinations with his brother Mel. Together they ran on Jamaica's fourth-place 4 x 400-meter relay team at the 1964 Tokyo Games. Malcolm's best of 46.4 seconds was 0.4 faster than Mel's. Malcolm Spence was a member of the Commonwealth Games' 4 x 440-yard winning relay team in 1962 with a 3:10.2. He had won his Olympic medal earlier, at the Rome Games in 1960.

Sources: British Virgin Islands, Olympic Committee; *Complete Book of the Olympics; Guinness Book of Olympic Records*.

SPINKS, LEON (USA). Born July 11, 1953, in St. Louis, Missouri.

1976 Gold Medal: Light Heavyweight Boxing

Leon Spinks had fought in 135 amateur bouts before the 1976 Olympics. Considered a brawler rather than an accomplished boxer, he had won the 1975 AAU title and lost in the finals of the 1976 Pan Am Games. Spinks won all bouts with ease in Montreal, and knocked out Cuban World champion Sixto Soria in the finals. Leon Spinks grew into a heavyweight world champion. He put on a few pounds and turned professional. He took on Muhammad Ali on February 15, 1978, for the heavyweight title—after only 7 professional fights—and upset him. In September 1978, Ali regained the title in a close controversial decision. Spinks's reign of 212 days as heavyweight champion was the shortest in history. A new class for small heavyweights like Spinks was formed in the late 1970s. It was called the cruiserweight division. Spinks has continued to box professionally, although he has never matched his early professional success.

Sources: *Approved History of Olympic Games; Black Olympians; Guinness Book of Olympic Records;* "Olympic Summaries," *New York Times* (August 2, 1976); *Quest for Gold; United States Olympic Team, Games of the XXIst Olympiad.*

SPINKS, MICHAEL (USA). Born July 22, 1956, in St. Louis, Missouri.

1976 Gold Medal: Middleweight Boxing

Michael Spinks was not nearly so well known in 1976 as his older brother Leon. He had only one title at the time: 1976 Golden Gloves Association of America champion. But he joined his brother on the victory platform at Montreal by also winning a gold medal. Spinks grew into the light heavyweight world champion and has gone on to a more successful career than his brother since turning professional. Early in his career he won all his bouts, including the World Boxing Association light heavyweight championship in 1981 in which he defeated Eddie Mustafa Muhammed. Then, in 1981, Spinks won a much-ballyhooed unification title fight with World Boxing Commission champion Dwight Braxton. Spinks's career record then was 23 wins and no losses; it was later 86 wins and 5 losses. In 1985 Michael Spinks dethroned the previously unbeaten Larry Holmes to win the International Boxing Federation heavyweight title, and he defeated Holmes in a 1986 rematch, which effectively ended Holmes's career. He shared the heavyweight title with World Boxing Council champion Pinklon Thomas and World Boxing Association champion Tony Tubbs.

Sources: *Approved History of Olympic Games; Black Olympians;* British Virgin Islands, Olympic Committee; "Michael Spinks," *Ebony* (March 1986); *Guinness Book of Olympic Records;* "Olympic Summaries," *New York Times* (August 1, 1976); "5 Boxers from U.S. Hit Gold," *New York Times* (August 2, 1976); *Quest for Gold; United States Olympic Team, Games of the XXIst Olympiad.*

STADLER, JOSEPH F. (USA).

1904 Silver Medal: Standing High Jump (n.d.a.)
1904 Bronze Medal: Standing Long Jump (n.d.a.)

Little is known about this early Black Olympian. Joseph Stadler was from the Franklin Athletic Club in Cleveland and was one of two Black athletes to compete in the 1904 Olympics. Both of the events he participated in have been discontinued. Stadler won his first medal on the same day that George Poage won his, but Stadler was second in order of events.

Sources: *Approved History of Olympic Games;* California Afro-American Museum; *Quest for Gold.*

STANDARD, FRANKLIN (Cuba). Born June 8, 1949, in Havana, Cuba.

1972 Bronze Medal: Basketball

Franklin Standard, a lanky 6-foot 6-inch forward, was primarily an inside player. In 1971 he became embroiled in a chair-swinging incident at the Pan Am Games in Winnepeg, during the final when Cuba was playing the U.S. His volatile temper and rapidly declining skills combined to make his international career relatively brief. For a summary of the Cuban team's record at the 1972 Munich Games, see Calderón-Gómez.

Sources: *Approved History of Olympic Games;* British Virgin Islands, Olympic Committee; *Die Spiele, Official Report for the Games of the XXth Olympiad; Guinness Book of Olympic Records.*

STANFIELD, ANDREW WILLIAM (USA). Born December 29, 1927, in Washington, D.C.

1952 Gold Medal: 200-Meter Run (20.70, Olympic record)
1952 Gold Medal: 4 x 100-Meter Relay (40.26)
1956 Silver Medal: 200-Meter Run (20.97)

Andy Stanfield attended Seton Hall University, where he was national AAU 100-meter champion in 1949. Stanfield broke the world 200-yard and 200-meter records around a turn when on May 5, 1951, in Philadelphia, he was timed in 20.6 at both distances. On June 28, 1952, he ran in the Olympic trials at Los Angeles to tie his own mark. Stanfield concentrated on the 200 at the 1952 Olympics in Helsinki, and took the gold medal to equal Jesse Owens's Olympic mark of 20.7. Stanfield made the 1956 Olympic team in the 200 meters and finished a meter behind gold medal winner Bobby Morrow. In Sydney, shortly after the Melbourne Games, Stanfield ran on the U.S. 880-yard and 800-meter relay team that set world records of 1:23.8. Stanfield won four AAU titles during his career: he took the 100 and 200 meters in 1949, with 10.3 and 20.4 (wind-aided), and the 200 in 1952 and 1953. Dominating the eastern collegiate sprint scene at Seton Hall, he won the IC4A 100-meter and 220-yard titles in 1949 and 1951. He also took the 100-yard crown in 1950, with a wind-aided 9.6, and was IC4A indoor champion at 60 yards from 1949 through 1951. Stanfield was also an outstanding long jumper and combined with fellow Olympians Mal Whitfield of the U.S. and Jamaicans Herb McKenley and George Rhoden to form a fearsome mile relay quartet for the Grand Street Boys (New York) Track Club. Andy Stanfield died in the late 1980s in New Jersey after a long illness.

Sources: *Approved History of Olympic Games*; British Virgin Islands, Olympic Committee; *Guinness Book of Olympic Records*; *Quest for Gold*; *Track and Field: The Great Ones*; *United States Olympic Team, Games of the XVth Olympiad*; *Who's Who in Track and Field*.

STEBBINS, RICHARD (USA). Born June 14, 1945, in Los Angeles, California.

1964 Gold Medal: 4 x 100-Meter Relay (39.06, world record)

Dick Stebbins attended Grambling State University in Louisiana and was a member of the Southern California Striders. He was fifth in the National AAU Championships in 1964 at age 19. At the 1964 Olympics he ran the third leg on his 4 x 100-meter relay team, which was anchored by Bob Hayes. Stebbins had run third leg in both the first round and the semifinals.

Sources: British Virgin Islands, Olympic Committee; *Guinness Book of Olympic Records*; *United States Olympic Team, Games of the XVIIIth Olympiad*; *United States Track and Field Olympians*.

STEELE, WILLIAM S. (USA). Born July 14, 1923, in Seeley, California.

1948 Gold Medal: Long Jump (25 ft. 8 in. / 7.82 m)

Willie Steele was probably the top long jumper of the 1940s. He jumped 25 feet, 7¼ inches in 1942. Following a stint in the army, Steele returned to San Diego State University. He came close to Jesse Owens's record in 1947 at the NCAA Championships with a winning leap of 26 feet, 6 inches. He also took the AAU title both in 1946 and 1947 and the NCAA title in 1948. Steele's winning jump in the 1948 London Olympics of 25 feet, 8 inches was third best in Olympics history—behind Jesse Owens and Germany's Luz Long.

Sources: *Black Olympians*; *Guinness Book of Olympic Records*; *Official Report of the XIVth Olympiad*; *Quest for Gold*; *Who's Who in Track and Field*.

TEOFILO STEVENSON (Photo courtesy of Cuban Interests Section, Czech Embassy, Washington, D.C.)

STEVENSON, TEÓFILO (Cuba). Born March 23, 1952, in Antonio Guitanas, Jamaica.

1972 Gold Medal: Heavyweight Boxing
1976 Gold Medal: Heavyweight Boxing
1980 Gold Medal: Heavyweight Boxing

Teófilo Stevenson is called El Gigante (the giant) by loving Cubans, and some have said that he has the greatest right hand since Joe Louis. Stevenson was the outstanding amateur boxer of the 1970s. He won the World title in Havana in 1974 and in Belgrade in 1978. Had it not been for the boycott of the 1984 Olympics, he probably could have won a fourth gold medal, in Los Angeles. He has also been World amateur heavyweight champion on several occasions. Three men in Cuba are widely known by their first names only: Fidel, Che, and Teófilo. "Teófilo was our first great sports figure after the revolution," Luis Canabrerro, a government translator, said (*Los Angeles Times*). The Cuban boxing squad won 6 gold, 2 silver, and 2 bronze medals in the 11 weight classes at the 1980 Olympics. At age 35, Stevenson said, "I'm trying to be a more technically well-rounded boxer.... As athletes grow older, they learn and develop more technique."

Sources: *Approved History of Olympic Games; Die Spiele, Official Report for Games of XXth Olympiad; Games of the XXIInd Olympiad; Guinness Book of Olympic Records; Montreal 1976, Games of the XXIst Olympiad; Who's Who in the Olympic Games.*

STEWART, RAYMOND (Jamaica). Born March 18, 1965, in Jamaica.

1984 Silver Medal: 4 x 100-Meter Relay (38.62)

In 1984 Raymond Stewart became one of the youngest-ever Olympic 100-meter finalists. He burst on the international scene in 1983 when he was a 100-meter semifinalist at the World Championships and ran on the seventh-place 4 x 100-meter relay team. A fifth place in the Pan Am Games 100 made the Olympic silver medal he won anchoring Jamaica's sprint relay team in 1984 less than surprising. Stewart has a 100-meter best of 10.19 seconds and a 200-meter best of 20.92.

Sources: British Virgin Islands, Olympic Committee; *1984 Olympic Games*; "1984 Olympic Games," *Olympian* (October/November 1984).

TATE, FRANK (USA). Born August 27, 1964, in Detroit, Michigan.

1984 Gold Medal: Light Middleweight Boxing

Frank Tate graduated from Kettering High School in 1983. He was a product of Detroit's Kronk Gymnasium. Tate had been boxing for 8 years when he defeated Canada's Shawn O'Sullivan for the title at the 1984 World Challenge Championships in Los Angeles. He also won the 1984 Olympic boxing trials. In 1983 he won the U.S. Amateur and National Golden Gloves while taking third at the Pan Am trials. Also in 1983 he took second at the North American Championships, losing to O'Sullivan. In early 1984 he decisioned Pan Am champion Orestes Solano of Cuba.

Sources: "The 1984 Olympics," *Ebony* (October 1984); "Detroit Duo Advances," *Los Angeles Times* (August 1, 1984); "The Champions," *Los Angeles Times* (August 14, 1984); "Boxing," *Olympian* (October/November 1984); *United States Olympic Team, Media Guide.*

TATE, JOHN (USA). Born January 29, 1955, in Marion City, Arkansas.

1976 Bronze Medal: Heavyweight Boxing (tied)

As an amateur Johnny Tate never won the big title, although he had won 50 bouts (31 by knockout) and lost 6. He was runner-up in the 1975 Golden Gloves and in the 1975 Pan Am Games. In 1976, at the Olympics, the Cuban Teofilo Stevenson knocked him out in the semifinals. As a professional, Tate defeated Ken Norton in 1979 and laid claim to the World Boxing Association heavyweight title (after Muhammad Ali retired). But Tate held the title only 1 year before losing to Mike Weaver in a 15-round knockout. Larry Holmes was World Boxing Commission champion at the time and was popularly considered the real heavyweight champion. Tate has not fought since.

Sources: *Approved History of Olympic Games; Black Olympians; Guinness Book of Olympic Records; Quest for Gold; United States Olympic Team.*

JOHN BAXTER TAYLOR (Photo courtesy of Amateur Athletic Foundation, Los Angeles, California.)

TAYLOR, JOHN BAXTER, JR. (USA). Born November 3, 1882, in Washington, D.C.

1908 Olympic Gold Medal: 4 x 400-Meter Relay (3:29.4)

John Taylor was captain of his high school track team. He attended the University of Pennsylvania, where he set a new collegiate record for the 440-yard dash (48.8 seconds). Taylor won three IC4A 440-yard titles while in college, and his winning times in 1904 (49.2) and 1907 (48.8) were the fastest times recorded in the world for that time. He was also AAU champion in 1907. At the 1908 Olympics in London, he was a favorite in the 400-meter individual event, as well as in the 1,600-meter relay. However, the 400 race was marred by an incident involving an American and a British runner. Taylor is considered one of the first great Black quarter-milers. He was also the first Black to win a gold medal as a member of a U.S. team. He planned to become a veterinarian, but died of typhoid pneumonia December 2, 1908—5 months after winning the medal.

Sources: *Approved History of Olympic Games; Black Olympians; Negro Firsts in Sports; Negro in Sports; Quest for Gold*.

TAYLOR, MELDRICK (USA). Born October 19, 1966, in Philadelphia, Pennsylvania.

1984 Gold Medal: Featherweight Boxing

Competing at 112 pounds in 1982, Meldrick Taylor won both the U.S. Amateur and National Golden Gloves. He won the U.S. Jr. Championships, competing at 139 pounds, in 1983 and defeated Cuba's Adolfo Horta, five-time champion, in February 1984. Taylor became the first American to decision Horta since Rocky Lockridge in 1979. In 1985 Taylor fought with gold medalist Howard Davis to a lively draw at the Sands Hotel in Atlantic City. Even though 19-year-old Taylor followed an aggressive attack upon his 30-year-old adversary, he was unable to overpower him. Taylor, who is now a professional boxer, has a twin brother, Eldrick, who also boxes. Their older brother, Myron, is a professional boxer as well.

Sources: "The 1984 Olympics," *Ebony* (October 1984); "The Champions," *Los Angeles Times* (August 14, 1984); "Olympic Winners Fight," *New York Times* (August 17, 1986); *United States Olympic Team, Media Guide*.

TAYLOR, ROBERT (USA). Born September 14, 1948, in Tyler, Texas.

1972 Gold Medal: 4 x 100-Meter Relay (38.19, Olympic record/world record)
1972 Silver Medal: 100-Meter Run (10.24)

Robert Taylor graduated from Ernest H. Scott High School in Tyler and from Texas Southern University. Taylor was 1970 NAIA 100-yard champion and took second in the 1972 NAIA 100 meters for Texas Southern in 10.2 seconds. He won the AAU title in 1972. He ran 10.0 in the Olympic trials but finished third, behind Eddie Hart and Rey

Robinson. Because of a communications breakdown, he was the sole American to compete in the 1972 Olympics 100-meter final. He won the silver medal behind Soviet sprinter Valery Borzov.

Sources: *Black Olympians*; British Virgin Islands, Olympic Committee; *Guinness Book of Olympic Records; Quest for Gold; United States Olympic Team, Games of the XXth Olympiad; Who's Who in Track and Field*.

TEMU, NAFTALI (Kenya). Born April 20, 1945, in Kisii, Kenya.

1968 Gold Medal: 10,000-Meter Run (29:27.4)
1968 Bronze Medal: 5,000-Meter Run (14:06.41)

Naftali Temu, a slightly built Kisii tribesman, made a dramatic appearance on the international athletics stage in 1966 when, as a decided underdog, he won the Commonwealth Games 6-mile championship with a 27:14.6 performance. Two years later he won the Olympic 10,000—a development far less surprising than his bronze medal in the 5,000. There was the question of the high altitude at Mexico City—whether the athletes would be adversely affected by it. In the 10,000 the first surprise came after 8,000 meters when Kip Keino dropped out. Although 11 different men had led over the first 8,000 meters, the only runners still in contention were Mamo Wolde, Ronald Clarke, Naftali Temu, and Mohamed Gammoudi. One and a half laps from the finish, Clarke lost contact. A 64.4-second 24th lap by Temu defeated Gammoudi. Just after the bell, Wolde shot past Temu and opened up a gap of 5 yards. But having the most strength left, Temu caught Wolde 50 meters from the finish line and won by 4 yards. Four of the first five finishers were from high altitude countries. And all three medals were taken by Africans, the first time this had occurred in a single Olympic event. Temu had a 10,000-meter best of 28:27.8. A very gritty competitor, his times were not reflective of his ability, as he rarely left Kenya except for major championships. He was the first Kenyan to earn an Olympic gold medal.

Sources: *Approved History of Olympic Games*; British Virgin Islands, Olympic Committee; *Complete Book of the Olympics; Encyclopaedia of Track and Field Athletics; The Games*, Organizing Committee of the XIXth Olympiad, Mexico City; *Guinness Book of Olympic Records*.

THOMAS, DEBI (USA). Born March 25, 1967, in Poughkeepsie, New York.

1988 Bronze Medal: Figure Skating (Singles)

The first and only Winter Olympic Games at which an Afro-American or other person of African descent has won a medal was in 1988 at Calgary, Alberta, Canada. The winner of the bronze medal in figure skating was Californian

DEBI THOMAS (Both photos courtesy of Rich Clarkson, Denver, Colorado.)

Debi Thomas. The record reveals a fascinating and dedicated young woman. Debi Thomas is bright, self-confident, and determined to make her mark upon the world. She is successful both academically and athletically. Attracting attention since age 5, when she began ice skating, Thomas has had outstanding opportunities and experiences. Her maternal grandparents, Dr. and Mrs. Daniel Skelton, met at Cornell University where he trained for veterinary medicine. Her mother, Janice Thomas, majored in mathematics and minored in physics at Wichita State University (Kansas). She became a computer analyst and is now a senior programmer-analyst at Control Data in San Jose, California. Debi's father, McKinley Thomas (now divorced from her mother), is a program manager at Masstor Systems, Santa Clara, California. Thomas attended San Mateo High School and practiced skating at Redwood City Ice Lodge. Her mother drove her 150 miles a day for 4 years to accomplish this. Debi trained with transplanted Scot Alex McGowan, respected and dedicated coach, for 10 years. Academically she excelled and was accepted for admission to Harvard, Princeton, and Stanford universities. She chose Stanford. Asked on the application to the university to describe herself, she wrote "invincible." Janice Thomas has had to pay $25,000 a year for skating lessons and her salary is only $35,000. Debi's Stanford education costs $16,000 a year. However, they manage on various grants and loans, supplemented by contributions from Debi's father, her half brother (a high school mathematics teacher), and her grandparents. In winning the U.S. Championships in 1987, Thomas upset two-time world champion Katarina Witt of East Germany, in addition to bursting into first place at the U.S. National Championships. In the latter she performed a dazzling display of jumps. However, Katarina Witt came back tough in 1987, while Thomas struggled along with tendinitis-inflamed ankles. Living under pressure and on the edge has endowed Thomas with unusual inner strength. When conditions got tough she once considered quitting. But her mother told her, "You can quit skating. That's easy. But you can never quit life." Thomas has been fortunate to have had former Olympic champion Peggy Fleming work with her. She also has met with internationally acclaimed ballet dancer, choreographer, and director Mikhail Baryshnikov and American Ballet Theatre dancer George de la Pena. Besides winning the world and national titles, Thomas was: winner of the Women's Competition at Skate Canada; the Women's Sports Foundation's Amateur Sportswoman of the Year, 1986; gold medalist, National Sports Foundation, 1985; McDonald's Amateur Sportswoman of the Year, 1986; and first place winner of the Grand Prix International in France and the Nelhorn Trophy in West Germany. Thomas, whom the French press dubbed *La Perle Noire* (The Black Pearl), is the first Black, male or female, to win a senior national championship in figure skating and the first Black to win a world championship. She is also the first Black to win a medal in the Winter Olympics. Perhaps the most physically powerful performer ever seen in figure skating, Thomas makes spectacular vertical leaps and speed-of-light midair spins. Then, with the grace and élan of a ballerina, she lands effortlessly and completes the meld of artistry and athleticism demanded by the sport. Debi Thomas states: "I want to be an orthopedic surgeon, specializing in sports medicine.... I want to have a ... training center ... a huge complex with an ice rink.... It will have a ballet room, a weight room, and [a] sports medicine clinic" (*Ms*). Thomas designs her own routines, cuts and mixes her own music, designs and sews her own costumes, and puts together her own aerobics. Now that Debi has had the seeming misfortune of missing the gold and winning only the bronze medal at the Calgary Winter Olympics in 1988, she can now—with certainty—attain her self-professed goal of "getting on with my life." This was reinforced further when on March 26, 1988, she again won only the bronze medal at the World Figure Skating Championships in Budapest, Hungary. Thomas later revealed that she and Brian Vanden Hogen, University of Colorado student, had married on March 15, 1988. Thomas made her television debut as a professional skater in "The Ice Capades with Kirk Cameron" on December 29, 1988. On tour since September 1988, she has skated with "Stars on Ice" and "Benson and Hedges on Ice." In her first professional competitions, she won the World Professional Figure Skating Championships and placed third in the Challenge of Champions.

Sources: "With Style and Grace," *Black Enterprise*, (June 1986); "Debi Thomas, the Nation's No. 1 Skating Sensation," *Ebony* (May 1986); "Teen Skater Breaks Ice," *Jet* (February 25, 1985); "Debi Plans a Medical Career," *Jet* (March 10, 1986); "Debi Thomas Fulfills Her Promise," *Jet* (April 7, 1986); "Thomas Sees Pressure," *Jet* (October 13, 1986); "There's No Doubting Thomas," *Los Angeles Times* (February 11, 1988); "It's No Surprise," *Los Angeles Times* (February 29, 1988); "Witt Goes Out on Top," *Los Angeles Times* (March 27, 1988); "Debi Thomas Ready for TV Pro Debut," *Los Angeles Times* (December 26, 1988); "Debi Thomas," *Ms* (February 1987); "Familiar Figures Take Lead," *New York Times* (January 8, 1988); "Boitano, Thomas in Good Shape," *New York Times* (January 11, 1988); "On the Cutting Edge," *Seventeen* (March 1987); "Books or Blades," *Sports Illustrated* (February 17, 1986); "Another Miracle on Ice?" *Sports Illustrated* (March 17, 1986); "Cashing in on the Collywobbles," *Sports Illustrated* (March 31, 1986); "All That Glittered," *Sports Illustrated* (February 16, 1987); "Lighting Up the Late Shift," *Sports Illustrated* (January 18, 1988); "End of Ice Age," *Sports Illustrated* (April 4, 1988); "Cool on Ice," *Vogue* (August 1987); "Debi Thomas," *Women's Sports and Fitness* (December 1985); "Dark Cloud Over U.S. Skaters," *Women's Sports and Fitness* (March 1986); "That Championship Year: 1986," *Women's Sports and Fitness* (December 1986).

THOMAS, JOHN CURTIS (USA). Born March 3, 1941, in Boston, Massachusetts.

1960 Bronze Medal: High Jump (7 ft. ¼ in./2.14 m)
1964 Silver Medal: High Jump (7 ft. 1¾ in./2.18 m, Olympic record/tied world record)

John Thomas was selected to the All-Time American track team at Boston University. As a 17-year-old freshman he set a world indoor high jump record of 7 feet, 1¼ inches, which was superior to the outdoor record. In 1960, a year later, he came back to raise the indoor record to 7 feet, 2½ inches and then set an indoor record of 7 feet, 3¾ inches at the Olympic final trials. Thomas was a heavy favorite at the 1960 Rome Olympics, but he finished behind Soviets Shavlakadze and Brumel. In 1964, at Tokyo, Brumel usurped Thomas's title as the world's best high jumper. Thomas had a fine competitive record, even though he did not succeed in winning an Olympic gold medal. He won two AAU outdoor championships and five indoors. He was twice NCAA champion and won both the indoor and the outdoor high jump at IC4A for 3 years. He was a very versatile athlete and could possibly have become a top-notch decathlete. Upon retirement Thomas took a coaching appointment at Boston University and then became a regional sales manager with New England telephone company.

Sources: *Approved History of Olympic Games; Black Olympians;* British Virgin Islands, Olympic Committee; *Guinness Book of Olympic Records; Quest for Gold; Who's Who in Track and Field.*

THOMPSON, FRANCIS (DALEY) (Great Britain). Born July 30, 1958, in London, England.

1980 Gold Medal: Decathlon (8,495 pts.)
1984 Gold Medal: Decathlon (8,847 pts., new Olympic record)

Son of a Nigerian father and a Scottish mother, Daley Thompson's father called him by an African name, Ayodele, which was shortened to Dele and pronounced like "Daley." Francis Morgan Thompson is a talkative, outgoing man. This driven athlete's years of effort have given him a deep perspective of himself and his passion for the decathlon (*Track & Field News*). In the 1984 Olympics Thompson beat his arch rival, West Germany's Jurgen Hingsen 8,797 to 8,673. Initially it was thought that Thompson had failed to break Hingsen's world record of 8,798. But in 1986 the IAAF announced that close examination of the electric phototimer revealed that Thomas had completed the 110 meter hurdles in 14.33 seconds rather than 14.34 seconds. Thus, one more point was added to Thompson's Olympic total to match Hingsen's world record of 8,798. However, under a new decathlon scoring table implemented in April 1985, Thompson became the new world record holder with an upgraded score of 8,847 points to Hingsen's 8,832 points. Thompson won the Commonwealth Games title in 1978, 1982, and 1986; the European title in 1982 and 1986; the World Championships title in 1983; and, of course, two Olympic titles in 1980 and 1984. Although his ambition was to win three Olympic decathlon titles, his winning streak came to an end in Rome at the 1987 World Championships. Beset by injury, he finished ninth. At the 1988 Seoul Olympics, he finished fourth, hampered by injury as well. Thompson's 1980 Olympic record was: 100 meters,

FRANCIS MORGAN (DALEY) THOMPSON (Photo courtesy of Amateur Athletic Foundation, Los Angeles, California, and Robert Hagedohm, AAF/LPI 1984.)

Olympics and European championships, Thompson has no really weak event.

Sources: *Approved History of Olympic Games*; British Virgin Islands, Olympic Committee; *Complete Book of the Olympics*; *Games of the XXIInd Olympiad, Moscow 1980*; *Guinness Book of Olympic Records*; *International Athletics Annual*; "The Decathlon," *Los Angeles Times* (July 26, 1984); "Daley Thompson Gets Half of a World Record," *Los Angeles Times* (August 9, 1984); "Daley Still Reigns in Decathlon," *Los Angeles Times* (August 10, 1984); *Olympic Games*; *Sackville Illustrated Dictionary of Athletics*; "Thompson Consumed by the Decathlon," *Track & Field News* (October 1982); "Daley Thompson," *Track & Field News* (April 1984); "Daley Thompson," *Track & Field News* (May, 1987).

TIACOH, GABRIEL (Ivory Coast). Born September 10, 1963, in the Ivory Coast.

1984 Silver Medal: 400-Meter Run (44.54)

Gabriel Tiacoh, the son of an Ivory Coast diplomat, spent his formative years in France. He later attended Washington State University, where he received a degree in business and is now working on an M.B.A. Tiacoh's silver medal for the 400 was the first-ever medal won by an Ivory Coast competitor in any sport. His personal best in the 400 is his 1986 NCAA record 44.30, and he has also run 20.71 seconds in the 200. He ran on Africa's 4 x 400 relay team at the 1985 World cup. Tiacoh created one of the major surprises of the 1984 Olympics when he won the 400. He surprised again with a powerful win in the Pepsi Invitational 400. Even he was amazed that he had run a 44.32 in the Pepsi. Tiacoh was rated the world's best in the 400 in 1986. A week after the Pepsi, Tiacoh sped 44.58 to win the PAC-10 title. He also anchored Washington State's long relay team with a 43.7 burner.

Sources: British Virgin Islands, Olympic Committee; "The Champions," *Los Angeles Times* (August 14, 1984); *1984 Olympic Games; Sarajevo/Los Angeles*; "The Games," *Olympian* (October/November 1984); "One Lap to Go," *Track & Field News* (July 1986); "Tiacoh Knows Where He Stands Now," *Track & Field News* (July 1986).

TILLMAN, HENRY DURAN (USA). Born August 1, 1960, in Los Angeles, California.

1984 Gold Medal: Heavyweight Boxing

In 1981 Henry Tillman served about 10 months at the California Youth Authority for armed robbery. But he decided to turn his life around and began working seriously on a boxing career. He reached the Olympics 3 years later, which was unusual. He won the 1984 Olympic trials after withdrawing from the Golden Gloves semifinals because of a

10.62; long jump, 26 feet, 3 inches; shot put, 49 feet, 10 inches; high jump, 6 feet, 9¾ inches; 400 meters, 48.01; 110-meter hurdles, 14.47; discus, 138 feet, 7 inches; pole vault, 15 feet, 5 inches; javelin, 210 feet, 6 inches; 1,500 meters, 4:39.9. His 1984 Olympic record was: 100 meters, 10.44; shotput, 51 feet, 7 inches; long jump, 26 feet, 3½ inches; high jump, 6 feet, 8 inches; 400 meters, 46.97; discus, 152 feet, 9 inches; 1,500 meters, 4:35.0; pole vault, 16 feet, 4¾ inches; javelin, 214 feet; 110-meter hurdles, 14.34. A cocky, cheerful, bouncy character, but only when competing, Thompson, coached by Bruce Longden, is totally dedicated to the decathlon. Although Thompson lost his world record to the giant 6-foot 7-inch Hingsen, he is generally regarded as shoulder to shoulder with Jim Thorpe, Bob Mathias, Rafer Johnson, and Bill Toomey as one of the greatest decathletes the world has ever seen. A world-class sprinter (10.26 and 20.88) and long jumper (26 feet, 3¼ inches), who has also run on British sprint relay teams at the hand injury. In 1983 he won the Pan Am trials and took second at the Pan Am Games. At 6 feet, 3 inches and 201 pounds, Tillman has a quick, powerful jab and he is swift afoot, but his professional career has progressed rather slowly. Tillman has worked for Anheuser-Busch as part of Operation Gold and Job Opportunities.

Sources: British Virgin Islands, Olympic Committee; *The Complete Book of the Olympics*; "The 1984 Olympics," *Ebony* (October 1984); "The Champions," *Los Angeles Times* (August 14, 1984); "Boxing," *Olympian* (October/November 1984); *United States Olympic Team, Media Guide*.

TINKER, GERALD (USA). Born January 19, 1951, in Miami, Florida.

1972 Gold Medal: 4 x 100-Meter Relay (38.19, Olympic record/world record)

Gerald Tinker, a 9.3 sprinter and football player at Memphis State University, continued these activities when he transferred to Kent State in 1971. Tinker was second in the Kennedy Games 100 yards, running 9.4. In the AAU he finished fourth in 10.3. He also placed fourth in the Olympic trials, in 10.1, and ran the third leg for the U.S. team that won the 400-meter relay gold medal in the Munich Olympics. Another member of that team was Tinker's cousin, Larry Black, who ran the first leg. Tinker had a brief professional football career.

Sources: *Approved History of Olympic Games; Black Olympians*; British Virgin Islands, Olympic Committee; *Guinness Book of Olympic Records; Quest for Gold; Who's Who in Track and Field*.

TISDALE, WAYMAN (USA). Born June 9, 1964, in Tulsa, Oklahoma.

1984 Gold Medal: Basketball

Wayman Tisdale is the all-time leading scorer in University of Oklahoma history, with 1,720 points. He established a Big Eight scoring record in each of his first two seasons and set a Big Eight record with 61 points against Texas at San Antonio. In 2 years he hit 57.9 percent from the field and averaged 10 rebounds and 25.8 points per game. He was the second leading scorer and rebounder on the 1983 U.S. Pan Am team that won a gold medal. Tisdale was a first team All-American in 1983 and 1984, his freshman and sophomore years. The first player in history to be awarded such an honor, he was also two-time unanimous Big Eight All-Conference and back-to-tack Big Eight Player of the Year. Playing forward rather than the center position he played in college, Tisdale was perhaps keyed on by opponents at the 1984 Olympics as the leading scoring threat on the U.S. team. Tisdale turned professional with the Indiana Pacers of

the NBA in 1985 and although he has enjoyed some moments of success, he has not reached the "star" status some envisioned for him.

Sources: British Virgin Islands, Olympic Committee; "The 1984 Olympics," *Ebony* (October 1984); "The Champions," *Los Angeles Times* (August 14, 1984); "Basketball," *Olympian* (October/November 1984); *United States Olympic Team, Media Guide*.

THOMAS EDWARD TOLAN (Photo courtesy of Amateur Athletic Foundation, Los Angeles, California.)

TOLAN, THOMAS EDWARD (USA). Born September 29, 1908, in Detroit, Michigan.

1932 Gold Medal: 100-Meter Run (10.3, Olympic record)
1932 Gold Medal: 200-Meter Run (21.2, Olympic record)

Eddie Tolan graduated from the University of Michigan at Ann Arbor with a B.A. in education. "He was affable, kindly, and an excellent student" (*Famous American Athletes of Today*). He had hoped to study medicine but did not get the chance. "Little Eddie Tolan ... became the first Negro to win the fabled 100 meter dash" (*Negro Firsts in Sports*), an accomplishment that emotionally stirred people of color around the world. Tolan won 300 races and lost only 7 to become a superstar of track. Oddly enough, despite his two sprint victories at the 1932 Olympic trials, Tolan was not selected to run on the U.S. 4 x 100-meter relay team. Tolan was a Detroit High School city and state champion in the 100- and 200-yard dashes. After graduating from Michigan, he flashed through the 100-meter dash in 10.3 seconds, an Olympic record. He was the first man to be officially credited with the time of 9.5 seconds for 100 yards—on May 25, 1929. He was known as "The Midnight Express." Tolan held the world 100-meter and 100-yard records. He ran the record 10.4 in 100 meters twice in 1929 and was the first to run 9.5 in the 100 yards (Evanston, Illinois, 1929). While at Michigan, he won the 1931 NCAA 200 yards in 21.5 and took the 1929 and 1930 AAU 100-yard championships. In 1929 and 1931 he also won the AAU 220 yards. He finished second to rival Ralph Metcalfe in the 1932 Olympic trials in both the 100 meters and 120 yards. However, he set the Olympic record at the Games themselves, with 10.4 in the preliminaries. He edged Metcalfe by the smallest of margins in the finals—both were timed at 10.3. Tolan later went onto the vaudeville circuit with Bill (Bojangles) Robinson. He enrolled in law school and became a clerk in a county office in Detroit, where he was later promoted to accountant. In 1935 he became an elementary school teacher. Eddie Tolan (who was nearsighted and ran with spectacles taped to his head) was named to the Michigan Sports Hall of Fame, the first of a long procession of Black sprinters to win an Olympic gold medal. He died of a heart attack on January 31, 1967, in Detroit, at age 58.

Sources: *Approved History of Olympic Games*; *Black Olympians*; British Virgin Islands, Olympic Committee; *Famous American Athletes of Today*; *Guinness Book of Olympic Records*; *Negro Firsts in Sports*; *Negro in Sports*; *1980 Olympics Handbook*; *Quest for Gold*; *Track and Field: The Great Ones*; *Who's Who in the Olympic Games*; *Who's Who in Track and Field*.

TORRES, JOSÉ LUÍS (USA). Born May 3, 1936, in Playa de Ponce, Puerto Rico.

1956 Silver Medal: Light Middleweight Boxing

José Torres won his only amateur championships in army and inter-service bouts. He fought in the 1956 Olympics while serving in the U.S. Army. At the 1956 Olympics in Melbourne, it was José "Chegui" Torres's ill fortune to have been in the same class as Hungarian László Papp, for Torres was a fine boxer. Papp defeated Torres in the finals for his third consecutive boxing title. After the Olympics, Torres fought for 2 more years in the army as an amateur and won the 1958 AAU Championships. He turned professional and had a good career as a middleweight and light heavyweight. He won the light heavyweight world title in 1965 by knocking out Willie Pastrono in nine rounds. Torres defended his title 4 times before losing a 15-round decision to Dick Tiger in December 1966. Since retiring he has authored a good biography of Muhammad Ali. Torres, a national hero in Puerto Rico, became commissioner of boxing for the state of New York.

Sources: *Approved History of Olympic Games*; British Virgin Islands, Olympic Committee; *Guinness Book of Olympic Records*; *Official Report of the XVIth Olympiad, Melbourne, 1956*; *Quest for Gold*.

TOUSSAINT, CHERYL (USA). Born December 16, 1952, in Brooklyn, New York.

1972 Silver Medal: 4 x 400-Meter Relay (3:25.2)

Cheryl Toussaint graduated from Erasmus High School and, in 1974, from New York University. She was a member of the Atoms Track Club. Toussaint won the AAU 990-yard title in 1970 and 1971 but lost that title in 1972 to Carol Hudson. She also lost at the Olympic final trials, to Madeline Manning. Toussaint was eliminated in the heats of the 800 meters at the Olympics, but her fifth place in the 400 meters at the final trials earned her a spot on the relay team, where her 51.3 third leg made a significant contribution to the new U.S. record of 3:22.8. In addition to her team winning the Olympic silver medal in the 4 x 400-meter relay, Toussaint won the AAU indoor 800 yards in 1972 and 1973.

Sources: *Black Olympians*; *Guinness Book of Olympic Records*; *Quest for Gold*; *United States Olympic Team, Games of the XXth Olympiad*; *United States Track and Field Olympians*.

TURA, ESHETU (Ethiopia). Born January 19, 1950, in Ethiopia.

1980 Bronze Medal: 3,000-Meter Steeplechase (8:13.6)

Eshetu Tura was deprived of his first chance at Olympic glory because of the 1976 African boycott. Redemption came 4 years later when he placed third in the Moscow 3,000-meter steeplechase. An outstanding cross-country runner, Tura had bests of 7:43.18 for 3,000-meters, 8:13.57 for the steeplechase, and 13:23.8 for the 5,000. He ranked second in the world in the steeplechase in 1977.

Sources: *Approved History of Olympic Games*; British Virgin Islands, Olympic Committee; *Complete Book of the Olympics*; *Games of the XXIInd Olympiad, Moscow*; *Guinness Book of Olympic Records*.

TURNER, KIM (USA). Born March 21, 1961, in Detroit, Michigan.

1984 Bronze Medal: 100-Meter Hurdles (13.06)

Kim Turner attended the University of Texas at El Paso and was a member of the L.A. Mercurettes. Nationally ranked in 1982 and 1983, Turner enjoyed her best season in 1983, taking second at the NCAA meet and the Pan Am Games and fourth at TAC. She lowered her personal record to 12.95 in 1983. Turner's bronze for the 100-meter hurdles was later ruled a tie for third place with French hurdler Michelle Chardonnet, who received her medal a year later.

Sources: "The 1984 Olympics," *Ebony* (October 1984); "The Champions," *Los Angeles Times* (August 14, 1984); "The Games," *Olympian* (October/November 1984); *United States Olympic Team, Media Guide*; "Kim Turner," *Women's Sports* (October 1984).

WYOMIA TYUS (Photo courtesy of U.S. Olympic Committee, Colorado Springs, Colorado.)

TYUS, WYOMIA (USA). Born August 29, 1945, in Griffin, Georgia.

1964 Gold Medal: 100-Meter Run (11.49)
1964 Silver Medal: 4 x 100-Meter Relay (43.92)
1968 Gold Medal: 100-Meter Run (11.08, Olympic record/world record)
1968 Gold Medal: 4 x 100-Meter Relay (42.88, Olympic record/world record)

Wyomia Tyus graduated from Fairmont High School, Griffin, Georgia, in 1963 and then went on to Tennessee State University, where she earned a degree in recreation in 1967. She was a member of coach Ed Temple's legendary Tennessee State Tigerbelles, which is considered the most successful women's program in American track and field. Tyus was the first athlete, male or female, to win an Olympic sprint title twice. She beat or equaled world records twice at 100 yards and four times at 100 meters. She had the knack of putting on her greatest performances when they really counted—during the Olympics. She was clocked at an amazing 23 miles per hour at a meet in 1965. Tyus won two AAU titles at 200 meters/200 yards to add to her three victories at 100 meters/100 yards, although she never posted a world record in the longer sprint. She won the AAU indoor 60 yards three times and was the 200-meter champion at the 1967 Pan Am Games. Tyus won the 100-meter Olympic title in 1964 and established a new world record of 11.2 in the qualifying heats. In July 1965 she brought the record down to 11.1. Two weeks earlier she had tied the 100-yard record with a 10.3 clocking. She set a world record again when she won the 100 at the 1968 Olympics in 11.08. Tyus was the most successful of all U.S. women track and field athletes at the Olympics, with three gold medals and one silver. In 1974, 4 years after retiring from the amateur league, Wyomia Tyus joined the first professional track association and went undefeated for her 2 years on the circuit. She now holds clinics and is a coach and a public speaker. She has worked as a public relations representative for a major soft drink company and has served as U.S. goodwill ambassador to Africa (Jesse Owens had preceded her in this). She has been on the Advisory Board of the Women's Sports Foundation, served on the Post Fun and Fitness Council, and participated in Colgate-Palmolive's "Help Young America Campaign" with Billie Jean King and Arnold Palmer. Wyomia Tyus was inducted into the Women's Sports Hall of Fame in 1981, and in 1983, when track and field sportswriters and statisticians picked an All-Time team, the woman sprinter named was Tyus. A resident of Los Angeles, Tyus has two children, Simone Simberg and Tyus Tillman.

Sources: Tyus, Wyomia. Interview. 1984; *Black Olympians*; *Biographical Dictionary of American Sports: Outdoor Sports; For the Record; Golden Girls; Guinness Book of Olympic Records; 1980 Olympics Handbook; Quest for Gold; Tales of Gold; Sprint Team Profiles*, Los Angeles Olympic Organizing Committee; *Who's Who in the Olympic Games; Who's Who in Track and Field*; "Wyomia Tyus," *Women's Sports* (August 1984).

UGBISIEN, MOSES (Nigeria). Born December 11, 1964, in Nigeria.

1984 Bronze Medal: 4 x 400-Meter Relay (2:59.32)

Moses Ugbisien attended Seton Hall University, Wayland Baptist College in Plainview, Texas, and Texas Southern

University. Ugbisien ran an outstanding second leg of 44.5 seconds on Nigeria's 4 x 400-meter relay team at the 1984 Olympics, moving the squad into contention for a medal (a bronze as it turned out). He ran his personal best 400-meter time of 45.74 seconds while representing Wayland Baptist at the 1985 NAIA Championships.

Sources: British Virgin Islands, Olympic Committee; *1984 Olympic Games, Sarajevo/Los Angeles*; "The Games," *Olympian* (October/November 1984); "Olympic Winners," *New York Times* (August 13, 1984).

URGELLES, ALEJANDRO (Cuba). Born in Cuba.

1972 Bronze Medal: Basketball

A strongly built 6-foot 8-inch forward, Urgelles retired from playing internationally for Cuba after the 1982 Central American and Caribbean Games in Havana. For a summary of the Cuban team's record at the Munich Games in 1972, see Calderón-Gómez.

Sources: *Approved History of Olympic Games*; British Virgin Islands, Olympic Committee; *Die Spiele, Official Report for the Games of the XXth Olympiad; Guinness Book of Olympic Records*.

UTI, SUNDAY (Nigeria). Born October 23, 1962, in Nigeria.

1984 Bronze Medal: 4 x 400-Meter Relay (2:59.32)

Sunday Uti runs fast on any day of the week. World Student Games 400-meter champion in 1983, Uti atoned for a disappointing World Championships performance by reaching the 400 final in Los Angeles and winning a bronze medal as leadoff for Nigeria's 1,600-meter relay squad. Nigeria finished behind the U.S. and Great Britain in an African record time. Uti's personal bests are 44.83 seconds for 400 meters and 20.79 for the 200.

Sources: British Virgin Islands, Olympic Committee; *1984 Olympic Games, Sarajevo/Los Angeles*; "The Games," *Olympian* (October/November 1984); "Olympic Winners," *New York Times* (August 13, 1984).

VAILS, NELSON (USA). Born October 13, 1960, in New York City.

1984 Silver Medal: Cycling, 1,000-Meter Sprint (10.95)

Nelson Vails grew up in a housing project in Harlem, the youngest of 10 children. A 10th-grade high school dropout, Vails, known as "Cheetah" for his speed and competitiveness, supported himself as a bicycle messenger in Manhattan, earning sometimes $400 a week. He began competitive cycling at 16, participating in local races and then nationally with New York clubs. In 1982 he was named to the 10-man U.S. national team and became one of the few Blacks to race in the international cycling circuit. Vails won the gold medal at the Pan Am Games in 1983, setting a Pan Am record of 10.6 seconds in the match sprint preliminaries. In the 1983 national championships he finished second to Mark Gorski by inches on the third ride. Winning the silver medal in the 1984 Olympic Games in Los Angeles, with a time of 10.95 seconds, he once again was second to Gorski, who took the gold with a time of 10.49.

Sources: *Black Olympians*; British Virgin Islands, Olympic Committee; "The Champions," *Los Angeles Times* (August 14, 1984); "Cycling," *Olympian* (October/November 1984); "For Terror of the Streets Nelson Vails," *People Magazine* (April 1984); *United States Olympic Team, Media Guide*.

VALDES, CARMEN (Cuba). Born November 23, 1954, in Cuba.

1972 Bronze Medal: 4 x 100-Meter Relay (43.36)

Seventeen-year-old Carmen Valdes ran the second leg for Cuba's bronze medal winners in the 4 x 100 at Munich. Her best electronically timed 100 was recorded in Munich at 11.46 seconds. Valdes had manually timed performances of 11.1 and 23.4 seconds in 1976 but never achieved as much as expected in major international competition. She returned to domestic competition in 1986 but failed to qualify for Cuba's international squads.

Sources: British Virgin Islands, Olympic Committee; *Complete Book of the Olympics; Guinness Book of Olympic Records*.

VAN DER LIJDE, ARNOLD (The Netherlands). Born in the Netherlands.

1984 Bronze Medal: Heavyweight Boxing
1988 Bronze Medal: Heavyweight Boxing

Considered on paper a classic boxer, "Towering Tulip" Arnold Van der Lijde (6 feet, 7 inches) was defeated in Seoul by Ray Mercer of the U.S., who knocked him out in the second round. Also a bronze medalist at the Los Angeles 1984 Olympics, Van der Lijde was given his nickname by U.S. boxing writers.

Sources: "The Seoul Games," *Los Angeles Times* (September 29, 1988); "Seoul Games/Medal Winners," *Los Angeles Times* (October 3, 1988); *Seoul '88*; "Olympics Record," *USA Today* (October 3, 1988).

VARONA, OSCAR (Cuba). Born in Cuba.

1972 Bronze Medal: Basketball

A reserve guard, Oscar Varona was a relatively minor contributor to the Cuban effort. For a summary of the

Cuban team's record at the Munich Games in 1972, see Calderón-Gómez.

Sources: *Approved History of Olympic Games*; British Virgin Islands, Olympic Committee; *Die Spiele, Official Report for the Games of the XXth Olympiad*; *Guinness Book of Olympic Records*; *Munchen 1972: Results of the Games of the XXth Olympiad*.

VELASQUES, DANIEL ROGER (France). Born December 20, 1943, in Guadeloupe.

1972 Bronze Medal: 4 x 400-Meter Relay (3:00.65)

Roger Velasques's brief international career was highlighted when he ran the second leg for France's 4 x 400-meter relay at Munich in 1972. The French team finished with a time of 3:00.7, which is still a national record. Velasques, who had a personal best time of 46.0 seconds for 400 meters, ran 46.35 as a 32-year-old in 1976.

Sources: British Virgin Islands, Olympic Committee; *Complete Book of the Olympics*; *Guinness Book of Olympic Records*.

VIRCHES, RAUL (Cuba). Born in Cuba.

1976 Bronze Medal: Volleyball

Raul Virches was one of the leading contributors to Cuba's effort in winning the bronze medal at the 1976 Olympics. For a summary of the Cuban team's record in Montreal, see García.

Sources: *Approved History of Olympic Games*; British Virgin Islands, Olympic Committee; *Complete Book of the Olympics*; *Guinness Book of Olympic Records*; *Montreal 1976*; *Games of the XXIst Olympiad*.

WAKIIHURI, DOUGLAS (Kenya). Born September 26, 1963, in Mombasa, Kenya.

1988 Silver Medal: Marathon (2 hrs. 10:47)

A Kikuyu, Douglas Wakiihuri graduated from high school in the village of Nyeru and later had a rather odd odyssey. He went to New Zealand in search of a coach and then went to Japan where he became a disciple of two Japanese mystics. He now lives in Tokyo and trains there with Toshihiko Seko. An employee of a Japanese food company, he speaks Swahili, English, and Japanese. In addition to winning a silver medal at the 1988 Olympics, Wakiihuri won the marathon in the 1987 World Championships and was Japanese champion in the 5,000 meters in 1987.

Sources: British Virgin Islands, Olympic Committee; *International Amateur Athletic Federation*; "Seoul Games/Medal Winners," *Los Angeles Times* (October 3, 1988); *Seoul '88*; "Big Surprise by Wakiihuri," *Track & Field News* (November 1987); "Olympics Record," *USA Today* (October 3, 1988).

WALLINGTON, JAMES R., JR. (USA). Born July 28, 1944, in Philadelphia, Pennsylvania.

1968 Bronze Medal: Light Welterweight Boxing

Jim Wallington took a brilliant amateur record of 76 and 2 to Mexico City. During an amazing 3-year period he won 3 national AAU titles (1966-68), 3 inter-service championships (1966-68), 3 Golden Gloves titles (1966-68), and the 1967 Pan Am Games gold medal. However, at the 1968 Olympics he lost in the semifinals to Enrique Regueiferos of Cuba by a decision.

Sources: *Approved History of Olympic Games*; *Guinness Book of Olympic Records*; *Quest for Gold*; *United States Olympic Team, Games of the XIXth Olympiad*.

WANGILA, ROBERT (Kenya). Born in Kenya.

1988 Gold Medal: Welterweight Boxing (147 lbs./67 kg)

Robert Wangila of Kenya, defeated Laurent Boudouani of France. The referee stopped the fight at 2 minutes, 16 seconds into the second round.

Sources: "U.S. Wins Two Golds in Boxing," *Los Angeles Times* (October 1, 1988); "Seoul Games/Medal Winners," *Los Angeles Times* (October 3, 1988); *Seoul '88*; "Olympics Record," *USA Today* (October 3, 1988).

WARUINGE, PHILIP (Kenya). Born February 3, 1945, in Muranga, Kenya.

1968 Bronze Medal: Featherweight Boxing
1972 Silver Medal: Featherweight Boxing

In 1968, at Mexico City, Philip Waruinge took the bronze in featherweight boxing, but in 1972 he moved up to the silver in that category, behind Boris Kuznetsov of the Soviet Union. Waruinge later had a moderately successful career as a professional, fighting mainly in Scandinavia.

Sources: *Africa at the Olympics*; *Approved History of Olympic Games*; British Virgin Islands, Olympic Committee; *Complete Book of the Olympics*; *Die Spiele, Official Report for the Games of the XXth Olympiad*; *Games of the XIXth Olympiad, Mexico City, 1968*; *Guinness Book of Olympic Records, Mexico 68*; *Participants in the XIXth Olympiad*; *Olympic Games: The Records*.

WEATHERSPOON, TERESA (USA). Born December 12, 1965.

1988 Gold Medal: Basketball

Teresa Weatherspoon graduated from Louisiana Tech University in 1988 with a degree in physical education. She was a Kodak All-American for the 1986-87 season and made the all-tournament teams at the Midwest Regional and the Final Four as Tech finished second to Tennessee. At the FIBA World Championships and Goodwill Games, she played for the 1986 U.S. gold medal-winning teams. Weatherspoon also played for the U.S. at the World University Games in Zagreb, Yugoslavia. She led Louisiana Tech to a 32-2 record and to the 1988 NCAA Championship as the Lady Techsters defeated Auburn for the title. In the Final Four she was named MVP and, for the second consecutive year, Wade Trophy winner. Averaging 12.8 points and 7.8 assists per game, Weatherspoon finished her collegiate career as the all-time assists and steals leader at Louisiana Tech.

Sources: "Black American Medal Winners," *Ebony* (December 1988); "Seoul Games/Medal Winners," *Los Angeles Times* (October 3, 1988); *1988 United States Olympic Team, Media Guide; Seoul '88;* "Olympics Record," *USA Today* (October 3, 1988).

WEDDERBURN, JAMES EDWARD (British West Indies). Born June 23, 1938, in St. John, Barbados.

1960 Bronze Medal: 4 x 400-Meter Relay (3:04.13)

James Wedderburn attended Lodge School in St. John, Barbados and New York University. He has a B.S. and an M.A. degree and an advanced certificate in school administration. Wedderburn is a member of the Grand Street Boys Club in New York. Wedderburn was the only non-Jamaican on the British West Indies unit that won third in the 4 x 400 at the Rome 1960 Olympics. The other team members were Malcolm Spence, Keith Gardner, and George Kerr. Their time was 3:04.0, then a Caribbean record. Wedderburn, whose best time in the 400 meters was 46.5, also dabbled in the 400-meter hurdles and held the Barbados record at 54.3 seconds for some 20 years. He won an Eastern Collegiate Athletic Conference medal in 1962. Wedderburn coached the Barbados national team from 1964 to 1969 and an Olympian team in 1968. Currently vice principal of a secondary school in Rochester, New York, he is married to Maureen Wedderburn and has two children, Trudy and James, Jr.

Sources: Wedderburn, James. Questionnaire. 1984; British Virgin Islands, Olympic Committee; *Complete Book of the Olympics; Guinness Book of Olympic Records.*

WESTBROOK, PETER J. (USA). Born April 16, 1952, in St. Louis, Missouri.

1984 Bronze Medal: Fencing, Individual Sabre

Peter Westbrook graduated from Essex Catholic High School and New York University. He participated in fencing, boxing, and track in high school and became state champion. In college he was fencing NCAA champion and captain of the New York University team. He was 11 times national champion (1979-86). He belonged to the New York Fencing Club. In 1975 Westbrook was third in sabre competition at the Pan Am Games, in 1979 he was second, and in 1983 he won the gold medal. He was a member of the U.S. Olympic team in 1976, 1980 (the year of the American boycott), and 1984. In 1984 he was the first American in 24 years to win a medal in the individual sabre. Westbrook won silver medals in 1975, 1979, 1983, and 1987.

Sources: Westbrook, Peter. Questionnaire. 1984; British Virgin Islands, Olympic Committee; "The 1984 Olympics," *Ebony* (October 1984); "The Champions," *Los Angeles Times* (August 14, 1984); "The Games," *Olympian* (October/November 1984); *United States Olympic Team, Media Guide; 1988 United States Olympic Team, Media Guide.*

WHITAKER, PERNELL (USA). Born January 2, 1964, in Norfolk, Virginia.

1984 Gold Medal: Lightweight Boxing

Pernell Whitaker graduated from Booker T. Washington High School in 1982 and attended Norfolk State College. Whitaker had been boxing for 11 years at the time of the 1984 Olympics. As world champion he had won the 1984 Olympic trials and World Championships challenge and, in 1983, had won the Pan Am trials and Pan Am Games. He defeated Cuba's feared Angel Herrera three or four times. Whitaker won his first world title in 1983 at the World Championships. He won his U.S. title in 1982 and, in his first international competition, took second at the World Championships that year. Whitaker turned professional on November 15, 1984, at Madison Square Garden, along with Evander Holyfield and Mark Breland, his Olympic teammates. He has made slow but steady progress up the professional lightweight ranks, remaining unbeaten.

Sources: British Virgin Islands, Olympic Committee; "1984 Olympics," *Ebony* (October 1984); "Olympic Winners Fight to Lively Draw," *New York Times* (August 17, 1986); *United States Olympic Team, Media Guide.*

WHITE, JOSEPH (USA). Born November 14, 1946, in St. Louis, Missouri.

1968 Gold Medal: Basketball

Joseph ("JoJo") White graduated from McKinley High School in St. Louis in 1965 and from the University of

Kansas in 1969. He was a member of the U.S. Pan Am Games team in 1967 and was 1968 All-American and MVP in the Big Eight Conference. White won the Olympic gold medal in 1968 as a starting guard for the American basketball team, whose others stars were Spencer Haywood and Charlie Scott. His Olympic average was 16.4 points. White went on to star for several years with the Boston Celtics and played on two league championship teams. He also appeared in several NBA All-Star games.

Sources: *Black Olympians*; British Virgin Islands, Olympic Committee; *Guinness Book of Olympic Records; United States Olympic Team, Games of the XIXth Olympiad*.

WHITE, MARILYN ELAINE (USA). Born October 17, 1944, in Los Angeles, California.

1964 Silver Medal: 4 x 100-Meter Relay (43.92)

Marilyn White attended Bishop Comatry High School and UCLA, and graduated in 1967 from Pepperdine University, where she studied on a track scholarship. The L.A. Mercurettes claimed her membership. The indoor 220 yards was the only AAU title that Marilyn White of UCLA won in 1963. Nevertheless, she was in the top flight of U.S. sprinters for a number of seasons. She ran the third leg for the U.S. team in the 400-meter relays at the Tokyo Olympics and also placed fourth in the individual 100 meters. White stated in an interview: "In 1962 when I first started in track and field I was trained very hard by Fred Jones. Then in 1963 I beat Wilma Rudolph indoors and in the 60-yard dash. I found out what a real champion she was.... I liked the fact that a person who was of her caliber ... could still [be so gracious]." White ran third in the 100 meters at the Pan Am Games in São Paulo, Brazil in 19-- and won a gold medal in the 400-meter relay. More recently White was a bilingual specialist for the Los Angeles Unified School District. She also runs with Masters Track and Field and with the Southern California Masters team (the Striders).

Sources: White, Marilyn. Interview. 1984; *Black Olympians; Guinness Book of Olympic Records; Quest for Gold; United States Olympic Track and Field Games; United States Track and Field Olympians*.

WHITE, WILLYE B. (USA). Born January 1, 1939, in Money, Mississippi.

1956 Silver Medal: Long Jump (19 ft. 11¾ in./6.09 m)
1964 Silver Medal: 4 x 100-Meter Relay (43.92)

Willye "Red" White graduated from Tennessee State University and earned a degree in public health administration from Chicago State University. She is another of Ed Temple's Tennessee State Tigerbelles. White's Olympic career began in 1956 when she competed in the long jump in Melbourne. In Munich, 16 years later, she established a record of being

the only woman track and field athlete to represent the U.S. in five Olympics—Melbourne, Rome, Tokyo, Mexico City, and Munich. White won the AAU outdoor long jump 10 times between 1960 and 1972 and was indoor champion in 1962. She was also an outstanding sprinter, having won the AAU indoor 50 yards three times. She won the Pan Am Games long jump in 1963 and was on the winning relay team that year. White improved the U.S. long jump record numerous times, and she finally took it up to 21 feet, 6 inches in 1964. She led off the 400-meter relay in 1968. White competed for the Mayor Daley Youth Foundation of Chicago after graduating from Tennessee State. She took up nursing as a career, although she continued to be active as a coach for young women in Chicago. She became supervisor of physical fitness with the Chicago Department of Health. White has traveled to 150 countries as a member of 35 international teams. A member of the Black Sports Hall of Fame, she has been a consultant for the U.S. Olympic Job Opportunity Program and a member of the President's Commission on Olympic Sports. White had always gone out of her way to be fair to competitors, and in 1965 she became the first individual to receive the Pierre de Coubertin International Fair Play Trophy from France. She was the first American, first woman, and first individual to receive it.

Sources: *Approved History of the Olympic Games; Development of Negro Female Olympic Talent; Golden Girls; Guinness Book of Olympic Records; Hard Road to Glory; Quest for Gold; Spirit Team Profiles; United States Olympic Team, Media Guide; United States Track and Field Olympians*.

WHITFIELD, MALVIN GRESTON (USA). Born October 11, 1924, in Bay City, Texas.

1948 Gold Medal: 800-Meter Run (1:49.2, Olympic record)
1948 Gold Medal: 4 x 400-Meter Relay (3:10.4)
1948 Bronze Medal: 400-Meter Run (46.6)
1952 Gold Medal: 800-Meter Run (1:49.34, Olympic record)
1952 Silver Medal: 4 x 400-Meter Relay (3:04.21)

Mal Whitfield attended Ohio State University and graduated from Los Angeles State College in 1956. "The Carbon-Copy Two Lap Master" lost only 3 of 63 races over 2 laps between June 1948 and September 1954. Whitfield was the world's best over 800 meters for 6 years. Although he set world records for both 880 yards (1:48.6) and 1,000 meters (2:20.8), he was more concerned about winning. His range, greater than that of any other runner of his time, covered 10.7 for 100 meters to 4:12.6 for the mile. In the Wembly 800-meter final, he set an Olympic record of 1:49.2. Whitfield won 1948 and 1949 NCAA 880 titles for Ohio State. He also won AAU 880 titles in 1949-51, 1953, and 1954. In 1954 he was the first Black to win the Sullivan award. He failed in his bid for the 1956 Olympic team with 1:49.3, just 00.1 off his winning times in 1948 and 1952.

In 1950 Whitfield equaled Wooderson's long-standing world 880-yard record and then reduced it to 1:48.6 in 1953, when he also broke the 1,000-meter record in 2:20.8. Whitfield's career at 800 meters/880 yards included five AAU wins, two NCAA wins, and two Olympic and one Pan Am gold medal. In 1952 he also won the AAU 440 yards. The Ohio State Buckeye set U.S. records at 400 meters and 440 yards and three world records—two at 880 yards and one at 1,000 meters. He set world records at three different distances. Before 1954 Whitfield ran 9 of the 16 fastest 800/880 times ever recorded. Whitfield's greatest accomplishments as a doubler were winning the 800 in 1:50.6, running a heat of the 400 in 47.3, and winning the final in 46.6—all in one day of the 1948 final Olympic trials. He set a Madison Square Garden 880 record of 1:50.9 indoors in 1953 and then came back a little over an hour later with a world record 600 in 1:09.5. In Cologne, on July 29, he ran a 1:48.4 in the 800 and came back in 45 minutes with a 46.2 in the 400. In the early 1950s Whitfield flew 27 bomber missions in Korea as an air force sergeant. After retirement he traveled the world working for the U.S. Intelligence Service. For several years he has lived and worked in Africa, where he has been a sort of U.S. goodwill ambassador and has helped develop several world-class athletes.

Sources: *Approved History of the Olympic Games; Black Olympians;* British Virgin Islands, Olympic Committee; *Guinness Book of Olympic Records; Hard Road to Glory; Negro Firsts in Sports; 1980 Olympic Handbook; Quest for Gold; Track and Field: The Great Ones; United States 1952 Olympic Book; Who's Who in the Olympic Games.*

WILKES, RODNEY ADOLPHUS (Trinidad).
Born in Trinidad-Tobago.

1948 Silver Medal: Featherweight Weightlifting (699¾ lbs./ 317.5 kg)
1952 Bronze Medal: Featherweight Weightlifting (711 lbs./ 322.5 kg)

The primary contenders in the featherweight weightlifting contest in the 1943 London Olympics were Mahmoud Fayad of Egypt, who set a new world record, Rodney Wilkes, and Jaffar Salmassi of Iran. The breakdown for Wilkes in the 1952 contest was press 100.0, snatch 100.0, and jerk 122.5, for a total of 322.5 kilograms or 711 pounds.

Sources: *Approved History of Olympic Games;* British Virgin Islands, Olympic Committee; *Complete Book of the Olympics; XVth Olympiad, Helsinki, 1952; Guinness Book of Olympic Records.*

WILLIAMS, ARCHIBALD FRANKLIN
(USA). Born May 1, 1915, in Oakland, California.

1936 Gold Medal: 400-Meter Run (46.5)

Archie Williams graduated from the University of California, Berkeley, with a degree in mechanical engineering. He later earned a degree in aeronautical engineering from the Air Force Engineering School, and a degree in meteorology from UCLA. He also holds a commercial pilot's license with an instructor's rating. This virtually unknown track man made astounding progress in the 1936 Olympic year. In April he ran 47.4 for 440 yards, in May he clocked 46.8, and in June, in the heats of the NCAA Championships, he set a world 400-meter record of 46.1. Williams beat Britain's Godfrey Brown by inches at the 1936 Berlin Olympics to win the gold medal. However, he missed the Olympic record set 4 years earlier by fellow American Bill Carr. He was one of 10 men on the U.S. Olympic team (1936) referred to in the Nazi press as America's "black auxiliaries." Williams stayed in the service after World War II. (He had been at Tuskegee with the first Black airmen.) He flew B-29s overseas to Korea, Okinawa, and Japan and became staff weather officer to the 22nd Air Division in New York. In 1964 he was discharged from the Strategic Air Command in Riverside, California, as a lieutenant colonel.

Sources: *Approved History of the Olympic Games; Black Olympians;* British Virgin Islands, Olympic Committee; *Guinness Book of Olympic Records; Negro Firsts in Sports; Negro in Sports; Quest for Gold; Tales of Gold; Track and Field: The Great Ones; Who's Who in Track and Field.*

WILLIAMS, DESAI (Canada). Born June 12, 1959, in Basseterre, St. Kitts.

1984 Bronze Medal: 4 x 100-Meter Relay (38.70)

Desai Williams played end in (American) football at Northview High School in Toronto. He was an economics student at York University, Toronto, after briefly attending Clemson University. Williams has often made the finals of one or both short sprints in major championships, but he won his only individual medal, a silver, at the 1983 University Games in the 100 meters. He ran the third leg for Canada's 400-meter relays. His personal best times are 10.17 (100), 20.29 (200), and 45.92 (400). Williams was third in the Inaugural IAAF Grand Prix 200-meter rankings in 1985. He won a Commonwealth Games gold medal in 1986 as a member of Canada's 4 x 100-meter relay team. Williams now owns a sporting goods business in Toronto and lives in Downsview, near Toronto.

Sources: British Virgin Islands, Olympic Committee; Canadian Olympic Association; *1984 Olympic Games; Sarajevo/Los Angeles;* "The Games," *Olympian* (October/November 1984); *Research Information, Games of the XXIIIrd Olympiad.*

WILLIAMS, LUCINDA (USA). Born August 10, 1937, in Savannah, Georgia.

1960 Gold Medal: 4 x 100-Meter Relay (44.72)

When Lucinda Williams graduated from high school she held the state track championship record. She was also the outstanding senior athlete. She attended Tennessee State University, returned to college after the Olympics, and received a master's degree in physical education in 1961. She later taught physical education in a Dayton, Ohio, high school. Williams made her Olympic debut in 1956 and was eliminated in the heats of the 100 meters. She took the sprint double at the 1959 Pan Am Games, prior to making her second Olympic appearance in Rome. She ran in the 200 at the 1960 Olympics but failed to make the final. Williams had won the AAU 220 yards in 1958 and the indoor title in 1957 and 1959. She had also earned a position on the 1958 and 1959 AAU women's All-America track and field team. The Tigerbelles of Tennessee State won all six gold medals for U.S. track and field for women at the 1960 Olympics. Williams ran the second leg on the U.S. team that won the gold. She acted as chaperone for the U.S. track and field team during the European tour in 1963.

Sources: *Approved History of Olympic Games; Black Olympians; British Virgin Islands, Olympic Committee; Development of Negro Female Olympic Talent; Guinness Book of Olympic Records; Historical and Biographical Studies of Women Participants; 1960 United States Sports Teams; Quest for Gold; United States Track and Field Olympians.*

WILLIAMS, RANDY LUVELLE (USA). Born August 23, 1953, in Fresno, California.

1972 Gold Medal: Long Jump (27 ft. ½ in./8.24 m)
1976 Silver Medal: Long Jump (26 ft. 7¼ in./8.11 m)

Randy Williams led his fellow high school athletes in the long jump with 25 feet, 4½ inches and in the triple jump with 52 feet, 3½ inches. He won the 1970 California State triple jump title with 50 feet, 11¾ inches. Williams took the NCAA long jump title in 1972 with a wind-assisted 26 feet, 8¼ inches. He also ran leadoff on the University of Southern California's winning 440-yard relay team. He won the U.S. junior long jump title in 1972 with 26 feet, 4 inches. He went 27 feet, 4½ inches to win the U.S.-USSR junior meet. He was second with a jump of 26 feet, 4 inches in the U.S. 1972 Olympic trials. In 1972, a few days after his 19th birthday, Williams became the youngest Olympic long jump champion in history. He took the silver medal in Montreal in 1976 and later qualified for his third Olympics, in 1980. Williams continued to be an international-class long jumper until 1983, when he was selected for the Pan Am Games in Caracas but did not compete. He became a lieutenant in the U.S. Marines.

Sources: *Approved History of Olympian Games; Black Olympians; Guinness Book of Olympic Records; Quest for Gold; Who's Who in Track and Field.*

WILLIAMS, ULIS (USA). Born October 24, 1941, in Hollandale, Mississippi.

1964 Gold Medal: 4 x 400-Meter Relay (3:00.7, Olympic record/world record)

Ulis Williams attended Arizona State and graduated from California State, Los Angeles. He later received an M.A. from Antioch University. He was a member of the Southern California Striders. In 1961 Williams set the world's junior record of 46.1 seconds for the 400 meters. He won the AAU 440-yard relay in 1962-63 and the NCAA 400/440 in 1963. In 1962 he became one of the four athletes to set a world record of 3:04.5 in the mile relay. He was Freshman Athlete of the Year at Arizona State in 1962 and was chosen Amateur Athlete of the Year in 1963. Williams won a gold in the 4 x 400-meter relay in 1964, after placing a disappointing fifth in the individual event. Williams seemed to make his best marks in races he lost. In 1963 he ran a 45.6 440 behind Adolph Plummers's world record 44.9 at the Western Athletic Conference meet. He achieved his career best 400 meters in finishing second to a world record. Mike Larrabee set that record with 44.9 and Williams was runner-up at 45.0. Williams's present position is associate dean of Continuing Education and Athletics at Compton Community College, Compton, California. He has one son, Senon, and two daughters, Della and Beryl.

Sources: *Approved History of Olympic Games; Williams, Ulis. Interview. 1984; Black Olympians; British Virgin Islands, Olympic Committee; Guinness Book of Olympic Records; Quest for Gold; Spirit Team Profiles; Los Angeles Olympic Team Organizing Committee; United States Track and Field Olympians.*

WILSON, GEORGE (USA). Born May 9, 1942, in Meridian, Mississippi.

1964 Gold Medal: Basketball

A power forward, George Wilson was the star of the University of Cincinnati team after Oscar Robertson left. Wilson received All-American mention in both his junior and senior years. After graduating in 1964, he was drafted in the first round by the Cincinnati Royals, where he joined Robertson again. He was with the Royals for 3 years. Wilson's physical style of play made him ideally suited for international competition. He played with fair success as a professional for 7 years, with the Royals, the Bulls, the Suns, the SuperSonics, and the 76ers. He retired in Buffalo in 1971.

Sources: *Approved History of Olympic Games; Guinness Book of Olympic Records; Quest for Gold; United States Olympic Team, Games of the XVIIIth Olympiad.*

WILSON, JACK (USA). Born January 17, 1918, in Spencer, North Carolina.

1936 Silver Medal: Bantamweight Boxing

Jackie Wilson lost only one fight as an amateur, in the finals of the Olympics to Ulderico Sergo of Italy. Wilson left the amateur ranks with a 50 wins, 1 loss record. His titles as an amateur had included Golden Gloves champion in New York, Chicago, and Cleveland and 1936 AAU Flyweight champion. Wilson fought as a professional for 13 years with moderate success. He took on such great fighters as Ray Robinson and Jake LaMotta but never fought for a championship. He retired in 1949 with a final record of 69 wins, 19 losses, and 5 draws. He died March 10, 1956.

Sources: *Approved History of Olympic Games; XIth Olympic Games, Berlin, 1936; Guinness Book of Olympic Records; Quest for Gold.*

ARTHUR WINT (Photo courtesy of U.S. Olympic Committee, Colorado Springs, Colorado.)

WINT, ARTHUR (Jamaica). Born May 29, 1920, in Manchester, Jamaica.

1948 Gold Medal: 400-Meter Run (46.2, Olympic record)
1948 Silver Medal: 800-Meter Run (1:49.5)
1952 Gold Medal: 4 x 400-Meter Relay (3:03.09, Olympic record/world record)
1952 Silver Medal: 800-Meter Run (1:49.63)

Arthur Wint attended Calabar High School in Jamaica and received an M.D. degree from the University of London. He joined the Royal Air Force in 1942 and was commissioned in 1944. He was a member of both the 1948 and 1952 Olympic teams. Wint had his greatest hour in the 1948 London Olympic Games. Underdog to world record-holder Herb McKenley (also Jamaican), Wint won the semifinals with 46.3. In the finals he took the lead with 20 meters to go and defeated McKenley, 46.2 to 46.4. He had won the silver medal the day before in the 800 meters. In the Helsinki Olympics in 1952 he finished fifth in the 400 and second again, to Mal Whitfield, in the 800. Wint led off the Jamaican 1,600-meter relay team that set a world record and won the gold medal, timed in 3:03.9. He achieved his best time in the 800 (1:49.3) when he won the British AAA in 1951. Arthur Wint was one of the great Jamaican quarter-milers. He was also a fine half-miler. In 1948 he won the 800 at the fourth Central American and Caribbean Games in Panama, clocked at 1:56.3. He was third in the 400. In the fifth Central American and Caribbean Games, he beat Herb McKenley in the 400 with 48.0. Wint also won the 800, in 1:54.8. Wint was Jamaican high commissioner in the United Kingdom from 1974 to 1978. He is a surgeon by profession in his native Jamaica.

Sources: *Approved History of Olympic Games; Black Sportsmen; Encyclopaedia of Track and Field Athletics; Guinness Book of Olympic Records; Official Report for the XIVth Olympiad; Track and Field: The Great Ones; Who's Who in Track and Field; World's All Sports Who's Who for 1950.*

WOLDE, MAMO (Ethiopia). Born June 12, 1943, in Jirgalem, Ethiopia.

1968 Gold Medal: Marathon (2 hrs.20:26.4)
1968 Silver Medal: 10,000-Meter Run (29:27.75)
1972 Bronze Medal: Marathon (2 hrs.15:08.4)

Mamo Wolde's involvement in the Olympics was long and unusual. He first appeared in Melbourne in 1956 and finished last in both the 800 and the 1,500 meters. He also ran third leg for the Ethiopian 1,600-meter relay team, which finished last. Wolde did not compete in 1960 but did in 1964. He did not complete the marathon but placed fourth in the 10,000-meter run. In 1968, a week before the marathon, he finished a close second to Naftali Temu in the 10,000. In the marathon, Wolde and Temu let others set the pace without allowing the leaders to get too far ahead. They picked up the pace considerably at the halfway mark, and left the others behind. Before long, after 30 kilometers, Temu ran out of steam and fell back, finally finishing 19th. Now Wolde was left with almost a 2-minute lead at 35 kilometers. He went on to win easily. He had at last come out from under the shadow of his famous teammate Abebe Bikila and won an Olympic gold medal, at age 34. Wolde won the marathon in the African Games in

MAMO WOLDE (Photo courtesy of Amateur Athletic Foundation, Los Angeles, California.)

1973 with 2 hours, 27 minutes, 32 seconds. He had a best time in the marathon of 2 hours, 15 minutes, 8 seconds, but like most Ethiopian runners he was motivated by his competitors rather than by the clock.

Sources: *Approved History of Olympic Games*; British Virgin Islands, Olympic Committee; *Complete Book of the Olympics*; *Encyclopaedia of Track and Field Athletics*; *The Games, Organizing Committee of the XIXth Olympiad*; *Guinness Book of Olympic Records*.

WOOD, LEON (USA). Born March 25, 1962, in Santa Monica, California.

1984 Gold Medal: Basketball

Leon Wood attended the University of Arizona and California State University, Fullerton. He was a physical education major. Wood was chosen first team All-American by *Sporting News* and second team All-American by many other polls. He set 16 records at Fullerton after transferring from the University of Arizona. He set a recognized collegiate single-season assist record with 319, an average of 11 per game. This was during the 1983 season when he also averaged 18.1 points per game. Wood's 24 points per game scoring average in 1984 was 10th best in the NCAA. In his final 3 years at California State he hit 47.9 percent from the field and 81.1 percent from the line. He averaged 8.2 assists and 20.6 points. Wood played on the gold medal-winning U.S. team in the 1983 Pan Am Games. His position was starting point guard. Wood has played professionally with the Washington Bullets, the Philadelphia 76ers, and the New Jersey Nets without gaining a starting position.

Sources: "The 1984 Olympics," *Ebony* (October 1984); "The Champions," *Los Angeles Times* (August 14, 1984); "Basketball," *Olympian* (October/November 1984); *United States Olympic Team, Media Guide*.

WOODARD, LYNETTE (USA). Born August 12, 1959, in Wichita, Kansas.

1984 Gold Medal: Basketball

Lynette Woodard graduated from Wichita North High School in 1977 and from the University of Kansas in 1981. Her major was speech communications and human relations. A versatile player who has played every position in the game, Woodard has many achievements to her credit besides winning an Olympic gold medal. She was leading scorer in the history of women's college basketball (with 3,649 points) and ranked first among Kansas University's men and women athletes in all-time scoring and rebounding. She was named Outstanding Young Woman of the Year, 1985; National Role Model for the National Conference of Christians and Jews, 1985; Kansan of the Year, 1985; captain of the Olympic women's basketball team, 1984; and Basketball Woman Athlete of the Year, 1983. She has won many awards, such as the Wade Trophy and the Broderick Award, was the first woman to be elected to the University of Kansas Athlete Hall of Fame, and has had a recreation center named after her. Academically, she won the Undergraduate Minority Award; Academic All-American, 1980, 1981; and the Agnes Strickland Alumni Award. Woodard became a member of the U.S. Olympic Committee and the Athlete's Advisory Committee and was the first woman chosen to play with the Harlem Globetrotters (October 1985). She says of playing with the Globetrotters: "You have to control your game. It's not like competitive basketball. This is Globetrotter basketball.... That's just relax and have a good time. Take your 50-foot shot" (*Los Angeles Times*).

Sources: Woodard, Lynette. Questionnaire. 1984; "The 1984 Olympics," *Ebony* (October 1984); *For the Record*; "The Champions," *Los Angeles Times* (August 14, 1984); "Miss Globetrotter," *Los Angeles Times* (January 19, 1986); "Basketball," *Olympian* (October/November 1984); "Olympic Medal Results," *Sporting News* (August 13, 1984); *United States Olympic Team, Media Guide*; "Lynette Woodard," *Women's Sports* (November 1983).

WOODRUFF, JOHN YOUIE (USA). Born July 5, 1915, in Connellsville, Pennsylvania.

1936 Gold Medal: 800-Meter Run (1:52.9)

John Woodruff graduated from the University of Pittsburgh and obtained his master's degree in social work from New York University. When Woodruff won the 800 meters with

1:51.3 in the 1936 Olympic sectional trials, he came to national attention. As a Pitt freshman in 1936, he was second to Charles Beetham in the AAU. He blazed 1:49.9 in the semi heat in the 1936 final Olympic tryouts. Woodruff won easily from Beetham in the final heat: 1.51. In Berlin he took the lead (after much delay) and defeated Mario Lanzi by 2 meters with 1:52.9 for a zig-zag 800-meter gold medal. Woodruff was 1937 AAU champion with 1:50.3. He was unbeatable as a college star at Pitt. He took the 1937-39 IC4A titles in both the 440 yards and the 800 yards and was NCAA champion in the 880 in 1937-39. He ran anchor leg on the world record 2-mile and 3,200-meter relay team for the U.S. in London in 1936. He broke the American 800 record with 1:48.6 in 1940 and also ran 1:47.8 on a course 5 feet short of 800 meters. His world record was 1:48.4. Woodruff was one of the most respected athletes on the 1936 team. He was the first great American Black middle-distance runner. No athlete since has dominated the 800 meters and half mile as he did. Woodruff served 5 years as an officer in World War II. During the Korean War he was called back to active duty. Upon discharge in 1957, he had earned the rank of lieutenant colonel. He later worked in public service and with disadvantaged youth. Woodruff was awarded a medallion as one of the University of Pittsburgh's most distinguished alumni.

Sources: "More about Winning," *American Visions* (1988); *Approved History of Olympic Games; Black Americans; XIth Olympic Games, Berlin, 1936; Guinness Book of Olympic Records; Negro in Sports; Quest for Gold; Tales of Gold; Track and Field: The Great Ones; Who's Who in Track and Field; World's All Sports Who's Who for 1950.*

WRIGHT, LORENZO C. (USA). Born December 9, 1926, in Detroit, Michigan.

1948 Gold Medal: 4 x 100-Meter Relay (40.6)

Lorenzo Wright set a career best in the long jump of 25 feet, 11 inches in May 1948. However, he could not reproduce this form at the Olympics and finished fourth. Then he joined the sprint relay team to win the gold medal he had missed in his special event. He ran the second leg for a team that also included Barney Ewell, "Bones" Dillard, and Mel Patton. Their time of 40.6 seconds gave them the victory by 7 meters. Wright became supervisor of athletics for the Detroit Public Schools after earning a master's degree from Wayne State University. He was stabbed to death in 1972 and was posthumously inducted into the Michigan Sports Hall of Fame in 1973.

Sources: *Approved History of Olympic Games; Black Olympians; Guinness Book of Olympic Records; Lexikon der 12000 Olympioniken; Quest for Gold; United States Track and Field Olympians.*

MIRUTS YIFTER (Photo courtesy of Rich Clarkson, Denver, Colorado.)

YIFTER, MIRUTS (Ethiopia). Born in the mid-1940s, in Ethiopia.

1972 Bronze Medal: 10,000-Meter Run (27:40.96)
1980 Gold Medal: 5,000-Meter Run (13:21.0)
1980 Gold Medal: 10,000-Meter Run (27:42.7)

Miruts Yifter comes from Adegrat, a village in the Tigra province of Northeastern Ethiopia. He was a captain in the Ethiopian Air Force and the father of eight. "Yifter won the 5,000 with his trademark, a burst of speed over the final 300 meters that makes it look as if he has suddenly jumped on a bicycle while the others in the race are still merely running" (*New York Times*). In both 1977 and 1979, "Yifter the Shifter" won in a space of 3 days the 5,000 and 10,000 meters in the World Cup, demonstrating each time one of the fiercest kicks over the final lap at these distances. He had been prevented from challenging for medals in Montreal in 1976 by the Black African boycott. In 1980, on his third attempt, and 1 year after he swept the 5,000-10,000 double in the Spartakfad in Lenin Stadium, Yifter accomplished his goal. His winning time in the 5,000 of 13:21.0 was the second fastest in Olympic history. He was one of the greatest Olympic middle-distance runners. The diminutive Yifter's personal bests in the 5,000 (13:13.82 at the 1977 World Cup in Dusseldorf) and in the 10,000 (27:41.0 at the 1972 Munich Olympics) still rank high on the all-time African performers lists. However, Yifter was a runner who raced opponents rather than the clock and never deliberately set out to break a world record. Miruts Yifter is one of the most remarkable long distance competitors the world has ever seen.

Sources: *Approved History of Olympic Games*; British Virgin Islands, Olympic Committee; *Encyclopaedia of Track and Field Athletics; Games of the XXIInd Olympiad; Guinness Book of Olympic Records*; "Results of Yesterday's Competition," *New York Times* (July 28, 1980); "Bayi is Unbeaten," *New York Times* (August 1, 1980); "His Unusual Style Serves Yifter Well," *New York Times* (August 3, 1980); *1984 Olympics Handbook; Who's Who in the Olympic Games*.

Group Profiles

INTRODUCTION

In reviewing the various Olympic Games, I noted that there were many groups that were outstanding in their achievements. Two of them, which I highlight here, are the "Tigerbelles," the women track and field stars of Tennessee State University, and the East African middle and long distance runners.

TIGERBELLES

A very interesting phenomenon in Black female track and field is that of the Tigerbelles. They are women who have distinguished themselves nationally and internationally in track and field. They are all students at Tennessee Agricultural and Industrial State University in Nashville, and are coached by Edward Temple. The following eight are some of the Olympic medalists: Isabelle Daniels, Mae Faggs, Barbara Jones, Edith McGuire, Madeline Manning, Margaret Matthews, Wyomia Tyus, and Lucinda Williams. The most prominent Tigerbelle of all was Wilma Rudolph.

The summer track and field clinics and availability of work-aid scholarships appear to have been the common factors that have influenced these young women to attend Tennessee State.

Sources: *For the Record; Golden Girls*; "Born to Be a Champion," *Sports Illustrated*, Aug. 8, 1988; *Tales of Gold*.

EAST AFRICAN TRACK

East Africa contains one of the deepest reservoirs of track talent in the athletic world. Its track stars have set several world and Olympic records. Ethiopia, Kenya, Tanzania, and Uganda, in particular, have produced some of the most exciting long and middle distance runners to date.

In the 1960 and 1964 Olympiads, Ethiopia triumphed; in Mexico City in 1968, the Kenyans turned in stunning victories; for the Munich Games in 1972, the Ugandans had surprises for us; and at the 1974 Christchurch Commonwealth Games, the Tanzanians scored their first major victory.

As a result, the whole of Africa has generated unusual enthusiasm, self-confidence and national pride because of these performances. One wonders, why East Africa? In particular, why is Kenya so far ahead of the rest of the continent in the light athletics field? Is there a secret behind the East African track performances?

Kenya

Kenya is the most track-conscious nation in Africa today; its first real impact was felt in 1962 at the Commonwealth Games. Wilson Kiprugut and Kipchoge Keino placed Kenya securely on the athletics world scene. Keino inspired other Kenyans by his performances in the metric mile, for example, Ben Jipcho, Amos Biwott, Naftali Temu, Robert Ouko, Charles Asati, Hezekiah Nyamau, and Julius Sang. However, gaining fame as the first Kenyan to receive an Olympic medal was Wilson Kiprugut. He was awarded the bronze in the Tokyo 800 meters and then captured the silver medal in Mexico City.

Kenyan athletic official Charles Mkora had this to say about his country's achievements: "The reason why Kenya has produced and continues to produce astoundingly successful trackmen lies in part in the incentives our athletes are given. From the time of our first international competitors ... we opened new doors for our athletes. Their good performances were passports to the outside world.... This inspired the newcomers to strive hard to produce good results.

"Another reason we Kenyans, in particular, have done so remarkably well is the bursaries provided our athletes.... A number of our athletes have been and some still are studying and training in the United States."

Kenya's national athletics coach, Jim Wambua, observed: "The Kenyan AAA, the Government and the Ministry of Sports are all working hard to discover and develop new talent" (*Africa at the Olympics*).

Ethiopia

Ethiopian Abebe Bikila stunned the world in 1960 by winning the Olympic marathon in Rome to become the first East African to capture an Olympic gold medal.

In the Mexico City Olympics, Mamo Wolde not only won the marathon, but he also took the silver medal in the 10,000 meters.

Ethiopia is striving to fill the shoes of Abebe Bikila and Mamo Wolde.

Tanzania

Filbert Bayi dethroned the king of African track, Kenyan Kip Keino, with an unexpected victory in the 1,500 meters at the Lagos All-Africa Games in 1973. In 1974 Bayi smashed Jim Ryun's 7-year-old 1,500-meter world record and, later, the 8-year-old record in the mile.

Tanzania began to draw international attention in 1974 at the Christchurch Commonwealth Games. The most outstanding performance at those games was Filbert Bayi's fantastic metric mile in 3 minutes, 32.2 seconds.

THE HUNDRED-YARD BARRIER

Blacks have for years been known and admired for their prowess as sprinters and field events men. Jesse Owens, Ralph Metcalfe, and Harrison Dillard are three such all-time greats.

But this scene has changed rapidly. Kipchoge Keino of Kenya is perhaps most responsible for the increased success of Blacks in the distance events. In every event from 800 meters to 10,000 meters, he has run world-class times. He held world records in the 5,000 (13:24.2) and 3,000 (7:39.6). The latter record stood for at least 8 years. On July 2, 1965, Keino burst dramatically onto the distance running scene, when he sped to a 13:26.2 for 5,000 meters (then the second fastest 5,000 of all time). He won the gold medal in the 1968 Mexico Olympics in the 1,500 meters and the silver in the 5,000.

It was during the 1968 Olympics that Blacks annexed most of the long distance races. Kenyans besides Keino did well in these races. Naftali Temu won the 10,000 meters, and Amos Biwott conquered the grueling 3,000-meter steeplechase. The marathon, the ultimate in endurance contests, was captured by Ethiopian Mamo Wolde.

Blacks continued to make their presence felt in the 1972 Munich Olympics. In Keino's third Olympic Games, he struck gold and demolished the field in the 3,000-meter steeplechase.

This was in addition to gaining the silver medal in the 1,500. Kenyan Ben Jipcho won the steeplechase silver.

Perhaps the most sensational runner in 1973 was Filbert Bayi of Tanzania. He won seven of nine 1,500-meter (one-mile) events, all in excellent to superior times. The year's fastest 1,500 time was his 3:34.6 in Helsinki, which won the World Games title. This was in addition to running the year's second fastest mile of 3:52.6 in Stockholm, which made him the third best miler of all time.

Ben Jipcho's accomplishments were more phenomenal than Bayi's during 1973. Jipcho went down in history as the second fastest miler ever with a 3:52.0, which was surpassed only by Jim Ryun's world record 3:51.1. In addition, Jipcho once tied and twice broke the world record for the rugged 3,000-meter steeplechase. He blasted an unbelievable record of 8:14.0, a full 5.8 seconds under his own previous world mark. This was 6.8 seconds faster than anyone else had ever covered the distance. Mike Boit, also of Kenya, has turned in a 1:45.2 for the 800, a time exceeded by world rankings of only four others to date.

The main reason such athletes have excelled in the distance events is their East African environment. They have run in the high altitude of the highlands since childhood. They have worked long and hard on their family farms at the foot of Mount Kilimanjaro and surroundings.

So, after years of being categorized as sprinters and jumpers only, Blacks are running at a world-class level and showing the ability to endure the rigors of distance running.

Sources: *Africa at the Olympics; Black Sports*, Feb. 1974.

The 1988 Summer Games were phenomenal in that Kenyans won all the following distance running events: Paul Ereng (800 meters), Peter Rono (1,500 meters), Julius Kariuki (3,000-meter steeplechase), John Ngugi (5,000 meters), and Kipkemboi Kimeli (10,000 meters)—all gold! This was a magnificent follow-through on what the East Africans (especially the Kenyans) were able to achieve over the years.

Actually the first eight events in track and field during the Summer Olympics were all won by Blacks—either from Africa or the U.S. (short, middle, or long distance races).

"Games of Seoul will be remembered as Games of the African Runners. Above all, as the Kenyan Games. Rarely have the men's middle distance events been dominated by one country. The beauty of the Kenyans is the effortless rhythm of their stride" (*Seoul '88*).

Profile of Black Management in U.S. Professional Sports

BASEBALL

In the forty or more years since Jackie Robinson desegregated baseball, four Blacks have been major league managers in the field. They are Frank Robinson (Cleveland Indians, San Francisco Giants, and Baltimore Orioles), Larry Doby (Chicago White Sox), Maury Wills (Seattle Mariners), and Cito Gaston (Toronto Blue Jays).

There have been hundreds of managerial changes during the forty years, but the only Black man who had served as general manager up to 1987 was Bill Lucas of the Atlanta Braves. Only one American-born Black had coached third base.

Benjamin Hooks, Executive Secretary of the National Association for the Advancement of Colored People, said that, in 1987, of the top 879 administrative positions in baseball, only 17 were filled by Blacks and 15 by Hispanics and Asians. Four California teams: the Dodgers, Giants, Athletics, and Angels accounted for almost two-thirds of the minority hiring. Ten out of fourteen American League teams and five of twelve National League franchises had no Blacks in management positions.

Bill White is president of the National League and the highest-ranking Black executive in the history of professional sports. White played fourteen years in the majors with the New York and San Francisco Giants, St. Louis Cardinals, and Philadelphia Phillies. He was a broadcaster for the New York Yankees for eighteen years.

Other blacks in managerial positions include:

- Hank Aaron, Vice President and Special Assistant to the President, Atlanta Braves, 1990.

- Dusty Baker, Hitting Coach, San Francisco Giants, 1990

- Don Edward Baylor, Batting Coach, Milwaukee Brewers, 1990

- Alonza (Al) Bumbry, First Base Coach, Boston Red Sox, 1990

- Roy Campanella, Community Relations, Los Angeles Dodgers, 1990

- Clarence Edwin (Cito) Gaston, Manager, Toronto Blue Jays, 1990

- Tommy Hawkins, Vice President of Communications, Los Angeles Dodgers, 1990

- Elrod Hendricks, Substitute manager (for Frank Robinson), and Bullpen Coach, Baltimore Orioles, 1990

- Sharon Jones, Director of Outreach Activities, Oakland Athletics, 1989

- John Mayberry, Hitting Coach, Kansas City Royals, 1990

- Don Newcombe, Director of Community Relations, Los Angeles Dodgers, 1990

- Amos Otis, Batting Coach, San Diego Padres, 1990

- Vada Pinson, Hitting Coach, Detroit Tigers, 1990

- Frank Robinson, Manager, Special Assistant to the President, Baltimore Orioles, 1989

- Elaine Weddington, Assistant General Manager, Boston Red Sox, 1990

- Billy Williams, Coaching Assistant, Cleveland Indians, 1990

- Willie Mays and Willie McCovey, special assistants to the President and General Manager, San Francisco Giants, 1990

131

BASKETBALL

After an outstanding college career Bill Russell signed with the Boston Celtics in 1956. In the nine seasons ending in 1965-1966, the Celtics won the Eastern Division title nine times and the NBA championship eight consecutive times. During his thirteen years with the team, Russell was named to the East All-Star Team eleven times and won the NBA's MVP award five times. He was elected to the Naismith Memorial Basketball Hall of Fame in 1974 and to the NBA's twenty-fifth and thirty-fifth anniversary All-Time Teams in 1970 and 1980.

Bill Russell began coaching while still playing with the Celtics, and became the first Black ever to serve as head coach of an NBA team. In 1973 he contracted to become coach and general manager of the Seattle Supersonics. He signed a ten-year contract to coach the Sacramento Kings in 1987 and was named Kings vice president in March 1988.

Bertram Lee and Peter Bynoe, Chicago businessmen, became the first Black NBA team owners when they secured the financial backing necessary to complete the $65 million purchase of the Denver Nuggets basketball team. Robert Wusler, head of COMSAT Video Enterprises (Washington, D.C.), put up $17 million for 62.5% of the team and Lee and Bynoe will put up $8 million and own 37.5%, but will serve as the managing partners.

Other Blacks in managerial positions include:

- Al Attles, General Manager, Golden State Warriors, 1983-1989

- Elgin Baylor, General Manager/Executive Vice President, Los Angeles Clippers, 1986-1989

- Bernie Bickerstaff, Head Coach, Seattle Supersonics, 1989-1990

- Michele Savage-Brown, Licensing Coordinator, NBA Properties, Inc., 1989

- Don Chaney, Head Coach, Houston Rockets, 1989-1990

- Wayne Embry, Vice President/General Manager, Cleveland Cavaliers, 1989-1990; Vice President/Basketball Consultant, 1985-1987

- Walt Frazier, Radio Station WFAN, New York Knickerbockers, 1989-1990

- K. C. Jones, Head Coach, Boston Celtics, 1983-1987; Assistant Coach/Basketball Consultant, 1989-1990

- Stu Jackson, Head Coach, New York Knickerbockers, 1989-1990

- Willis Reed, Jr., Head Coach, New Jersey Nets, 1989-1990

- Wes Unseld, Vice President/Head Coach, Washington Bullets, 1989-1990

- Lenny Wilkins, Vice President and General Manager, Seattle Supersonics, 1985-1986; Head Coach, Cleveland Cavaliers, 1989-1990

FOOTBALL

Art Shell became the first NFL Black head coach in 64 years, when he was appointed coach of the Los Angeles Raiders. The league's only other Black head coach was Fritz Pollard, way back in 1923-1925, who handled the Hammond (Indiana) Pros.

Shell was named All-Pro three times and played in eight Pro Bowls in his fifteen seasons as a Raider player (1968-1982). He played in 207 games—third on the team's alltime list. He was elected to the Hall of Fame in January 1989.

Other Blacks in managerial positions include:

- William Nunn, Assistant Director, Player Personnel, Pittsburgh Steelers, 1968-1986

- Clarence Shields, Team Physician, Los Angeles Rams, 1989

- Gene Upshaw, Executive Director, National Football League Players Association, 1989

- Paul "Tank" Younger, Assistant General Manager, San Diego Chargers, 1975-1986

Sources: *Baseball Guide*, 1990 edition. St. Louis, MO., *The Sporting News*; *Biographical Dictionary of American Sports*. (Basketball and Other Indoor Sports). Edited by David L. Porter. New York, Greenwood Press, 1989; *Ebony Man*, "Black Baseball Coaches and Managers," Vol. 5, No. 10, pages 52-53, August 1990; *Jet*, "Orioles, Blue Jays, Put Black Managers on the Spot," Vol. 77, No. 2, page 51, October 16, 1989; *Jet*, "Red Sox Name Black Female Assistant General Manager," Vol. 77, No. 20, page 52, February 26, 1990; *Official NBA Guide*, 1989-1990 edition. St. Louis, MO., *The Sporting News*; *Pro Football Guide*, 1989 edition. St. Louis, MO., *The Sporting News*; *Sports Illustrated*, "Dreams Do Come True," Vol. 71, No. 17, pages 74-78, October 23, 1989; *Sports Illustrated*, "Welcome to the Owner's Club," Vol. 71, No. 4, page 12, July 24, 1989; *Total Baseball*, edited by John Thorn and Pete Palmer (Baseball Ink Book). New York, Warner Books, 1989; *NBA Register*, 1989-1990 edition. St. Louis, MO., *The Sporting News*; *Los Angeles Clippers 1988-89 Media Guide*. Los Angeles.

Statistics

BLACK TRACK AND FIELD OLYMPIC MEDALISTS, UNITED STATES AND INTERNATIONAL BY EVENT (MEN)

100 Meters

YEAR	GOLD	SILVER	BRONZE
1920			Harry Edward (Gbr) 11.0
1928		Jack London (Gbr) 10.9	
1932	Eddie Tolan (USA) 10.38, Olympic record	Ralph Metcalfe (USA) 10.38, Olympic record	
1936	Jesse Owens (USA) 10.3, Olympic record	Ralph Metcalfe (USA) 10.4	
1948	Harrison Dillard (USA) 10.3, Olympic record	Norwood Ewell (USA) 10.4	Lloyd LaBeach (Pan) 10.4
1952		Herb McKenley (Jam) 10.8	E. McDonald Bailey (Gbr) 10.83
1964	Bob Hayes (USA) 10.06, Olympic/world records	Enrique Figuerola (Cub) 10.25	Harry Jerome (Can) 10.27
1968	James Hines (USA) 9.95, Olympic/world records	Lennox Miller (Jam) 10.04	Charlie Greene (USA) 10.07
1972		Robert Taylor (USA) 10.24	Lennox Miller (Jam) 10.33
1976	Hasely Crawford (Tri) 10.06	Don Quarrie (Jam) 10.08	
1980		Silvio Leonard (Cub) 10.25	
1984	Carl Lewis (USA) 9.99	Sam Graddy (USA) 10.19	Ben Johnson (Can) 10.22
1988	Carl Lewis (USA) 9.92, Olympic record	Linford Christie (Gbr) 9.97	Calvin Smith (USA) 9.99

200 Meters

YEAR	GOLD	SILVER	BRONZE
1920			Harry Edward (Gbr) 22.2
1932	Eddie Tolan (USA) 21.12, Olympic record		Ralph Metcalfe (USA) 21.5
1936	Jesse Owens (USA) 20.7, Olympic record	Mack Robinson (USA) 21.1	
1948		Norwood Ewell (USA) 21.1	Lloyd LaBeach (Pan) 21.2
1952	Andrew Stanfield (USA) 20.81, Olympic record		James Gathers (USA) 21.08
1956		Andrew Stanfield (USA) 20.97	
1960		Les Carney (USA) 20.69	Abdoulaye Seye (Fra) 20.83
1964	Henry Carr (USA) 20.36, Olympic record	Paul Drayton (USA) 20.58	Edwin Roberts (Tri) 20.63
1968	Tommie Smith (USA) 19.83, Olympic/world records		John Carlos (USA) 20.10
1972		Larry Black (USA) 20.19	
1976	Don Quarrie (Jam) 20.23	Millard Hampton (USA) 20.29	Dwayne Evans (USA) 20.43
1980			Don Quarrie (Jam) 20.29
1984	Carl Lewis (USA) 19.80, Olympic record	Kirk Baptiste (USA) 19.96	Thomas Jefferson (USA) 20.26
1988	Joe DeLoach (USA) 19.75, Olympic record	Carl Lewis (USA) 19.79, Olympic record	

400 Meters

YEAR	GOLD	SILVER	BRONZE
1936	Archie Williams (USA) 46.66		James LuValle (USA) 46.84
1948	Arthur Wint (Jam) 46.2, Olympic record	Herb McKenley (Jam) 46.4	Mal Whitfield (USA) 46.6

YEAR	GOLD	SILVER	BRONZE
1952	George Rhoden (Jam) 46.09, Olympic record	Herb McKenley (Jam) 46.20, Olympic record	Ollie Matson (USA) 46.94
1956	Charles Jenkins (USA) 46.85, Olympic record		
1960	Otis Davis (USA) 45.07, Olympic/world records		
1964		Wendell Mottley (Tri) 45.24	
1968	Lee Evans (USA) 43.86, Olympic/world records	Larry James (USA) 43.97	Ronald Freeman (USA) 44.41
1972	Vincent Matthews (USA) 44.66	Wayne Collett (USA) 44.80	Julius Sang (Ken) 44.92
1976	Alberto Juantorena (Cub) 44.26	Fred Newhouse (USA) 44.40	Herman Frazier (USA) 44.95
1984	Alonzo Babers (USA) 44.27	Gabriel Tiacoh (Ivc) 44.54	Antonio McKay (USA) 44.71
1988	Steve Lewis (USA) 43.87	Butch Reynolds (USA) 43.93	Danny Everett (USA) 44.09

800 Meters

YEAR	GOLD	SILVER	BRONZE
1932			Phil Edwards (Can) 1:51.5
1936	John Woodruff (USA) 1:52.9		Phil Edwards (Can) 1:53.6
1948	Mal Whitfield (USA) 1:49.2, Olympic record	Arthur Wint (Jam) 1:49.5	
1952	Mal Whitfield (USA) 1:49.34, Olympic record	Arthur Wint (Jam) 1:49.63	
1960			George Kerr (Jam) 1:47.25
1964			Wilson Kiprugut (Ken) 1:45.9
1968		Wilson Kiprugut (Ken) 1:44.57	

YEAR	GOLD	SILVER	BRONZE
1972			Mike Boit (Ken) 1:46.01
1976	Alberto Juantorena (Cub) 1:43.5, Olympic/world records		
1984	Joaquim Cruz (Bra) 1:43.00, Olympic record		Earl Jones (USA) 1:43.83
1988	Paul Ereng (Ken) 1:43.45	Joaquim Cruz (Bra) 1:43.90	Saïd Aouita (Mor) 1:44.06

1,500 Meters

YEAR	GOLD	SILVER	BRONZE
1968	Kipchoge Keino (Ken) 3:34.91, Olympic record		
1972		Kipchoge Keino (Ken) 3:36.81	
1988	Peter Rono (Ken) 3:35.96		

5,000 Meters

YEAR	GOLD	SILVER	BRONZE
1968		Kipchoge Keino (Ken) 14:05.16	Naftali Temu (Ken) 14:06.41
1980	Miruts Yifter (Eth) 13:21.0	Suleiman Nyambui (Tan) 13:21.6	
1984	Saïd Aouita (Mor) 13:05.59, Olympic record		
1988	John Ngugi (Ken) 13:11.70		

10,000 Meters

YEAR	GOLD	SILVER	BRONZE
1968	Naftali Temu (Ken) 29:27.4	Mamo Wolde (Eth) 29:27.75	
1972			Miruts Yifter (Eth) 27:40.96

YEAR	GOLD	SILVER	BRONZE
1980	Miruts Yifter (Eth) 27:42.7		Muhammed Kedir (Eth) 27:44.7
1984			Mike Musyoki (Ken) 28:06.46
1988	Brahim Boutaib (Mor) 27:21.46, Olympic record		Kipkemboi Kimeli (Ken) 27:25.16

Marathon

YEAR	GOLD	SILVER	BRONZE
1960	Abebe Bikila (Eth) 2 hrs. 15:16.2, Olympic/world records		
1964	Abebe Bikila (Eth) 2 hrs. 12:11.2, Olympic/world records		
1968	Mamo Wolde (Eth) 2 hrs. 20:26.4		
1972			Mamo Wolde (Eth) 2 hrs. 15:08.4
1988		Douglas Wakihuri (Ken) 2 hrs. 10:47.0	Ahmed Saleh (Dji) 2 hrs. 10:59.0

4 x 100-Meter Relay

YEAR	GOLD	SILVER	BRONZE
1928			Great Britain (41.8) Jack E. London
1936	United States (39.8, Olympic/ world records) Jesse Owens Ralph Metcalfe		
1948	United States (40.6) Norwood Ewell Lorenzo Wright Harrison Dillard		
1952	United States (40.26) Harrison Dillard Andrew Stanfield		

YEAR	GOLD	SILVER	BRONZE
1956	United States (39.60, Olympic/ world records) Ira Murchison Leamon King		
1964	United States (39.06, Olympic/ world records) Paul Drayton Richard Stebbins Bob Hayes		
1968	United States (38.24, Olympic/ world records) Charles Greene Mel Pender Ronnie R. Smith James Hines	Cuba (38.40) Hermes Ramírez Juan Morales Pablo Montes Enrique Figuerola	France (38.43) Roger Bambuck
1972	United States (38.19, Olympic/ world records) Larry Black Robert Taylor Gerald Tinker Eddie Hart		
1976	United States (38.33) Harvey Glance John Jones Millard Hampton Steve Riddick		
1980			France (38.53) Hermann Panzo
1984	United States (37.83, Olympic/ world records) Sam Graddy Ron Brown Calvin Smith Carl Lewis	Jamaica (38.62) Albert Lawrence Gregory Meghoo Don Quarrie Raymond Stewart	Canada (38.70) Ben Johnson Tony Sharpe Desai Williams Sterling Hinds
1988		Great Britain (38.28) Linford Christie	

4 x 400-Meter Relay

YEAR	GOLD	SILVER	BRONZE
1908	J. B. Taylor 3:29.4		
1928			Canada (3:15.4) Phil Edwards

YEAR	GOLD	SILVER	BRONZE
1932			Canada (3:12.8) Raymond Lewis Phil Edwards
1948	United States (3:10.4) Mal Whitfield		
1952	Jamaica (3:04.04 Olympic/world records Arthur Wint Leslie Laing Herb McKenley George Rhoden	United States (3:04.21) Ollie Matson Mal Whitfield	
1956	United States (3:04.81) Lou Jones Charlie Jenkins		
1960	United States (3:02.37, Olympic record) Otis Davis		Jamaica (3:04.13) Malcolm Spence Jimmy Wedderburn Keith Gardner George Kerr
1964	United States (3:00.7, Olympic/world records) Ulis Williams Henry Carr		Trinidad (3:01.7) Edwin Skinner Kent Bernard Wendell Mottley Edwin Roberts
1968	United States (2:56.16, Olympic/world records) Vincent Matthews Ron Freeman Larry James Lee Evans	Kenya (2:59.64) Daniel Rudisha Hezekiah Nyamau Naftali Bon Charles Asati	
1972	Kenya (2:59.83) Charles Asati Hezekiah Nyamau Robert Ouko Julius Sang		France (3:00.65) Roger Velasquez
1976	United States (2:58.65) Maxie Parks Benny Brown Fred Newhouse Herman Frazier		
1984	United States (2:57.91) Sunder Nix Ray Armstead Alonzo Babers Antonio McKay	Great Britain (2:59.13) Kriss Akabusi Phil Brown	Nigeria (2:59.32) Sunday Uti Moses Ugbisi Rotimi Peters Innocent Egbunike

YEAR	GOLD	SILVER	BRONZE
1988	United States (2:56.16, Olympic record) Danny Everett Steve Lewis Kevin Robinzine Butch Reynolds	Jamaica (3:00.30) Winthrop Graham Bert Cameron	

110-Meter Hurdles

YEAR	GOLD	SILVER	BRONZE
1936			Fritz Pollard, Jr. (USA) 14.4
1952	Harrison Dillard (USA) 13.91, Olympic record		
1956	Lee Calhoun (USA) 13.70, Olympic record		
1960	Lee Calhoun (USA) 13.98	Willie May (USA) 13.99	Hayes Jones (USA) 14.17
1964	Hayes Jones (USA) 13.67, Olympic record		
1968	Willie Davenport (USA) 13.33, Olympic record	Ervin Hall (USA) 13.42	
1972	Rodney Milburn (USA) 13.24, Olympic/world records		Thomas Hill (USA) 13.48
1976		Alejandro Casañas (Cub) 13.33	Willie Davenport (USA) 13.38
1980		Alejandro Casañas (Cub) 13.40	
1984	Roger Kingdom (USA) 13.20, Olympic record	Greg Foster (USA) 13.23	
1988	Roger Kingdom (USA) 12.98, Olympic record	Colin Jackson (Gbr) 13.28	Tonie Campbell (USA) 13.38

200-Meter Hurdles

YEAR	GOLD	SILVER	BRONZE
1904			George Poage (USA) 25.2

400-Meter Hurdles

YEAR	GOLD	SILVER	BRONZE
1904			George Poage (USA) 54.8
1956			Josh Culbreath (USA) 51.74
1972	John Akii-Bua (Uga) 47.82, Olympic/world records		
1976	Edwin Moses (USA) 47.63, Olympic/world records		
1984	Edwin Moses (USA) 47.75	Danny Harris (USA) 48.13	
1988	Andre Phillips (USA) 47.19, Olympic record	Elhadjdia Ba (Sen) 47.23	Edwin Moses (USA) 47.56

3,000-Meter Steeplechase

YEAR	GOLD	SILVER	BRONZE
1968	Amos Biwott (Ken) 8:51.02	Ben Kogo (Ken) 8:51.56	
1972	Kipchoge Keino (Ken) 8:23.64, Olympic record	Ben Jipcho (Ken) 8:24.62	
1980		Filbert Bayi (Tan) 8:12.5	Eshetu Tura (Eth) 8:13.6
1984	Julius Korir (Ken) 8:11.80		
1988	Julius Kariuki (Ken) 8:05.51, Olympic record	Peter Koech (Ken) 8:06.79	

20-Kilometer Walk

YEAR	GOLD	SILVER	BRONZE
1976	Daniel Bautista (Mex) 1 hr. 24:40.6, Olympic record		

High Jump

YEAR	GOLD	SILVER	BRONZE
1936	Cornelius Johnson (USA) 6 ft. 7¾ in. (2.03 m.), Olympic record	Dave Albritton (USA) 6 ft. 6¾ in. (2 m.)	
1952			José Telles da Conceição (Bra) 6 ft. 6 in. (1.98 m.)
1956	Charles Dumas (USA) 6 ft. 11½ in. (2.12 m.), Olympic record		
1960			John Thomas (USA) 7 ft. ¼ in. (2.14 m.)
1964		John Thomas (USA) 7 ft. 1¾ in. (2.18 m.), Olympic record, tied world record	John Rambo (USA) 7 ft. 1 in. (2.16 m.)
1968		Edward Caruthers (USA) 7 ft. 3¼ in. (2.22 m.)	
1988		Hollis Conway (USA) 7 ft. 8¾ in. (2.36 m.)	

Broad Jump (Long Jump)

YEAR	GOLD	SILVER	BRONZE
1924	DeHart Hubbard (USA) 24 ft. 5 in. (7.44 m.)	Edward Gourdin (USA) 23 ft. 10¼ in. (7.27 m.)	
1928		Silvio Cator (Hai) 24 ft. 10¼ in. (7.58 m.)	
1932	Edward Gordon (USA) 25 ft. ¾ in. (7.64 m.)		
1936	Jesse Owens (USA) 26 ft. 5½ in. (8.06 m.), Olympic record		
1948	Willie Steele (USA) 25 ft. 8 in. (7.82 m.)		Herbert Douglas (USA) 24 ft. 8¾ in. (7.54 m.)
1952	Jerome Biffle (USA) 24 ft. 10 in. (7.57 m.)	Meredith Gourdine (USA) 24 ft. 8¼ in. (7.53 m.)	
1956	Gregory Bell (USA) 25 ft. 8¼ in. (7.83 m.)		

YEAR	GOLD	SILVER	BRONZE
1960	Ralph Boston (USA) 26 ft. 7¾ in. (8.12 m.), Olympic record	Irv Roberson (USA) 26 ft. 7¼ in. (8.11 m.)	
1964		Ralph Boston (USA) 26 ft. 4 in. (8.03 m.)	
1968	Bob Beamon (USA) 29 ft. 2½ in. (8.90 m.), Olympic/ world records		Ralph Boston (USA) 26 ft. 9¼ in. (8.16 m.)
1972	Randy Williams (USA) 27 ft. ½ in. (8.24 m.)		Arnie Robinson (USA) 26 ft. 4 in. (8.03 m.)
1976	Arnie Robinson (USA) 27 ft. 4¾ in. (8.35 m.)	Randy Williams (USA) 26 ft. 7¼ in. (8.11 m.)	
1984	Carl Lewis (USA) 28 ft. ¼ in. (8.54 m.)		
1988	Carl Lewis (USA) 28 ft. 7½ in. (8.72 m.)	Michael Powell (USA) 27 ft. 10¼ in. (8.49 m.)	Larry Myricks (USA) 27 ft. 1¾ in. (8.27 m.)

Triple Jump

YEAR	GOLD	SILVER	BRONZE
1952	Adhemar Ferreira da Silva (Bra) 53 ft. 2¾ in. (16.22 m.), Olympic/world records		Arnoldo Devonish (Ven) 50 ft. 11 in. (15.52 m.)
1956	Adhemar Ferreira da Silva (Bra) 53 ft. 7¾ in. (16.35 m.), Olympic record		
1968		Nelson Prudencio (Bra) 56 ft. 8 in. (17.27 m.)	
1972			Nelson Prudencio (Bra) 55 ft. 11¼ in. (17.05 m.)
1976		James Butts (USA) 56 ft. 4½ in. (17.18 m.)	Joao Carlos de Oliveira (Bra) 55 ft. 5½ in. (16.90 m.)
1980			Joao Carlos de Oliveira (Bra) 56 ft. 6 in. (17.22 m.)
1984	Al Joyner (USA) 56 ft. 7½ in. (17.26 m.), Olympic record	Mike Conley (USA) 56 ft. 4½ in. (17.18 m.)	

Discus Throw

YEAR	GOLD	SILVER	BRONZE
1980			Luis Mariano Delis (Cub) 217 ft. 7 in. (66.32 m.)

Javelin Throw

YEAR	GOLD	SILVER	BRONZE
1952		Bill Miller (USA) 237 ft. 9 in. (72.46 m.)	

Decathlon

YEAR	GOLD	SILVER	BRONZE
1952		Milton Campbell (USA) 6,975 pts.	
1956	Milton Campbell (USA) 7,937 pts., Olympic record	Rafer Johnson (USA) 7,587 pts.	
1960	Rafer Johnson (USA) 8,392 pts., Olympic record		
1980	Daley Thompson (Gbr) 8,495 pts.		
1984	Daley Thompson (Gbr) 8,798 pts., equaled world record		

BLACK TRACK AND FIELD OLYMPIC MEDALISTS, UNITED STATES AND INTERNATIONAL BY EVENT (WOMEN)

Women's 100 Meters

YEAR	GOLD	SILVER	BRONZE
1960	Wilma Rudolph (USA) 11.18, Olympic record		
1964	Wyomia Tyus (USA) 11.49	Edith McGuire (USA) 11.62	
1968	Wyomia Tyus (USA) 11.08, Olympic/world records	Barbara Ferrell (USA) 11.15	

YEAR	GOLD	SILVER	BRONZE
1972			Silvia Chivás (Cub) 11.24
1984	Evelyn Ashford (USA) 10.97, Olympic record	Alice Brown (USA) 11.13	Merlene Ottey-Page (Jam) 11.16
1988	Florence Griffith-Joyner (USA) 10.54, Olympic record	Evelyn Ashford (USA) 10.83	

Women's 200 Meters

YEAR	GOLD	SILVER	BRONZE
1948			Audrey Patterson (USA) 25.2
1960	Wilma Rudolph (USA) 24.13		
1964	Edith McGuire (USA) 23.05, Olympic record		
1980			Merlene Ottey-Page (Jam) 22.20
1984	Valerie Brisco-Hooks (USA) 21.81, Olympic record	Florence Griffith-Joyner (USA) 22.04	Merlene Ottey-Page (Jam) 22.09
1988	Florence Griffith-Joyner (USA) 21.34, Olympic record	Grace Jackson (Jam) 21.72	

Women's 400 Meters

YEAR	GOLD	SILVER	BRONZE
1984	Valerie Brisco-Hooks (USA) 48.83, Olympic record	Chandra Cheeseborough (USA) 49.05	

Women's 800 Meters

YEAR	GOLD	SILVER	BRONZE
1968	Madeline Manning (USA) 2:00.92, Olympic record		
1984		Kim Gallagher (USA) 1:58.63	
1988			Kim Gallagher (USA) 1:56.91

Women's 4 x 100-Meter Relay

YEAR	GOLD	SILVER	BRONZE
1952	United States (46.14, Olympic record) Mae Faggs Barbara Jones Catherine Hardy		
1956			United States (45.04) Mae Faggs Margaret Matthews Wilma Rudolph Isabelle Daniels
1960	United States (44.72) Martha Hudson Lucinda Williams Barbara Jones Wilma Rudolph		
1964		United States (43.92) Willye White Wyomia Tyus Marilyn White Edith McGuire	
1968	United States (42.88, Olympic/world records) Wyomia Tyus Barbara Ferrell Margaret Bailes Mildrette Netter	Cuba (43.36) Marlene Elejarde Fulgencia Romay Violeta Quesada Miguelina Cobian	
1972			Cuba (43.36) Marlene Elejarde Carmen Valdes Fulgencia Romay Silvia Chivas
1980			Great Britain (42.43) Heather Oakes Beverley Goddard-Callender Sonia Lannaman
1984	United States (41.65) Chandra Cheeseborough Alice Brown Jeanette Bolden Evelyn Ashford	Canada (42.77) Angela Bailey Marita Payne Angella Taylor	Great Britain (43.11) Simone Jacobs Beverley Goddard-Callender Heather Oakes
1988	United States (41.98) Alice Brown Sheila Echols Florence Griffith-Joyner Evelyn Ashford		

Women's 4 x 400-Meter Relay

YEAR	GOLD	SILVER	BRONZE
1972		United States (3:25.15) Madeline Manning Mable Fergerson Cheryl Toussaint	
1976		United States (3:22.81) Rosalyn Bryant Sheila Ingram Pamela Jiles Debra Sapenter	
1980			Great Britain (3:27.5) Joslyn Hoyte-Smith
1984	United States (3:18.29, Olympic record) Lillie Leatherwood Sherri Howard Valerie Brisco-Hooks Chandra Cheeseborough	Canada (3:21.21) Charmaine Crooks Molly Killingbeck Jillian Richardson Marita Payne	
1988		United States (3:15.51) Denean Howard Diane Dixon Valerie Brisco-Hooks Florence Griffith-Joyner	

Women's 100-Meter Hurdles

YEAR	GOLD	SILVER	BRONZE
1984	Benita Fitzgerald-Brown (USA) 12.84		Kim Turner (USA) 13.06

Women's 400-Meter Hurdles

YEAR	GOLD	SILVER	BRONZE
1984		Judi Brown (USA) 55.20, American record	

Women's High Jump

YEAR	GOLD	SILVER	BRONZE
1948	Alice Coachman (USA) 5 ft. 6 in. (1.68 m.), Olympic record		
1956	Mildred McDaniel (USA) 5 ft. 9¼ in. (1.76 m.), Olympic/ world records		

Women's Broad Jump (Long Jump)

YEAR	GOLD	SILVER	BRONZE
1956		Willye White (USA) 19 ft. 11¾ in. (6.09 m.)	
1976		Kathy McMillan (USA) 21 ft. 10¼ in. (6.66 m.)	
1988	Jackie Joyner-Kersee (USA) 24 ft. 3½ in. (7.40 m.), Olympic record		

Women's Shot Put

YEAR	GOLD	SILVER	BRONZE
1960			Earlene Brown (USA) 53 ft. 10¼ in. (16.42 m.)

Women's Javelin Throw

YEAR	GOLD	SILVER	BRONZE
1980	María Colón (Cub) 224 ft. 5 in. (68.40 m.), Olympic record		
1984	Tessa Sanderson (Gbr) 228 ft. 2 in. (69.56 m.), Olympic record		

Women's Heptathlon

YEAR	GOLD	SILVER	BRONZE
1984		Jackie Joyner-Kersee (USA) 6,385 pts.	
1988	Jackie Joyner-Kersee (USA) 7,291 pts., Olympic/world records		

U.S. BLACK TRACK AND FIELD OLYMPIC MEDALISTS, 1904-1988, BY PLACE AND DATE

PLACE/YEAR	EVENT	ATHLETE	MEDAL/RESULT
St. Louis, 1904	200-Meter Hurdles	George C. Poage	Bronze (25.2)
	400-Meter Hurdles	George C. Poage	Bronze (54.8)
London, 1908	4 x 400-Meter Relay	J. B. Taylor	Gold (3:29.4)
Paris, 1924	Long Jump	DeHart Hubbard Edward Gourdin	Gold (24 ft. 5 in./7.44 m.) Silver (23 ft. 10¼ in./7.27 m.)
Los Angeles, 1932	100 Meters	Eddie Tolan Ralph Metcalfe	Gold (10.38, Olympic record) Silver (10.38)
	200 Meters	Eddie Tolan Ralph Metcalfe	Gold (21.12, Olympic record) Bronze (21.5)
	Long Jump	Edward Gordon	Gold (25 ft. ¾ in./7.64 m.)
Berlin, 1936	100 Meters	Jesse Owens Ralph Metcalfe	Gold (10.3) Silver (10.4)
	200 Meters	Jesse Owens Matthew Robinson	Gold (20.7, Olympic record) Silver (21.1)
	400 Meters	Archie Williams James LuValle	Gold (46.66) Bronze (46.84)
	800 Meters	John Woodruff	Gold (1:52.9)
	110-Meter Hurdles	Fritz Pollard, Jr.	Bronze (14.4)
	High Jump	Cornelius Johnson David Albritton	Gold (6 ft. 8 in./2.03 m., Olympic record) Silver (6 ft. 6¾ in./2.0 m.)
	Long Jump	Jesse Owens	Gold (26 ft. 5½ in./8.06 m., Olympic record unbroken for 24 years)
	4 x 100-Meter Relay	Jesse Owens Ralph Metcalfe	Gold (39.8, Olympic/world records)

PLACE/YEAR	EVENT	ATHLETE	MEDAL/RESULT
London, 1948	100 Meters	Harrison Dillard Norwood Ewell	Gold (10.3, Olympic record) Silver (10.4)
	200 Meters	Norwood Ewell	Silver (21.1)
	400 Meters	Mal Whitfield	Bronze (46.6)
	800 Meters	Mal Whitfield	Gold (1:49.2, Olympic record)
	4 x 100-Meter Relay	Harrison Dillard Norwood Ewell Lorenzo Wright	Gold (40.6)
	4 x 400-meter Relay	Mal Whitfield	Gold (3:10.4)
	Long Jump	Willie Steele Herbert Douglas	Gold (25 ft. 8 in./7.82 m.) Bronze (24 ft. 9 in./7.54 m.)
	Women's 200 Meters	Audrey Patterson	Bronze (25.2)
	Women's High Jump	Alice Coachman	Gold (5 ft. 6¼ in./1.68 m., Olympic record)
Helsinki, 1952	200 Meters	Andrew Stanfield James Gathers	Gold (20.81, Olympic record) Bronze (21.08)
	400 Meters	Ollie Matson	Bronze (46.94)
	800 Meters	Mal Whitfield	Gold (1:49.34, Olympic record)
	110 Meters	Harrison Dillard	Gold (13.91, Olympic record)
	4 x 100-Meter Relay	Harrison Dillard Andrew Stanfield	Gold (40.26)
	4 x 400-Meter Relay	Ollie Matson Mal Whitfield	Silver (3:04.21)
	Long Jump	Jerome Biffle Meredith Gourdine	Gold (24 ft. 10 in./7.57 m.) Silver (24 ft. 8½ in./7.53 m.)
	High Jump	Walter Davis	Gold (6 ft. 8½ in./2.04 m., Olympic record)
	Javelin	Bill Miller	Silver (237 ft. 9 in./72.46 m.)
	Decathlon	Milton Campbell	Silver (6,975 pts.)
	Women's 4 x 100-Meter Relay	Catherine Hardy Mae Faggs Barbara Jones	Gold (46.14)

PLACE/YEAR	EVENT	ATHLETE	MEDAL/RESULT
Melbourne, 1956	200 Meters	Andrew Stanfield	Silver (20.97)
	400 Meters	Charles Jenkins	Gold (46.85)
	110-Meter Hurdles	Lee Calhoun	Gold (13.70, Olympic record)
	400-Meter Hurdles	Josh Culbreath	Bronze (51.74)
	4 x 100-Meter Relay	Ira Murchison Leamon King	Gold (39.60, Olympic/world records)
	4 x 400-Meter Relay	Lou Jones Charles Jenkins	Gold (3:04.81)
	High Jump	Charles Dumas	Gold (6 ft. 11½ in./2.12 m., Olympic record)
	Long Jump	Gregory Bell	Gold (25 ft. 8¼ in./7.83 m.)
	Decathlon	Milton Campbell	Gold (7,937 pts., Olympic record)
		Rafer Johnson	Silver (7,587 pts.)
	Women's 4 x 100-Meter Relay	Mae Faggs Margaret Matthews Isabelle Daniels Wilma Rudolph	Bronze (45.04)
	Women's High Jump	Mildred McDaniel	Gold (5 ft. 9¼ in./1.76 m., Olympic/world records)
	Women's Long Jump	Willye White	Silver (19 ft. 11¾ in./6.09 m.)
Rome, 1960	200 Meters	Les Carney	Silver (20.69)
	400 Meters	Otis Davis	Gold (45.07, Olympic/world records)
	110-Meter Hurdles	Lee Calhoun Willie May Hayes Jones	Gold (13.98) Silver (13.99) Bronze (14.17)
	4 x 400-Meter Relay	Otis Davis	Gold (3:02.37)
	High Jump	John Thomas	Bronze (7 ft. ¼ in./2.14 m.)
	Long Jump	Ralph Boston	Gold (26 ft. 7¾ in./8.12 m., Olympic record)
		Irvin Roberson	Silver (26 ft. 7¼ in./8.11 m.)
	Decathlon	Rafer Johnson	Gold (8,392 pts., Olympic record)
	Women's 100 Meters	Wilma Rudolph	Gold (11.18, Olympic record; wind-assisted world record disallowed)

PLACE/YEAR	EVENT	ATHLETE	MEDAL/RESULT
	Women's 200 Meters	Wilma Rudolph	Gold (24.13, Olympic record)
	Women's 4 x 100-Meter Relay	Martha Hudson Lucinda Williams Barbara Jones Wilma Rudolph	Gold (44.72)
	Women's Shot Put	Earlene Brown	Bronze (53 ft. 10¼ in./ 16.42 m.)
Tokyo, 1964	100 Meters	Bob Hayes	Gold (10.06, Olympic/world records)
	200 Meters	Henry Carr Paul Drayton	Gold (20.33, Olympic record) Silver (20.58)
	110-Meter Hurdles	Hayes Jones	Gold (13.67)
	4 x 100-Meter Relay	Paul Drayton Bob Hayes Richard Stebbins	Gold (39.06, Olympic/world records)
	4 x 400-Meter Relay	Ulis Williams Henry Carr	Gold (3:00.7, Olympic/ world records)
	High Jump	John Thomas John Rambo	Silver (7 ft. 1¾ in./2.18 m., Olympic record/tied world record) Bronze (7 ft. 1 in./2.16 m.)
	Long Jump	Ralph Boston	Silver (26 ft. 4¼ in./8.03 m.)
	Women's 100 Meters	Wyomia Tyus Edith McGuire	Gold (11.49) Silver (11.62)
	Women's 200 Meters	Edith McGuire	Gold (23.05, Olympic record)
	Women's 4 x 100-Meter Relay	Willye White Wyomia Tyus Marilyn White Edith McGuire	Silver (43.92)
Mexico City, 1968	100 Meters	James Hines Charles Greene	Gold (9.95, Olympic/world records) Bronze (10.07)
	200 Meters	Tommie Smith John Carlos	Gold (19.83, world record) Bronze (20.10)
	400 Meters	Lee Evans Lawrence James Ronald Freeman	Gold (43.86) Silver (43.97) Bronze (44.41)
	110-Meter Hurdles	Willie Davenport Ervin Hall	Gold (13.33, Olympic record) Silver (13.42)

PLACE/YEAR	EVENT	ATHLETE	MEDAL/RESULT
	4 x 100-Meter Relay	James Hines Mel Pender Charles Greene Ronnie R. Smith	Gold (38.24, Olympic/world records)
	4 x 400-Meter Relay	Lee Evans Ronald Freeman Vincent Matthews Lawrence James	Gold (2:56.16, Olympic/world records)
	High Jump	Edward Caruthers	Silver (7 ft. 3¼ in./2.22 m.)
	Long Jump	Bob Beamon Ralph Boston	Gold (29 ft. 2½ in./8.90 m., Olympic/world records) Bronze (26 ft. 9¼ in./8.16 m.)
	Women's 100 Meters	Wyomia Tyus Barbara Ferrell	Gold (11.08, Olympic/world records) Silver (11.15)
	Women's 800 Meters	Madeline Manning	Gold (2:00.92)
	Women's 4 x 100-Meter Relay	Wyomia Tyus Barbara Ferrell Margaret Bailes Mildrette Netter	Gold (42.88, Olympic record)
Munich, 1972	100 Meters	Robert Taylor	Silver (10.24)
	200 Meters	Larry Black	Silver (20.19)
	400 Meters	Vincent Matthews Wayne Collett	Gold (44.66) Silver (44.80)
	110-Meter Hurdles	Rodney Milburn Thomas Hill	Gold (13.24, Olympic record/equaled world record) Bronze (13.48)
	4 x 100-Meter Relay	Eddie Hart Robert Taylor Gerald Tinker Larry Black	Gold (38.19, Olympic/world records)
	Long Jump	Randy Williams Arnie Robinson	Gold (27 ft. ¼ in./8.24 m.) Bronze (26 ft. 4 in./8.03 m.)
	Women's 4 x 400-Meter Relay	Madeline Manning Mable Fergerson Cheryl Toussaint	Silver (3:25.15)
Montreal, 1976	200 Meters	Millard Hampton Dwayne Evans	Silver (20.29) Bronze (20.43)
	400 Meters	Fred Newhouse Herman Frazier	Silver (44.40) Bronze (44.95)

PLACE/YEAR	EVENT	ATHLETE	MEDAL/RESULT
	110-Meter Hurdles	Willie Davenport	Bronze (13.38)
	400-Meter Hurdles	Edwin Moses	Gold (47.63, Olympic/world records)
	4 x 100-Meter Relay	Millard Hampton Steve Riddick John Jones Harvey Glance	Gold (38.33)
	4 x 400-Meter Relay	Maxie Parks Benny Brown Fred Newhouse Herman Frazier	Gold (2:58.65)
	Long Jump	Arnie Robinson Randy Williams	Gold (27 ft. 4¾ in./8.35 m.) Silver (26 ft. 7¼ in./8.11 m.)
	Triple Jump	James Butts	Silver (56 ft. 4½ in./17.18 m.)
	Women's 4 x 400-Meter Relay	Rosalyn Bryant Sheila Ingram Pamela Jiles Debra Sapenter	Silver (3:22.81)
	Women's Long Jump	Kathy McMillan	Silver (21 ft. 10¼ in./6.66 m.)
Los Angeles, 1984	100 Meters	Carl Lewis Sam Graddy	Gold (9.99) Silver (10.19)
	200 Meters	Carl Lewis Kirk Baptiste Thomas Jefferson	Gold (19.80, Olympic record) Silver (19.96) Bronze (20.26)
	400 Meters	Alonzo Babers Antonio McKay	Gold (44.27) Bronze (44.71)
	800 Meters	Earl Jones	Bronze (1:43.83)
	110-Meter Hurdles	Roger Kingdom Greg Foster	Gold (13.20, Olympic record) Silver (13.23)
	400-Meter Hurdles	Edwin Moses Danny Harris	Gold (47.75) Silver (48.13)
	4 x 100-Meter Relay	Sam Graddy Ron Brown Calvin Smith Carl Lewis	Gold (37.83, Olympic/world records)
	4 x 400-Meter Relay	Sunder Nix Ray Armstead Alonzo Babers Antonio McKay	Gold (2:57.91)

PLACE/YEAR	EVENT	ATHLETE	MEDAL/RESULT
	Long Jump	Carl Lewis	Gold (28 ft. ¼ in./8.54 m.)
	Triple Jump	Al Joyner	Gold (56 ft. 7½ in./17.26 m., Olympic record)
		Mike Conley	Silver (56 ft. 4½ in./17.18 m.)
	Women's 100 Meters	Evelyn Ashford	Gold (10.97, Olympic record)
		Alice Brown	Silver (11.13)
	Women's 200 Meters	Valerie Brisco-Hooks	Gold (21.81, Olympic record)
		Florence Griffith-Joyner	Silver (22.04)
	Women's 400 Meters	Valerie Brisco-Hooks	Gold (48.83, Olympic record)
		Chandra Cheeseborough	Silver (49.05)
	Women's 800 Meters	Kim Gallagher	Silver (1:58.63)
	Women's 100-Meter Hurdles	Benita Fitzgerald-Brown	Gold (12.84)
		Kim Turner	Bronze (13.06)
	Women's 400-Meter Hurdles	Judi Brown	Silver (55.20, American record)
	Women's 4 x 100-Meter Relay	Chandra Cheeseborough Alice Brown Jeanette Bolden Evelyn Ashford	Gold (41.65)
	Women's 4 x 400-Meter Relay	Lillie Leatherwood Sherri Howard Valerie Brisco-Hooks Chandra Cheeseborough	Gold (3:18.29, Olympic record)
	Women's Heptathlon	Jackie Joyner-Kersee	Silver (6,385 pts.)
Seoul, 1988	100 Meters	Carl Lewis	Gold (9.92, Olympic record)
		Calvin Smith	Bronze (9.99)
	200 Meters	Joe DeLoach	Gold (19.75, Olympic record)
		Carl Lewis	Silver (19.79, Olympic record)
	400 Meters	Steve Lewis	Gold (43.87)
		Butch Reynolds	Silver (43.93)
		Danny Everett	Bronze (44.09)
	110-Meter Hurdles	Roger Kingdom	Gold (12.98, Olympic record)
		Tonie Campbell	Bronze (13.38)
	400-Meter Hurdles	Andre Phillips	Gold (47.19, Olympic record)
		Edwin Moses	Bronze (47.56)
	4 x 400-Meter Relay	Danny Everett Steve Lewis Kevin Robinzine Butch Reynolds	Gold (2:56.16, Olympic record)

PLACE/YEAR	EVENT	ATHLETE	MEDAL/RESULT
	Long Jump	Carl Lewis Mike Powell Larry Myricks	Gold (28 ft. 7½ in./8.72 m.) Silver (27 ft. 10¼ in./8.49 m.) Bronze (27 ft. 1¾ in./8.27 m.)
	High Jump	Hollis Conway	Silver (7 ft. 8¾ in./2.36 m.)
	Women's 100 Meters	Florence Griffith-Joyner Evelyn Ashford	Gold (10.54, Olympic record) Silver (10.83)
	Women's 200 Meters	Florence Griffith-Joyner	Gold (21.34, Olympic record)
	Women's 800 Meters	Kim Gallagher	Bronze (1:56.91)
	Women's 4 x 100-Meter Relay	Alice Brown Sheila Echols Florence Griffith-Joyner Evelyn Ashford	Gold (41.98)
	Women's 4 x 400-Meter Relay	Denean Howard Diane Dixon Valerie Brisco-Hooks Florence Griffith-Joyner	Silver (3:15.51)
	Long Jump	Jackie Joyner-Kersee	Gold (24 ft. 3½ in./7.41 m., Olympic/world records)
	Heptathlon	Jackie Joyner-Kersee	Gold (7,291 pts., world record)

INTERNATIONAL BLACK TRACK AND FIELD OLYMPIC MEDALISTS, 1904-1988, BY PLACE AND DATE

PLACE/YEAR	EVENT	ATHLETE/COUNTRY	MEDAL/RESULT
Antwerp, 1920	100 Meters	Harry Edward (Gbr)	Bronze (11.0)
	200 Meters	Harry Edward (Gbr)	Bronze (22.2)
Amsterdam, 1928	100 Meters	Jack London (Gbr)	Silver (10.9)
	4 x 100-Meter Relay	Jack London (Gbr)	Bronze (41.8)
	4 x 400-Meter Relay	Phil Edwards (Can)	Bronze (3:15.4)
	Long Jump	Silvio Cator (Hai)	Silver (24 ft. 10¼ in./ 7.58 m.)
Los Angeles, 1932	800 Meters	Phil Edwards (Can)	Bronze (1:51.5)
	4 x 400-Meter Relay	Phil Edwards (Can)	Bronze (3:12.8)
Berlin, 1936	800 Meters	Phil Edwards (Can)	Bronze (1:53.6)

PLACE/YEAR	EVENT	ATHLETE/COUNTRY	MEDAL/RESULT
London, 1948	100 Meters	Lloyd LaBeach (Pan)	Bronze (10.4)
	200 Meters	Lloyd LaBeach (Pan)	Bronze (21.2)
	400 Meters	Arthur Wint (Jam) Herb McKenley (Jam)	Gold (46.2, Olympic record) Silver (46.4)
	800 Meters	Arthur Wint (Jam)	Silver (1:49.5)
Helsinki, 1952	100 Meters	Herb McKenley (Jam) McDonald Bailey (Gbr)	Silver (10.8) Bronze (10.83)
	400 Meters	George Rhoden (Jam) Herb McKenley (Jam)	Gold (46.09, Olympic record) Silver (46.20, Olympic record)
	800 Meters	Arthur Wint (Jam)	Silver (1:49.63)
	4 x 400-Meter Relay	Arthur Wint (Jam) Leslie Laing (Jam) Herb McKenley (Jam) George Rhoden (Jam)	Gold (3:04.04, Olympic/world records)
	High Jump	José Telles da Conceição (Bra)	Bronze (6 ft. 6 in./1.98 m.)
	Triple Jump	Adhemar Ferreira da Silva (Bra) Arnoldo Devonish (Ven)	Gold (53 ft. 2¾ in./16.22 m., Olympic/world record) Bronze (50 ft. 11 in./15.52 m.)
Melbourne, 1956	Triple Jump	Adhemar Ferreira da Silva (Bra)	Gold (53 ft. 7¾ in./16.35 m., Olympic record)
Rome, 1960	200 Meters	Abdoulaye Seye (Fra)	Bronze (20.83)
	800 Meters	George Kerr (Jam)	Bronze (1:47.25)
	Marathon	Abebe Bikila (Eth)	Gold (2 hrs. 15:16.2, Olympic/world records)
	4 x 400-Meter Relay	Malcolm Spence (Jam) Jimmy Wedderburn (Jam) Keith Gardner (Jam) George Kerr (Jam)	Bronze (3:04.13)
Tokyo, 1964	100 Meters	Enrique Figuerola (Cub) Harry Jerome (Can)	Silver (10.25) Bronze (10.27)
	200 Meters	Edwin Roberts (Tri)	Bronze (20.63)
	400 Meters	Wendell Mottley (Tri)	Silver (45.24)
	800 Meters	Wilson Kiprugut (Ken)	Bronze (1:45.9)

PLACE/YEAR	EVENT	ATHLETE/COUNTRY	MEDAL/RESULT
	Marathon	Abebe Bikila (Eth)	Gold (2 hrs. 12:11.2, Olympic/world records)
	4 x 400-Meter Relay	Edwin Skinner (Tri) Kent Bernard (Tri) Edwin Roberts (Tri) Wendell Mottley (Tri)	Bronze (3:01.7)
Mexico City, 1968	100 Meters	Lennox Miller (Jam)	Silver (10.04)
	800 Meters	Wilson Kiprugut (Ken)	Silver (1:44.57)
	1,500 Meters	Kipchoge Keino (Ken)	Gold (3:34.91, Olympic record)
	5,000 Meters	Kipchoge Keino (Ken) Naftali Temu (Ken)	Silver (14:05.16) Bronze (14:06.41)
	10,000 Meters	Naftali Temu (Ken) Mamo Wolde (Eth)	Gold (29:27.40) Silver (29:27.75)
	Marathon	Mamo Wolde (Eth)	Gold (2 hrs. 20:26.4)
	4 x 100-Meter Relay	Hermes Ramírez (Cub) Juan Morales (Cub) Pablo Montes (Cub) Enrique Figuerola (Cub) Roger Bambuck (Fra)	Silver (38.40) Bronze (38.43)
	4 x 400-Meter Relay	Daniel Rudisha (Ken) Hezekiah Nyamau (Ken) Naftali Bon (Ken) Charles Asati (Ken)	Silver (2:59.64)
	1,500 Meters	Kipchoge Keino (Ken)	Gold (3:34.91, Olympic record)
	3,000-Meter Steeplechase	Amos Biwott (Ken) Ben Kogo (Ken)	Gold (8:51.02) Silver (8:51.56)
	Triple Jump	Nelson Prudencio (Bra)	Silver (56 ft. 8 in./17.27 m.)
	Women's 4 x 100-Meter Relay	Marlene Elejarde (Cub) Fulgencia Romay (Cub) Violeta Quesada (Cub) Miguelina Cobian (Cub)	Silver (43.36)
Munich, 1972	100 Meters	Lennox Miller (Jam)	Bronze (10.33)
	400 Meters	Julius Sang (Ken)	Bronze (44.92)
	800 Meters	Mike Boit (Ken)	Bronze (1:46.01)
	1,500 Meters	Kipchoge Keino (Ken)	Silver (3:36.81)
	10,000 Meters	Miruts Yifter (Eth)	Bronze (27:40.96)

PLACE/YEAR	EVENT	ATHLETE/COUNTRY	MEDAL/RESULT
	Marathon	Mamo Wolde (Eth)	Bronze (2 hrs. 15:08.4)
	4 x 400-Meter Relay	Charles Asati (Ken) Hezekiah Nyamau (Ken) Robert Ouko (Ken) Julius Sang (Ken)	Gold (2:59.83)
	4 x 400-Meter Relay	Roger Velasques (Fra)	Bronze (3:00.65)
	400-Meter Hurdles	John Akii-Bua (Uga)	Gold (47.82, Olympic/ world records)
	3,000-Meter Steeplechase	Kipchoge Keino (Ken) Ben Jipcho (Ken)	Gold (8:23.64, Olympic record) Silver (8:24.62)
	Triple Jump	Nelson Prudencio (Bra)	Bronze (55 ft. 11¼ in./ 17.05 m.)
	Women's 100 Meters	Silvia Chivás (Cub)	Bronze (11.24)
	Women's 4 x 100-Meter Relay	Marlene Elejarde (Cub) Carmen Valdes (Cub) Fulgencia Romay (Cub) Silvia Chivás (Cub)	Bronze (43.36)
Montreal, 1976	100 Meters	Hasely Crawford (Tri) Don Quarrie (Jam)	Gold (10.06) Silver (10.08)
	200 Meters	Don Quarrie (Jam)	Gold (20.23)
	400 Meters	Alberto Juantorena (Cub)	Gold (44.26, Olympic record)
	800 Meters	Alberto Juantorena (Cub)	Gold (1:43.5, Olympic/ world records)
	110-Meter Hurdles	Alejandro Casañas (Cub)	Silver (13.33)
	20 Kilo Meter Walk	Daniel Bautista (Mex)	Gold (1 hr. 24 min. 40.6, Olympic record)
	Triple Jump	Joao Carlos de Oliveira (Bra)	Bronze (55 ft. 5½ in./ 16.90 m.)
Moscow, 1980	100 Meters	Silvio Leonard (Cub)	Silver (10.25)
	200 Meters	Don Quarrie (Jam)	Bronze (20.29)
	5,000 Meters	Miruts Yifter (Eth) Suleiman Nyambui (Tan)	Gold (13:21.0) Silver (13:21.6)
	10,000 Meters	Miruts Yifter (Eth) Mohammed Kedir (Eth)	Gold (27:42.7) Bronze (27:44.7)

PLACE/YEAR	EVENT	ATHLETE/COUNTRY	MEDAL/RESULT
	4 x 100-Meter Relay	Hermann Panzo (Fra)	Bronze (38.53)
	110-Meter Hurdles	Alejandro Casañas (Cub)	Silver (13.40)
	3,000-Meter Steeplechase	Filbert Bayi (Tan) Esketu Tura (Eth)	Silver (8:12.5) Bronze (8:13.6)
	Triple Jump	Joao Carlos de Oliveira (Bra)	Bronze (56 ft. 6 in./ 17.22 m.)
	Discus Throw	Luis Delis (Cub)	Bronze (217 ft. 7 in./ 66.32 m.)
	Decathlon	Daley Thompson (Gbr)	Gold (8,495 pts.)
	Women's 200 Meters	Merlene Ottey-Page (Jam)	Bronze (22.20)
	Women's 4 x 100-Meter Relay	Heather Oakes (Gbr) Beverley Goddard-Callender (Gbr) Sonia Lannaman (Gbr)	Bronze (42.43)
	Women's 4 x 400-Meter Relay	Joslyn Hoyte-Smith (Gbr)	Bronze (3:27.5)
	Women's Javelin Throw	María Colón (Cub)	Gold (224 ft. 5 in./ 68.40 m., Olympic record)
Los Angeles, 1984	100 Meters	Ben Johnson (Can)	Bronze (10.22)
	400 Meters	Gabriel Tiacoh (Ivc)	Silver (44.54)
	800 Meters	Joaquim Cruz (Bra)	Gold (1:43.00, new Olympic record)
	5,000 Meters	Saïd Aouita (Mor)	Gold (13:05.59, new Olympic record)
	10,000 Meters	Mike Musyoki (Ken)	Bronze (28:06.46)
	4 x 100-Meter Relay	Albert Lawrence (Jam) Gregory Meghoo (Jam) Don Quarrie (Jam) Raymond Stewart (Jam)	Silver (38.62)
		Ben Johnson (Can) Tony Sharpe (Can) Desai Williams (Can) Sterling Hinds (Can)	Bronze (38.70)
	4 x 400-Meter Relay	Kriss Akabusi (Gbr) Phil Brown (Gbr)	Silver (2:59.13)
		Sunday Uti (Ngr) Moses Ugbisbie (Ngr) Rotimi Peters (Ngr) Innocent Egbunike (Ngr)	Bronze (2:59.32)
	3,000-Meter Steeplechase	Julius Korir (Ken)	Gold (8:11.80)

PLACE/YEAR	EVENT	ATHLETE/COUNTRY	MEDAL/RESULT
	Triple Jump	Keith Connor (Gbr)	Bronze (55 ft. 4¼ in./ 16.87 m.)
	Decathlon	Daley Thompson (Gbr)	Gold (8,798 pts., Olympic record/equaled world record)
	Women's 100 Meters	Merlene Ottey-Page (Jam)	Bronze (11.16)
	Women's 200 Meters	Merlene Ottey-Page (Jam)	Bronze (22.09)
	Women's 4 x 100-Meter Relay	Angela Bailey (Can) Marita Payne (Can) Angella Taylor (Can)	Silver (42.77)
	Women's 4 x 100-Meter Relay	Simone Jacobs (Gbr) Beverley Goddard-Callender (Gbr) Heather Oakes (Gbr)	Bronze (43.11)
	Women's 4 x 400-Meter Relay	Charmaine Crooks (Can) Molly Killingbeck (Can) Jillian Richardson (Can) Marita Payne (Can)	Silver (3:21.21)
	Women's Javelin Throw	Tessa Sanderson (Gbr)	Gold (228 ft. 2 in./ 69.56 m., Olympic record)
Seoul, 1988	100 Meters	Linford Christie (Gbr)	Silver (9.97)
	800 Meters	Paul Ereng (Ken) Joaquim Cruz (Bra) Saïd Aouita (Mor)	Gold (1:43.45) Silver (1:43.90) Bronze (1:44.06)
	1,500 Meters	Peter Rono (Ken)	Gold (3:35.96)
	5,000 Meters	John Ngugi (Ken)	Gold (13:11.70)
	10,000 Meters	Irahim Boutaib (Mor) Kipkemboi Kimeli (Ken)	Gold (27:21.46) Bronze (27:25.16)
	Marathon	Douglas Wakihuri (Ken) Ahmed Saleh (Dji)	Silver (2 hrs. 10:47.0) Bronze (2 hrs. 10:59.0)
	3,000-Meter Steeplechase	Julius Karuiki (Ken) Peter Koech (Ken)	Gold (8:05.51, Olympic record) Silver (8:06.79)
	110-Meter Hurdles	Colin Jackson (Gbr)	Silver (13.28)
	400-Meter Hurdles	Elhadjdia Ba (Sen)	Silver (47.23)
	4 x 100-Meter Relay	Linford Christie (Gbr)	Silver (38.28)
	4 x 400-Meter Relay	Winthrop Graham (Jam) Bert Cameron (Jam)	Silver (3:00.30)
	Women's 200 Meters	Grace Jackson (Jam)	Silver (21.72)

BLACK BASKETBALL OLYMPIC MEDALISTS (MEN)

PLACE/YEAR	GOLD	SILVER	BRONZE
London, 1948	Don Barksdale (USA) R. Jackie Robinson (USA)		
Melbourne, 1956	K. C. Jones (USA) Bill Russell (USA)		
Rome, 1960	Oscar Robertson (USA) Bob Boozer (USA) Walter Bellamy (USA)		
Tokyo, 1964	Jim Barnes (USA) Joe Caldwell (USA) Walter Hazzard (USA) Lucius Jackson (USA) George Wilson (USA)		
Mexico City, 1968	Calvin Fowler (USA) Spencer Haywood (USA) James King (USA) Charles Scott (USA) Joseph White (USA)		
Munich, 1972		James Brewer (USA) Michael Bantom (USA) Ed Ratleff (USA) James Forbes (USA) Thomas Henderson (USA) Dwight Jones (USA)	Conrado Pérez (Cub) Ruperto Herrera (Cub) Alejandro Urgelles (Cub) Pedro Chappé (Cub) Franklin Standard (Cub) Juan Ortega (Cub) Tomás Herrera (Cub) Oscar Varona (Cub) Miguel Calderón (Cub) Rafael Canizares (Cub)
Montreal, 1976	Phil Ford (USA) Steve Sheppard (USA) Adrian Dantley (USA) Walter Davis (USA) Scott May (USA) Phil Hubbard (USA)		
Los Angeles, 1984	Michael Jordan (USA) Patrick Ewing (USA) Leon Wood (USA) Wayman Tisdale (USA) Vern Fleming (USA) Sam Perkins (USA) Alvin Robertson (USA)		

PLACE/YEAR	GOLD	SILVER	BRONZE
Seoul, 1988			Willie Anderson (USA) Vernell Coles (USA) Jeff Grayer (USA) Hersey Hawkins (USA) Danny Manning (USA) J. R. Reid (USA) Mitch Richmond (USA) David Robinson (USA) Charles D. Smith (USA) Charles E. Smith (USA)

BLACK BASKETBALL OLYMPIC MEDALISTS (WOMEN)

PLACE/YEAR	GOLD	SILVER	BRONZE
Montreal, 1976		Luisa Harris (USA) Charlotte Lewis (USA) Gail Marquis (USA) Patricia Roberts (USA)	
Los Angeles, 1984	Cheryl Miller (USA) Pam McGee (USA) Lynette Woodard (USA) Janice Lawrence (USA) Cathy Boswell (USA) Teresa Edwards (USA)		
Seoul, 1988	Jennifer Gillom (USA) Bridgette Gordon (USA) Katrina McClain (USA) Teresa Weatherspoon (USA) Cindy Brown (USA) Vicki Bullet (USA) Cynthia Cooper (USA) Teresa Edwards (USA)		

BLACK BOXING OLYMPIC MEDALISTS

YEAR	GOLD	SILVER	BRONZE
	Light Flyweight		
1976	Jorge Hernández (Cub)		
1980		Hipolito Ramos (Cub)	
	Flyweight		
1952	Nathan Brooks (USA)		
1968			Leo Rwabwogo (Uga)
1972		Leo Rwabwogo (Uga)	Douglas Rodríguez (Cub)

YEAR	GOLD	SILVER	BRONZE
1976	Leo Randolph (USA)	Ramón Duvalon (Cub)	
1984	Steven McCrory (USA)		Ibrahim Bilali (Ken)

Bantamweight

YEAR	GOLD	SILVER	BRONZE
1936		Jack Wilson (USA)	
1968		Eridari Mukwanga (Uga)	
1972	Orlando Martínez (Cub)		
1980	Juan Hernández (Cub)		Ricardo Carreras (USA), tied
1988	Kennedy McKinney (USA)		Ricardo Carreras (USA)

Featherweight

YEAR	GOLD	SILVER	BRONZE
1964			Charles Brown (USA)
1968			Philip Waruinge (Ken)
1972		Philip Waruinge (Ken)	
1976	Angel Herrera (Cub)		
1980		Adolfo Horta (Cub)	
1984	Meldrick Taylor (USA)	Peter Konyegwackie (Ngr)	

Lightweight

YEAR	GOLD	SILVER	BRONZE
1964			Ronnie Harris (USA)
1968	Ronnie Harris (USA)		
1972			Samuel Mbugua (Ken)
1976	Howard Davis (USA)		
1980	Angel Herrera (Cub)		
1984	Pernell Whitaker (USA)		Martin Ebanga (Cam)
1988			Romallis Ellis (USA)

Light Welterweight

YEAR	GOLD	SILVER	BRONZE
1952	Charles Adkins (USA)		
1960		Clement Quartey (Gha)	Quincy Daniels (USA)
1964			Eddie Blay (Gha)
1968		Enrique Regueiferos (Cub)	
1972	Ray Seales (USA)		
1976	Ray Leonard (USA)	Andrés Aldama (Cub)	
1980			José Aguilar (Cub)
1984	Jerry Page (USA)		

YEAR	GOLD	SILVER	BRONZE

Welterweight

YEAR	GOLD	SILVER	BRONZE
1968		Joseph Bessala (Cam)	
1972	Emilio Correa (Cub)		Dick Murunga (Ken)
1976		Pedro Gamarro (Ven)	
1980	Andrés Aldama (Cub)	John Mugabi (Uga)	
1984	Mark Breland (USA)		
1988	Robert Wangila (Ken)		Kenneth Gould (USA)

Light Middleweight

YEAR	GOLD	SILVER	BRONZE
1960	Wilbert McClure (USA)		
1964			Nojim Maiyegun (Ngr)
1968		Rolando Garbey (Cub)	John Baldwin (USA)
1980	Armando Martínez (Cub)		
1984	Frank Tate (USA)		
1988		Roy Jones (USA)	

Middleweight

YEAR	GOLD	SILVER	BRONZE
1952	Floyd Patterson (USA)		
1960	Edward Crook (USA)		
1968			Alfred Jones (USA)
1972			Prince Amartey (Gha)
1976	Michael Spinks (USA)		Luis Martínez (Cub)
1980	José Gómez (Cub)		
1984		Virgil Hill (USA)	
1988		Egerton Marcus (Can)	

Light Heavyweight

YEAR	GOLD	SILVER	BRONZE
1952	Norvel Lee (USA)		
1960	Cassius Clay (USA)		
1972		Gilberto Carrillo (Cub)	Isaac Ikhouria (Ngr)
1976	Leon Spinks (USA)	Sixto Soria (Cub)	
1980			Ricardo Rojas (Cub)
1984			Evander Holyfield (USA)
1988	Andrew Maynard (USA)		

YEAR	GOLD	SILVER	BRONZE

Heavyweight

YEAR	GOLD	SILVER	BRONZE
1952	Ed Sanders (USA)		
1964	Joe Frazier (USA)		
1968	George Foreman (USA)		
1972	Teófilo Stevenson (Cub)		
1976	Teófilo Stevenson (Cub)		Clarence Hill (Ber)
1980	Teófilo Stevenson (Cub)		
1984	Henry Tillman (USA)		
1988	Ray Mercer (USA)		Arnold Van der Lidje (Hol)

Superweight

YEAR	GOLD	SILVER	BRONZE
1984	Tyrell Biggs (USA)		
1988	Lennox Lewis (Can)	Riddick Bowe (USA)	

BLACK CYCLING OLYMPIC MEDALISTS

PLACE/YEAR	EVENT	ATHLETE/COUNTRY	MEDAL
Los Angeles, 1984	Cycling Match Sprints	Nelson Vails (USA)	Silver

BLACK FENCING OLYMPIC MEDALISTS

PLACE/YEAR	EVENT	ATHLETE/COUNTRY	MEDAL
Los Angeles, 1984	Fencing, Individual Sabre	Peter Westbrook (USA)	Bronze

BLACK JUDO OLYMPIC MEDALISTS

PLACE/YEAR	EVENT	ATHLETE/COUNTRY	MEDAL
Moscow, 1980	Judo, Up to 78 kg	Juan Ferrer (Cub)	Silver
	Judo, Up to 60 kg	Rafael Rodríguez (Cub)	Silver
Los Angeles, 1984	Judo, Extra Lightweight	Edward Liddie (USA)	Bronze
Seoul, 1988	Judo, Heavyweight	Aurelio Miguel (Bra)	Gold

BLACK ROWING OLYMPIC MEDALISTS

PLACE/YEAR	EVENT	ATHLETE/COUNTRY	MEDAL
Montreal, 1976	Rowing Eights	Anita DeFrantz (USA)	Bronze

BLACK SWIMMING OLYMPIC MEDALISTS

PLACE/YEAR	EVENT	ATHLETE/COUNTRY	MEDAL
(Men) Seoul, 1988	Swimming, 100-Meter Butterfly	Anthony Nesty	Gold
(Women) Montreal, 1976	Swimming, 100-Meter Freestyle	Enith Brigitha (Hol)	Bronze
	Swimming, 200-Meter Freestyle	Enith Brigitha (Hol)	Bronze

BLACK TENNIS OLYMPIC MEDALISTS

Seoul, 1988	Tennis, Women's Doubles	Zina Garrison (USA)	Gold
	Tennis, Women's Singles	Zina Garrison (USA)	Bronze

BLACK VOLLEYBALL OLYMPIC MEDALISTS

(Men) Montreal, 1976	Volleyball	Leonel Marshall (Cub) Victoriano Sarmientos (Cub) Ernesto Martínez (Cub) Victor García (Cub) Raul Virches (Cub) Jesús Savigne (Cub) Lorenzo Martínez (Cub) Jorge Pérez (Cub)	Bronze
(Women) Los Angeles, 1984	Volleyball	Flo Hyman (USA) Rita Crockett (USA) Rose Magers (USA)	Silver

BLACK WEIGHTLIFTING OLYMPIC MEDALISTS

Moscow, 1980	Weightlifting, Bantam	Daniel Nuñez (Cub)	Gold
London, 1948	Weightlifting, Featherweight	Rodney Wilkes (Tri)	Silver
Helsinki, 1952	Weightlifting, Middle Heavyweight	Lennox Kilgour (Tri)	Bronze
Rome, 1960	Weightlifting, Middle Heavyweight	Louis Martin (Gbr)	Bronze
Tokyo, 1964	Weightlifting, Middle Heavyweight	Louis Martin (Gbr)	Silver
London, 1948	Weightlifting, Heavyweight	John Davis (USA)	Gold

PLACE/YEAR	EVENT	ATHLETE/COUNTRY	MEDAL
Helsinki, 1952	Weightlifting, Heavyweight	Louis Martin (Gbr)	Bronze
	Weightlifting, Heavyweight	John Davis (USA)	Gold
	Weightlifting, Featherweight	Rodney Wilkes (Tri)	Bronze

BLACK WRESTLING OLYMPIC MEDALISTS

Montreal, 1976	Wrestling, Freestyle Lightweight	Lloyd Keasor (USA)	Silver
Seoul, 1988	Wrestling, Freestyle Lightweight	Nate Carr (USA)	Bronze
	Wrestling, Freestyle Welterweight	Kennedy Monday (USA)	Gold

BLACK DOMINANCE OF 1988 OLYMPIC RUNNING EVENTS

All Black, All U.S.

EVENT	GOLD	SILVER	BRONZE
100 m.	Carl Lewis (USA)	Linford Christie (Gbr)	Calvin Smith (USA)
200 m.	Joe DeLoach (USA)	Carl Lewis (USA)	
400 m.	Steve Lewis (USA)	Butch Reynolds (USA)	Danny Everett (USA)

All Black

800 m.	Paul Ereng (Ken)	Joaquim Cruz (Bra)	Saïd Aouita (Mor)
110 m.H	Roger Kingdom (USA)	Colin Jackson (Gbr)	Tonie Campbell (USA)
400 m.H	Andre Phillips (USA)	Elhadjdia Ba (Sen)	Edwin Moses (USA)

All African

800 m.	Paul Ereng (Ken)
1500 m.	Peter Rono (Ken)
5000 m.	John Ngugi (Ken)
3000 m. St	Julius Kariuki (Ken)
10,000 m.	Brahim Boutaib (Mor)

Additional Black Winners

EVENT	GOLD	SILVER	BRONZE
1500 m.	Peter Rono (Ken)		
3000 m. St.	Julius Kariuki (Ken)	Peter Koech (Ken)	
5000 m.	John Ngugi (Ken)		
10,000 m.	Brahim Boutaib (Mor)		Kipkemboi Kimeli (Ken)
Marathon		Douglas Wakihuri (Ken)	Ahmed Saleh (Dji)
4 x 100		Linford Christie (Gbr)	
4 x 400	Danny Everett (USA) Steve Lewis (USA) Kevin Robinzine (USA) Butch Reynolds (USA)	Winthrop Graham (Jam) Bert Cameron (Jam)	

International Black Olympians by Sponsoring Country

BARBADOS
Jimmy Wedderburn

BERMUDA
Clarence Hill

BRAZIL
Joaquim Cruz, José da Conceição, Adhemar Ferreira da Silva, Joao Carlos de Oliveria, Aurelio Miguel, Nelson Prudencio

CAMEROON
Jean Bessala, Martin Ebanga

CANADA
Angela Bailey, Charmaine Crooks, Philip Edwards, Sterling Hinds, Harry Jerome, Ben Johnson, Molly Killingbeck, Lennox Lewis, Raymond Lewis, Marita Payne, Jillian Richardson, Tony Sharpe, Angella Taylor, Desai Williams

CUBA
José Aguilar, Andrés Aldama, Miguel Calderón, Rafael Canizares, Gilberto Carillo, Alejandro Casañas, Pedro Chappé, Silvia Chivás, Miguelina Cobian, María Colón, Emilio Correa, Luis Delis, Ramón Duvalon, Fulgencia Elejarde, Juan Ferrer, Camue Enrique Figuerola, Rolando Garbey, Victor García, José Gómez, Jorge Hernández, Juan Hernández, Angel Herrera, Ruperto Herrera, Tomás Herrera, Adolfo Horta, Alberto Juantorena, Silvio Leonard, Leonel Marshall, Pablo Montes, Juan Morales, Daniel Nuñez, Juan Ortega, Jorge Pérez, Conrado Pérez, Violeta Quesada, Hermes Ramírez, Hipolito Ramos, Enrique Regueiferos, Rafael Rodríguez, Luis Rodríguez, Ricardo Rojas, Fulgencia Romay, Victoriano Sarmientos, Jesús Savigne, Sixto Soria, Franklin Standard, Teófilo Stevenson, Alejandro Urgelles, Carmen Valdes, Oscar Varona, Raul Virches

DJIBOUTI
Ahmed Saleh

ETHIOPIA
Abebe Bikila, Muhammed Kedir, Eshetu Tura, Mamo Wolde, Miruts Yifter

FRANCE
Roger Bambuck, Hermann Panzo, Abdoulaye Seye, Roger Velasques

GHANA
Prince Amartey, Eddie Blay, Clement Quartey

GREAT BRITAIN
Kriss Akabusi, E. MacDonald Bailey, Phil Brown, Beverley Goddard-Callender, Linford Christie, Keith Connor, Harry Edward, Colin Jackson, Simone Jacobs, Sonia Lannaman, Heather Hunte-Oakes, Tessa Sanderson, Daley Thompson

GUYANA (BRITISH GUIANA)
Michael Anthony, Jack London

HAITI
Silvio Cator

IVORY COAST
Gabriel Tiacoh

JAMAICA
Bert Cameron, Winthrop Graham, Grace Jackson, George Kerr, Leslie Laing, Albert Lawrence, Herb McKenley, Gregory Meghoo, Lennox Miller, Merlene Ottey-Page, Don Quarrie, George Rhoden, Malcolm Spence, Raymond Stewart, Arthur Wint

KENYA
Charles Asati, Irahim Bilali, Amos Biwott, Michael Boit, Naftali Bon, Paul Ereng, Benjamin Jipcho, Julius Kariuki, Kipkemboi Kimeli, Wilson Kiprugut, Peter Koech, Benjamin Kogo, Julius Korir, Samuel Mbugua, Dick Murunga, Mike Musyoki, John Ngugi, Hezekiah Nyamau, Robert Ouko, Peter Rono, Daniel Rudisha, Julius Sang, Naftali Temu, Douglas Wakihuri, Robert Wangila, Philip Waruinge

MOROCCO
Saïd Aouita, Moblay Brahim Boutaib

NETHERLANDS
Enith Brigitha, Arnold Van der Lidje

NIGER
Issaka Daborg

NIGERIA
Innocent Egbunike, Isaac Ikhourea, Peter Konyegwackie, Nojim Maiyegun, Rotimi Peters, Moses Ugbisie, Sunday Uti

PANAMA
Lloyd LaBeach

SENEGAL
Elhadjdia Ba

SURINAM
Anthony Nesty

TANZANIA
Filbert Bayi, Suleiman Nyambui

TRINIDAD
Kent Bernard, Hasely Crawford, Lennox Kilgour, Wendell Motley, Edwin Roberts, Edwin Skinner, Rodney Wilkes

UGANDA
John Akii-Bua, Eridari Mukwanga, Leo Rwabwogo

UNITED STATES
Charles Adkins, Dave Albritton, Muhammad Ali, Willie Anderson, Ray Armstead, Evelyn Ashford, Stacey Augmon, Alonzo Babers, Margaret Bailes, John Baldwin, Michael Bantom, Kirk Baptiste, Don Barksdale, Jim Barnes, Bob Beamon, Gregory Bell, Walter Bellamy, Jerome Biffle, Tyrell Biggs, Larry Black, Jeannette Bolden, Bob Boozer, Ralph Boston, Cathy Boswell, Riddick Bowe, James Boyd, Jim Bradford, Mark Breland, James Brewer, Valerie Brisco-Hooks, Nathan Brooks, Alice Brown, Benjamin Brown, Charles Brown, Cindy Brown, Earlene Brown, Judi Brown, Ron Brown, Rosalyn Bryant, William Q. Buckner, Vicki Bullett, James Butts, Carl Cain, Joe Caldwell, Lee Q. Calhoun, Milton Campbell, Tonie Campbell, John Carlos, Lester Carney, Henry Carr, Kenneth Carr, Nate Carr, Ricardo Carreras, Michael Carter, Edward Caruthers, Chandra Cheeseborough, Alice Coachman, Allen Coage, Vernell Coles, Wayne Collett, Mike Conley, Hollis Conway, Cynthia Cooper, Rita Crockett, Edward Crook, Joshua Culbreath, Isabelle Daniels, Quincy Daniels, Adrian Dantley, Willie Davenport, Howard Davis, John Davis, Otis Davis, Walter Davis, Anita DeFrantz, Joe DeLoach, Harrison Dillard, Diane Dixon, Herbert Douglas, Otis Drayton, Charles Dumas, Sheila Echols, Teresa Edwards, Romallis Ellis, Dwayne Evans, Lee Evans, Danny Everett, Henry Ewell, Patrick Ewing,

Heriwentha Faggs, Mable Fergerson, Barbara Ferrell, Benita Fitzgerald, Vern Fleming, Jim Forbes, Phil J. Ford, George Foreman, Greg Foster, Calvin Fowler, Herman Frazier, Joseph Frazier, Ronald Freeman, Kim Gallagher, Zina Garrison, James Gathers, Greg Gibson, Jennifer Gillom, Harvey Glance, Bridgette Gordon, Edward Gordon, Kenneth Gould, Edward Gourdin, Meredith Gourdine, Sam Graddy, Jeff Grayer, Charles Greene, Florence Griffith-Joyner, Ervin Hall, Millard Hampton, Catherine Hardy, Danny Harris, Lusia Harris, Ronald Harris, Eddie Hart, Hersey Hawkins, Bob Hayes, Spencer Haywood, Walter Hazzard, Thomas Henderson, Thomas Hill, Virgil Hill, Jim Hines, Evander Holyfield, Denean Howard, Richard Howard, Sherri Howard, Joslyn Hoyte, Philip Hubbard, W. DeHart Hubbard, Martha Hudson, Flo Hyman, Sheila Ingram, Lucius Jackson, George L. James, Thomas Jefferson, Charles Jenkins, Pam Jiles, Cornelius Johnson, Marvin Johnson, R. Earl Johnson, Rafer Johnson, Alfred Jones, Barbara Jones, Dwight Jones, Earl Jones, Hayes Jones, John W. Jones, K. C. Jones, Louis Jones, Roy Jones, Michael Jordan, Al Joyner, Jackie Joyner-Kersee, Lloyd Keasor, James King, Leamon King, Roger Kingdom, Janice Lawrence, Lillie Leatherwood, Norvel Lee, Ray Leonard, Carl Lewis, Charlotte Lewis, Steve Lewis, Edward Liddie, James LuValle, Rose Magers, Danny Manning, Madeline Manning, Harlan Marbley, Gail Marquis, Ollie Matson, Margaret Matthews, Vince Matthews, Scott May, William May, Andrew Maynard, Katrina McClain, Wilbert McClure, Steve McCrory, Mildred McDaniel, Pam McGee, Edith McGuire, Antonio McKay, Kennedy McKinney, Kathy McMillan, Ray Mercer, Ralph Metcalfe, Rodney Milburn, Cheryl Miller, Bill Miller, Kennedy Monday, Charles Mooney, Edwin Moses, Ira Murchison, Larry Myricks, Mildrette Netter, Fred Newhouse, Sunder Nix, Jesse Owens, Jerry Page, Maxie Parks, Audrey Patterson, Floyd Patterson, Melvin Pender, Sam Perkins, Andre Phillips, George Poage, Fritz Pollard, Mike Powell, John Rambo, Leo Randolph, Ed Ratleff, J. R. Reid, Butch Reynolds, Mitch Richmond, Steven Riddick, Irvin Roberson, Patricia Roberts, Alvin Robertson, Oscar Robertson, Albert Robinson, Arnie Robinson, David Robinson, Matthew Robinson, Kevin Robinzine, Wilma Rudolph, Bill Russell, Ed Sanders, Debra Sapenter, Charles Scott, Ray Seales, Steve Sheppard, Calvin Smith, Charles D. Smith, Charles E. Smith, Ronnie Ray Smith, Tommie Smith, Leon Spinks, Michael Spinks, Joseph Stadler, Andrew Stanfield, Richard Stebbins, William Steele, Frank Tate, John Tate, John Taylor, Meldrick Taylor, Robert Taylor, Debi Thomas, John Thomas, Henry Tillman, Gerald Tinker, Wayman Tisdale, Thomas Tolan, Cheryl Toussaint, Kim Turner, Wyomia Tyus, Nelson Vails, James Wallington, Teresa Weatherspoon, Peter Westbrook, Pernell Whitaker, Joseph White, Marilyn White, Willye White, Mal Whitfield, Archibald Williams, Lucinda Williams, Randy Williams, Ulis Williams, George Wilson, Jack Wilson, Leon Wood, Lynette Woodard, John Woodruff, Lorenzo Wright

VENEZUELA
Arnoldo Devonish, Pedro Gamarro

Bibliography

BOOKS

Adkins, Vivian B. L. *The Development of Negro Female Olympic Talent* (Ph.D diss., Indiana University). Ann Arbor, Mich.: University Microfilms, 1967.

Ali, Ramadhan. *Africa at the Olympics*. London: Africa Books, 1976.

American Athletics Annual. Indianapolis: Athletics Congress of United States, 1984.

Arbott, John, ed. *Oxford Companion to World Sports and Games*. New York: Oxford University Press, 1975.

Ashe, Arthur R., Jr. *A Hard Road to Glory: A History of the African-American Athlete, 1619-Present*. 3 vols. New York: Warner Books, 1988.

Bateman, Hal., ed. *United States Track and Field Olympians, 1896-1980*. Indianapolis: Athletics Congress/U.S.A., n.d.

Benagh, Jim. *Incredible Olympic Feats*. New York: McGraw-Hill, 1976.

Benn, Gale D. *Olympic Gold, Summer and Winter Games, Official Record of Championship Performances since 1896*. New York: Golden Press, 1972.

The Black Olympians, 1904-1984. Los Angeles: Afro-American Museum, 1984.

Carlson, Lewis H., and Fogarty, John J. *Tales of Gold*. Chicago: Contemporary Books, 1987.

Cashmere, Ernest. *Black Sportsmen*. Boston: Routledge & Kegan Paul, 1982.

Chester, David. *Olympic Games Handbook*. New York: Charles Scribner, 1975.

Coe, Sebastian, with Mason, Nicholas. *The Olympians: A Quest for Gold Triumphs, Heroes and Legends*. London: Pavilion Books, 1984.

Compton's Gift to the Olympic Games. Robinson's Research. Compton, California: Enterprise Savings and Loan Association, 1984.

Coote, James. *Picture History of the Olympics*. New York: Macmillan, 1972.

Davis, John P., ed. *American Negro Reference Book*. Englewood Cliffs, N.J.: Prentice-Hall, 1966.

Davis, Lenwood G., and Daniels, Belinda S., comps. *Black Athletes in the United States: A Bibliography of Books, Articles, Autobiography and Biography on Black Professional Athletes in the United States, 1800-1981*. Westport, Conn.: Greenwood Press, 1981.

Die Spiele, Official Report of Organizing Committee for the Games of the XXth Olympiad. Munich, Germany, 1972.

Eller, Buddy. *U.S.A. and the Olympics, 1984*. Atlanta: Philmay Enterprises, 1983.

Emery, David, ed. *Who's Who in the 1984 Olympics*. London: Pelham Books, 1984.

Famous American Athletes of Today. Revised, 14 Series. Boston: L. C. Page, 1956.

Foreman, Thomas E. *Discrimination against the Negro in American Athletics*. San Francisco: R & E Associates, 1975.

Games of the (IV-XXII) Olympiad. Official Report of the Organizing Committee, 1908-1972. Colorado Springs, Colorado.

Giller, Norman. *The 1984 Olympics Handbook*. New York: Holt Rinehart & Winston, 1983.

Green, Tina Sloan; Oglesby, Carole A.; Alexander, Alpha; and Franke, Nikki. *Black Women in Sport*. Reston, Virginia: Aahperd Publications, 1981.

Greenberg, Stan. *Olympic Games: The Records*. London: Guinness Books, 1987.

Hanley, Reid M. *Who's Who in Track and Field*. New Rochelle, N.Y.: Arlington House, 1973.

Helsingin Olympiakisat, 1952. Helsinki: Kustannuso-sakeyhtio Kivi, 1952.

Henderson, Edwin Van Croft. *The Negro in Sports*. Washington, D.C.: Associated Publishers, 1939.

Henry, Bill. *An Approved History of the Olympic Games*. Los Angeles: Southern California Committee for the Olympic Games, 1981.

Hickok, Ralph. *New Encyclopedia of Sports*. New York: McGraw-Hill, 1977.

The History of the Olympics: A Pictorial Review of the World's Greatest Sporting Event. New York: Galahad Books, 1980.

Hollander, Phyllis, and Hollander, Zander. *The Complete Book of the Olympic Games*. New York: Signet Books, New American Library, 1984.

_____. *100 Greatest Women in Sports*. New York: Grosset & Dunlap, 1976.

How to Watch the Olympic Games, Summer 1976. (Complete ABC/Montreal Star/New York Times Guide). Ottawa: Quadrangle/New York Times Book Company, 1975.

The IAAF/ATS Statistics Handbook for the Track and Field Events of the Olympic Games. Los Angeles: International Amateur Athletic Federation, 1984.

Information Please: Almanac, Atlas and Yearbook, 1989. 42d ed. Boston: Houghton Mifflin, 1989.

Jenner, Bruce, and Abraham, Mark. *Bruce Jenner's Guide to the Olympics*. New York: Andrews & McMeel, 1979.

Johnson, William, Jr. *All That Glitters Is Not Gold: The Olympic Games*. New York: G. P. Putnam, 1972.

Kamper, Erich. *Lexikon der 14000 Olympioniken* (Who's Who at the Olympics). Graz, Austria: Leykam-Verlag, 1983.

_____. *Lexikon der 12000 Olympioniken* (Who's Who at the Olympics). Graz, Austria: Leykam-Verlag, 1975.

Killanin, Lord, and Rodda, John, eds. *Olympic Games 1980, Moscow and Lake Placid*. New York: Macmillan, 1979.

_____. *The Olympic Games, 1984, Los Angeles and Sarajevo*. Salem, N.H.: Rainbird Publishing Group, 1983.

Laklan, Carli. *Golden Girls: True Stories of Olympic Women Stars*. New York: McGraw-Hill, 1980.

Lincoln Library of Sports Champions. 14 vols. Columbus, Ohio: Sports Resources Company, 1974.

The Los Angeles Times Book of the 1984 Olympic Games. New York: Abrams, 1984.

Mallon, Bill, and Buchanan, Ian. *Quest for Gold: The Encyclopedia of American Olympians*. New York: Leisure Press, 1984.

Mallon, Bill. *The Olympic Record Book*. New York: Garland Publishing Company, 1988.

_____. *The Olympics, a Bibliography*. New York: Garland Publishing, 1984.

Markel, Robert, et al. *For the Record: Women in Sports*. New York: World Almanac Publication, 1985.

Matthews, Peter. *Guinness Book of Athletics Facts and Feats*. London: Guinness Superlatives, 1982.

_____. *International Athletics Annual, 1985, 1986*. (Association of Track & Field Statisticians). Sports World Publication, Ltd., London.

Maxwell, Jocko, comp. and ed. *Great Black Athletes*. Largo, Florida: Snible Publications, 1971.

McWhirter, Norris, ed. and comp. *Guinness Book of Olympic Records*. Toronto, New York: Bantam Books, 1983.

Mexico 68: Participants in the XIXth Olympiad. Mexico City: El Comite Organizador de los Juegos de la XIX Olimpiada, 1968.

Miller, David. *Seoul '88: The Official Book of the Games of the XXIVth Olympiad*. London: William Collins, 1988.

Mullan, Harry. *The Illustrated History of Boxing*. New York: Crescent Books, 1987.

The Negro Handbook. Compiled by editors of *Ebony*. Chicago: Johnson Publishing, 1966.

Nelson, Cordner. *Track and Field, the Great Ones*. London: Pelham Books, 1970.

The 1980 Olympic Handbook: A Guide to the Moscow Olympics and a History of the Games. London: Arthur Barker, 1980.

1960 U.S. Sports Teams, Games of the XVIIth Olympiad, Rome. Chicago: Presented through The American Dairy Association in cooperation with the U.S. Olympic Committee, 1960.

Official Report of XIVth Olympiad. London: 1948.

Official Report of the Games of the XXIIIrd Olympiad. Vol. 2. Los Angeles: Los Angeles Olympic Organizing Committee, 1985.

The Olympic Games: Athens 1896 to Los Angeles 1984. London: Optimism Books, 1983.

Ploski, Harry, and Brown, Roscoe C. *Negro Almanac.* New York: Belwether, 1971.

Porter, David L., ed. *Biographical Dictionary of American Sports, Outdoor Sports.* New York: Greenwood Press, 1988.

Pratt, John L., and Benagh, Jim. *The Official Encyclopedia of Sports.* New York: Franklin Watts, 1964.

Pursuit of Excellence: The Olympic Story, by Associated Press & Grolier. New York: Franklin Watts, 1979.

Report of the U.S. Olympic Committee, 1904-1980. Colorado Springs, Colo.

Research Information, Games of the XXIIIrd Olympiad. Los Angeles: Los Angeles Olympic Organizing Committee, 1985.

Schaap, Richard. *An Illustrated History of the Olympics.* 3d edition. New York: Knopf, 1975.

_____. *The 1984 Olympic Games: Sarajevo/Los Angeles.* New York: Charles Scribner, 1984.

Spirit Team Profiles. Los Angeles: Los Angeles Olympic Organizing Committee, 1985.

Toomey, Bill, and King, Barry. *The Olympic Challenge 1988.* Costa Mesa: Calif.: HDL Publisher, 1988.

United States: Olympic Book, Report of the U.S. Olympic Committee, 1948-1980. Colorado Springs, Colo.

Wallechinsky, David. *The Complete Book of the Olympics.* Middlesex, England and New York: Penguin Books, 1984.

Watkins, Mary Belle Sanders. *Historical and Biographical Studies of Women Olympic Participants at Tennessee State University, 1948-1980.* Ann Arbor, Mich.: UMI Dissertation Information Service, 1980.

Watman, Mel, comp. *Encyclopaedia of Athletics.* New York: St. Martin's Press, 1977.

_____. *Encyclopaedia of Track and Field Athletics.* New York: St. Martin's Press, 1981.

Webster's Sports Dictionary. Springfield, Mass.: G. & C. Merriam, 1976.

Willoughby, David P. *The Super-Athletes.* New York: A. S. Barnes, 1970.

World Almanac and Book of Facts. New York: Newspaper Enterprise Association, 1986, 1989.

World Encyclopedia of Sports. "The High Jump." Paris, France: Editions de Vaillant, n.d.

Young, Andrew S. N. *Negro Firsts in Sports.* Chicago: Johnson Publishing, 1963.

NEWSPAPERS AND PERIODICALS

Black Sports, 1975
Ebony, 1984-1988
Herald News (Joliet, Illinois), July 28, 1984
Jet, various issues
(London) *Times,* October 3, 1988
Long Beach Press Telegram, September 24, 1984
Los Angeles Herald Examiner, "Olympic Special," August 13, 1984
Los Angeles Sentinel, August 2, 1984
Los Angeles Times, 1980-1989
New York Times, 1960-1986
Newsweek, January 6, 1969
The Olympian, various issues
People Magazine, April 1984
Runners World, July 1988; October 1988
Sport Magazine, July 1988
Sporting News, August 13, 1984
Sports Illustrated, August 29, 1984; June 4, 1988; August 1, 1988
Time, June 9, 1967; March 29, 1968
Track & Field News, 1980-1989
USA Today, August 4, 1986; October 3, 1988
Women's Sports, 1983-1984
Women's Track and Field World, various issues

MISCELLANEOUS SOURCES

American Visions, "More about Winning," vol. 3, 1988

British Virgin Islands, Olympic Committee

Canadian Olympic Association

First Interstate Bank Athletic Foundation, "Special Release," August 1984

Sportsworld, "Official Report of the Olympic Games," London, British Olympic Association, 1972

Uganda Olympic Committee

VIDEO

1988 Summer Olympics, Seoul: Track and Field (Men); Track and Field (Women); Watersports; Boxing; Volleyball. NBC Sports Wood Knapp Video.

Index

This index covers names of individuals, teams, clubs, and organizations; sports competitions, special events or occurrences; and schools, colleges, and universities as they are mentioned in the biographies of athletes.